The Kiowas &
the Legend of Kicking Bird

Kicking Bird. Battey, *Life and Adventures*. Courtesy University of Oklahoma Press.

The Kiowas &
the Legend of Kicking Bird

Stan Hoig

with three Kiowa tales by Col. W. S. Nye

University Press of Colorado

Copyright © 2000 by the University Press of Colorado
International Standard Book Number 0-87081-564-4

Published by the University Press of Colorado
5589 Arapahoe Avenue, Suite 206C
Boulder, Colorado 80303

The University Press of Colorado is a cooperative publishing enterprise supported, in part, by Adams State College, Colorado State University, Fort Lewis College, Mesa State College, Metropolitan State College of Denver, University of Colorado, University of Northern Colorado, University of Southern Colorado, and Western State College of Colorado.

The paper used in this publication meets the minimum requirements of the American National Standard for Information Sciences—Permanence of Paper for Printed Library Materials. ANSI Z39.48-1984

Library of Congress Cataloging-in-Publication Data

Hoig, Stan
    The Kiowas and the legend of Kicking Bird / Stan Hoig
        p. cm.
    Includes bibliographical references and index.
    ISBN 0-87081-564-4 (cloth : alk. paper)
    1. Kicking Bird, d. 1875. 2. Kiowa Indians—Kings and rulers—Biography. 3. Kiowa Indians—Wars. 4. Kiowa Indians—Government relations. I. Title.

E99.K5 K535 2000
978'.00497490092—dc21
[B]   99-088349

Designed by Laura Furney
Typeset by Daniel Pratt

08 07 06 05 04 03 02 01 00 99   10 9 8 7 6 5 4 3 2 1

Contents

Contents

Illustrations

MAPS

Preface

During the nineteenth century, the changing world doomed the old ways of tribal existence on the Central Plains of North America. The onslaught of Euro-American influence that swept onto and across the Plains brought with it a societal upheaval that meant a certain end to the unrestrained existence of the nomadic tribesman. The often unprincipled but irrepressible force of America's westward movement; the rampant, government-unhindered destruction of the great buffalo herds by white hunters; the growing propensity of tribes for the food products and manufactured goods of the white man; devastation by diseases once foreign to the prairies; and the superior military power of the United States all combined against the old ways of tribal life that the Kiowas and others had always known.

Many tribal leaders of the day were caught squarely in the epicenter of this conflict between the native cultures of America and the United States and were forced to seek a solution for the survival of their people through compromise with the white man. Tohawson (the original of that name) was the most prominent peace leader during the Kiowas' early contact with whites. Although Satanta and Lone Wolf would become noted for their resistance to white intrusion, it was the superb warrior and tribal leader Kicking Bird who would take up Tohawson's mantle of peaceful diplomacy.

The problem of maintaining peace on the Plains was not a simple one. The complicating factors of both state and national expansion were

Kicking Bird (Tene Angopte). Courtesy Western History Collection, University of Oklahoma.

underlaid with a primary problem of organizational control by both the federal government and the tribes themselves. In 1863 President Abraham Lincoln held an interview with a Plains Indian delegation to Washington led by Cheyenne chief Lean Bear and Kiowa chief Yellow Wolf. He observed that even as president he could not always control the actions of his troops or citizens in the field. This fact, especially true on the frontier, was starkly illustrated by the murder of Cheyenne chief Lean Bear on the Kansas prairie by U.S. troops the following year and the ensuing massacre of Black Kettle's Cheyenne village at Sand Creek in Colorado by Col. John M. Chivington on November 29, 1864.

Tribal leaders, likewise, often had scant control over the war factions of their tribes. War parties were normally independent operations over which a chief could exercise little restraint. In 1873 Kicking Bird and the Kiowa chiefs loyal to him did temporarily curb warring into Texas. They threatened to kill the war horses; burn the saddles, bridles, and other accouterments; and destroy the lodges of would-be raiders. This, however, was an exceptional act rarely exercised by tribal leaders.

Peacemaking could be a dangerous undertaking from forces both outside and inside the tribe. Those tribal leaders who dared to seek peaceful compromises were not only at times betrayed and victimized by whites, but just as often they were mortally endangered by their own war element. The Cheyenne Dog Soldiers issued dire threats against Black Kettle when he was invited to attend treaty talks following Sand Creek. The murder of Lakota chief Spotted Tail went unavenged, largely because of his reputation as a favorite of the white man. Even the more socially advanced Cherokees and Creeks of the South suffered intense trauma from intratribal assassinations over the issue of making accommodations with the United States.

It was a long-standing ploy of U.S. officials to invite tribal leaders to Washington, D.C., where they could be impressed with the magnitude and might of the white people. Although this plan was often effective in persuading the individual chiefs, it did little to influence the tribal warriors who, having not been there to see for themselves, concluded that the chiefs had been bewitched or duped.

Following the death of Tohawson in 1866, a number of the tribe's war leaders vied to replace him as head chief. Among them were Satanta, Lone Wolf, and the youthful Kicking Bird. None of these men, however, was able to establish a firm position above all the other chiefs of Kiowa bands such as Tohawson had held.

Satanta was lauded by whites for his power of personality and his oratory in speaking of the Indian's love for the land and way of life. Largely because of the publicity he received at the Treaty of Medicine Lodge and that provided afterward by western writers, he became the symbolic Kiowa figure by modern reputation. But in the end, Satanta's warring proclivities led him to be arrested by the military and eventually imprisoned.

Lone Wolf, who had twice visited Washington and avowed his desire for peace to the White Father, made an effort to take up the peace mantle of Tohawson. Tragically, however, he could not overcome his deep, all-consuming despair when his favorite son was killed during a war-party raid in Texas. The old tribal compulsion for blood revenge led Lone Wolf back to the war path and ultimately, like Satanta, to prison.

Kicking Bird began to emerge as a peace leader during the 1870s, winning more and more of a following among the chiefs of other Kiowa bands. His designation as the Kiowa head chief was made by U.S. officials and not by a consensus of the Kiowa people, although evidence indicates he had a majority following of the tribe before his untimely death. During the critical years of 1874 and 1875, however, it was he, not Satanta or Lone Wolf, who wrestled with the heavy burden of peace versus war, of social advancement versus traditional tribal culture, and of the ultimate welfare of his people versus the inclination for bloody revenge and personal gratification.

Although he had a relatively short life, Kicking Bird played a prominent role in the Kiowa events of his lifetime. As a young man, he was a Kiowa warrior supreme—an "onde." As he matured during his late thirties, he ceased his raiding and followed the pattern of many former warriors who, having assumed the responsibility of tribal leadership, counseled their people away from the often aimless raiding that dominated Plains Indian societies during the nineteenth century.

Kicking Bird's role among the Kiowas can also be compared with that of Bull Bear among the Cheyennes. Bull Bear, brother to Lean Bear, was leader of the Cheyennes' famed Dog Soldiers during much of that tribe's early conflicts with whites on the Central Plains. His warrior credentials were beyond question. Still, it was he who dared to accompany Black Kettle to Denver in 1864 to seek peace; and it was he who was among the first to send a child, his son Leonard Tyler, off to Carlisle, Pennsylvania, to be educated. Similarly, Kicking Bird led the Kiowas into the world of formal education by arranging for Quaker teacher Thomas C. Battey to come to his village and teach his daughter Topen. Educated, articulate Kiowas of today are inescapably endebted to Kicking Bird's courage as the first to challenge the antischooling mores of his tribe.

As a chief, Kicking Bird already lived on a level above other Kiowas in terms of a better lodge, a large horse herd, and a choice position when annuities were issued. The charge that he bettered himself personally from cultivating white favor seems weak, however, in that before he died he had lost his entire horse herd and was reduced to riding a lowly mule.

The Cheyennes, Comanches, and Kiowas were essentially compatible with one another at this time. But historically the tribes of the Central Plains warred with one another exclusive of the white man. Young males among the Plains tribes rose to recognition, prestige, and wealth through acts of war. At times these actions were more figurative than real, as in the case of counting coup by merely touching the enemy. But in the fuller sense, warring involved killing the enemy, taking the victim's scalp, stealing his horses, destroying his camp or village, capturing his women and children, and committing other acts of violence.

War was often conducted as a matter of tribal or personal vengeance. Tribal feuds were long-standing: the Kiowas with the Utes, Apaches, and Pawnees; the Cheyennes with the Pawnees, Utes, and Snakes; the Osages with the Comanches, Kiowas, Wichitas, and Cherokees; the Pawnees and Kaws with the Osages. At times the larger issue of competition over territory was at stake, particularly the vital buffalo hunting regions. The Lakota Sioux won control over the country north of the Missouri River by overwhelming the Assiniboines and Crees. The Sioux, Cheyennes, and Arapahos fought the Kiowas and Crows for the country west of the Black Hills. The Comanches and Kiowas forced the Apaches out of northern New Mexico and Texas. The Osages drove the Wichitas from Kansas into southern Oklahoma. Eventually, the Cheyennes and Arapahos pushed south of the Arkansas River to contest the Kiowas and Comanches for hunting privileges there.

From their prairie bastion in the Texas Panhandle and western Kansas and Oklahoma, the Kiowas joined the Comanches in conducting raids against white settlements in south Texas and Mexico, returning with stock and women and children captives. As the Santa Fe Trail between Missouri and New Mexico developed into a trade route during the first half of the nineteenth century, Kiowa war parties found the passing wagon trains a lucrative source for obtaining goods of the white man's world, especially food.

In addition to other factors, the societal influences transmitted through contact with missionaries, the military, traders, and other whites helped to alter the conditions of tribal life. This reshaping of the world tribespeople knew eventually posed the ultimate choice for tribal leaders: Should they follow their tradition of warring and contest the United States in a struggle that would likely mean the annihilation of their tribe; or should they, for the welfare and survival of their people, make peace and accept a drastically changed mode of life as demanded by a dominant white society?

It was not a simple or easy matter for the chiefs. Most of them had risen to prominence among their people on the basis of their fighting prowess as younger men. But being a war leader and being a civil chief, both of which existed as dual positions in most tribes, called for vastly different concerns. A civil leader was responsible for maintaining the peace both within and without the tribe. Yet his authority, rarely supported by any regulatory body, was generally based on his force of character and personal reputation among the people and other chiefs. The issue of peace and war often separated those leaders who acted with reasoned intellect from those who responded through the raw emotions generated by the thrill and excitement of battle or vindictive hatred of the enemy.

Tribal war societies, which acted independent of the civil chiefs, exercised great dominance over young males who yearned to gain recognition and reputations as warriors and war leaders. Not only was the warrior tradition the medium for rising in social standing, but its basic calling was to protect the tribe from its enemies. This last was a constant requirement, for danger from other tribes never ceased. The war societies were thus a self-perpetuating and powerful element of Plains Indian culture.

Indeed, the tribal warrior, abhorred as he was by frontier whites, played a vital role during the early years of U.S. movement westward. Had he not been there to resist white expansion, the fate of the tribe would surely have been at even greater risk. Our national history offers solid evidence that acquiescence by native peoples not uncommonly resulted in greater loss of territorial rights, decimation of their people, or even total annihilation. In the Southern Plains region, the Wichitas serve as a prime example of a tribe who lost out badly because it did not militarily oppose U.S. pressure. Peacemaking and war making are often interrelated activities of competing societies. Without such a counterforce as the tribal warrior offered, government officials were little inclined to hold treaties or make concessions.

There were those determined Kiowas who chose to fight as long as they could—possibly, it could be argued, beyond the limits of effective resistance. Ultimately, most Kiowa hostiles—men such as Satanta, Lone Wolf, Maman-ti, Woman's Heart, Big Bow, and White Horse—were forced to make the same choice of compliance Kicking Bird, Stumbling Bear, and other Kiowa leaders had made earlier.

In truth, the efforts of the militants were seldom more than individual revenge strikes or raiding for personal gain. No evidence exists of any organized attempt by the tribes on the Southern Plains to defeat the U.S. military or even to drive whites away in any systematic manner. When such a move was once considered in a Kiowa-Comanche war council, Kicking Bird effectively argued it down.

Without a dominant peace leader during the uprising of 1874-1875, the Kiowas would surely have suffered an even greater loss of life and tribal prominence. In the end, the imprisonment of twenty-seven militants for three years was a small matter compared to the starvation and deaths of Kiowa tribespeople that would have occurred with continued resistance. It should be well noted that the main Kiowa chiefs who were incarcerated at Fort Marion, Florida, in 1875 had surrendered fully aware that they might be sent to prison as Satanta had been earlier. Without food, adequate clothing, shelter, or ammunition, they capitulated because the only alternative for them and their people was to starve or freeze to death on the prairie.

It would be difficult to gauge the attitude of the Kiowa people toward Kicking Bird today. The old rivalry between him and Satanta lives on in modern competition for historical recognition. Kiowa interviews in the Duke Collection of the University of Oklahoma Western History Collection reveal little awareness of Kicking Bird other than what was written by Colonel Nye in *Carbine and Lance*. Most meaningful, however, are accounts from that generation of Kiowas who knew Kicking Bird personally, most of whom loved and admired him.

In writing this book, I have been unable to escape a strong personal belief that any society is far better served with formal education of its young than without. This bias leads me unfailingly to the opinion that, for whatever role he played in the selection of the Fort Marion prisoners (many of them Mexican captives and lesser figures), Kicking Bird was a progressive and positive factor in the evolution of his tribe by being the first to see the value of schooling for Kiowa children.

It is not likely, however, that the controversy concerning Kicking Bird will fade. Even with the same information, people often come to different conclusions. The following pages will have to speak for themselves, and those who read them can reach their own determinations. Perhaps, like many other prominent men of the past, he will remain forever caught in limbo between these opposing societal views. Still, with well over a century having passed since Kicking Bird's death, it is time to take a fuller look at the life and being of this important Native American leader.

A number of people were very helpful to me in my research. These include Towanda Spivey, director, Fort Sill Museum; John Lovett, librarian, Western History Collection, University of Oklahoma; Bill Welge, director, Archives/Manuscript Division, Oklahoma Historical Society; staff, Max Chambers Library and Oklahoma Collection, University of Central Oklahoma; Alfred Mueller, Beinecke Rare Book and Manuscript Library, Yale University; Alison Deeprose of the British Museum; Peter Harrison of Southhampton, England; and my good friends of literary note, Fred Grove and Brent Ashabranner. My sincere thanks to them and to my wife, Patricia Corbell Hoig, who, as always, contributed immeasurably to this book.

Kicking Bird, wearing a military coat with epaulets. Courtesy
Kansas Historical Society.

Prologue—Tales of a Legend

His name was T'ené-angópte.[1] The white man called him Kicking Bird, but the name really translated something more like "Eagle Who Strikes With His Talons" or "Striking Eagle." He was given that name for a reason. They said it was the way he fought his enemies. He was a Kiowa, although his father's father had been of the Crow tribe. As a young man, he was an intrepid warrior; as a leader of his people, he became their most prominent peace chief, taking up the mantle of his predecessor, Tohawson. Those who knew him described him as slender, lithe, graceful, and handsome. They also said he was highly intelligent and a natural leader—one who acted in the interest of his people and protected them.

Others insist that Kicking Bird was a traitor to his tribe, a man who played up to the whites for his own benefit and gain. Because he often visited the Kiowa-Comanche agency at Fort Sill and chatted with the Quaker staff, Kicking Bird's enemies among the Kiowa war element called him a "coffee chief" or an "aw day tallee" (all-day talker)—the white man's favorite child.[2] Most significantly, he was known by some Kiowas as the chief who helped send other Kiowas to prison in Florida.

Which was he, this man whom history has shunted off into the shadows of Satanta and Lone Wolf? Was he a traitor to his people for leading the Kiowas on the path of peace while others made war? Or was he, as Indian agent James M. Haworth declared him to be, "the noblest Kiowa of them all."[3]

The tales others tell give some clue to the man that Kicking Bird was. Many of his enemies in the tribe had not been in battle with him during his warrior days and did not understand why he was called Striking Eagle. They may not have known of the time when a Kiowa woman dared to complain about her husband being killed during a raid. During the celebration on the war party's return, she had commented bitterly that while the others were dancing and laughing, she wept in despair.

One of the young warriors heard of this and was very angry. He vowed that if the woman took part in any victory celebration before her year of mourning was over, he would kill her. The woman waited a year, then one day she took part in a victory celebration, joining the other women in their luluing. Even though she had waited, the vengeful warrior killed her.

Kicking Bird was furious, but he was not related to the woman and by tribal law he could do nothing about the situation. When the warrior was told of Kicking Bird's displeasure, he was insulted. Carrying a carbine, he went to Kicking Bird's tent and challenged him to a fight. It was a mistake. Before the man could cock his weapon, Kicking Bird placed three arrows in his chest.[4]

Luther Sahmaunt was a half-brother of Chief Big Bow, whom Kicking Bird saved from being sent to prison. Sahmaunt told the story of how Kicking Bird was persuaded to become friends with the white people and work for peace. Tsa-la-am, or Chasing Calves, was the son of Kicking Bird's cousin Stumbling Bear (Set-Imkla, Pushing Bear, or Bear-that-runs-over-a-man). The boy, who was very dear to his father, became seriously ill. None of the Kiowa medicine men were able to make him well again. Finally, Kicking Bird said he would go to Fort Sill and secure the help of a white doctor.

Kicking Bird's friends were afraid for him to go. They said the soldiers would kill him. But Kicking Bird was determined; he feared if he did not go, the boy would die. Goon-daule, or the Cat, and Goo-oolie, or Chases Some One, rode with him as far as a trader's store on Cache Creek. Kicking Bird said he would go on alone from there on foot.

"If I am killed," he said, "you can have my horse."

He walked the two miles farther to Fort Sill. When the post guard challenged him, he thought for certain that he would be shot and killed. Instead, some soldiers came out from the fort and were friendly to him. They led him into the fort and had him tell the post interpreter why he had come. When the commanding officer learned about Chasing Calves, he ordered some soldiers to go back with Kicking Bird and bring the sick boy to the base hospital. Kicking Bird was given a white flag that he could carry as a sign of peace for protection.

"This so impressed both Kicking Bird and Stumbling Bear that thereafter they made every effort to keep peace between the Kiowas and the Government. By doing so they were often called 'Traitors' by the more warlike chiefs."[5]

Another Kicking Bird story was related by Lt. Richard Henry Pratt, who served with the Tenth Cavalry at Fort Supply, Fort Arbuckle, and Fort Sill. Pratt was the officer who escorted the Plains Indian prisoners to Fort Marion, Florida, in 1875 and remained there as the officer in charge over them. While at Fort Sill, he knew and was friends with virtually all of the leading chiefs of the area, including Kicking Bird. In his book *Battlefield and Classroom* (edited by Robert M. Utley),[6] Pratt related an interesting encounter with Kicking Bird in the field.

During the summer of 1870, most of the Kiowas went on a big buffalo hunt along the Sweetwater River west of the Wichita Mountains. In doing so, they drifted beyond the 100th Meridian into the Texas Panhandle and off their reservation area. Learning of this, Col. B. H. Grierson formed a command from the majority of the buffalo-soldier Tenth Cavalry at Fort Sill and went looking for the Kiowas. In his search, Grierson divided his command, one portion under himself and the other under Capt. Louis H. Carpenter.

It was Carpenter who first contacted the Kiowas when he spotted their warriors formed in a line of battle on a distant hilltop. Through field glasses, Carpenter could see that the tribesmen were wearing their war bonnets and their bodies were stripped and painted for action. To Carpenter and his men, it appeared that the Kiowas were defiant and prepared to fight.

The officer placed his men in a cavalry formation and began moving toward the Indians at a steady walk with weapons ready and prepared for a charge. When they were within about half a mile, a Kiowa came riding forth with a white flag tied to the end of his lance. Pratt was sent forward with an interpreter to meet the messenger. The man told him the Kiowas did not want a fight and that Chief Kicking Bird wished to talk with the commander of the troops. Pratt escorted the Kiowa to the cavalry line to talk with Carpenter.

When the Indians were first spotted, a courier had been sent galloping to Grierson, who now arrived with his portion of the command. Taking charge, he sent word back for Kicking Bird to meet him. Grierson, Carpenter, Pratt, and a few others rode out to mid-distance between the two lines. Kicking Bird came forward with a like number of men. After a long talk, a peace accord was agreed upon. Kicking Bird sent word to his lines, and the Indians quickly vanished from the hilltop.

Kicking Bird proved to be a good host. He offered to lead Grierson and his troops to a good camping place. On the way, however, a large herd of buffalo was encountered. Grierson asked Kicking Bird if Indians could actually kill a buffalo with a bow and arrow.

Kicking Bird laughed and assured him they could. In fact, he said, he would show them how it was done. Kicking Bird stripped both himself and his horse. Taking his rope, he looped it over the horse's nose and around its neck. With the rein in one hand and his bow and arrows in the other, he galloped into the buffalo herd. Selecting a fat buffalo, he herded it off to one side. The buffalo charged him time and again, but each time Kicking Bird deftly maneuvered his pony to avoid the charge. Finally, the discouraged and fatigued buffalo stopped and stood snorting at his tormentor, wheeling about to face Kicking Bird as he circled around the animal.

When Grierson and his staff came riding up, Kicking Bird forced the buffalo to run away and followed in a hot chase. As he closed on the animal, Kicking Bird loosed an arrow into its forequarters. Soon the buffalo stopped running and stood motionless for a short time before it finally tottered and fell over. The officers dismounted and looked over the huge carcass. They saw that the arrow had entered the buffalo behind the shoulder and protruded from a lower position on the other side.

It had been great entertainment for Grierson and his men. But another part of the story was discovered later. Since the Kiowas were off their reservation, they had feared the troops might attack them. Kicking Bird's maneuver on meeting the troops and his demonstration of buffalo hunting had given the camp time to take down their tepees and move onto their reservation where they were safe.

Kicking Bird and Satanta were contemporaries and competitors for the role of Kiowa principal chief. The latter was several years older than Kicking Bird and held a more dominant leadership position with the tribe for a time. But Kicking Bird was clearly Satanta's equal as a warrior, and he challenged him as an orator in speaking the cause of the Kiowas. In the end, he may have had a far larger influence on Kiowa history than Satanta had. A view into the personal relationship between the two men is provided in a story by Old Iseeo as recounted by Wilbur S. Nye in *Bad Medicine and Good*.[7]

The incident occurred during a summer buffalo hunt near the North Fork of the Red River west of the Wichita Mountains. It was a Kiowa custom to assign warriors to keep independent hunters from the camp

Satanta, wearing a military coat and peace medal. Custer,
My Life on the Plains. Courtesy University of Oklahoma
Press.

from going out on their own and scaring the buffalo. They called this
"holding the buffalo." On this occasion there were over fifty men of the
Rattle band, headed by Satanta, who acted as guards over a huge herd that
filled the valley below.

The Kiowa soldiers were sitting on their horses atop a hill when they
spotted three riders approaching the herd. The three apparently intended
to make a run on the buffalo. Satanta hailed the men. One of them was
Kicking Bird's brother, and one was the chief's brother-in-law. Satanta
demanded they go back to the village, but the two who were Kicking
Bird's relatives refused. They chased the herd, although they were merely
firing their guns in the air, not even trying to kill buffalo.

Satanta ordered his guards after them, and they shot and killed the
two men's horses. Then, after having all of the men's arrows broken and

their robes slashed, Satanta ordered each of his men to ride up and strike the pair across the face and shoulders with his quirt.

"Now I leave you here afoot," Satanta said. "No one is allowed to take you up and give you a ride."

It was a long way back to the village. The two very hot and thirsty men finally came walking in, hiding their swollen faces beneath blankets. They said Kicking Bird had told them to scare the herd. Presently, another man came to the camp. He said Kicking Bird, whose wife was sick, was very angry over what had happened and that he was going to whip Satanta.

Several days passed, however, and Kicking Bird did not come. Satanta waited and fretted, and finally he called his warriors together in a council. He said he had decided to go to Kicking Bird and make peace. He and his men took some presents with them: four horses, a white mule, two saddles and bridles, a gun, and blankets.

They found Kicking Bird sitting under his shade. He asked, "What have you come here for? To fight?"

Satanta said he had come to make peace. When the presents had been laid out, Kicking Bird relented.

"I began the trouble," he admitted. "But I do not feel that my heart stabbed anywhere."

He explained he had sent the men because he was angry that the village had moved against his orders while the buffalo were being held. He shook hands with Satanta and the others.

"Satanta was a big man," Old Iseeo observed, "and he was older than Kicking Bird. But he was not as wise. Furthermore, I think that Kicking Bird had the stronger medicine."

A report by Capt. C. H. Carlton, Tenth Cavalry, to agent Haworth on May 8, 1874, tells of another incident at Fort Sill that reflects on the relationship between Kicking Bird and Satanta.[8] By Carlton's report, Satanta, who was on parole from the Texas penitentiary at Huntsville, was in the habit of pursuing women who worked at the post. On this particular evening he was following a woman from the post laundry to the stable when he was ordered to halt by a sentry. When Satanta persisted, the sentry aimed his weapon at the Kiowa chief and placed him under arrest.

Satanta reacted by backing away from the guard and yelling "Kicking Bird! Kicking Bird!" He then turned and ran to the nearby Kiowa camp and began shouting that the soldiers were coming to attack. The camp was greatly alarmed and, even though it was night, began to pack up and break camp. Kicking Bird and a few other Kiowas were sleeping at the post trader's store. Some young men from the camp came to him and told him what Satanta was doing. Kicking Bird immediately sent word back for everyone to stay in camp and remain calm. He thereby quieted a situation that Satanta had created.

A significant issue in Kiowa history concerns the attitude of the people to Kicking Bird as a peace chief. In *Ten Grandmothers*,[9] Alice Marriott tells the story of a woman who bore a child in the Fort Sill horse corral while temporarily being held as one of the Kiowa captives by the U.S. Army during the winter of 1874 and 1875. The story does not directly involve Kicking Bird, but it reflects the attitude of some tribespeople toward him during this critical period.

The horse corral was a high-walled rock square stuck against the side of a hill with a lean-to shelter rimming the inside perimeter and leaving a small open space at the center. It was in this open area that the Kiowas had to kill and butcher the cattle driven in for them to eat. There was little room for drying the meat for cooking, so much of what they ate was raw. The place soon began to smell bad. One family at a time was permitted to go outside to a well and get water.

Every day the prisoners were counted. The people did not like to be counted. But the worst part was that there was very little they could do to keep busy inside the corral. Some of the men carved and polished bones and made a gambling game that kept them occupied. A few of the women tried to tan the cow hides, but the cows were so lean and sparse of tallow that tanning was difficult.

Spear Woman, however, persisted. Bow Woman, her co-wife to Hunting Horse, was going to have a baby, and Spear Woman wanted her to have a cradle. She had been forced to leave the one her mother had made and given her on the prairie when they were brought back from Texas. Hunting Horse wanted to help make the cradle. He and Spear Woman cut the stiff, hard center out of a cowhide to use for a board. Together they sliced long strips of leather to use for thongs.

Spear Woman needed something soft to put inside for the baby to lie in, but there was nothing soft about the cowhides. Hunting Horse came up with an idea. Their friend Wood Smoke was outside the corral helping the military as an interpreter and in making the daily count of people in the corral. Hunting Horse asked Smoke if he would go to Kicking Bird's camp and find something soft for the cradle. In a few days, Smoke returned with four fluffy rabbit pelts that had been prepared.

Spear Woman and Hunting Horse were very proud and happy as they stood looking at the finished cradle. Hunting Horse took off his long silver earrings and fastened them to the side of the cradle. The baby was born, a bright-eyed girl, and spring finally came. Spear Woman could peer through the square holes at the top of the wall and see the trees and brush along Cache Creek turning green.

Finally, the last bands to surrender were brought in, and the soldiers let the people out of the corral. The former inmates were required to camp away from Kicking Bird's band so there would be no fighting between those who had been prisoners and those who had not—also so they could still be counted. Spear Woman's mother, one of the old ones who had lived through the winter outside the walls, brought Spear Woman's children to her. One of them was a young son who had never been named.

Hunting Horse decided that now that his son had a little sister he should be named. He deeply regretted that he had no horses to give away in his son's honor. Also, he had hoped to have the famous war chief Sitting Bear (Satank) give his son a strong war name, but Sitting Bear had been killed. Spear Woman suggested that since it looked as though the warring was over, the war names were also dead. Perhaps they should find a peace name for the boy.

Hunting Horse agreed. He said he would find a peace name and ask Kicking Bird to give it to him. Spear Woman was doubtful about asking Kicking Bird. Many of the people who had been held in the corral blamed him for their having been there. Some were going to be angry if Kicking Bird gave the boy a peace name. But Hunting Horse was stubborn. The others did not have to like it, he said. If his son needed a peace name to live with, that was the kind of name he would get. The hating and warring would have to end, and the Kiowas needed to make a new kind of life for themselves.

During late 1874, Kicking Bird became an accepted figure at Fort Sill. Lieutenant Pratt related an occasion when the military officers and their wives decided to hold a banquet and dance in celebration of the completion of their new base hospital. The committee of officers in charge of the event came up with the idea of inviting six of the principal Kiowa and Comanche chiefs to attend. Pratt was delegated to go to their camps and give escort to the chiefs.[10]

When Pratt arrived at Kicking Bird's lodge, the chief was being attired and painted by his two wives. Pratt was struck with the notion of having himself adorned and feathered in a similar fashion. The idea amused Kicking Bird and his wives, and they agreed. Pratt was outfitted in Kiowa garments that included a beaded shirt, leggings, and moccasins. His face was painted vividly, and his head was adorned with a beautiful war bonnet. Kicking Bird and the women were immensely pleased with the result. When Pratt entered the large ward of the hospital where the dance was under way, some of his close acquaintances did not recognize him.

No white man knew Kicking Bird better than did Quaker school-teacher Thomas Battey, who resided among the Kiowas in the wilds of the Indian Territory for many months. Battey's four-year contact with the tribe is recounted in his book, *The Life and Adventures of a Quaker Among the Indians.* Battey's letters, taken from observations recorded in his private journal, were first published in *The Friend* of Philadelphia from May 15, 1875, through February 26, 1876. Of Kicking Bird, Battey wrote in 1872:

> Kicking Bird is a chief of some distinction, not only among his own tribe, but has great influence with other tribes, particularly the Apaches. He is not a full Kiowa, his grandfather being a Crow Indian, who was captured while young, and brought up among the Kiowas, married a Kiowa woman, and raised a family of children, one [Tsain-hay-te, or Big Horse] of whom became the father of Kicking Bird, who is distinguished for eloquence, bravery, good sound practical sense, military capacity, and his friendship to the white people. He might be considered the first chief of the tribe; although no chief is amenable to another; still there are, at the present time not less than twelve chiefs who look to him for counsel in all matters of importance.[11]

The fact that Kicking Bird was a favorite of the whites who knew him contributed strongly to his being disliked by some of his own people. Still, in the months before his death he was clearly the leading chief of the Kiowas and was followed by a majority of the tribe that wanted the warring to end. Like many important men in history, he remains controversial and legendary even today. Without question, Kicking Bird was a pivotal figure in the fate of his people. Oral legends, anecdotes, and personal observations offer valuable insight to the man Kicking Bird was. In the end, however, he can be aptly measured and rightly understood only against the play of Kiowa history.

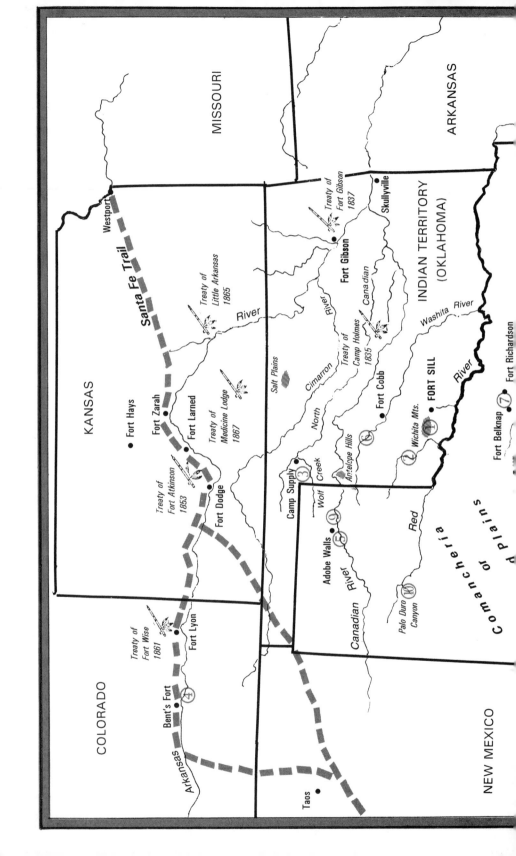

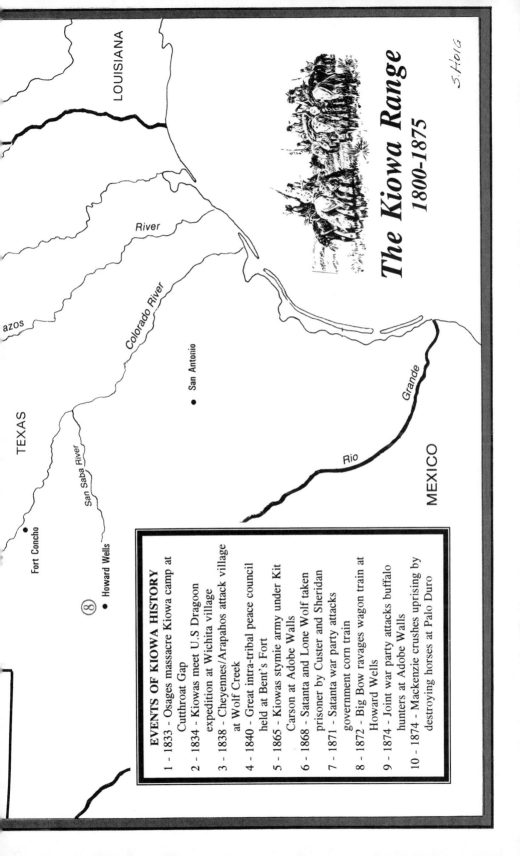

TEXAS

LOUISIANA

MEXICO

azos

San Saba River

Colorado River

River

Rio Grande

• Fort Concho

• Howard Wells

⑧

• San Antonio

The Kiowa Range
1800-1875

5.4616

EVENTS OF KIOWA HISTORY

1 - 1833 - Osages massacre Kiowa camp at
    Cutthroat Gap

2 - 1834 - Kiowas meet U.S Dragoon
    expedition at Wichita village

3 - 1838 - Cheyennes/Arapahos attack village
    at Wolf Creek

4 - 1840 - Great intra-tribal peace council
    held at Bent's Fort

5 - 1865 - Kiowas stymie army under Kit
    Carson at Adobe Walls

6 - 1868 - Satanta and Lone Wolf taken
    prisoner by Custer and Sheridan

7 - 1871 - Satanta war party attacks
    government corn train

8 - 1872 - Big Bow ravages wagon train at
    Howard Wells

9 - 1874 - Joint war party attacks buffalo
    hunters at Adobe Walls

10 - 1874 - Mackenzie crushes uprising by
    destroying horses at Palo Duro

The Kiowas &
the Legend of Kicking Bird

1

Tribe of the Unknown

In his *Carbine and Lance*, W. S. Nye tells a story of the Fort Sill Kiowa and Comanche prisoners as they were being loaded aboard army wagons to be sent to Fort Marion, Florida, on the morning of April 28, 1875.[1] According to Nye, Kiowa peace chief Kicking Bird (Striking Eagle or Kicking Eagle, T'ené-angópte), who had assisted the military in selecting the Kiowas to be imprisoned, rode forward and spoke to the prisoners, saying in effect: "Brothers, the time has come to say goodbye. I am sorry for you. But because of your stubbornness, I have failed to keep you out of trouble. You will have to be punished by the government."[2]

Kiowa war leader and medicine man Maman-ti (Mamän'-te, Man-Who-Walks-Above-the-Ground or Sky Walker, also known as Dahä'-ti or the Owl Prophet) is said to have answered: "You have become a big man with the whites, Kicking Bird. But you will pay the price soon enough."[3]

Upon this account is built the legend of Kicking Bird's mysterious death that was soon to follow, a legend many Kiowas still believe today. During their camp on the second night from Fort Sill, the story goes, the prisoners were smoking the calumet. When passing the pipe to Maman-ti, Eagle Chief suggested that the Kiowa medicine man use his magical powers to issue a prayer of vengeance for the death of Kicking Bird. Maman-ti agreed to do so, but reluctantly, for he believed if he so used his hexing power against a fellow tribesman, his own life would soon end.[4]

It is recorded fact that on May 3, 1875, only five days after the prisoners departed, Kicking Bird, who was still a young man of around forty

years, died suddenly and unexpectedly in his lodge near Fort Sill.[5] Most of
the military and agency workers at the post conjectured that he had been
poisoned, and such was surmised in the post surgeon's belated report,
made without examination of the body. The most popular and often-
repeated scenario of published accounts by writers is that a Mexican
servant brought Kicking Bird a cup of coffee, he drank it, and he died
soon after. Still another version of Kicking Bird's demise put forth by a
man who visited Fort Sill during the spring of 1875 was that the Kiowa
chief had been poisoned by one of his wives for having delivered her
brother as one of those sent to Fort Marion.[6]

Maman-ti did die that same year, but not immediately as many have
claimed. His death came on July 29, 1875, three months after departing
from Fort Sill. He was one of three Kiowas who perished that year at Fort
Marion. Some believe Maman-ti's death came as a penalty for his curse
on Kicking Bird; others think he succumbed to the dank, unprairie-like
conditions inside the walls of the ancient fortress, which had been built
by the Spanish many years earlier as the Castillo de San Marcos.[7]

Hearsay account, speculation, and casual opinion are often disput-
able, and it is not expected that any theory of Kicking Bird's death will
ever be proved or disproved to the satisfaction of all. Indeed, the coinci-
dental closeness of the departure of the prisoners and Kicking Bird's
death is difficult to ignore. Nonetheless, it is regretful that the intrigue
and mystery of his death should so override the true measure of Kicking
Bird's existence both as a noted Kiowa warrior and as a leading peace
advocate during the critical struggles of peace and war on the Central
Plains. By whatever means he died and for whatever negative attitude is
held toward him, there is no question that the white men—of both the
Indian Bureau and the U.S. military—who knew Kicking Bird best believed he was a courageous and key participant in the compelled transition of the Kiowas to an accommodation with the white man and his way
of life. It is understandable, however, that some Kiowas might see the
matter differently.

Precisely what year Kicking Bird was born is unrecorded. It is thought
he was about forty years of age when he died in 1875;[8] thus the date of his
birth is placed around 1835. This was very close to the time of the first
formal relations between the United States and the Kiowas. Kicking Bird's
life thus spanned one of the most critical and volatile eras of known Kiowa
history, the period in which the tribe was forced from its life of freedom
on the prairie to the confinement and suppression of a reservation.

A half century before Kicking Bird was born, the Kiowas arrived on
the Southern Plains to take up a nomadic life in an area centered by

western Kansas and Oklahoma and the Texas Panhandle. Originally a northern mountain tribe, they first emerge into known history as residents of southern Montana and members of the Plateau Salish confederacy that included the Blackfeet and Crows. A Kiowa creation tradition tells how they believe they first came into being as the Gai'gwu, the Principal People on Earth.

> In the beginning, darkness surrounded the people who were killing one another until Coyote, with the help of Swift Hawk, Prairie Chicken, and another kind of hawk, brought the sun and put it on top of their tepee so it would light the earth. It was not high enough. After all creatures had failed to get the sun high enough to light everything, Spider Old Woman placed it on her foot and kicked it up, saying, "Sun go up and give light to all the world."
>
> With the sun up and light everywhere, all the people (tribes) on Earth came together at a big body of water from which some sharp points protruded. The leader said, "Whoever jumps in here, his people will be above all others. Others will be afraid of them."
>
> Several creatures started to jump in, but it looked too dangerous and they backed away. Finally, a Kiowa man dove in and the leaders said, "Now, since he dove in, he shall be above all of us. This is his land, and after the life of the Kiowa is ended there is to be no more life on Earth."[9]

In his lodge during the spring of 1873, Kicking Bird explained the Kiowa concept of death and afterlife to Quaker teacher Thomas C. Battey. The Kiowa spirit, he said, was thought to have originally made a long journey westward toward the sunset, crossing over a high chain of mountains and coming to a large body of water. On the opposite shore, the spirit met with all of its former friends and loved ones. The spirit land was a place where the grass was always green, the horses large and beautiful, and the game fat and plentiful. There was no sickness or pain, and there was constant joy. Sentinels kept watch from a mountain top for spirits of the dead or dying so others could prepare their lodges and go to meet them.[10]

On another occasion, while sitting around a campfire and viewing the night sky during a journey between villages, Kicking Bird joined others in conveying the Kiowa notion of the heavens to Battey. The moon, the Kiowas said, was the Great White Man, while the white man's Pleiades were to them the Great Kiowa. The Great Kiowa was a very large and powerful man who had created all the lakes, rivers, mountains, and prairies, as well as all the animals. He had once traveled westward until he came to a large, hollow tree lying on the ground.

The Great Kiowa struck the tree forcefully, and a group of Kiowa people came out. These proved to be disfigured, so he sent them away and struck the log again. This time the true Kiowa people came out, first men and women and then children. The Great Kiowa discovered, however, that evil had been done in the log, and he vowed he would make no more Kiowas. After providing them with bows and arrows and sharp stones for dressing skins, he taught them how to slay animals for food and to make clothes and lodges from the skin of the animals.[11]

Leaving the tribe, the Great Kiowa traveled east until he came to a great water. There he met the Great White Man, who was well clothed and rode a fine horse. The man had many children living beyond the waters for whom he had provided books and fine houses. He had also taught them to plant in the ground and produce food to eat. The Great Kiowa returned to his people and told them of his meeting with the Great White Man. But he reminded them that he had given the prairie to the Kiowas. If the children of the Great White Man should come to the prairie, the Kiowas must fight them as enemies and never make peace with them. Afterward, the Great Kiowa and the Great White Man went back into the heavens where they could watch over the earth.[12]

The moral of the story, though, was troubling to Kicking Bird. He confessed to Battey that he felt the Great Kiowa was wrong in telling his children to never make peace with the white people. The tale, he observed, was taught to children when they were very young, and it remained with them all of their lives.

"This big man [the Great Kiowa] is the father of them [the Kiowas]," Kicking Bird once said to agent Lawrie Tatum, "and he went to the moon one night and we can see him every night; he watches by our camp-fires and some day (don't know when) he will get tired of watching and kill them all, and white men too, may be so by water, may be so by fire, I don't know how."[13]

The pre-Plains existence of the Kiowas remains obscure and mysterious. We are largely dependent upon tribal traditions for accounts of them prior to recorded history. Almost all such oral histories, passed from one generation to the next, tend to vary over time with retelling. Still, these accounts provide the framework of beliefs within which the Kiowas existed as a people. Ethnologist James Mooney states that the earliest tradition of the tribe places it in western Montana on the headwaters of the Missouri and Yellowstone Rivers: "They describe it as a region of great cold and deep snows, and say that they had the Flatheads near them, and that on the other side of the mountains was a large stream flowing westward, evidently an upper branch of the Columbia. These mountains they still call Gâ'i K'op, 'Kiowa mountains.' "[14]

Kiowa legend tells of their early migration from the north that occurred as a result of a quarrel between two chiefs over the division of a hunt. The entire tribe became involved in the argument, causing one faction to migrate to the northwest and, supposedly, becoming lost to historical record. The relationship of Satank and other older Kiowas with the Sarsi or Pakiage tribe of western Canada may well be tied to this northward-moving faction. Mooney, in *Calendar History of the Kiowas*, states that Satank's maternal grandmother was a Sarsi who married a Kiowa man as a result of friendly visits between the two tribes.[15]

The remainder of the Kiowas, the tradition states, migrated southeastward across the Yellowstone. There they took up close alliance with the Crows who taught them the ways of the Plains Indians and instilled cultural elements such as the buffalo skin tepee, the soldier societies, the medicine lodge, the Sun Dance, the Ten Grandmother medicine bundles, the sacred lances, and the three carved sacred images known as the "Taime."

In 1929 Kiowa elder Alukah, hereditary keeper of the Taime, told a story of how his people came to possess the sun god emblem.

> The Kiowas, when they lived in the north, a long time ago, received the sun god from the Crows, who worshipped it. An Arapaho youth visited the Crows. He was poor; he had no ponies. The Crows were holding a

Kiowas hunting buffalo. Whipple, *Reports of Exploration.*

sun dance and the Arapaho joined in the dance. He danced long and earnestly before the sun god in hope that it would pity him and make him prosperous. The chief priest of the Crows rewarded him by giving him the taime image, notwithstanding the protests of the other Crows, who were angry at seeing such a favor conferred upon a stranger. Fortune smiled upon the Arapaho; he stole many horses and won new blessings for himself by tying numerous ponies to the medicine lodge as a sacrifice to the taime, until at last his herd was of the largest. Being now wealthy, when his own people visited the Crows, he gathered his herd of ponies and went back with them. He married a Kiowa woman and went to live with her tribe, and the taime became the medicine, or sun god of the Kiowas. Since that time the taime has been handed down to his family, of which I am a descendant.[16]

C. E. Campbell, who worked among the Kiowas at Fort Sill during their early reservation days, offered another Kiowa tale of how the tribe came to possess the Taime. The story, which contains elements of the creation legend, relates that sometime in their forgotten past, the Great Spirit called together representatives from all the Indian tribes, as well as a white man, a yellow man (a Mexican), and a black man. They were shown a great pit where the "true medicine," encased in painted skins, lay surrounded by sharpened spears. The spears were so close together that even the smallest animal could not pass between them.

The men were told that the medicine would belong to the one who was brave enough to jump into the pit. The white man, the yellow man, the black man, and red men of many tribes came to the pit but refused to jump down onto the spears and what appeared to be certain death. But finally a Kiowa with a brave heart came forth. He decided that he was willing to give his life so his people could have the true medicine.

He ran forward and made a great leap into the pit. As he did so, the spears all swung back, and the Kiowa landed unhurt. For this he was rewarded with the sacred Taime that "would make them invincible in war, successful in the hunt and would ward off sickness and calamity from them."[17]

If, as Battey states, Kicking Bird's grandfather was a Crow captive of the Kiowas, it would indicate a period of warfare between the two tribes. The long association between the Kiowas and the Crows, however, is clear evidence that a strong alliance flourished between them during the late eighteenth and early nineteenth centuries. Even after moving south, the Kiowas made sojourns up along the Rocky Mountains to the north country to visit with relatives and friends.[18]

Scholars remain uncertain as to the meaning of the fact that the Kiowa language is of the Tanoan stock and akin to that spoken by the

Whipple expedition view of Kiowas on the move. Whipple, *Reports of Exploration.*

Tiwa (Taos, Picuris, Sandia, Isleta), Tewa (San Juan, Santa Clara, San Ildefonso, Nambe, Tesuque), and Towa (Jemez) pueblos of New Mexico.[19] Mooney, who conducted interviews with the Kiowas prior to 1900, states that elderly tribal members had a firm memory of lost relatives who lived in the north, but they were positive that they had no kindred in the south or elsewhere.[20]

Another migration account was recited by Kicking Bird, who obviously learned it as part of his people's folklore. The story recounts how the Kiowas once lived in a country to the north of the Crows and the Lakota Sioux where it was very cold for most of the year. They knew nothing of horses then, using dogs to pull the lodgepole travois that carried their goods. This habit of the past was still evident in 1845 when the Abert party, which had happened onto a Kiowa band in the Texas Panhandle, noted that the Kiowas still had great numbers of dogs that "look most uncanine and have more the exterior of a wolf than that of the domestic quadruped. . . . Their bark resembles that of the prairie wolf."[21]

Kicking Bird's migration account also told of a Kiowa man who wandered far southward and was taken prisoner by the Comanches, who had never seen anyone like him. He was spared from being put to death when a head man argued that it would be wise to treat him well and send him back to his tribe. Then, if a Comanche were captured by the man's people, he would be befriended in return. The Kiowa was given a horse, saddle, and bridle that won him great attention when he arrived back among his people. When spring came, most of the tribe left their dogs with friends and began a migration to the south.[22]

It was nearly two decades into the nineteenth century before whites made recorded contacts directly with the Kiowas. Although there are undoubtedly transcending societal elements between their prehistory existence and that which is known of them afterward, it is clear that during the late seventeenth century the tribe underwent a drastic change through its adaptation to the buffalo-hunter culture of the Plains.

Apparently the tribe had become almost totally acculturated to the regimen of the prairie by the time the first white men ventured among them. Their principal food was meat, generally boiled in a kettle—with buffalo, antelope, or deer much preferred. When these were unavailable and hunger stalked the camps, the horse, mule, dog, or wolf became subsistence. The bear, a principal mountain game, was considered bad medicine and was never eaten. The land tortoise, cooked among the ashes of a campfire, was a favorite dish. The Kiowas did not eat fish or bird. The wild turkey was hunted only for its feathers, which were used to wing arrows.[23]

Undoubtedly, it was during their Montana period in the mid- or late 1700s that the Kiowas first experienced and acquired the horse. The new buffalo culture the Crows taught them was dependent on the chase of buffalo on horseback rather than by the old method of surrounding the herd on foot. Possession of the horse was a virtual prerequisite for their move from the mountains onto the Plains to take up a buffalo-hunting existence west of the Black Hills of South Dakota prior to 1800.

The horse also gave them new war-making potential. It equated them with other tribes as a fighting force, offered their villages movability and better seclusion from attack, and provided them with an invaluable tool in hunting the buffalo, which produced many necessities of life. Being small in numbers, the Kiowas had been much at the mercy of larger tribes in previous times. By joining with others, however, they could strike back.

Early tradition indicates that prior to 1775 the Gens du Serpents were defeated and driven from south of the Black Hills by a force of Kiowas, Arikaras, Crows, and possibly Kiowa-Apaches.[24] The Kiowas' alliance with the Crows and other tribes helped, but not enough, as Lakota chief Black Hawk indicated during the 1851 Treaty of Fort Laramie:

> These lands [the Platte River country] once belonged to the Kiowas and
> Crows, but we whipped these nations out of them, and in this did what

the white men do when they want the lands of the Indians. We met the Kiowas and Crows and whipped them, at the Kiowa Creek just below where we now are. We met them and whipped them again, this time at Crow Creek. This last battle was fought by the Cheyennes, Arapahoes and Ogallahlala combined, and the Ogallahlala claim their share of the country.[25]

One account, which may refer to the same incident, states that the Lakota Sioux attacked the K'úato band of Kiowas in about 1790. When the leader of the K'úatos ordered his people to stand and fight, they were completely wiped out except, perhaps, for one woman survivor.[26]

The historical path of the Kiowas is attached by mythology to the great thimble-shaped butte in northeastern Wyoming known as Devils Tower. Kiowa legend relates the story of a spirit that once transformed a Kiowa girl into a giant Bear Girl. Beset with power, the Bear Girl threatened to devour her seven siblings. The siblings took refuge on a small rock and prayed to the Great Spirit to be saved. The rock then began to grow higher and higher until those on top were beyond the Bear Girl's reach. She clawed the sides of the tower furiously, leaving deep vertical cleavages in its sides. Eventually the siblings rose into the heavens where they became the seven stars of the Pleiades.[27]

The Kiowas resided in close contact with the Crows and, like them, traded with the Hidatsa (Gros Ventres), Arikara, and Mandan at the Great Bend of the Missouri River near present Bismarck, North Dakota. Ethnologist James Mooney states that the Kiowas were once such good friends with the Arikara that one division of the Kiowa tribe was called the K'at'a, or Arikara band.[28] While on a trading visit to the Missouri River, however, a complete band of Kiowas was attacked and annihilated by the Teton Sioux. In 1795 French trader Trudeau reported that the Kiowas were staying far up the Cheyenne River, fearful to resume their trade.[29]

Pressure from the Lakotas, who were pushing westward into the Platte River country, was one cause of the Kiowa migration southward to the Arkansas River of present Colorado shortly before 1800. There may have been other reasons as well. The availability of horses to steal in New Mexico and the potential of trade there were undoubtedly factors. Bernard Mishkin, in *Rank and Warfare Among the Plains Indians*, contends that while wild horses were abundant on the early Plains, the raiding of Texan and Mexican rancherias was the principal method of acquiring horses by the tribes.[30] The "Cayguas" (Kiowas) along with the Comanches, Apaches, Navajos, and Utes were listed in 1748 by Spanish historian Jose Antonio Vello Senor y Sanchez as special enemies of New Mexico.[31]

Debenneville R. Keim, correspondent companion of Gen. Phil Sheridan during his 1868–1869 sojourn to the Indian Territory, became acquainted with the tribes at Fort Cobb and Fort Sill. On the subject of the Kiowa migration, he recounted:

> The Kiowas claim that their primitive country was in the far north. That other tribes coming upon them, a long and sanguinary war ensued, in which both parties were nearly used up. Seeing their condition, and still too proud to offer or to accept terms of peace, both withdrew. After remaining for a while in their old country, continually harassed by their enemies, their hunters brought back stories of extensive regions to the south, and inhabited by a people much weakened by wars. The entire tribe resolved to drive out these prior occupants, and take possession of these new lands. The families were collected and the removal commenced. Their effects were carried on dogs, or sledges drawn by that animal. From the north they reached a river, now the south fork of the Platte. Their residence upon the borders of this stream is within the recollection of the old men of the tribe.
>
> Not satisfied with the Platte country, they moved on across the Republican and Smoky Hill until they reached the Arkansas. Thence they moved upon the head waters of the Cimarron. Here they permanently located their council fire, and after much fighting secured control of all the country south of the Arkansas, and north of the Wichita mountains and head waters of the Red river.
>
> There are many evidences in the names of tributary streams on the upper Missouri indicating that the Kiowas at one time were in that vicinity. Kiowa pride would not descend to an admission that the tribe was compelled to leave. . . . The Cheyennes and Arrapahoes claim some years ago, to have had severe wars with the Kiowas, and that they whipped them to such an extent that they left the country.[32]

Following their move as a tribe to the Arkansas River, the Kiowas aggressively plundered Spanish settlements in New Mexico. In the fall of 1800 Kiowa warriors were among a large combined force of 300 to 500 northern Indians that raided frontier settlements south of the Arkansas River. The invaders ravaged the Spanish villas, burning, looting, and taking stock and captives. Spanish troops, supported by Jicarilla Apaches and Utes, arrived too late to intercept them.[33]

The Kiowas' move southward was made just behind the much larger Comanche migration, and for a time the two tribes competed for territory. During the summer of 1802 a Comanche force struck a Kiowa camp on the Arkansas, killing twenty-four people and retaking much of the property that been stolen from them earlier. In the spring of 1806 Kiowa chief Guik'áte, second to head chief Bule, met with the Comanches at the Double Mountain Fork of the Brazos and worked out a permanent peace between the two tribes. Guik'áte may have been the Kiowa known to the Spaniards as El Ronco, who in 1806 married the daughter of a Comanche chief and thereafter lived with that tribe.[34]

Little is recorded of the Kiowa chiefs of this date and before. Three that have been named are Poliakya, or Hare-Lip, who was also named Kagiatse, or Thick Blanket; Tsonbohon, or Feather Cap; and A'date (Guik'áte).[35]

While in Colorado, the Kiowas were involved in constant warfare with the Utes of northeastern Colorado and the Pawnees of the Loup River in Nebraska. They also conducted sojourns to trade with the French on the Missouri River even as they raided in New Mexico. Overtures from the Spanish governor eventually persuaded them of the trading advantages in New Mexico. In August 1807 Chief Bule led a party of fourteen Kiowas to Santa Fe where they entered into a peace and trade treaty with the New Mexicans at the Palace of the Governors. The governor draped a large silver medal around Bule's neck and presented him with a silver-headed cane.

The Kiowa presence in New Mexico is established by New Mexico church records that reveal thirty-five baptisms and six burials of Kiowas from 1727 to 1800.[36] It is possible that these were captives, but other evidence indicates that an era of peaceful coexistence with the New Mexicans may have taken place. In 1848, however, Maj. William Gilpin referred to the Kiowas as long the scourge of Mexico and Taos as well as the road to Santa Fe.[37]

In a manuscript concerning Stumbling Bear, Kicking Bird's fellow chief and cousin, Lucille Gilstrap recounts a descendant story of a Kiowa party that supposedly visited Chihuahua, Mexico, around 1804. At that time, the story goes, the Kiowa chief was awarded a silver medal that became known as the Sun Medal. Since it is improbable that the Kiowas would have a peace agreement with Mexico immediately preceding the one of 1807, this descendant story likely refers to the latter affair.[38]

Once the arrangement was made, the Kiowas enjoyed harmonious relations with the New Mexicans, who entertained them lavishly and made a large variety of trade goods available to them. In February 1809 Kiowas under chief Dos Hachas were among a large multitribal delegation that visited Santa Fe.[39]

It was during this period of history, however, that Anglo-Americans began to influence the course of Kiowa existence on the Plains. Some of the Anglos were from a place in the east known as the United States; others from the south were called Texicans. To the Kiowas, they were separate and distinct peoples.

2

First U.S. Contact

The Lewis and Clark expedition did not meet the Kiowas during their stay at Fort Mandan through the winter of 1804–1805. From information supplied by the Mandans, Hidatsas, and others, however, the explorers were able to list the Kiowas as residing on the Paduca Fork of the Platte River in present Wyoming.[1] The tribe reportedly had a population of about 700 persons, possessed around seventy lodges, and could field about 200 warriors. They were described as a wandering, well-disposed tribe who conducted trade with the Mandans and Hidatsas.[2]

In 1806 an exploring party under Capt. Zebulon Pike marched south from the Pawnee villages of Nebraska to the Big Bend of the Arkansas River in Kansas. At that point, Pike and the main group continued on toward the Rocky Mountains of Colorado while Lt. James B. Wilkinson and a small detachment turned eastward down the river toward Arkansas. In passing through the buffalo prairie of southern Kansas, the Wilkinson men encountered a Pawnee war party returning home from a revenge raid on the Kiowas.[3]

Pike and his men reached the mountains and began exploring along the South Platte. On December 16 they discovered the remnants of a large camp marked by a cross. Later it would be learned that this had been the campsite of a party of around 3,000 Kiowas and Comanches accompanied by a few white hunters and traders on a tour of the region. The trading party had been led by James Purcell (Pike called him Pursley), a former captive of the Kiowas who, after escaping, had been hired to go back to the region with trade goods. An attack by the Lakotas drove the party from the Plains into the mountains where Pike and his men found their signs in abundance. The Kiowas and Comanches eventually sent Purcell in to Santa Fe to see if the New Mexicans would be willing to establish trade relations.[4]

Pike reported that the nomadic Kiowas then roved the headwaters of the Platte and Arkansas Rivers of present Colorado and among the mountain regions of northern New Mexico. Their warriors, estimated at about 1,000 men, still fought with the bow, arrow, and lance. The tribe lived off the buffalo and possessed immense horse herds. Pike was mistaken, however, in stating that they spoke the same language as the Comanches and Utes.[5]

No record is available of U.S. contact with the Kiowas during the ensuing nine years. A Dakota (Sioux) calendar, however, tells of an incident that took place between that tribe and the Kiowas on Horse Creek of eastern Wyoming during the winter of 1814–1815. There the Kiowas, Arapahos, Kiowa Apaches, Cheyennes, Crows, and Dakotas met and traded horses and other goods. Trade had barely gotten under way when a quarrel erupted and a Dakota Indian split open a Kiowa's head with a war ax. The Dakotas then attacked Kiowas and others and drove them into the mountains, ending the conclave.[6]

During 1816 the Kiowas and other tribes of the Plains were struck by a decimating smallpox epidemic brought by war parties returning from the settlements of New Mexico. The disease annihilated nearly half of the Kiowa people.[7]

In its exploration westward up the Platte and Loup Rivers of Nebraska in June 1820, the Stephen H. Long expedition visited a Pawnee village. There they found the village chief in mourning for a brother who had been killed in a recent battle. A Pawnee Loup war party of ninety-three men had gone south on foot to steal horses. South of the Arkansas River, the Pawnees were attacked by a large combined force of Kiowas, Comanches, and Arapahos and in desperate hand-to-hand combat were severely defeated.[8]

Later, the Long party had the first official U.S. meeting with the Kiowas. After marching up the Platte and then the South Platte Rivers, the group moved south down the eastern slopes of the Rockies. Upon reaching the Arkansas River, Long and his men encountered a Kaskaia Indian man and woman.[9]

The Kaskaias are believed to have been Kiowa-Apaches. Anthropologist James Mooney claims, however, that the tribe was not the product of a Kiowa-Apache union in the south as is generally thought. He insists that they were of Athapascan stock and migrated south with the Kiowas after a long association in the north.[10] During the years to follow, the Kiowa-Apaches would become known as Prairie or Plains Apaches, playing a shadowy and lesser role with the Kiowas and Comanches and being included in a secondary way to treaties with those two tribes.

The two Kaskaias met by Long were on their way to the mountains, having just left a large encampment of Kiowas, Cheyennes, Arapahos, and other tribes several days downriver. The man, who was known as the Calf, said that a combined force of warriors from the camp had recently defeated the Spaniards in a battle on the Red River.[11]

Shortly after this meeting, Long divided his party for the return march eastward. While one group under Capt. John R. Bell returned east down the Arkansas River, Long led the other segment of twenty-two men farther south into New Mexico in search of the Red River as a route to follow back to the United States. In doing so, however, he mistook the headwaters of the Canadian River for those of the Red and followed the former stream eastward. Near the New Mexico–Texas Panhandle border, the expedition met a sizable group of Kaskaias preparing to cross the stream.[12]

The cavalcade of thirty-two lodges and 250 tribespeople was returning from a hunting expedition on the upper Brazos and Colorado Rivers of northwestern Texas. At the advance were the women of the band who led the way on horseback, each herding a remuda of extra horses. Some of the horses were dragging lodge poles fully loaded either with children or with buffalo meat. Expedition chronicler Edwin James described the scene:

> We were amused at observing many small children, too young to be able by their own strength to sit on a horse, lashed by their legs to the saddle, and riding on in entire unconcern. As they passed the deepest part of the river, many stopped to fill their vessels with water. These were of the most primitive kind, being formed almost without exception of the stomach or bladder of a bison or other animals.[13]

Of special interest to the explorers were numerous images of alligators among the Indians, possibly indicating the tribe's penetration well into Texas.[14] These carved-wood reptile figures, leather covered and ornamented with beads, were considered to be great medicine and were often worn dangling about the neck. The leader of the band, a large, ferocious-looking man called Red Mouse, employed a small image of the alligator to treat a wound he had recently received when an arrow had passed through his arm.

Although the visit was brief, James provided an interesting description of the band who had experienced little contact with whites other

Kaskaia camp met by Long Expedition in Texas Panhandle. Thwaites, *Stephen H. Long Expedition*.

than occasional Spanish traders. One child of Mexican descent was seen among the band. The Indians were amused by the difference in the skin color of the Long party. The Kaskaias knew of tobacco but could not tolerate it unmixed with other substances. James saw but one iron pot among them, although some of the women wore beads and brass or pewter rings. Some of the young females, he observed, were not unattractive. His description of the Kaskaia warriors compares favorably with that of the Kiowas: "The men of this band wear the hair long and suffer it to hang negligently about the shoulders. Some of them have a braid behind which is garnished with bits of red cloth, small pieces of tin, &c., and descends nearly to the ground, being sometimes eked out with the hair of a horse's tail."[15]

The Long group met no more Indians on their journey across the Indian Territory to Arkansas. The other division of the Long expedition under Bell, however, enjoyed a peaceful encounter with the Kiowas proper. Two days after separating from Long near the mouth of the Purgatoire River, Bell's party of twelve men came onto the consolidated encampment of tribes mentioned by the Calf. They were warmly welcomed, and Bell responded by inviting several of the chiefs to visit his camp. He presented a few knives, combs, and other gifts to the tribal leaders and

Kiowa encampment visited by Captain Long on the Arkansas River in eastern Colorado. *Stephen H. Long Expedition.*

promised that the white father would send out more goods. Afterward, virtually the whole Indian camp came forth, eager to trade jerked meat, skins, hair ropes, and other articles for trinkets of the white men.[16]

Before leaving the encampment, the travelers were visited by an elderly Kiowa chief who happily pronounced Kiowa words for ethnologist Thomas Say to enter in the expedition record. The chief also made a gift of a horse to the group. Interpreter Bijeau, who had lived among those tribes for three years, indicated that the Kaskaia and Kiowa languages were among the most difficult to understand and learn. Curiously, although those two tribes were constantly together, they appeared totally unable to speak or understand one another's tongue.[17]

Farther down the river, the explorers met a war party of nine Indians. One was a young Kiowa who attempted to take the horse Bell had purchased from the Kaskaia. He was repulsed without any disturbance being created among the other Kiowas.[18] The group met other war parties composed of Cheyennes and Comanches, but no additional Kiowas or Kaskaias were encountered.

Even closer white contact with the Kiowas came the following year when frontiersman Hugh Glenn led a hunting and trapping party from Arkansas Territory to the upper Arkansas River of present Colorado. The over-winter excursion was chronicled by Jacob Fowler, a member of the party. Among the numerous Indians frequenting the river east of the mountains was a band of Kiowas under their principal chief.

The chief proved to be a friendly and hospitable man. He was unhappy, however, to learn that the trade goods of the party were not those Major Long had promised would be sent out. The Kiowa chief claimed he had refused a Comanche invitation to join in a war against the Osages and the whites. Fowler was impressed with the great number of excellent horses owned by both the Kiowas and Comanches. Glenn presented the chief with a medal bearing the likeness of Gen. Andrew Jackson. The Kiowa promised that he would treat with kindness any white men he met.

"It is but Justice to Say," Fowler wrote, "we find the Kiawa the best Indeans poss[ess]ing more firmness and manly deportment than the arrapoho and less arogrance and Hatey Pride than the Ietan [Comanche]."[19]

Likely, the Kiowas were drawn to the Arkansas River in part for reasons of trade with the other tribes and with any whites who came forth. The Bent brothers and Ceran St. Vrain would soon erect the trading post known as Fort William, or Bent's Fort, near present La Junta, Colorado.

Thomas James, a trader who traversed the upper North Canadian on his way to Santa Fe in 1821, told of a Kiowa-related incident while crossing Kansas on his way home from Santa Fe. His group was met by a large body of Kiowa and Pawnee Indians, then on friendly terms, who said they were on the way to the Salt Plains to make peace with the Comanches, Arapahos, and other tribes. The Indians badly wanted to kill two Mexicans with James's party, and a Kiowa chief made a violent harangue to that purpose. James, however, was able to intercede, and some older chiefs calmed the situation.[20]

James came west again in 1823 to build a temporary fort and conduct trade at (it is believed) the conflux of Beaver and Wolf Creeks in present northwest Oklahoma. In his book *Three Years Among the Mexicans and Indians,* he mentions the Comanches and Wichitas but says nothing of any contact with the Kiowas during his trading operations on the North Canadian.

A curious account of the early Kiowas was provided by Capt. W. E. Doyle, who said he was told by the Comanches at Fort Sill that when first known on the headwaters of the Platte and Arkansas Rivers, the Kiowas lived in holes in the ground. This habit was confirmed to him by Col. Albert G. Boone who said that when he was with Ashley's trapping party in 1822, he and his comrades were observing a group of Indians who suddenly and mysteriously disappeared. Upon investigation they found the Indians to be Kiowas who resided in subterranean habitations eight feet in diameter, the holes neatly lined with grass and buffalo robes. The Kiowas called themselves "a-tool-pay."[21]

The Atkinson-O'Fallon expedition, which worked its way up the Missouri River in 1825 to make treaty arrangements with the resident tribes, was told of the Kiowas. At the foot of the river's great bend in present North Dakota, the expedition established a log-cabin fort called Fort Kiaway. Although the expedition did not contact the Kiowas directly, its journal referred to them as residing on the headwaters of the Arkansas and Platte.[22]

Indications are that the Kiowas remained close to the Arkansas River at this time, in part because of the transportation that had begun to pass along its banks after 1821 when William Becknell took the first wagons over the route. Other traders followed, and by 1824 both American and Mexican trade caravans were passing regularly between Westport, Missouri, and Santa Fe, New Mexico. During 1825 and 1826 a three-man U.S. commission surveyed and marked the famous commercial link between the United States and Mexico.

The ever-increasing traffic on the road offered the Kiowas the potential of procuring foodstuff and tobacco as bribes for passage; of finding metal objects and other items of value left behind at campsites; and, at times, for preying on careless or vulnerable travelers. Trading caravans were hit particularly hard during 1828. One caravan was robbed of nearly a thousand horses and mules; the men of another, which lost all of its animals, was forced to abandon its wagons and walk home.[23]

Major B. Riley, an early veteran of the trail, clashed with Indians at Chouteau's Island near the present town of Lakin in Kearny County, Kansas, while escorting a trading caravan westward in July 1829 with three companies of infantry and one of riflemen. When a three-man party of hunters went out from the traders' camp, one was killed by a war party. Later, a discharged soldier was slain when he and three others attempted to return east to the settlements. When Riley dispatched a search party to find and bring in the soldier's body, his camp was attacked by 300 mounted warriors armed with guns, bows and arrows, and spears. Riley lost one man, fifty-four oxen, twenty horses, and a few mules: "I have reason to believe that there was a part of the Camanchies, Arapahoes, and Hiaways, as one of my men's tin pans was found with some of these three nations that attacked the traders on their return."[24]

The huge Kiowa horse herds witnessed by Fowler indicate that the tribe already regularly ranged south of the river into New Mexico, north Texas, and western Oklahoma. Jean Louis Berlandier, who visited among the Comanches of southern Texas in 1830, wrote that little was known about the "Caihuas," or Kiowas, who resided in the furthermost reaches of Texas and in New Mexico and camped with the Comanches there. He also told of Plains Apaches who first appeared in the Texas deserts during the early 1800s.[25]

Soon, however, the Kiowas would be conducting regular sorties into southern Texas and Mexico, seeking more horses, mules, and captives. Tribal position and personal wealth resulted, and the raids became an integral part of life for the prairie tribesmen.

The development of trade between Missouri and Santa Fe, New Mexico, created an ever-increasing flow of wagon caravans through the heart of the Kiowa range. Most traders traveled the Arkansas River route across Kansas to Colorado that became known as the Santa Fe Trail, but some followed a course that traced the Canadian River crossing of the Indian Territory and Texas Panhandle.

It was virtually inevitable that clashes between these merchant expeditions and the prairie tribes would occur. One such incident took place in December 1832 when the Kiowas attacked a company of twelve Missouri traders returning from Santa Fe along the Canadian River of the Texas Panhandle. The group's pack mules were loaded with $10,000 in Mexican specie. Two of the traders were killed during a thirty-six hour standoff before the others finally fled, leaving behind all their goods including the specie, which they buried. Five of the men eventually staggered into the Creek settlements in eastern Indian Territory, and all but two of five others perished on the prairie. Behind them, the Kiowas looted their camp and found the buried specie. Having never encountered money, the Kiowas hammered the coins into disks to be used as silver decorations for themselves and their horses.[26]

At this point, however, the Kiowas were less concerned with white intrusion into their country than they were with their feuding with other tribes. The Osages in particular were their much-hated enemies. Two Osage bands, one under Clermont and another under White Hair, had migrated from Missouri to take up residence on the Verdigris River of northeastern Indian Territory and southeastern Kansas. Warriors from these villages commonly raided the Kiowa, Comanche, Wichita, and Plains Apache horse herds and, whenever the opportunity presented itself, killed or took captives.

In the spring of 1833, a large Kiowa war party of nearly 200 men left their villages on Cache, Otter, and Rainey Mountain Creeks near the Wichita Mountains and rode northeastward on a revenge raid. Their objective was the more northerly of the two Osage villages, which was under Chief White Hair. Before reaching the Osage town, however, the mounted Kiowas, armed with bows and arrows and lances, were intercepted by a like number of Osage warriors.

The Osages were on foot, but they were armed with flintlock rifles secured from Missouri traders. As the two forces closed for combat, a heavy rainstorm blew in. Unable to use their bows in the heavy rain, the Kiowas withdrew. Not long after this incident, a party of Kiowas was engaged by a party of Osage hunters, each side losing two men in the ensuing confrontation.[27]

Even as these events were taking place, a far greater tragedy was befalling one of the Kiowa home camps. A large Osage war party from the village of Clermont, located to the south of White Hair, was on its way westward to the Salt Plains along the Cimarron River when it came onto the trail of the Kiowa expedition. Enterprisingly, the Osages began backtracking the trail toward the Kiowa home camp in the Wichita Mountains.

When the Kiowa warriors departed, an elderly chief named Ah-da-te had been left in charge. He led his band of Kiowas to just beyond a pass in the mountains along Otter Creek known today as Cutthroat Gap where the Osages found the undefended Kiowa village and fell on it without mercy. Kiowa women, children, and old men alike attempted to flee into the mountains, but an estimated 150 were killed. The Osages cut off the heads of their victims and placed them around the destroyed camp in brass buckets the Kiowas had obtained in trade with the Pawnees. The Osages then burned the tepee village to the ground and absconded with the Kiowas' sacred Taime medicine, as well as over 100 scalps, seven captives, and more than 400 horses. They also carried off battered, sand-rusted Mexican coins found on the corpses of the dead Kiowas. The Osage attack became known in Kiowa calendars as the "Summer that they cut off their heads."[28]

U.S. officials, who still knew very little about the Kiowas and other tribes of western Indian Territory, were alarmed at the increasing disturbances on the Plains. "It is deemed indispensable to the peace and security of the frontier," Secretary of War Lewis Cass wrote, "that a respectable force should be displayed in that quarter, and that the wandering and restless tribes who roam through it should be impressed with the power of the United States by the expedition of a corps so well qualified to excite their respect."[29]

Accordingly, during the spring of 1834 a sizable military expedition of First U.S. Dragoons was formed at Fort Gibson under the command of Brig. Gen. Henry Leavenworth. In preparation, three Indian captives were purchased from the Osages, eventually to be used as tokens of friendship in contacting the prairie tribes. One was an eighteen-year-old Wichita girl who had been captured five or six years before. The other two were a Kiowa girl of fourteen years (Wun-pan-to-mee, or the White Weasel) and her younger brother (Tunk-aht-oh-ye, or the Thunderer), both of whom had been taken the year before at Cutthroat Gap. The day after Indian artist George Catlin had painted his portrait, the boy was killed when he was butted into a fence by a belligerent ram at a trading post near Fort Gibson.[30]

In addition to presenting a show of force, U.S. officials further hoped to rescue a young white boy named Matthew Martin who had been captured and his father killed by unknown Indians while hunting along the Red River in eastern Indian Territory. Also taken off was one of the family's slaves. The dragoons further hoped to learn the fate of an officer of their First Dragoon regiment, Lt. George B. Abbay, who had been carried off by Indians during a scouting mission to the Washita in 1833.

When it marched from Fort Gibson on June 15, 1834, the Leavenworth expedition consisted of nine companies of U.S. First Dragoons. The officer list included many names that would become famous

Left: Catlin sketch of medicine man Quay-ham-kay, or Stone Shell. Catlin, *Letters and Notes. Right:* The Kiowa boy, an Osage captive, was killed at Fort Gibson. Catlin, *Letters and Notes.*

in the American West and elsewhere: Col. Henry Dodge, Lt. Col. Stephen W. Kearny, Maj. Richard B. Mason, and Lt. Jefferson Davis, among others. Catlin accompanied the march, and German botanist Count Beyrick would join it en route.

Serving as guides, hunters, and interpreters were eleven Osages, eight Cherokees, six Delawares, and seven Seminoles. These men would also speak for their tribes in making peace arrangements with the prairie bands. The woodland Indians wished to bring an end to raids on their settlements, to arrange for trade in horses and mules that the prairie tribes held in great numbers, and to gain unmolested entry to the buffalo range for their hunters.

The expedition marched southwestward to the juncture of the Washita and Red Rivers. A portion of the command—men, horses, and mules alike—was hit by a deadly, decimating sickness there. The sick included General Leavenworth, who in addition to being ill had been injured during a buffalo hunt on the Blue River. The reorganized, still healthy unit continued west under the command of Colonel Dodge. Later, Leavenworth would make a valiant effort to rejoin his command, only to perish on the trail.[31]

On July 14 the Dodge command encountered a large force of Comanche warriors riding eastward to do battle with the Caddos. The Comanches were friendly to the dragoons and led them to their village of over 200 lodges, encamped beside a stream on the northeastern slopes of the Wichita Mountains. After a brief visit, Dodge established a sick camp for those who had become too ill to travel, then led his command westward to a Wichita village. The Wichitas' rounded grass huts, estimated at 400 in number, lay nestled below a towering granite bluff that banked the North Fork of the Red River. Well-cultivated and neatly fenced fields of corn, beans, melons, and squashes surrounded the village.[32]

There Dodge found and rescued both Matthew Martin and his family's slave. He was told, however, that Lieutenant Abbay had been captured and killed by Comanches from Texas. The two captives were turned over to Dodge, who reciprocated by returning the Wichita girl he had brought from Fort Gibson to her people. He also presented a gun to a Wichita man who had saved Matthew Martin from being killed by others of his party. The Wichita chief admitted that there were also captive Osages in his village. But, he insisted, they had been raised among his people and did not wish to leave.[33]

Talks with the Wichitas and Comanches, who had followed the dragoons to the village, were under way when a Kiowa war party galloped into the camp and pulled to a halt before Dodge's tent. Bold and ready for battle, they sat their prancing horses with the grace of the superior horsemen they were, their bows strung and stone-tipped arrows in hand. The Kiowas had learned there were Osages in the camp, and they had come to kill them.[34]

The inhabitants of the Wichita encampment scattered in great alarm when the Kiowas appeared. Dodge quickly ordered the dragoons to stand by their arms. With their makeshift force of 250 men having been further reduced around 60 or 70 by the persisting malady, both men and officers were reminded that they were a long, long way from their home base at Fort Gibson.

Dodge pacified the Kiowas by informing them that he had with him a Kiowa girl whom he had ransomed from the Osages and intended to return to her family. This would be done, he said, on the following day in a general council with chiefs of the tribes. A site for the meeting was selected in the woods not far from the Wichita village.

At midmorning over 2,000 tribesmen, women, and children arrived at the meeting area. Sixty Kiowas led by their principal chief Tiche-toche-cha joined the council. The Kiowa chief was handsomely dressed in "a Spanish red cloth mantle, prodigious feathers, and leggings that followed his heels like an ancient train."[35]

The tribal leaders seated themselves in the great council circle with a "dignity and grace that would well become senators of a more civilized conclave."[36] After the traditional calumet had been passed among the chiefs, Dodge presented Wa-ha-sep-ah to the Kiowas as an offering of friendship from the United States. An uncle of the girl, a chief, threw his arms around Dodge, weeping in gratitude. He made an emotional speech to his people praising the officer.[37] Women of the tribe, also tearfully grateful, came forward in succession to embrace the girl. The girl's father begged Dodge to accept a gift as a reward, but the officer refused. Tiche-toche-cha rose to speak.

"The American captain has spoken well today," he said through a translator. "The white men have shown themselves as our friends; if a white man ever comes to my country, he shall be kindly treated; if he wants a horse, or anything that I have, he shall not pay for it; I will give him what he wants."[38]

The Americans were highly impressed with the Kiowas. One officer described them as "chivalric, impulsive and daring, [the Kiowa] reminds one of the bold clannish highlander."[39] Artist Catlin, one of those left at the sick camp, relied on a comrade to make sketches of the Kiowa village and take notes. The friend penned an excellent narrative of the difficult journey. He wrote of the Kiowas:

Left: Kiowa head chief Teh-toot-sah (Tiche-toche-cha), sketched by Catlin at Fort Gibson. Catlin, *Letters and Notes. Right:* Kiowa chief Bon-son-gee, or the New Fire. Catlin, *Letters and Notes.*

The Kioways are a much finer looking race of man than either the Comanches or Pawnees [Wichitas]—are tall and erect, with an easy and graceful gait—with long hair, cultivated oftentimes so as to reach nearly to the ground. They have generally the fine and Roman outline of head that is so frequently found at the North—and decidedly distinct from that of the Camanchees and Pawnee Picts [the Taovaya branch of the Wichitas].

The head chief of the Kioways, whose name is Tech-toot-sah, we found to be a very gentlemanly and high-minded man, who treated the dragoons and officers with great kindness while in his country. His long hair, which was put up in several large clubs, and ornamented with a great many silver broaches, extended quite down to his knees.[40]

After insisting that to achieve a permanent peace "a large white paper be written and signed by the President, and the hands of the chiefs,"[41] Dodge invited the chiefs of the three tribes to accompany him back to Fort Gibson. Although the prairie Indians expressed great concern about traveling through the forested area that lay to the east, they accepted Dodge's invitation. Tiche-toche-cha and fourteen other Kiowas, along with five Comanche men, one Comanche woman, a Mexican captive now a Comanche warrior, one Waco, and three Wichitas, all mounted on mules, rode with the dragoon command as it formed in three columns and headed wearily back to Fort Gibson.

During the journey the dragoons were highly impressed with the Kiowas' hunting skills, particularly when they observed a Kiowa who dashed among a herd and killed three buffalo using only three arrows. The march to Fort Gibson was extremely punishing, however, with several dragoons becoming so ill they were carried on litters. The Comanche party turned back because their woman was sick, although the Mexican-Comanche warrior known as the Spaniard continued on. When the group reached Fort Gibson at the conflux of the Verdigris, Grand, and Arkansas Rivers, another council was convened on September 2, 1834. Its purpose was to conduct a dialogue for peace among the United States, the tribes of eastern Indian Territory, and the visitors from the prairies.

Dodge; Col. William Armstrong, superintendent of Indian Affairs, who had recently arrived from Washington, D.C.; and commissioner Montford Stokes represented the United States. Lt. T. B. Wheelock, First U.S. Dragoon Regiment, transcribed the meeting word for word, while Sgt. Hugh Evans, orderly to Colonel Dodge, penned observations in his personal journal. Evans was greatly intrigued by the "motly collection of severally toungs . . . with their different dresses and ornaments."[42] Still another transcriber of the council was Col. S. C. Stambaugh, secretary to a board of Indian commissioners. Catlin busied himself with sketching portraits of the various tribal personalities in attendance. He wrote: "We brought with us to this place, three of the principal chiefs of the Pawnees, fifteen Kioways, one Comanche and one Waco chief. The group was undoubtedly one of the most interesting that ever visited our frontier; and I have taken pains in painting the portraits of all of them, as well as seven of the Comanche chiefs who came part of the way with us, and turned back."[43]

Representing the tribes lately removed to the Indian Territory were Choctaw chief Moosh-la-tu-bee, Creek leaders Rolly McIntosh and Benjamin Perryman, and Thomas Chisholm and John Rogers, chiefs of the Western Cherokees. Delawares and Senecas were also in attendance. The headmen of the prairie tribes were Tiche-toche-cha for the Kiowas, Me-ter-ra-sharro of the Wichitas, We-ta-ra-yah of the Wacos, and the Spaniard for the Comanches. Osage chief Clermont, who arrived at the head of a large Osage presence, was initially disturbed by the presence of his longtime enemies in his country. A crowd of curious fort residents and warriors surrounded the council gathering of whites and tribesmen in the fort's old garrison compound.

Thomas Chisholm presented tobacco and white beads as gifts from the Cherokees to the prairie visitors: the tobacco for friendship, the beads as emblems of peace and purity, he said. After a brief debate on the issue, Chief Rogers decided that the honor of filling the pipe would go to the "Eldest of all Red men," the Senecas. The ceremony of smoking the calumet was delayed briefly, however, by Tiche-toche-cha. The Kiowa chief would not allow the tobacco in the pipe to be touched, nor would he allow it to be lighted or passed with the right hand, only with the left.[44]

The commissioners spoke, saying that the purpose of the council was to establish peace among the tribes and to have each extend the hand of friendship to all. Clermont and Tiche-toche-cha, inveterate enemies, were reluctant to shake hands. Dodge finally persuaded them to do so and even to embrace.[45]

When asked to speak his mind, Tiche-toche-cha said: "I have not much to say. I have shaken hands with you. I wish to continue at peace with you. I am not fond of words. The road is now open to all our Red Brethren. They shall come to us in safety and we will receive them with open hearts."

Eventually, Clermont spoke to the prairie chiefs in support of the white people and their efforts to establish peace: "You must listen to our Father; we shall not be happy if we do not listen to his words. My children will not grow if we shut our ears to his words. Our race will be no more. It will vanish away."

On the third and final day of the council, Tiche-toche-cha answered at length.

> I am not young, but my word will live forever. My children will be your friends as I am now. I came to make peace with all the Red men here. I have seen, and am satisfied. When I go home I shall tell my people all that has passed in this Council House, The road, as I said before, is open. You can travel it in safety. We, too, can come to you in safety. I have seen the "houses" of the white men, but I have not seen many horses. When you come to my country, you shall see vast numbers of horses. They will show for themselves. I came here with my friend [Colonel Dodge]. I came in good heart. I gave my word to my people, that I would return. My time has arrived. I would depart tomorrow. The presents that were promised, I hope to receive.[46]

Three silver medals—one each for the Kiowas, Wichitas, and Comanches—and a United States flag were presented to the prairie chiefs. A medal and a flag were provided for the Spaniard to take back to the Comanche chief Tabaqueena, or Big Eagle. Colonel Dodge presented the medals as tokens of the white man's friendship. He told the chiefs:

On the one side of the medal you see the face of your Great Father, the President of the United States [Andrew Jackson, presumably]. Look upon it, and remember that he is your friend; that he knows your wants; that he has the power to gratify them; that he loves to be kind to the Red Men. On the other side, two hands are locked together in friendship; you see *they do not part*; the white man's hand will never part from yours, so long as you heed his counsels and remain his friend as he is your friend.[47]

Colonel Armstrong ended the meeting by indicating that a general council would be held during the coming spring in the buffalo country. Dodge wished to send the Indians to visit President Jackson at his Hermitage, Tennessee, home, but the tribesmen refused the invitation.[48] Tiche-toche-cha further rejected an offer for a Cherokee escort to take him back to his country, saying that he and his people could find a better road than the road on which they came.

The Leavenworth-Dodge expedition and the ensuing council at Fort Gibson in 1834 were significant steps in establishing a faction among the strongly militant Kiowas that supported peace with the United States. Good relations with the tribe were advanced further when a company of around eighty traders and trappers accompanied the Kiowa delegation back to the upper Washita and Red Rivers.[49]

Tiche-toche-cha is the only Kiowa chief mentioned in the records of the Fort Gibson council. It is possible, however, that it was attended as well by Tohawson who would soon take his place as the Kiowa principal chief and leading proponent for peace, a role to which Kicking Bird would ultimately become heir.

3

Enemies to the North

During the years 1835 to 1845, Kicking Bird would have grown from a babe to a boy of about ten years. Although we know little directly of his life during this decade, the nature of Kiowa culture tells us something of his activities as a youngster. Sons were generally the favorite of Kiowa men. Although they could love their daughters dearly, as Kicking Bird did his daughter Topen, Kiowa parents looked with special fondness upon sons, who stood to be great warriors or tribal leaders.

The warrior tradition was a primary element of Plains Indian society, and certainly so with the Kiowas. An Englishwoman who visited Fort Marion at St. Augustine, Florida, and viewed drawings left on the walls by the Kiowa and Cheyenne prisoners who had been there observed of the nineteenth-century tribesman: "An Indian never represents himself as standing, dancing, or walking; he is always on horseback, and always fighting against fabulous numbers, and always a conqueror, riding victorious over a score of prostrate foes."[1]

Little girls helped their mothers in the upkeep of the lodge and by gathering wood or carrying water from the nearby creek or pond. Boys, on the other hand, were pretty much free to play, usually at games that developed their physical and competitive skills.[2] They wrestled, ran foot races, fought with sticks, played leapfrog, and practiced throwing tomahawks or shooting headless arrows. They learned to ride and handle horses at an early age.

At times the boys imitated the activities of adult life in their games by putting up small tepees, hobbling dogs like their fathers did the horses,

Kiowa warrior, the Smoked Shield (c. 1834), stood almost seven feet tall and was the fastest runner in his tribe. Catlin, *Letters and Notes*.

holding sham battles with playmates, and conducting pretended raids. Alice Marriott tells of a group of Kiowa children who dug a ditch and piled up a dirt wall behind which the girls took refuge. The boys then proceeded to attack the redoubt by throwing clods and loose dirt to simulate guns firing.[3]

Young Kiowa boys of about six years of age could belong to the Rabbits, the primary of six Kiowa warrior societies. This involved the Rabbit Dance when the boys would hop around inside the dance ring, making rabbit sounds and wagging their hands at the sides of their faces to imitate the flop of rabbit ears.[4] The boys were taught the duties of warriors under the direction of two grown males who told stories of past Kiowa battle victories.

Training for Kiowa boys to become warriors began at a very early age. Lt. Richard H. Pratt recounted an incident that occurred during the surrender of Kiowa hostiles under Big Bow on the North Fork of the Red River in February 1875. All of the warriors of the band had come forward to lay down their guns, bows and arrows, spears, and shields in a pile on the ground. After turning in his weapons, one younger Kiowa man hurried back to his lodge. He soon returned with a small furry quiver along with miniature bow and arrows he had made for his four- or five-year-old son. There were amused smiles among whites and Indians alike as Pratt returned the toy weapons to the father.[5]

A visitor to Fort Sill that same year described the children at play in a Kiowa-Comanche-Apache camp along Medicine Bluff Creek.

> Crowds of children gambolled and shouted, and seemed to enjoy themselves intensely. . . . They threw their arms about and "kicked loose legs" as naturally and with as much *abandon* as any white children could have done. Some, more industriously inclined, built little *tepies*, or lodges; others made tiny camp-fires, playing "war party"; others, with miniature bows and arrows, skipped along, shooting at the small birds that crossed their path.[6]

Kicking Bird may well have been an infant peering from his mother's cradleboard when the Kiowas came to attend a treaty council on the Canadian River at the western edge of the Cross Timbers near present Lexington, Oklahoma, in 1835. In late June of that year, Maj. Richard B. Mason and a unit of U.S. dragoons had selected a site on the headwaters of Little River, a tributary of the Canadian, for a grand council between the United States and the prairie and woodland tribes of Indian Territory. Dubbed Camp Mason at first and then named Camp Holmes, the short-lived post would later win official designation as Fort Holmes.[7]

Earlier, at a Fort Gibson meeting, a visiting group of Plains Indians had been told that the treaty council would be held "when the grass next grows after the snows shall have melted away."[8] There had also been promises of much food and many gifts. The three-man peace commission party was held at Fort Gibson, however, by the illness and eventual death of member Maj. F. W. Armstrong. By then the torrid sun had dried up the rivers, left the scorched prairie brown, and made game very scarce.

During early July 1835 the Kiowas came forth from the prairie along with the Comanches, Wichitas, Wacos, Kichais (Keechis), and Tawakonis. The Indians camped along Chouteau Creek and waited through the long, hot days with few buffalo to hunt and their families becoming increasingly hungry. Finally, the Kiowas felt they could wait no longer. The meeting was supposed to have been held when the grass was in the *blade*, they told Mason in disgust, and not in the *leaf*. They struck their tepees and trailed off to the prairie.[9]

Mason reported on July 8 that according to the Comanches, the Kiowas were not far off, hunting and drying meat to live on while at the treaty. All of the tribes who hunted the area between the council site and the Red River were present, he noted, except the Kiowas, and he expected them back in a short time.[10]

Commissioners Montford Stokes and Gen. Matthew Arbuckle, accompanied by an entourage of wagons loaded with presents and trade goods, finally arrived at the council site from Fort Gibson on August 19, 1835. When the commissioners discovered the Kiowas were absent, they asked if the principal Kiowa chiefs could be found and brought in within ten days. The Comanche and Wichita chiefs shook their heads. It would be impossible, they said.

"The Kiowas are like wolves, so difficult to find."[11]

A detachment of dragoons sent out to search for the tribe soon found this all too true. Later, after the council had ended, a Kiowa and his wife appeared in camp for a brief visit, causing assistant surgeon Leonard McPhail to comment in his diary, "They are the finest looking savage folks I have seen."[12]

The council got under way on August 19 without the Kiowas. After a series of speeches by the commissioners and by chiefs of various tribes, a friendship treaty was entered into by the Cherokees, Creeks, Choctaws, Osages, Senecas, Quapaws, Comanches, and Wichitas. The pact promised full indemnification for theft of horses and other property, free hunting and trapping west of the Cross Timbers, and unmolested passage for U.S. citizens across the hunting grounds of the tribes.[13]

Even though the Comanches assured them that the absent Kiowas would also abide by the Fort Holmes pact, the commissioners had not given up on making an agreement with the tribe. In the spring of 1836 Paul L. Chouteau, brother to Col. Auguste P. Chouteau who had established a trading post on Chouteau Creek near the Camp Mason site, was sent to search for the Kiowas.[14]

Chouteau went first to Coffee's trading house on the Red River near present Preston, Texas. He failed to find any Kiowas there, as he had expected. Coffee said that he, too, had been unable to locate them the year before. Chouteau proceeded on up the Red River to Cache Creek. Again he found no Indians, but he followed a trail southward into Texas for two days and came onto a group of Tawacaros and Wacos. They said the Kiowas were either on the headwaters of the Big Wichita or on the Colorado River of Texas. Chouteau scoured the country between the Red and the Colorado for twenty-two days. On returning to the Indian Territory, at Cache Creek he finally encountered bands of Kiowas, Comanches, and Plains Apaches (he called them Cah-tash-kahs) on their annual migration northward with the buffalo.

Alexander Le Grand, who accompanied Chouteau on his tour, noted that Comanche chief She-co-ney was adamantly opposed to any peace agreement because of the continued approach of whites onto his hunting grounds. So long as he saw that happening, the chief had declared, so long would he believe the whites ultimately intended to deprive the Indians of their country and "so long would he continue to be the enemy of the white race."[15] At one point, She-co-ney issued a threat to destroy Fort Holmes.

Chouteau, however, found the Kiowas agreeable to meeting with the U.S. commissioners, preferably in early May. He reported that the Kiowas, closest allies to the Comanches, ranged from the Arkansas River to the Mexican settlements of Texas. Their warriors numbered around 1,500.[16] A less optimistic view was voiced in a letter to the *Daily National Intelligencer* in Washington, D.C., by a man who said he had spent the past five years in contact with the Comanches. He wrote:

> The different tribes are Camanches, Kyawas, Towash, Southern Pawnee, Caddoes, Wacoes, and Skiddies. They number about thirty-five thousand in all, and can muster from seven to eight thousand restless warriors in this great Western prairie. Free as the buffalo themselves, they acknowledge no superior—depredating upon the Mexicans of the interior states, ravaging and burning their towns, murdering their people, sometimes taking prisoners, which they either torture to death or make *slave* of, carrying off immense herds of mules and horses.[17]

During April 1836 a company of eight Missouri-bound traders was attacked fifty miles below Chouteau's Island on the Arkansas River in western Kansas. Three of the men were killed by the 200-strong war party, who fought with guns, bows, arrows, and spears—but, uniquely, they were on foot.

"The Indians who committed this outrage, had their faces painted red, wore long hair tied down their backs, which I know to be the fashion of the Kioways; and as they are represented to be tall, handsome men, I should pronounce them at once belonging to that nation, if they had not made the attack on foot, as the Kioways generally fight on horseback."[18]

The traders, some of whom were from Vasquez and Sublette's post on the South Platte and were familiar with all of the northern prairie tribes, discounted the attackers being Blackfeet, Snake, Arapaho, Cheyenne, Arickara, Sioux, Cut-throat, or Gros Ventre. It was thus assumed that the Indians were either Comanche, Pawnee Pict, or Kiowa.

It was 1837 before the Kiowa treaty council was finally arranged. Paul Chouteau's son Edward again went out to the prairie in January 1837 with a party of four. He eventually located the Kiowas and secured a new promise from the Kiowa chief to come to Fort Gibson. He reported seeing a number of white captives among the prairie tribes. The Comanches held two white women, one of whom said her youngest child had been killed because it could not keep up with the captors. The Kiowas also had white captives among them.[19]

On May 8, 1837, Paul Chouteau left Camp Mason for Fort Gibson with twenty-four Kiowa chiefs, seven Plains Apaches, and two Wichitas who had arrived there. A Tawacaro chief followed behind with a group of his people.[20] During the period May 24–26, a peace and friendship treaty was worked out and signed between the United States and the Kiowas, Plains Apaches (listed as Ka-ta-kas), and Tawacaros. The Comanches, Wichitas, Cherokees, Creeks, Choctaws, Osages, Senecas, and Quapaws were also represented at the council.

The leading Kiowa to sign the treaty was Ta-ka-to-couche, or the Black Bird. Whether this was the same man as Chief Tiche-toche-cha is not known. His name was followed on the document by Cha-hon-de-ton, or the Flying Squirrel; Ta-ne-congais, or the Sea Gull; Bon-congais, or the Black Cap; To-ho-sa (Tohawson), or the Top of the Mountain; Sen-son-da-cat, or the White Bird; Con-a-hen-ka, or the Horne[d] Frog; He-pan-ni-gais, or the Night; Ka-him-hi, or the Prairie Dog; and Pa-con-ta, or My Young Brother. Montford Stokes and A. P. Chouteau officiated for the United States.[21]

With this pact, the Kiowas agreed to maintain perpetual peace with citizens of the United States, to pay for any property of U.S. citizens taken or destroyed in their country, and to freely permit other tribes to hunt and trap west of the Cross Timbers. The Kiowas would receive $1,176.98 in presents immediately after signing the treaty.[22]

Later, the Kiowa and Comanche chiefs complained that they had not been given flags and medals at the treaty such as the Mexican officials had proffered in negotiations with them. Reports had surfaced that several Mexican officers had been among the Comanches and other prairie tribes in an effort to recruit their assistance in Mexico's war with the revolutionists in Texas. The tribes were asked to remain neutral until Mexico could supply them arms and ammunition, then they were to conduct a war of extermination against the Texans.[23]

Former Secretary of War Lewis Cass, who was present at the treaty council, observed that the pact would save traders on the St. Louis road from further molestation.[24] No assignment of territory was made. With some degree of naïveté, the treaty stated that the agreement would in no respect interrupt the prairie tribes' friendly relations with the Republics of Mexico and Texas.

Even as these negotiations were being worked out, the Kiowas and Comanches were under pressure from new intruders from the north. The Pawnees of Nebraska, notorious horse stealers, were raiding the Kiowa, Comanche, and Wichita herds, as were tribesmen from eastern Indian Territory. Colonel Chouteau, who spent the winter of 1837–1838 at Camp Mason, reported persistent Pawnee raids on Indian Territory horse herds.[25]

One Kiowa chief complained that while he was willing to go after the Pawnees, he did not have the mounts to do so.[26] An old Pawnee charged that the Kiowas were cowards because they would give up the chase after only two days, then simply set fire to the prairie in hopes the Pawnee horse thieves would be entrapped.[27]

Although the Kiowa-Pawnee relationship was essentially hostile, it was not unusual for the Pawnees to send delegations south to trade guns and ammunition for horses.[28] An early Kiowa romantic incident involved the two tribes. A Kiowa warrior and the young wife of another had taken advantage of the husband's absence to flee to a Pawnee village on the Platte River where they were given refuge. They were observed there by John Treat Irving, Jr., nephew of Washington Irving, who wrote of the warrior:

> He was slight and beautifully formed; but there was a fire in his eye; a swell of the nostril; and a proud curve of the lip, which showed a spirit that brooked no opposition, shunned no danger, and could only be quenched by the chill of the grave. His long black hair, which trailed behind him on the ground, was plaited together, and ornamented with about twenty plates of massive silver. A band of silver was fastened round his throat, and several large medals of the same hung upon his breast. Upon his arms were bands of silver, and rings of the same upon his fingers. His leggings, though more finely wrought, like those of the chiefs, were fringed with scalps. A scalp consisting of the entire upper part of a human head, hung from the bit of his fiery horse.[29]

Irving described the beautiful young Kiowa girl as having "the step of a queen."[30] She wore a beaded and lace-trimmed jacket of scarlet cloth and a long blue skirt. Like the warrior, she was ornately decked with silver plates and bracelets. Her moccasins were ornamented more finely than those of the Pawnee women.

The loosely confederated Cheyennes and Arapahos, who originally resided north of the Platte, were likewise drawn southward from the Black Hills country to raid the horse remudas of the southern tribes.

Kiowa warrior, contemporary of Kicking Bird.
Courtesy Western History Collection, University of
Oklahoma.

Although the Cheyennes and Arapahos usually camped apart, they often
made war together. The Cheyennes were the more aggressive; they and
the Kiowas had done battle many times over the years.

One factor of their conflict was the Kiowas' desire to visit their
friends of old in the north, the Crows. Some families, like that of Kicking Bird, had relatives among the Crows. During the summer months
Kiowa parties would make the long journey to the Bear Tooth country of
Montana, following what became known as the Kiowa Trail close along
the mountains. They were cautious to avoid the Cheyennes to the east as
well as the Kiowas' longtime enemies, the Utes, who resided to the northwest across the mountains and with whom they often traded warring
forays.

Occasionally, while conducting their visits to the Crows, the Kiowas
were discovered en route by the Cheyennes, and conflicts resulted. One

such took place in 1835 in the sand hills east of Denver. It was there that White Cow Woman, then only three or four years of age, was taken from the Kiowas by the Cheyennes. Actually, White Cow Woman was white, having been captured by the Kiowas only a year or two earlier. She lived out her life as a Cheyenne.[31]

But the principal issue of trouble was the raiding of Kiowa and Comanche horse herds by the northern tribes. The matter took on serious proportions in 1837 when forty-eight Cheyenne Bow String warriors attempted to run off with a Kiowa horse herd on the Washita River. The Bow Strings had come south on foot expecting to ride the Kiowa ponies back to their camp. By bad luck they were spotted by the Kiowas before they could secure any horses for the return north. Like angry wasps protecting the hive, the mounted Kiowa warriors rushed after the Cheyennes and surrounded them in a ravine. The Bow Strings were killed and scalped to the man.

With no survivors of the ill-fated party, the news of the massacre did not reach the Cheyenne camps for some time. The event became known only when a party of Arapahos visited a Kiowa village in the Texas Panhandle. While observing a Kiowa war dance, the Arapahos recognized the ornaments of two Bow String braids. They reported the matter to the Cheyennes.[32]

To lose their warriors was one thing to the Cheyennes; to have their scalps danced derisively was another. Immediately, the infuriated tribe sent out runners to all Cheyenne and Arapaho camps, calling for a joint strike against the Kiowas. Throughout the winter preparation was made for vengeance. By April 1838, with their horses well fed on the fresh spring grass, the great Cheyenne and Arapaho war party moved south from the Arkansas River into northwestern Oklahoma.

The Kiowa home range was essentially between the Cimarron River and the Red River in western Indian Territory, extending into the Texas Panhandle.[33] Wolf Creek, a sandy, low-banked stream that flowed northeastward from the ravine-sliced country of the Panhandle to join the Beaver and form the North Canadian River, was a favorite Kiowa camping area.

Cheyenne and Arapaho scouts located their prey, a Kiowa-Comanche buffalo-hunt encampment nestled on the north bank of Wolf Creek not far from its conflux with the Beaver. The main body of the Cheyenne-Arapaho force launched its attack shortly after sunrise. The results were reported by Lt. Lucius B. Northrop, who by chance was on a march in that direction at the time and arrived at the scene two days after the fight occurred:

As the Cheyennes advanced to attack their enemies, they were met by the latter about a mile from the encampment. The latter were slowly beaten back into their encampment, though disputing desperately every inch of ground. The whole scene was in an open prairie. The women dug holes in the earth, in which to hide themselves and their children. The Cheyennes continued to make dreadful havoc of their wretched enemies. . . . Fifty-eight of the Kiowas and Comanches were killed. More than a hundred horses lay dead on the ground, chiefly within the encampment.[34]

The attack on their camp on Wolf Creek was a severe blow to the security of the Kiowas' home range. Already pressed from the northeast by the Osages, Pawnees, and Kaws, the Kiowas could do without more formidable enemies like the Cheyennes and Arapahos. It would be up to a new Kiowa principal chief to step forward as a peacemaker and alleviate this new danger.

4
Tohawson the Peacemaker

It is expected that the records would fail to tell us much directly of Kicking
Bird during his years as a youth in the country south of the Arkansas
River. Despite the lack of direct mention of him, however, it takes little
imagination to visualize a young Kicking Bird against descriptions of the
Kiowas of that day or to see the influence on his life of tribal culture and
leadership.

Kiowa chief Ta-ka-to-couche disappears from record following the
Treaty of 1837. Just what caused his demise is not known; perhaps he was
killed in the Battle of Wolf Creek. We do know, however, that the Kiowa
principal chief for the next three decades was Tohawson (or Dohawson).
His name has been translated variously as Top of the Mountain, Little
Bluff, Over-the-Mountain, and Overhanging Butte, but he was best known
to whites as Little Mountain.[1] Lt. James W. Abert, who met him in the
Texas Panhandle, described him as "a man of middling stature, quite fat,
with a very wide mouth, upon which there played a constant smile, and
his whole face showed an intriguing character. We found him very intelligent."[2]

Indian agent Samuel G. Colley knew Tohawson on the Arkansas
and was likewise impressed, both with the chief and his wife. "To-hau-
san," Colley wrote, "the head chief of the Kiowas is a very good man. His
counsels to his young men is worthy of emulation by the whites. . . . His
wife is a splendid housekeeper and many white women would be benefit-
ted by taking lessons from her."[3]

During his long reign as Kiowa principal chief, Tohawson earned a high reputation as a peacemaker among both Indians and whites. "I caught the hands of my children," he told the whites as he neared his end, "and tried to hold them."[4]

Tohawson likely headed the Kiowa delegation that set forth to visit the Great Father at Washington in the spring of 1839. Responding to the persuasion of U.S. emissaries, a party of sixty Kiowa, Comanche, and other prairie chiefs with their women and children arrived at Chouteau's post near Fort Holmes during May. They had come in anticipation of meeting Colonel Chouteau there and continuing on to Washington.

As they neared the post, the Indians met a large caravan of wagons headed westward along the Canadian River. This was the trading expedition of Josiah Gregg, whose classic book, *Commerce of the Prairies*, would serve as a guide across the Plains for many travelers of the Canadian route in the years ahead.[5] The Comanches were led by Tabbaqueena, or Big Eagle, head Comanche chief. Tabbaqueena, who spoke some Spanish, bartered for mules with the trader party. From Gregg they learned that Chouteau had died the previous December. Delaware frontiersman John Connor agreed to escort the delegation on to Fort Gibson. A number of the Indians turned back, reducing the number to seventeen men and seven women mounted on stout mules. Records indicate that the head chief of the Kiowas, which was probably Tohawson by then, continued on with the group.[6]

En route, the Kiowa-Comanche delegation visited the Little River home of their friend, Cherokee trader Jesse Chisholm. Chisholm supplied them with beef, corn, and bacon. At Webbers Falls on the Arkansas River, Chisholm's half-brother George gave them three more beef cows for food.[7] From Fort Gibson the Plains Indians received a dragoon escort to the Choctaw agency at Skullyville.

The chiefs were received there by agent William Armstrong, who expressed concern about their continuing on. He pointed out that they would be confined in steamboats and stages and would undergo a harsh change of diet, climate, and environment. The chiefs finally decided to turn back. During their brief visit at the agency, however, the prairie visitors watched with great delight as the Choctaws and the Chickasaws competed in a traditional stick ball contest. Before they returned home, Armstrong supplied his guests with provisions that included blankets, scarlet cloth and prints, tin cups, thread, calico, combs, butcher knives, handkerchiefs, bridles, brass kettles, buckets, axes, tobacco, gunflints, lead for bullets, and gunpowder.[8]

Gregg's trading caravan met by Indians in Texas Panhandle. Gregg, *Commerce of the Prairie.*

Tohawson emerges with certainty as the Kiowa head chief in 1840. Following the Wolf Creek attack, he sent word through some Plains Apaches that the Kiowas would return the Bow String scalps if the Cheyennes and Arapahos would agree to make peace. The Cheyennes and Arapahos discussed the matter and eventually accepted the offer. Tohawson, accompanied by Satank, led a small party north to Two Butte Creek, met with the Cheyennes, and made arrangements for a great feast and exchange of presents. "We will make a strong friendship which will last forever," Tohawson said.[9]

During the summer of 1840, a great encampment of the five tribes gathered on the banks of the Arkansas River at Bent's Fort near present La Junta, Colorado. The Cheyennes and Arapahos were on one side of the river and the Kiowas, Comanches, and Prairie Apaches on the other. The Cheyenne chief put up a special lodge and invited the Kiowa, Comanche, and Apache chiefs to a feast. Tohawson responded by asking all of the Cheyenne people to come to his camp in the morning and seat themselves in one long row with the men in front of their families. He said he wanted them to come on foot, and they would all return on horseback.

When the Cheyennes and Arapahos arrived, Satank led the way in presenting gifts. He went down the long line, his arms loaded with sticks. He gave a stick to each man in the line, telling them that if they would bring the sticks to his camp they would receive a horse. The Kiowas and

Comanches gave their former enemies a great number of horses; Satank reportedly presented 250 of his own. Some of the Cheyenne and Arapaho people received as many as 6 horses each, while the chiefs reaped even more.

The Cheyennes responded with guns, calico, beads, brass kettles, and blankets by the pile. The tribes jointly feasted, sang, danced, and drummed all day and night, and many presents were exchanged. In council the chiefs agreed that from then on the tribes could freely and safely visit one another's camps and conduct trade.

These five tribes never warred with one another again. The Kiowas could now visit Bent's Fort and travel north of the Arkansas River without fear of attack from the Cheyennes. In return, the Cheyennes and Arapahos were free to range south of the Arkansas River without molestation. Eventually, under pressure from the whites, the Southern divisions of those two tribes would take up permanent residence there as neighbors and allies to the Kiowas and Comanches.[10]

Tohawson's peaceful inclinations notwithstanding, the Kiowa 1837 treaty with the United States had little effect on the Kiowa-Comanche relationship with the newly established Republic of Texas. Although there had been periods of tranquil trading relations when the Spanish ruled there, the Kiowas and Comanches had always been able to raid at will even beyond the Rio Grande. They struck haciendas, burned structures,

Bent's Fort on the Arkansas River, once a favorite resort for Kiowas. Inman, *The Old Santa Fe Trail.*

and took stock and captives. The Anglo rebellion against Mexican rule in Texas, however, brought a great change. The people who now called themselves Texans were far more resistive and determined than the Spanish had been. This was well illustrated in a disastrous affair that occurred at San Antonio.

In March 1840 a large group of Comanches, led by chief Mook-war-tuh, or the Spirit Talker, came to San Antonio under a flag of truce to talk peace. They brought a white captive, sixteen-year-old Matilda Lockhart, as a peace offering. The sight of the badly scarred girl, however, infuriated the Texans. Once the chiefs were inside the courthouse council room, the Texans attempted to take the Comanches as prisoners. The chiefs, still with their weapons at hand, resisted. A bloody fight resulted in which thirty-three Comanche chiefs, women, and children were killed. Thirty-two women and children were taken prisoner. The Texans lost seven men, and ten others were badly wounded.[11]

This betrayal of a flag of truce and the murders of their people infuriated the Plains tribes. The Comanches responded with an invasion of the Texas Gulf Coast region under Chief Buffalo Hump. They ravaged several towns, burning buildings, killing stock and people, and looting homes. On their way back to the prairie, however, they were ambushed by a force of Texas Rangers and their Tonkawa allies at Plum Creek in central Texas. The Comanches were badly defeated and routed, leaving behind around eighty of their dead and most of their spoils.

The Kiowas are not known to have been involved in these actions, but their passions were severely aroused. Their hatred for and distrust of the Texans would last for many years. Evidence of this was quickly apparent when in 1841 Texas launched a trade expedition from Austin to Santa Fe. Wandering misguided and bewildered in the tribal-dominated cross-timber country of north Texas, the caravan of merchants and soldiers of fortune was attacked by Kiowas southwest of present Childress. Five of the Texas party were killed and scalped, their bodies stripped and mutilated in contempt.[12] George W. Kendall, who accompanied the expedition, commented on the Kiowas based on his observations and interviews with Mexicans who regularly traded with the tribe.

> The Caygüas appear to be a powerful tribe. They lead a roving life, esteem the whites as their natural enemies, and never give them quarter. Like the Comanches, they are expert on horseback to an extraordinary degree, leaping from one horse to another while at full speed, and performing many feats upon the prairies never undertaken even by the best equestrians of the circus.

>   They have a small number of rifles among them, and these are
>   ineffective and useless in their hands: the larger portion of them are
>   armed with shield, lances, and bows and arrows, weapons they use with
>   surprising dexterity.[13]

In general, the Kiowas were more receptive to citizens of the United
States, although they sometimes had difficulty differentiating them from
Texans. In April 1843 Edward and William Glasgow, traders on their way
from Mexico to the States, encountered two large camps, one Kiowa and
one Arapaho, near the Cimarron River in the Oklahoma Panhandle.
The traders were received in a friendly fashion by the Indians: "The men
were generally dressed in Moccasins & leggings made of dressed Buffaloe
skins, no shirts, but with a loose Robe wrapped around their bodies. The
women, were dressed in the same manner and rode astride their horses
like the men & without a saddle. We seated them upon the ground and
made them presents of Corn, Tobacco, flour and dried bread."[14]

A more revealing encounter with the Kiowas occurred during the
fall of 1845. On this occasion, Lt. James W. Abert led a thirty-five-man
U.S. topographical party southward from Bent's Fort. Guided by the renowned mountain man Thomas Fitzpatrick, they turned eastward at the
Canadian River and began working their wagons over an Indian trail
that wound through the gypsum-streaked buttes and deep ravines that
banked the stream. On September 12 a group of eight to ten Indians
appeared on a bluff above the river. The Indians fired their guns in the
air and yelped in salute as they rode boldly down the river bank into
Abert's camp, hailing the travelers in a friendly fashion.[15]

The visitors were Kiowas and Crows who had just returned from the
headwaters of the Missouri River. They dismounted and seated themselves in a circle for a talk. John Hatcher, a Bent's Fort trader traveling
with Abert, rolled the Indians some "segaritos," which they enjoyed very
much. The Indians chatted, joked, and laughed "much to the astonishment of us, who possessed preconceived notions which were, doubtless,
obtained from the popular writers of the day."[16]

Abert penned an excellent description of the Kiowas and what could
well have been the home camp of the youthful Kicking Bird. Abert noted
that the Kiowas and Crows were by tradition from the far North:

>   In dress the Kioways resemble the other roving tribes of the great desert,
>   being habited in buckskin. Their moccasins are furnished with a fringed
>   appendance 8 or 10 inches in length, which is attached to the heel,
>   which could not be conveniently worn by other than mounted Indians
>   and is said to be peculiar to their tribe. They all have blanket or buffalo
>   robe, and their long hair is braided so as to form a queue, sometimes

lengthened by means of horsehair until it reaches the ground; and this queue is often ornamented with convex silver plates, which they procure from the Spaniards. The dress of the women differs little from that of the northern tribes—the same leathern cape, tunic, leggings, and beaded moccasins. We were particularly struck with the profusion of trappings with which the men ornamented themselves and their horses.[17]

With the party was a captive Mexican youth of about twenty years of age who wore leggings and breech clout and carried both a Spanish gun and a bow. The chief of the group—unnamed but from the description quite likely Tohawson—was "a merry faced, confident old fellow, whose whole body shook when he felt pleased." He said that most of his warriors had gone to Mexico where, a member of Abert's party indicated, the Kiowas "carry on their warfare in North Mexico, against the Cavejardes and Ranchos."[18]

On September 15 Abert's party camped not far from the abandoned Bent trading post, which, now in crumbled condition, had become known as Adobe Walls. "To this fort," a member of Abert's party noted, "would the Camanches and Cayquas [Kiowas] annually resort to traffick their hunting spoils, for beads, bells, wire, vermillion, cotton handkerchiefs, tobacco & trinkets."[19] The Bent traders at Fort Adobe, including Hatcher and the noted plainsman and Cheyenne interpreter John Simpson Smith, had abandoned the remote post when it came under attack from the Kiowas and Comanches. Twenty years later the Kiowas would do battle with Kit Carson and his New Mexico army at the site.[20]

Hatcher vouched highly for the Kiowas' bravery, energy, and honesty, and Abert noted that during his party's encounter with the tribe not a single item was stolen.[21]

After leaving the Canadian and marching south, Abert's party met a small group of mounted Indians who appeared atop a nearby butte. Fitzpatrick quickly hoisted the American flag, and some of the men called out in Spanish, "Americano! Americano!" The warriors responded with "Kiowah! Kiowah!" With this exchange pleasantly made, the Kiowas rode down from the butte and dismounted at Abert's tent. After turning their mounts loose to graze, they were treated to breakfast and improvised cigars. The Kiowas then seated themselves in a circle in the grass to smoke and talk with the visitors. Many had never met a white man and were surprised to know that the Americans and the Texans spoke the same tongue. A member of the exploring party—Isaac Cooper, who published an account of the journey under the pen name François des Montaignes—described the Kiowas:

These Indians had several elegant horses.—They had spears ten or 12 feet in length,—shields,—bow & arrows, & several had short Mexican guns. They were accoutered like the Indians we had seen before, but appeared to be a more sensible set. Although one old fellow, among them having over his shoulders, a well-dressed elkskin, shrugged his shoulders, when pressed by us to exchange it for something else, and gave as his reason, that it was proof against bullets, & no Texian could shoot through it.[22]

Shortly after this meeting, the exploring party was joined in camp by Tohawson and the entire Kiowa village. The chief had many questions and was particularly pleased at seeing Hatcher, a familiar figure to the Kiowas and a great favorite with them. One ancient Kiowa woman who had known Hatcher since he first began trading with the Kiowas had wept for joy upon meeting him and called him her son.[23]

The Indians brought leather ropes and robes for trade. The Americans had no goods for bartering, but they did make gifts of some tobacco. Among the band was a young Spanish woman of great beauty, the wife of Tohawson's wrinkled father who wore a tattered Mexican uniform and a unique sealskin cap on his head. The woman said she had been with the Kiowas for four years and that they held a number of Texas captives.[24]

The Kiowa women often wore blue and pink Navajo blankets, while black Mexican blankets were common for men. Warriors dressed much fancier. One of them, The Wolf Who Looks Over the Hill, who along with his Crow wife served as Abert's guide for a time, was typical. "He had vermillion on his face, brass wire wrapped many times around his brawny wrists, & with his ornamented queue, his Spanish bridle, his leggings,—his fantastic stirrups, his Mexican guns and his bows and arrows, he looked the beau ideal of an American Bedouin of the Rio Rojo."[25]

Another member of Tohawson's band who caught the attention of the Americans was a young chief named Bear. When his orders were disobeyed by a tribal member, he was quick to grab his spear, make a threatening charge at the culprit, and demand respect. It has been speculated that this chief, who appeared to be contesting for Tohawson's position, could have been Satanta (Set-tainte), or White Bear.[26] Whoever he was, it was men of such fierce warrior spirit who would challenge for leadership in the days ahead.

During his reign as head chief of the Kiowas, Tohawson established a strong peace tradition to counterbalance the intense warrior ethic of his tribe. This conflict of peace and war would be severely agitated among the Kiowas and other Plains tribes as the number of whites entering the Plains accelerated greatly in the days ahead. The Kiowas still had need for their warriors, but their destiny would soon depend far more on men who could bring them peace.

5

White Men Marching

Kicking Bird would have been about twelve in 1847, eighteen in 1853, and thirty in 1865. During this period he became a warrior and probably a subchief. As a youngster he surely underwent initiation rites in male warrior societies. The society beyond the Rabbits for young teenagers was known as the Shepherd's or Herder's Society. A dance and feast were held to initiate male youths into it, with fathers of new members giving away buffalo robes, blankets, and even horses in honor of their sons. At this age a Kiowa boy usually took on the task of watering horses for his band, as was needed three times a day.[1] (For the story of a war-party adventure by two Kiowa youths, see "The Mountain Route" by W. S. Nye in the Appendix.)

As a teenager Kicking Bird likely accompanied older warriors on raids, serving them, like Kiowa boys often did, as an attendant. The leader of the war party generally required that boys secure their father's permission to go along. The boys guarded the extra horses and equipment that were left at a safe location while the raid was undertaken. They did not participate in the fighting, but they gained experience by observing.

During his 1845 encounter with the Kiowas, Abert observed a young aide who would spread a buffalo robe for the chief to sit on, light his pipe, and address his every need. Such servitude by young boys to older males was traditional among the Kiowas.[2] At about age fifteen boys began to look for opportunities to display their bravery and win their place in the sun. It was not unusual, however, for young teenagers to strike off on their own in pairs or small parties on foot to steal horses and mules in Texas and Mexico. They would live off the land, proving themselves as self-sufficient foragers and returning home with their prizes to receive the praise of all the tribe.[3]

Abert and his men witnessed Kiowa youths, sixteen to eighteen years of age, who were well equipped with shield, bow, lance, and gun. As the youngsters rode along beside Abert's wagons, they would gallop off in mock attack on a grazing antelope as though it were a tribal enemy. The explorers were amazed at the archery skills of the Kiowa youths. One Plains Indian training feat was to see who could launch arrows the fastest and keep the most in the sky at one time. It is possible that Kicking Bird, now about ten, was among the boys observed by the Abert party who "shewed scientific marksmanship and adroitness, & striking buttons with their arrows, 20 steps distance."[4]

In his study "Rank and Warfare Among the Plains Indians," Bernard Mishkin lists several acts of warrior valor that contributed to status in the tribe. These included the counting of first coup, charging the enemy or rescuing a comrade when in retreat, dismounting and fighting on foot, killing enemy warriors, being wounded in hand-to-hand combat, stealing horses successfully, and serving obediently as a member of a war party or demonstrating ability as a war-party leader.[5]

A young Kiowa male, who would become a warrior at about twenty years of age, gained stature in the tribe by performing at least four such deeds. From there, he could rise in succession into the other warrior societies: the Horse Headdresses, the Crazy Horses, the Black Legs, or the Real or Principal Dogs. These societies cut across band lines, and they did not meet until the tribe united. These annual gatherings involved dancing to drums and rattles, recitations of war deeds by older men, and initiation rituals, each society exercising its own style of dance and dress.[6]

The Kiowas consisted of twelve to fifteen bands. These essentially lived apart as extended family groups that came together once a year during late June or early July to celebrate their Sun Dance and hold the tribal medicine lodge. At that time, the people offered sacrifices, made pledges, and issued petitions to the medicine bundles of the Ten Grandmothers of the priests. Also, it was often at this consolidation of the tribe that the large revenge expeditions—as contrasted to smaller horse-stealing parties—were organized.[7]

The size of a man's horse herd, his greatest facet of wealth, was testimony to his success as a war leader. But a rise to Kiowa leadership was influenced by other factors. To become an "Onde," the highest rank of Kiowa warriors, required that a man be wealthy, be of proven generosity, make a handsome appearance on a horse, have an aristocratic bearing, and, most important, own an outstanding war record.[8] Kicking Bird, from all historical evidence, exemplified these five attributes as much as any known Kiowa leader.

Kicking Bird was undoubtedly present at or active in many of the Kiowa historical events of the period preceding the end of the American Civil War. As a warrior he fought against the Utes of Colorado, the Pawnees of Nebraska, and possibly against other tribal enemies such as the Navajos of New Mexico. He joined in raids against wagon trains along the Santa Fe Trail, went on horse-stealing incursions, killed both whites and Indians who were considered enemies, and took scalp trophies. Such activities were essential roles in Kiowa culture and prerequisite for the high position he held in the tribe when he first emerged into public notice at the Treaty of the Little Arkansas in 1865.

Kicking Bird's entry into manhood came during a time of special conflict and change for the Kiowas. This period of his life coincided with the early stage of American expansion westward, a day when the Kiowas were both contesting and adapting to the influences of white civilization. Prior to the Civil War, U.S. military power on the Plains was wanting. The Kiowas and other prairie tribes were still able to strike with impunity against the whites who crossed the Plains and invaded their hunting grounds. At the same time, the tribespeople increasingly desired manufactured goods and weaponry, almost to the point of dependency. It was in large part the opportunity to obtain the white man's goods that led tribes both to make war (that is, to raid) and to attend peace councils, where presents were always promised.

The 1840 Kiowa and Comanche pact with the Cheyennes and Arapahos served all of those four tribes well. Without the threat of attack from the tribes of western Kansas and eastern Colorado, the Kiowas and Comanches could again range freely northward to the Arkansas River country. There Kiowa warriors, who were seldom constrained by agreements their chiefs made on paper with the white man, found both a new sport and a ripe field of enterprise in raiding the sparsely protected wagon trains along the Santa Fe Trail.

The Kiowas were noticeably absent from several treaty councils and agreements conducted with the Comanches and other prairie tribes by Texas and U.S. officials during the 1840s. They were not party to the meeting at newly established Torrey's Trading Post on Tehuacana Creek near present Waco, Texas, in March 1843 or at Bird's Fort north of present Fort Worth the following September. Nor were they present at Tehuacana

Creek in October 1844 when President Sam Houston personally attended or the 1846 Treaty of Comanche Peak, which initially met on the Brazos southwest of Fort Worth but was culminated at Council Springs near Waco. The Kiowa absence is explained in the report of U.S. commissioners Pierce M. Butler and M. G. Lewis on the Comanche Peak proceedings:

> Besides the tribes enumerated above, there is one other tribe in friendly intercourse with the United States and her friendly Indians—the Ki-o-ways, numbering about four thousand souls. They reside high upon the Canadian River, between that and the Arkansas, extending their rambles to the Rio Grande towards Mexico. Through our runners, we received friendly messages from these people, with a request to meet them next fall in council, to hold a friendly talk and smoke the pipe. They are to some extent in intercourse with the Comanches, and form a link in the great chain of the prairie Indians.[9]

Creek Indians returning from a visit to the prairie reported to their agent Marcellus Duval that they met with the Kiowas and Comanches. The two tribes, they said, were suffering once again from smallpox and were very hostile to other tribes. The Creeks said also that they saw guns among the Kiowas that had formerly belonged to a small party under a Captain Leavitt that had left Little River along the Canadian at an earlier time. It was feared that the party had been murdered by the Kiowas.[10]

Through its treaties, Texas won a temporary respite from Comanche raiding. Indian agent Robert Neighbors reported that in August 1847, at the Clear Fork of the Brazos, Comanches met a band of around 600 Kiowas on its way to raid in Texas. When the Kiowas stated that their purpose was to raid in Texas, the Comanches objected strongly. They said that if the Kiowas continued, they would make war on them. This, Neighbors claimed, had influenced the Kiowas to renounce their hostile intentions and express a desire for their own treaty with the whites.[11]

To the north, newly appointed U.S. agent for the Cheyennes and Arapahos Thomas Fitzpatrick reported from Bent's Fort in September 1847. He wrote that the Comanches and Kiowas had been marauding on the Santa Fe road all spring and summer and had been "endeavoring to induce those [Cheyennes and Arapahos] here to join them in the war, representing the great advantages as well as the profits, without incurring the least risk."[12] The whites who travel the Santa Fe road, the warriors had declared, were as easily killed as elk or buffalo—not like the Texans. Fitzpatrick estimated that twenty-seven white men had fallen victim to Indians on the trail during the past spring and summer. An Arapaho claimed that the Kiowas and Comanches alone had sixty scalps.

Losses from Indian attacks on the Santa Fe Trail during that summer were estimated at 47 persons killed, 330 wagons destroyed, and 6,500 head of stock plundered. Much of this involved government trains to and from New Mexico. Not only were the Kiowas and Comanches believed to have been involved but also the Cheyennes and Arapahos, the Lakotas from north of the Platte, Pawnees of the Loup River in Nebraska, and Kiowa-Apaches from the Canadian River.[13]

To better protect transportation on the Santa Fe Trail, the U.S. Army established a small stockade called Fort Mann near present Dodge City, Kansas. During the spring of 1848, the new post's commanding officer, Maj. William Gilpin, took to the field with his infantry troops mounted on mules. Driving westward down the Santa Fe Trail to El Moro, New Mexico, he then turned back eastward along the Canadian River across the Texas Panhandle to the Antelope Hills.

From there, he and his men scoured the Kiowa country, veering north and crossing Wolf and Beaver Creeks and the Cimarron River to Fort Mann. He reported that he found the country burned off and saw no Indians or game. When he reached Fort Mann on May 30, however, he discovered the chiefs of the Kiowas, Cheyennes, and Arapahos waiting for him there. They expressed their desire to make a new treaty of peace.[14]

Having no authority to treat with the tribes, Gilpin ordered them away from the Santa Fe road until he had heard from the White Father in Washington. In August 1848 he reported that the Kiowas had taken up residence at Bent's Fort in association with the Cheyennes and Arapahos. Those tribes had invited the Kiowas to give up their alliance with the Comanches and unite with them in establishing peaceful relations with the whites. Fitzpatrick wrote in October that they had done so and were living in "perfect amity with the surrounding tribes."[15]

In November 1848 Fitzpatrick was back at Bent's place, where a sizable encampment of Kiowas, Kiowa-Apaches, Cheyennes, and Arapahos had arrived to make peace. With no presents to give them, the agent put them off. Although they remained peaceful, the Indians complained strongly about the destruction of game and the cutting of their timber by the flood of whites crossing their hunting grounds. More than 3,000 gold-rush wagons passed Fort Mann during the summer of 1848 on their way to California.[16]

Explorer John C. Fremont, also on a march to California, observed that Fitzpatrick had "succeeded in drawing out from among the Comanches the whole Kiowa nation, with the exception of six lodges . . . in a few years he could have them all farming on the Arkansas."[17]

Fitzpatrick headed off north to deal with bands on the South Platte. En route he was overtaken by a party of Kiowas, who reported that trouble was brewing on the Santa Fe Trail. The Comanches had been told that troops were on the way to liberate all the captives they held, and they were very excited. Fitzpatrick returned to the Arkansas and managed to quiet the situation.[18]

The discovery of gold in California greatly accelerated the flood of white travelers across the Indian Territory as well as Kansas during the spring and summer of 1849. The camp of Capt. Randolph B. Marcy, who was surveying a route along the Canadian River from Fort Smith to Santa Fe, was visited on the evening of June 1, 1849, by four Kiowa Indians just west of the Antelope Hills.

The Kiowas, who were dressed in their war costume and well armed with rifles, bows, lances, and shields, were friendly. Through Delaware guide Black Beaver, they told Marcy that they were headed for Chihuahua, Mexico, to capture horses and mules. They expected to be gone a year or more. Marcy fed the four, made them gifts of tobacco, pipes, and sugar. He told them the United States wished to be on friendly terms with them. The Kiowas, whose village was forty miles to the north on Wolf Creek, said they were pleased to know this and promised to convey Marcy's talk to their people.[19]

Forty-niners traveling to California by way of the Santa Fe Trail constantly encountered Kiowas among the prairie tribes they met. On June 10, 1849, members of a train camped near Fort Mann looked across the Arkansas to see a large body of mounted Indians. The travelers prepared for trouble, but the Kiowa, Arapaho, and Cheyenne warriors carried a Fitzpatrick letter of introduction and were friendly. A month later a group of traders reached Independence over the Santa Fe road and reported that the crossing of the Arkansas at Fort Mann was lined with Indian lodges and animals. The tribesmen were so congenial as to help retrieve a stalled wagon from the waters of the Arkansas.[20]

Trader Thomas Aird, who ran a trading post near the juncture of Little River and the Canadian River in the Indian Territory, wrote to the *Fort Smith Herald* on August 18, 1849, to report an encounter that was far less happy: "This will be handed to you by one of the poor fellows, attacked in the Prairies by the Kiowa band of Comanches; they have suffered extremely, and now with nothing left in the world, are making their way to the settlements. One was badly wounded in two places when they came in, but by care, the wounds are nearly healed."[21]

Capt. Abraham Buford, returning over the Santa Fe Trail after making a gold-rush reconnaissance to Santa Fe from Fort Gibson by way of the

Intrepid Delaware frontiersman and peacemaker Black Beaver exerted a strong influence on Kicking Bird. Courtesy British Museum.

Cimarron River, likewise came onto three to four thousand Indians of various tribes near Pawnee Fork, Kansas. The Indians were camped peacefully, awaiting the arrival of Fitzpatrick.[22]

The gold-rush migration brought with it a deadly and dreaded disease, cholera. It struck the Kiowas and other tribes who had gathered at a great encampment on Bluff Creek south of present Dodge City, Kansas, during the summer of 1849.

The Kiowas had been celebrating a peace pact with the Osages by holding a medicine lodge event. In addition to the Kiowas and Osages there were bands of Prairie Apaches, Comanches, and Arapahos.[23] While Kiowa dancers performed one day, an Osage man suddenly fell to the ground, writhing in agony. He was dead within a few minutes. Immediately, the shout went up that it was the dreaded "cramps," and panic

William Bent. Courtesy Colorado Historical Society.

spread through the encampment. Instantly, the lodges were dismantled, and Indians began fleeing in all directions. Many deaths occurred among all of the tribes. It was said that almost half of the Cheyennes died that summer. Also, travelers reaching Independence from Santa Fe in July reported that "the Cholera was committing great ravages among those who remained [along the Arkansas], particularly the Kiowas."[24]

Fitzpatrick continued his efforts to work out new treaties with the Plains tribes. Assisting him was William Bent, who in April 1851 was at Fort Atkinson, a newly established post on the Santa Fe road twenty miles from the now abandoned Fort Mann, which had been sacked and burned by the Pawnees. Bent had sent out runners to the Kiowas, Comanches, Cheyennes, Arapahos, and Plains Apaches inviting them to come in and trade and treat with him. The tribes responded and in early May arrived at Fort Atkinson (then still known as Fort Mackay), Kansas, to conduct a peace council with Lt. Col. William Hoffman, commander of the post. An observer noted that both sides of the Arkansas River were crowded with lodges for about fifteen miles.[25]

In June Fitzpatrick arrived to hold a council with the tribes and ask them to attend a great assembly of tribes at Fort Laramie, Wyoming. The Cheyennes and Arapahos agreed to do so, but the Kiowas, Comanches, and Kiowa-Apaches were fearful of taking their horses among the northern tribes, who constantly raided their herds. They indicated, however, that they were willing to hold a treaty council in their own country.[26]

News of the meeting of tribes at Fort Laramie and the many wonderful gifts the Great Father had sent undoubtedly reached the Kiowas and Comanches through the Cheyennes and Arapahos. All four of these tribes, their total estimated at over 10,000, gathered at Fort Atkinson again in July 1852 fully expecting Fitzpatrick to arrive with presents. For a time the Indians enjoyed the gathering at Atkinson, as one soldier wrote: "Here we spent some two months or more with the Kiowas camped near by. These Indians were great horsemen, and would run races, bet their tepees and everything they had on their favorite horse."[27]

But as the hot days of midsummer dragged on, the grass, firewood, and game grew more and more scarce. The tribespeople and their horses became increasingly starved, and the agent did not arrive. Suspicion that the Big Chief in Washington was trying to cheat them increased. The situation became more and more precarious for the tiny cedar-palisade fort isolated in the sea of Kansas prairie. Its dried-mud buildings were roofed with canvas, and the garrison of ninety infantrymen and twenty dragoons was only lightly armed with a few small artillery pieces that were of questionable value against the overwhelming Indian force.

The young men of the several tribes became greatly aroused and demonstrative, and the fear of an attack grew inside the fort. Sentries were placed on patrol with orders to shoot any Indian who tried to pass. This, however, did not stop a very large Kiowa warrior who wished to enter the fort. When a smallish guard challenged him, the muscular, six-foot-three Kiowa simply knocked him down and walked in. Other Indians followed and began investigating the fort like any set of tourists but causing no disturbance.

Indignant and somewhat embarrassed by the audacious Kiowa, the fort's commanding lieutenant mustered his forces and with two artillery pieces marched to the Kiowa camp. There, surrounded by hundreds of hooting, weapon-brandishing warriors, he demanded that Tohawson turn over the man who had knocked down the sentry. Presently, the Kiowas brought the man forward, presenting him with an amused attitude of "Here's the rascal—let's see you take him!"[28]

The lieutenant was aware of the precarious situation he had unwittingly marched into. Now suddenly much wiser, he stepped forward, shook hands with Tohawson, and thanked him for showing his willingness to cooperate. He said he would not press the matter further, and he and his men retreated to the fort. They were followed the distance by yelling, dirt-throwing tribespeople. Some have seen the warrior as a young Satanta, but there is no evidence of that being so.

Percival Lowe, who was stationed at Fort Atkinson as a U.S. dragoon during this period, penned a description of the famous Kiowa:

> Satanta, the war chief of the Kiowas, always came rather neatly dressed in fine buckskin, and wore a handsome cavalry saber and belt. He was a man about five feet ten, sparely made, muscular, cat-like in his movements—more Spanish than Indian in his appearance—sharp features, thin lips, keen restless eyes, thin mustache and scattering chin whiskers that seemed to have stopped growing when one to three inches long. At the time of which I write he was about thirty-five years old.[29]

In September, European Julius Fröbel passed by Fort Atkinson with a westward-bound train. He met and wrote descriptively of several Kiowa and Comanche chiefs, all of whom were friendly. The Kiowas were on their way eastward to hunt and made inquiries concerning the hunting grounds there with special emphasis on the Pawnee presence. One ranking Kiowa chief came forth with a Mexican interpreter to tell of his expeditions into Mexico. "Caballos, mulas, muchachos, muchachas,—mucho!—bueno!" he reported. On the Arkansas, however, there was "Nada!"[30] Fröbel named several Comanche chiefs but identified none of the Kiowas. According to Andrew Stumbling Bear, Kicking Bird's father, Big Horse (Tsain-hay-te) led a raid into Mexico during this period.[31]

Fitzpatrick returned to Fort Atkinson on June 20, 1853, this time with presents. Again waiting for him were the Kiowas, Comanches, and Kiowa-Apaches. The tribes had only recently met at the Salt Plains in northern Indian Territory with the Cherokees and Creeks, who had encouraged them to give up their raiding into Texas. The Kiowa chiefs, led by Tohawson and Satank, were prepared to hold talks with Fitzpatrick and initiate a new treaty. Neither Satanta nor Kicking Bird was important enough as yet to be among the eight other Kiowa signators to the treaty, but they were undoubtedly present.

This was principally a friendship treaty, but it also attended to restitution for injuries to U.S. citizens by the tribes, gave the United States the right to lay off roads and establish forts in the country of the

Kiowa chief Satanta (Set-tainte, or White Bear) and Kicking Bird competed for tribal leadership. Courtesy Western History Collection, University of Oklahoma.

tribes, and promised the restoration of future captives. In turn, the United
States promised to protect and defend the tribes and to provide annuities
on Beaver Creek in northwestern Indian Territory each July. One clause
also foresaw the future possibility of providing farms in lieu of annuities.[32]

The treaty further stipulated that the three tribes would refrain from
conducting incursions into Mexico. The Kiowas and Comanches both
requested letters of safe conduct for one or two of their chiefs, who set
out at once to the south to assure the Mexicans that they were no longer
enemies. When the pact had been signed, the agent presented the treaty
presents and departed to meet with the Cheyennes and Arapahos at Fort
St. Vrain on the South Platte of Colorado.[33]

On July 16 an exploring party under Capt. John W. Gunnison camped a mile west of Fort Atkinson, finding 280 lodges of Comanches encamped there. The Kiowa camp on the south bank of the Arkansas was composed largely of old men, women, and children, the warriors having gone north with other tribes to attack the Pawnees.[34]

These Kiowa warriors had joined a large 1,000-man Cheyenne-led force, which also included Arapahos, Comanches, and a few Lakotas and Apaches for this war excursion. Sixty miles southwest of Fort Kearny, Nebraska, they engaged 400 Pawnee warriors whose families had taken shelter in a ravine. The tide of battle was turned when 40 Pottawatomis, armed with rifles, arrived to support the Pawnees. It was reported that of the 150 killed or wounded among the Cheyenne force, the dead included 2 Kiowas, 17 Cheyennes, and 5 Arapahoes along with 170 of their horses. The Pawnees suffered only about a fifth that many casualties.[35]

In September of that year, a railroad surveying expedition under Lt. Amiel W. Whipple found a small band of Kiowas along the Canadian River in the Texas Panhandle. The band had recently returned from meeting with Fitzpatrick, and most of the people possessed blue blankets they had been given at that meeting. They were disappointed, though, that Whipple could offer few presents other than a red blanket and some beads and tobacco for each of five chiefs in the camp. Tohawson, the Kiowas said, was away to the north hunting buffalo.[36] Whipple wrote:

> Some, who appeared to be sub-chiefs, with faces painted yellow, had colored the tops of their heads, where the long black hair was parted, with vermilion. Their noses were long and aquiline, chins beardless, and eyes small, bright and sparkling. Their foreheads were retreating, and their cheek-bones high and ugly. They carried superb bows of bois d'arc, ornamented with brass nails, silver plates and tinted feather trimmings. The quiver and belt, of wolfskin, were wrought with beads. They wore moccasins and buckskin leggings, covered with wampum and bead-work, and fastened with silver buckles. From the crown of their heads was suspended a queue of horse-hair, reaching nearly to the ground, orna-mented with ten circular plates, from one to three inches in diameter, and terminated by a silver crescent and wampum. They wore no pen-dants from the nose, but in their ears were brass rings, from which hung chains and bugle-beads of bone or iridescent shells, reaching far down upon the shoulders. Similar ornaments were worn around the neck. All had bracelets of brass-wire or silver bands.[37]

Whipple and his men attempted to purchase one of the Kiowa's long, colorful war bonnets, but they had nothing of equal beauty to trade. Baldwin Möllhausen, a German artist who accompanied the survey, wrote of the great number of horses and mules owned by the Kiowas that enabled them to move rapidly about the prairie. He concluded that their mobility and capacity to live off the land would make them difficult to defeat.[38]

During a council with the chiefs, Whipple said he wished to restore to their own people some of the Mexican captives held by the band. The suggestion shocked an old chief (Tohawson's father, perhaps), whose third and favorite wife, Jose Maria, was a comely Mexican woman. She had been captured at age twenty and had been with the Kiowas for seven years. The marriage had produced a blue-eyed, three-year-old son. The chief was beset with rage at Whipple. Friends, he charged, would not come among them and attempt to separate wives and children from husbands and fathers. It took a gift of a cow from the expedition herd to finally calm him.

Whipple's interpreter was Vincente, a young former captive of the Comanches who had been rescued and adopted by trader Jesse Chisholm. Later known on the frontier also as George Chisholm or Caboon, Vincente greatly feared the Kiowas for the witchcraft he believed they practiced in sending puffs of smoke toward the sun. Further efforts to rescue Jose Maria and a Mexican man of five years' captivity proved fruitless.

Their defeat at the hands of the Pottawatomis and the loss of a tribesman led the Kiowas to conduct another warring expedition to the north during the summer of 1854. This was another revenge raid against the Pawnees, but it was also directed against the immigrant tribes the U.S. government had removed to west of the Mississippi River. The Kiowas and Comanches went from camp to camp among the Cheyennes and passed the pipe to solicit aid against the Pawnees.

Indian agent J. W. Whitfield, replacing Fitzpatrick, who had died while on a visit to Washington, D.C., was witness to a gathering of the tribes during the summer of 1854.

> The Indians were camped on Pawnee Fork, at the crossing of the Santa Fé Road, where they were collected in larger numbers than have ever been known to assemble on the Arkansas river before. Old traders estimate the numbers at from twelve to fifteen hundred lodges, and the horses and mules at from forty to fifty thousand head. The entire Kiowa and Prairie Comanche were there; several hundred of Texas or Woods Comanche had come; the Prairie Apache, one band of Arapahoe, and two bands of Cheyennes, and the Osages composed the grand council. They had met for the purpose of forming their war party in order, as they say in their language, as if to "*wipe out*" all frontier Indians they could find on the plains.[39]

This war expedition also met defeat. Driving northeast, they contested a force of around a hundred Sac and Fox Indians. Like the Pottawatomis, the Sac and Fox warriors were well armed with modern rifles that were overpowering at long range against the bows and arrows and lances of the prairie bands. The Kiowas and their allies were forced to retreat after 16 of them had been killed, over a hundred wounded, and a large number of their horses dropped by the firepower of the Sac and Fox.[40]

These intertribal battles reflected the enormity of the white man's influence on the balance of power among the tribes of the West. It had become imperative for the Kiowas and others to procure their own explosive weapons. This, along with their desire for more of the cloth, sugar, coffee, pots, pans, knives, and other goods of the white men that passed by, would continue to incite them to raid along the Santa Fe Trail, as well as in Texas and New Mexico. Thus far there had been no out-and-out warfare between the prairie tribes and the intruding whites. But that would soon change.

6

Promises Are a Poor Thing

When Whitfield met with the prairie tribes at the Pawnee Fork in 1854, he found them very unruly. They had been exacting a toll of sugar, coffee, and other articles from passing wagons, he reported, and evidenced little respect for the United States. There had, however, been no major depredations reported along the Santa Fe Trail.[1]

Whitfield talked with the chiefs regarding a U.S. Senate amendment to the 1853 treaty. The amendment gave the president of the United States the right to amend the annual annuity clause of the treaty. Instead of providing goods, the government would give the tribe land for farms within an assigned reservation and provide farming help. When this alteration was explained to Tohawson, the percipient Kiowa replied that he was pleased that the Great Father was going to take pity on his people and send them farmers, but he hoped the president would also send the Kiowas some land that would produce corn, as they had none such. Whitfield shared the opinion that the entire country occupied by the Kiowas was worthless for agricultural purposes.[2]

Whitfield again returned to the Arkansas River with his wagon train of annuity goods in July 1855. He was met by Tohawson's band of 150 lodges and some Comanches twenty-five miles above Fort Atkinson. When he attempted to distribute all of the Kiowas' annuities, Tohawson refused them. The chief said that half of the goods belonged to Satank, who, angry at Whitfield's tardiness, had already taken his half of the tribe back to the prairie. Satank had been talking bad, he said, and both Tohawson and Whitfield feared there would be trouble if that chief's share of the goods was provided to others.[3]

Writing from Bent's Fort on August 15, Whitfield made the following estimates. Of a total population of 2,400, there were about 600 adult Kiowa males, of whom 500 were warriors. They possessed around 1,100 lodges and 15,000 horses. In an attempt to calculate their worth in dollar terms, he estimated that their annual income from the chase was $7,000, based on a year's killing of 20,000 buffalo, 1,500 deer, 600 elk, and 300 bears—these last pointing possibly to hunting sojourns in the Rockies.[4]

In Texas, meanwhile, Indian superintendent Robert Neighbors, reporting from the Brazos reserves, decried the serious depredations committed by the Kiowas and Comanches in Texas during forays into Mexico. Both tribes, he charged, held a great many captives and horses and mules they had stolen from the Texas frontier and Mexico. It was up to the federal government, he said, to use its military force to restore the captives and stolen property and to force the tribes to abandon their roving life on the prairie.[5]

When Robert C. Miller, who had replaced Whitfield as agent, arrived at Fort Atkinson in 1856, he was met by a delegation of Kiowas and Comanches. They insisted that he deliver the goods to their camps thirty or forty miles distant, and Miller complied. As he later proceeded down the trail toward Bent's Fort, a group of Kiowas came up and began annoying the wagonmaster. The Indians charged into his cattle herd, shooting some of the cows with arrows and cutting off the tails of others to make them stampede. They drove off four of the animals, Miller's men not daring to interfere while looking into the face of drawn bows.[6]

The next year Miller sent out runners in advance from Westport, Missouri, to notify the tribes that he was coming with presents. When he reached Fort Atkinson with his annuity train in July, he found a sizable encampment waiting for him. Some of the main bands were still out, however, and Miller decided to hold up the distribution of goods. The Kiowas became very angry and surrounded the train with their lances and bows ready and demanded that their goods be issued immediately. Just as Miller was about to give in, some Comanche chiefs arrived and said they would help him protect the train. Miller felt the Kiowas were contemptuous of the United States for giving them presents after they had conducted raids.[7]

Miller continued on to Bent's Fort with the Cheyenne and Arapaho annuities. While he was there, word arrived of the Cheyennes' defeat on the Solomon River in western Kansas by U.S. troops under Col. Edwin V. Sumner. The Cheyennes' village had been destroyed, five or six chiefs had been killed, and they had been forced to flee and leave behind 150 horses.[8]

The new agent held the Kiowas responsible for attacks on wagon trains in New Mexico. Four of five Kiowas or Comanches, he was told at Bent's, had tagged behind a mail stage from Santa Fe for a time before killing the driver. They then cut the mules loose from their harness and fled.[9]

Settlers in northern Texas were up in arms about the stock they had been losing to horse thieves. Generally, Indians were blamed, either those at the two Brazos reserves west of Fort Belknap or the tribes who resided in the Indian Territory. White gangs of horse thieves were active against both white settlers and the Indians, but most Texans still held the Comanches and Kiowas responsible for losses that occurred.[10] In Texas, Neighbors complained that while the Kiowas and Comanches were way-laying the transportation and mails along the route to El Paso, their agent on the Arkansas River was issuing them arms and ammunition.[11]

During 1857 a military survey led by Lt. Col. Joseph E. Johnston worked its way westward along the southern boundary line of Kansas. On July 30, in the vicinity of present Forgan, Oklahoma, two or more Kiowas attacked an advance party of the surveyors, killing the driver of a wagon and running off its two mules. The Indians were tracked to Fort Atkinson, where the tribes had gathered to receive their annual treaty awards, but no further action was taken.[12]

More Kiowas, this group friendly, were met on September 7 near Aubrey's Cutoff in the far western tip of the Oklahoma Panhandle. On September 25 while on their return march, Johnston's party encountered a Kiowa camp of fifty or more lodges near present Texhoma, Oklahoma. This was Tohawson's party, and he again vowed to abide by the Kiowas' treaty with the United States. He also promised that he would surrender the two murderers of the wagon driver when he learned who they were.[13]

On April 15, 1858, Wichita agent A. H. McKisick reported from western Indian Territory that Jesse Chisholm had just returned from a trading venture among the prairie tribes. Chisholm said he found the tribes in an angry and belligerent mood. He claimed that Mormons had been among them, and the Indians spoke of a "great chief" who was able to destroy the people of the United States. Chisholm assumed this power-ful chief was Brigham Young.[14]

Only a month later a Texas Ranger force under Capt. John S. "Old Rip" Ford, supported by Indians from the two Brazos reserves, drove northward along the 100th meridian that separated the Indian Territory from the Texas Panhandle. On May 11 Ford located a Comanche village encamped on Little Robe Creek, which fed into the Canadian River from the northwest just beyond the Antelope Hills. He attacked the camp, killing a number of its occupants and capturing much of its horse herd. A Comanche chief who was shot from his horse during the attack was later found to be wearing a coat of mail.[15]

During the following September the Comanches were again hit hard, this time by a force of U.S. cavalry from Texas. After having established Camp Radziminski west of the Wichita Mountains, Maj. Earl Van Dorn learned of a large entourage of Comanches that had stopped to visit the Wichitas while on the way to Fort Arbuckle to hold peace talks. Making an overnight forced march eastward around the mountains, Van Dorn launched a surprise attack against the village, killing numerous Comanches and Wichitas. Fortunately for them, the Kiowas were well to the north on the Arkansas River. In July 1858 agent Miller found them waiting for him en masse at the mouth of Pawnee Fork.

The Indians were very hungry, and Miller found that Sumner's defeat of the Cheyennes had made the Cheyennes, Arapahos, and Kiowa-Apaches anxious to have a new treaty enacted. Their chiefs said they realized it was useless to oppose the white man "who would soon with his villages occupy the whole prairie."[16] They were not blind, they said, and knew the buffalo would soon disappear entirely. They wanted peace and no longer listened to their young men who clamored continually for war.

The mood of the Kiowas and Comanches was much different, however. Comanche chief Buffalo Hump was still very angry over Ford's surprise attack on his band at Little Robe Creek. He declared that he intended to lead a united Comanche force back against the "white man of the south," the Texans, once the annuity distribution was made. The Kiowas had no desire to make a new treaty. They did agree reluctantly to send a delegation to Washington to hear what the Great Father had to say. They said, though, that they did not believe his heart was strong and placed little confidence in what he had to say.[17]

Miller talked threateningly. He said that if the tribes did not cease their depredations, the Great Father would withhold their presents and send troops to burn their villages and take their women and children captive. The Kiowas listened in silence, but they did not take insulting threats lightly. When Miller had finished, Tohawson, normally the peace-maker, rose to his feet. He motioned angrily toward the countless lodges and horses in the valley below. He said:

> The white chief is a fool; he is a coward; his heart is small—not larger than a pebble stone; his men are not strong—too few to contend against

Annuity distribution at Bluff Creek, Kansas. *Harper's Weekly*, March 27, 1869.

my warriors; they are women. There are three chiefs—the white chief, the Spanish chief, and myself. The Spanish and myself are men; we do bad towards each other sometimes, stealing horses and taking scalps, but we do not get mad and act the fool. The white chief is a child, and like a child gets mad quick. When my young men, to keep their women and children from starving, take from the white man passing through our country, killing and driving away our buffalo, a cup of sugar or coffee, the "white chief" is angry and threatens to send his soldiers. I have looked for them a long time, but they have not come; he is a coward; his heart is a woman's. I have spoken. Tell the "great chief" what I have said.[18]

When the annuities had been issued, one group of Kiowas headed south with the Comanches under Buffalo Hump, one group rode up the Pawnee Fork to hunt for buffalo, and another group went eastward in search of the Osages. Fearing more attacks from Texas, however, Buffalo Hump moved north to southern Kansas. He was camped on Crooked Creek in Clark County, Kansas, when once again he was struck by surprise during May 1859. And once again the attacker was Van Dorn, who had marched north from Camp Radziminski across western Indian Territory into Kansas looking for Indians. Forty-nine Comanches were killed and thirty-six taken prisoner.[19]

James Brice, who operated a mail station at the Pawnee Fork stop on the Santa Fe Trail, described the tentative relationship with the Kiowas.

The tribe, he said, had long used the site as a regular camping ground and continued the practice after Fort Larned was established there in 1859. Capt. Julius Hayden, commander of the foundling post, instructed Brice to bring to his office any Indians who wanted to see him. Brice wrote:

> They would come to the mail Station at all hours. Santanta, a Kiowa leader of young desperados on the frontier days, a dog soldier, and more feared than loved by his pale faced brethren, came along about midnight with eighteen or twenty of his band. He would knock on the door; I would get up out of bed, not knowing who was knocking; opening the door to see, I was facing those Indians mounted in single file like cavalry soldiers waiting orders from the commander, wanting to stop with me and get a pass on the stage to Council Grove, 200 miles, where he and his men were going to see the Comanche Indians. I would tell him that the commanding officer gave me orders to inform him when Indians came to the mail station, and that he would have to go and see him. After telling my wife to bolt the doors, we would start for headquarters. Santanta was a large man and would crouch behind me for protection from stray bullets; if any should come our way, he preferred them to reach me first. When we reached the sentinel, he asked: "Who comes there?" and I answered, Brice, from the mail station with Santanta to see the commanding officer. Halt! he would call the sergeant of the guard; after all the preliminaries, we would be told to advance. The sergeant would wake up the commander from his bed, telling him Santanta with eighteen or twenty of his band wanted to stop all night; he would direct the sergeant to let the men sleep in the guard house and turn their ponies into the corral. Santanta would decline the invitation and return with me. While we were seeing the captain the Indians, waiting our return, tied their ponies in a ravine close to the mail station. Sitting around a camp fire, I would bring them bread and all the cooked victuals I could find, remaining with them until their camp fires went out and that there was no danger of burning the mail companies hay stacks.[20]

Brice, who knew many of the Kiowa leaders personally, gave his estimation of the leading Kiowa chiefs of the day.

> Setank and Dehosin [Tohawson] were the leading chiefs of the Kiowa Indians when I first began to run with the Santa Fe mail. The former was said to be vicious and always inclined to the warpath. Dehosin was said to be the opposite and always advised his people against going to war with the government. After that Santanta became a power in his tribe and had a bad reputation. Kicking Bird [only in his mid-twenties by now] was said to be a good Indian by white men that knew him and would some day become influential with his people and the government.[21]

The flood of whites across the prairie during the Colorado gold rush of 1858 and 1859 and the increased presence of U.S. troops along the Santa Fe Trail soon led to conflicts. One incident involved the killing of a well-liked young Kiowa chief named Pawnee, who with two other Kiowas had obtained some whiskey on the trail at Walnut Creek. This was reported to the commander of a military unit en route to Fort Riley, who, fearing trouble, placed Pawnee under arrest. The troops were taking him back to their camp when he began riding off in another direction. A young officer, thinking Pawnee was trying to escape, yelled for him to stop and fired a shot over his head. Not understanding, Pawnee rode on. The officer then shot and killed him.[22]

Following this incident, the Kiowas reportedly attacked a mail party and murdered some gold seekers on their way to Pike's Peak. Capt. Lambert B. Wolf, with the First U.S. Dragoons under Maj. John Sedgwick at Fort Larned, told of other conflicts. When three white men reported that fifteen Kiowas had threatened them, a cavalry troop rushed out, found two Kiowas, and killed them, bringing six captured ponies back to camp. On November 3, 1859, two men, a woman, and two children on their way to the States from New Mexico arrived at Fort Larned. They claimed the Kiowas had attacked them at Santa Fe Crossing, taken their oxen and cow, and plundered their wagon. The Kiowas, they said, were about to torture one of their men when some Cheyennes came up, stopped the proceedings, and made the Kiowas return their loot.[23]

William Bent, who was appointed a U.S. Indian agent in 1859, defined the situation of the Central Plains tribes in his annual report: "These numerous and warlike Indians, pressed upon all around by the Texans, by the settlers of the gold region, by the advancing people of Kansas, and from the Platte, are already compressed into a small circle of territory, destitute of food, and itself bisected athwart by a constantly marching line of emigrants."[24]

The Kiowas and Comanches, Bent noted, had appeared in large numbers and for long periods on the Arkansas River of Kansas and Colorado. This had been brought on in part by the hostile front in Texas, which had forced them northward. Bent had recently encountered about 2,500 warriors of those two tribes at the conflux of the Arkansas and Walnut Creek. He felt they would remain peaceful only so long as U.S. troops were in the area. Jesse Chisholm, who traded among eight to nine thousand Kiowas and Comanches below the Antelope Hills in early 1860, said the Indians wanted a trader to be sent among them. They also wished to make peace and join the other tribes in the Leased District, an area to which the Texas Indians had been relocated in southwestern Indian Territory in 1859.[25]

The First Cavalry spent the winter at Fort Riley. But in the spring of 1860, Sedgwick set out to punish the Kiowas for their winter depredations—"all caused by, or at least commencing with, the killing of Pawnee."[26] On July 12 four companies of Sedgwick's First Dragoon regiment were camped near Bent's Fort on the Arkansas. From there, Capt. William Steele, commanding a hundred men and guided by a Cheyenne, was sent on a scout toward the Smoky Hill River in pursuit of the Kiowas. Two days later, Bent informed Sedgwick that Kiowa war chief Satank had been there a short time earlier with his family and a few warriors.[27]

Lt. J. E. B. Stuart was immediately put in pursuit with twenty dragoons. Stuart soon came across the Kiowas and was joined in the chase by Steele's unit. Some of the Kiowas managed to escape, but fifteen women and children were captured and taken to camp. Among the prisoners were the wives and children of Satank.[28] When Sedgwick and his command departed down the Arkansas to their station at the Pawnee Fork, the captured Kiowas were turned over to Bent. The Indians returned, however, and angrily surrounded Bent's post in battle array to demand the release of the captives. Bent had no choice but to comply.

A messenger sent by Bent to inform the troops of the situation was shot, mangled, and scalped by a Kiowa war party. Still alive, the man was taken by friendly Arapahos back to Bent's, where he eventually recovered.[29] Bent recommended that the Kiowas be soundly whipped, and the secretary of war obligingly ordered the army in the West to chastise them.[30]

Even as these events were taking place, Capt. Samuel D. Sturgis led a First Dragoon command from Fort Cobb, Indian Territory, north into western Kansas in search of the Kiowas. His force consisted of 430 troops, 100 Indians, and 70 wagons. He reported an intended march to the Antelope Hills and across the Canadian northward to Rabbit Ear Creek. Instead, he marched into western Kansas and crossed Sedgwick's trail on the Smoky Hill. On August 6 and 7 he engaged 600 Kiowa and Comanche warriors near the Republican River. By his claim, Sturgis killed 20 or 30 of them while losing one dragoon and 5 Indian guides. The Indians, Sturgis said, had tried to avoid a fight.[31]

In the fall of 1860 the government constructed a new military post just above where Bent's Fort stood perched on a stone bluff along the Arkansas River. For a time the new post would be called Fort Wise after the governor of Virginia. At the same time, Albert G. Boone, who resided at Booneville just up the Arkansas, was appointed to succeed Bent as agent for the tribes of the upper Arkansas.

Bent had recommended that new treaties be initiated with the Cheyennes and Arapahos. In response, Commissioner of Indian Affairs A. B.

Greenwood visited Fort Wise in September 1860 and made tentative agreements with the Cheyenne and Arapaho leaders. By the proposed treaty, the Cheyennes and Arapahos were assigned to a small, gameless reserve in eastern Colorado.

With the Civil War under way in 1861 and the Confederacy working to win the support of the tribes of the Indian Territory, a new urgency was placed on like efforts by the North. Capt. Elmer Otis reported from Fort Wise in August 1861 that word had reached him of Confederate tampering with the tribes in the Territory. He said the Kiowas, then gathered at Wise, were friendly and had never behaved better. The tribe was anxious, however, over a new treaty that had been promised them the previous winter. "Promises are a poor thing to live on," they said.[32]

In response, Boone met with the main chiefs of the Kiowas and some lesser chiefs of the Comanches at Fort Wise on September 6 and initiated a formal agreement in which a full treaty was promised at Fort Larned the next September. Until that time, the Kiowas pledged themselves to an armistice period of friendship with white citizens and to the protection of their property. They also agreed not to pass through any white settlements on the Arkansas in making war on the Utes. In return, they were assured of faithful delivery of their annuities.[33]

It was clear from those chiefs signing the treaty that they represented the majority of the Kiowas. The Kiowa signatories were, as listed: To-hauson, or Little Mountain; Sa-tanka, or Sitting Bear; Te-nat-ton, or Little Heart; Pah-tall-ye, or Bald Bear; Quey-pah-kah, or Lone Wolf; Sa-tainte, or White Bear; Quo-i-qui,[34] or Yellow Wolf; and Tah-quoy-ye pool, or Stinking Ahisamore. This would indicate that although he had begun to emerge into public notice, Kicking Bird was not yet among the principal tribal leaders.

Just as it did for all the other tribes, the war among the white men, the Civil War, changed much for the Kiowas. Responding to pressures from Texas citizens, the federal government had closed its two Indian reserves near Fort Belknap in 1859 and moved virtually all of its Plains tribes to a district in western Indian Territory leased from the Choctaw and Chickasaw Indians. With the Union abandonment of the Indian Territory, the protection and subsistence promised by treaties with the United States quickly vanished. This separation was soon formalized by treaties initiated between the Confederacy and the Indian Territory tribes by Gen. Albert Pike. The Kiowas were the only tribe of the region that refused to sign with Pike, although some Comanche bands also held out.

Still another effort to persuade the Kiowas to the side of the South was made during July 1861 when former Texas Ranger Gen. Henry McCulloch and five companies of Texas Mounted Rifles, guided by

Tonkawa scouts, marched from the Wichita agency to the Antelope Hills where they met with Satank, Satanta, and Lone Wolf of the Kiowas and Red Bear and Eagle Chief of the Comanches. Neither tribe, however, had any desire to take up with the Texans or the Confederacy, and they rejected McCulloch's overtures.[35]

In his report to Confederacy president Jefferson Davis, Pike noted that the Kiowas had quarreled with the Comanches over treating with the Confederacy, of which Texas was a member. When Comanche chief Buffalo Hump went to talk with the other chiefs about it, they drove him off.[36] On December 15, 1861, Buffalo Hump and others wrote to Seminole chief John Jumper saying that a Kiowa named Pea-o-popicult had recently visited the Wichita agency. He had expressed his friendly intentions and returned to his people to consult with them.[37]

The Kiowas remained aloof, however, declaring that as soon as their young men returned from a raid into Mexico, they would attack and kill other prairie Indians who had signed treaties with the Confederates and would plunder the Texas frontier. This pointed to the fact that with the outbreak of the war, neither the North nor Texas could do much to restrain such activity. Pike sent a message to the Kiowas saying they would have to choose between peace and war.[38]

Rebel commissioner S. S. Scott reported that a Kiowa named Testoth-cha, identified as a principal chief, returned to the agency to say that his band would like to make their home on Elk Creek in the Wichita Mountains. The name is similar in enunciation to Tiche-toche-cha, and it may be that the former head chief was still alive. On July 4, 1862, he signed a treaty with Confederate authorities pledging the Kiowas' friendship and willingness to abide by the stipulations Pike had made in treaties with the other tribes.[39]

It soon became evident to all of the tribes that the Confederacy could and would do little to fulfill the treaty obligations. Some beef was purchased and driven in from Texas, but it was hardly enough to feed the hungry Indians. More often, the Indians crossed the Red River and got their own. The herds that had been created by the now absent tribes of the Leased District were also vulnerable to marauders from both the prairie tribes and cattle thieves from Kansas. Following a destructive raid and massacre of the Wichita agency by Union-aligned Indians that same month, that agency essentially disintegrated, although Texas troops continued to garrison Forts Arbuckle and Cobb. Most of the agency's Wichita, Shawnee, Caddo, and other residents fled into Kansas.

In late 1861 Samuel G. Colley was named to replace Boone as agent for the tribes of the upper Arkansas. The following June he reported that the Kiowas, Comanches, and Apaches had spent the past winter and spring on the Arkansas River near the crossing of the Santa Fe road.[40] In August Colley was upset to learn that the commanding officer at Fort Larned had halted a train on its way to Fort Lyon (formerly Fort Wise) with the annual annuity goods and threatened to distribute them himself. Colley and Col. Jesse Leavenworth, son of Gen. Henry Leavenworth and a West Point graduate who had recently been assigned command of both Lyon and Larned, hurried to Larned and took charge of the goods.[41]

The treaty promised for September did not develop. The tribes were peaceful, however, when Colley issued annuity goods to them at the Cimarron Crossing on October 30. The agent reported that the Indians were highly delighted and pledged their friendship.[42] As he had been instructed to do, Colley worked to assemble a delegation of his Indian charges for a visit to Washington, D.C. John Simpson Smith, interpreter at Fort Lyon who had been associated with the Cheyennes for many years, was sent among the tribes to recruit members.[43]

The Kiowas chosen to go were Lone Wolf, Yellow Wolf, White Bull, Yellow Buffalo, and Little Heart, plus two women whose names were given as Coy and Etla. Chiefs Lean Bear, War Bonnet, and Standing-in-the-Water represented the Cheyennes; Spotted Wolf and Neva for the Arapahos; Ten Bears and Prickled Forehead for the Comanches; Poor Bear for the Plains-Apaches; and Jacob for the Caddos. Neither Satanta nor Kicking Bird was with the delegation.

The family of Yellow Wolf pleaded with him not to go, even following the delegation for miles from their camps near Fort Larned, wailing and lamenting in their effort to dissuade him. But the much respected chief was determined to follow in the footsteps of an ancestor who had been awarded a peace medal that had been handed down from father to son since the time of Thomas Jefferson.[44]

Under the escort of Colley and Smith, the delegation arrived in Washington, D.C., on March 26, 1863. They went on sight-seeing tours around the town, visiting the Capitol and attending a play at Grover's Theatre. An interview was arranged with President Abraham Lincoln in the East Room of the White House. Lean Bear of the Cheyennes acted as orator for the tribesmen and expressed amazement at what he and the others had seen.

The president brought forth a world globe and asked a learned professor to explain it and where the Indians lived on it. He then explained that the pale-faced people were so numerous and prosperous because they cultivate the soil. "We make treaties with you, and will try to observe

John Simpson Smith with (*left to right*) Cheyenne chief Standing Water, Kiowa chief Yellow Wolf, and Cheyenne chief Lean Bear. Courtesy British Museum.

them; and if our children should sometimes behave badly, and violate these treaties, it is against our wish."[45]

He leaned forward toward Lean Bear with a kindly smile on his face and spoke. His words would hold a prophetic truth for the Cheyenne chief, who would be shot down by U.S. troops within a year's time, and for the prairie tribes in general. "You know it is not always possible for any father to have his children do precisely as he wishes them to do."

After the interview, photographs of the tribesmen, along with Washington dignitaries including Mrs. Lincoln, were made in the White House conservatory by an artist from Matthew Brady's studio.[46]

The trip was not without incident, however. Kiowa chief Yellow Wolf became ill with pneumonia while in Washington and died there on April 5. He was buried in the Congressional Cemetery, where the great Choctaw chief Pushmataha had been interred in 1824 and Western Cherokee chief John Rogers in 1846.[47] The *Washington Evening Star* described Yellow Wolf's death:

> Yellow Wolf, chief of the Kiowa Indians, and who was sent here as one of the delegates to see the President, died on Saturday afternoon after a short illness, and was buried yesterday afternoon at the request of the surviving Indians, "as the white brethren were." The government furnished the coffin, which was a very fine one. About half an hour before the breath left [the] deceased, his companions commenced to paint his face, hands, and feet with a red paint, and then securing new clothing and new blankets, they arrayed the dying chief in them.
>
> A few moments before expiring Yellow Wolf sent for Maj. S. G. Colley, the Indian agent for that and other tribes, and taking the agent's hands, said to him, "We have come a great way to see our Great Father, and make peace. I have seen the big father, and am at peace with every one—with the Great Spirit and with the Great Father, and I am now going to lay down and sleep with him here."
>
> As soon as the chief expired, his companions took his bow and arrows and broke them in half. They were then made up in a bundle together with his other effects and will be buried with him, as also will his

Members of the 1863 Kiowa delegation include Lone Wolf, top center; Yellow Buffalo, far right; and Coy and Etla, seated. Courtesy British Museum.

buffalo robes and blankets, and all that he owned at the time of his death. A large silver medal, a present from President Jefferson to Yellow Wolf's ancestors, will be buried with him also.[48]

The delegation's adventure in the East did not end at the capital city. P. T. Barnum, the famous showman, invited Colley to bring his Indian charges to New York City. Colley accepted, and the Indians were escorted there by way of Baltimore and Philadelphia. Barnum arranged for tours on horse-drawn omnibuses to let the chiefs view all the wondrous sights of the city.

On one occasion they were driven down Broadway to a public school where 1,500 children performed by singing and doing calisthenics. Afterward the chiefs stood in line while interpreter Smith introduced them, giving their names and tribes and making personal comments about each. He gave his view that Kiowa Yellow Buffalo was the best Indian in the delegation, while Kiowa Little Heart was the worst.[49]

Barnum had a purpose behind his generosity. For two weeks he advertised the prairie natives and put them on public display in his museum of oddities before crowds of gaping New Yorkers—for a fee, of course.

"They are the genuine article," a *New York Times* reporter observed. "Paint, feathers and trinkets cover their exterior; but their interior is, metaphorically speaking, filled with dead men's bones. They are a hard set, and, if Barnum is permitted to remain unscalped, he will do well."[50]

The trip to the East had been an effort to smooth relations between the tribes of the Plains and the white man. However much it may have impressed the Indians, it did not alter the fact that affairs in the West were deteriorating rapidly. The ever-increasing white population of Kansas and Colorado and the rising wartime military power of the United States boded certain trouble and misfortune for the tribes.

7

Raiding the Santa Fe Trail

The truth of Lincoln's lament that he could not completely control his troops in the field would soon produce tragic consequences on the Plains. The peace leaders of the various tribes often suffered the same inability to restrain their warriors. As a result, open warfare, not peace, would ensue following the delegation's return from the East.

Matters had been heating up along the Santa Fe Trail, where transportation was ever increasing. Settlers were moving westward to the Colorado, California, and other Western regions; and with the emigrants lumbered ox trains loaded with supplies and trade goods. Wagons carried gold and silver eastward from the Rocky Mountains to help finance the cost of war for the Union. All this activity served as a magnet to the Kiowas and other tribes of western Kansas and the Indian Territory. During the months of June and July, the great buffalo herds crossed the Arkansas River near Fort Larned in their summer migration. The annual distribution of annuity goods along the trail was still another draw for the tribes.

Fort Larned was garrisoned by one company of cavalry and one of infantry—147 men equipped with one piece of field artillery. It was a sparse force indeed to maintain control of the long, desolate, and dangerous road through western Kansas and on to New Mexico. On June 11, 1863, Leavenworth reported from Larned that a sizable band of Comanches had just arrived on the trail with three to four thousand horses, many of them large American animals. There they joined the Kiowas, Apaches,

Sutler store at Fort Dodge, Kansas. *Harper's Weekly*, May 25, 1867. Courtesy Western History Collection, University of Oklahoma.

Cheyennes, Arapahos, and Caddos already present. The Indians were estimated to number between four and five thousand lodges.[1] The situation was exacerbated by wagon caravans carrying loads of whiskey through the region. Many of these were Mexican trains returning from Missouri to Santa Fe. Even the post sutlers along the trail openly sold spirits to all comers.

"There is enough whisky in one train that I met today," Leavenworth complained, "to intoxicate every Indian on the plains."[2]

Two weeks later, a wagon train arrived at Larned to report that the Kiowas and Comanches had given it a good deal of trouble along the road. The wagon master said he had never known the Indians to be so impudent and insulting.

"They stripped his mule of his saddle," the base adjutant reported, "took all the blankets from his men, cut open sacks in his wagons, from which he could not keep them, and committed many other outrages."[3]

The situation erupted to the point of imminent danger at Fort Larned on July 9, 1863, when a sentinel shot and killed an Indian. The tribesman had used up his whiskey, and at one o'clock in the morning he headed to the sutler's store for more. He ignored the sentry's order to halt and made a fatal effort to run his horse over the guard. He was shot and killed.[4]

No one knew to which tribe of all those camped near the post the dead Indian belonged, and there was great fear that the Indians would attack the fort. Runners were sent out for scouts to return to the post, and chiefs of the tribes were called in for a council. The chiefs were instructed to keep their warriors away. The Kiowas, however, were very excited. They ignored the order and stormed into the post. Fortunately, the victim was eventually identified as Little Heart, a Cheyenne, whose tribe was not camped in the area.

Leavenworth was perturbed that Col. John M. Chivington, a former Methodist minister now commanding the military District of Colorado,

Col. John M. Chivington. Courtesy Colorado Historical Society.

would not permit his troops to assist in the protection of the road or even to help escort mail carriers from Fort Larned to Fort Lyon. Both Chivington and Colorado Territory governor John Evans had grown increasingly concerned over reported difficulties with the Cheyennes.

Evans dispatched Elbridge Gerry, namesake grandson of the signer of the Declaration of Independence, to set up a meeting for him with the Cheyennes. The Cheyennes, however, were suffering badly from a decimating siege of whooping cough and dysentery and failed to meet Evans when he came out to the Arikaree River. Further, the Cheyennes were unhappy with the Treaty of Fort Wise, calling it a swindle, and pointed to the killing of Little Heart as proof that the white man's hand dripped with blood.[5]

From Fort Lyon, Maj. Scott J. Anthony reported that three trains arriving there had been robbed of provisions by Kiowas and Comanches on the Larned-Lyon stretch of the road. In September he led his First Colorado troops to Larned where he visited camps of the Kiowas, Comanches, Plains Apaches, Caddos, and Arapahos. The Indians professed to be friendly but said that the Lakotas, who held their own grudges over white intrusion of their country, were trying to incite their warriors to attack white transportation on both the Arkansas and Platte roads.[6]

During the winter of 1863–1864, the Kiowas, Comanches, and Plains Apaches retreated south into western Indian Territory and made their camps well away from any interference from either the Union troops or the Texas rebel forces. There the tribesmen conducted their winter hunts, and their women prepared pelts and buffalo robes to trade for flour, sugar, coffee, dry goods, and trinkets with the American and Mexican traders who came into the country. Raiding into the scantly defended Texas frontier further produced horses and mules for the trade.

The Kiowas returned to the Arkansas River during the spring of 1864. Special agent H. T. Ketcham, sent out by the government to vaccinate the Indians, estimated that the various tribes would furnish 15,000 robes that season. Ketcham also proposed that all intoxicating liquor be banned from the country.

> Until it is done there can be no security for emigrants and freighters passing over the roads leading through the Indian country, and no permanent improvement in the condition of the Indian. Dissipation, licentiousness, and venereal diseases prevail in and around all the military posts that I have visited to an astonishing extent. Exclude spirituous liquor from the posts and from this country, and prohibit sutlers from trading directly or indirectly with the Indians, and there will be no inducement for them to bring in their women for prostitution.[7]

Ketcham spent two weeks during March and April among the Kiowas on the Arkansas River forty miles above Fort Larned. For four days he was a guest in Satanta's village, where he slept in the lodge of Yellow Buffalo. Ketcham was very impressed with Satanta.

> He is a fine-looking Indian, very energetic, and as sharp as a brier. He and all his people treated me with much friendship. I ate my meals regularly three times a day with him in his lodge. He puts on a good deal of style; spreads a carpet for his guests to sit on, and has painted fire-boards, twenty inches wide and three feet long, ornamented with bright brass tacks driven all around the edges, which they use for tables; he has a brass French horn, which he blew vigorously when the meals were ready.[8]

The congeniality of Ketcham's visit with the Kiowas, however, belied the friction that was erupting between the Indians and the rapidly increasing white population throughout Kansas and Colorado Territory. Evans and Chivington, insisting that the Indians were set to conduct a "war of extermination" against whites, had commenced an aggressive campaign against the Cheyennes in particular. Acting under Chivington's mandate to "kill Cheyennes whenever and wherever found,"[9] Lt. George S. Eayre led a unit of eighty-four Colorado troops with two mountain howitzers and fifteen wagons eastward from Denver, crossing district lines into Kansas.

There, on May 16 near the Smoky Hill River, he came onto a Cheyenne buffalo hunt under Chief Lean Bear. When Lean Bear and another tribesman named Star approached Eayre's advance unit to display Lean Bear's peace medal and a letter from President Lincoln testifying that he was friendly, the two men were shot from their saddles without warning.[10] The enraged Cheyennes attacked Eayre's scattered command and drove it from the field to Fort Larned.

The wanton killing of Lean Bear and Star unleashed the fury of the Cheyenne Dog Soldiers against frontier whites. It was Kansas, not Colorado, however, that took the brunt of their anger. On May 17 a man arrived at Larned to report Indian attacks on ranches between there and Fort Riley. A party of Cheyennes visited a Walnut Creek ranch, told the owner to leave immediately or he would be killed, and took away the man's Cheyenne wife. They said their chief had just been killed and they intended to kill all the whites they could find. A detail sent from Fort Larned to search for the mail found the arrow-ridden body of a man at Cow Creek and buried him.[11]

The Fort Larned commanding officer immediately called a council of the Kiowa, Arapaho, and Comanche chiefs who were camped around the post. The chiefs said they were all against going to war, even though the Kiowas and Arapahos sympathized with the Cheyennes. William Bent, passing on his way to Leavenworth, learned of Eayre's attack. After talking with Cheyenne chief Black Kettle, who wanted to know what the Eayre fight was about, Bent turned around and met Chivington at Fort Lyon. His attempts to advise the officer against inciting an Indian war went nowhere. Chivington said he himself was "on the warpath."[12] Bent was eventually persuaded to carry a proclamation issued by Governor Evans out to the tribes and explain it to them.

Evans's proclamation was designed to separate the hostile from the friendly Indians. It was an impossible notion. Addressed to all friendly Indians, the statement was nonetheless bellicose, threatening to hunt out those who had gone to war and punish them. Friendly Cheyennes and Arapahos were directed to go to Fort Lyon, where they would be given provisions and safety. Friendly Kiowas and Comanches would go to Fort Larned for the same. The proclamation concluded: "The object of this is to prevent friendly Indians from being killed through mistake. None but those who intend to be friendly with the whites must come to these places. The families of those who have gone to war with the whites must be kept from the friendly Indians. The war on hostile Indians will be continued until they are effectively subdued."[13]

At about this same time, Maj. T. I. McKenny was making an inspection tour of posts along the Arkansas River. He was at Fort Larned during mid-June and visited the Kiowas and Arapahos who were camped nearby. He reported:

> I have met La-how-san [Tohawson], a venerable Indian chief of the Kiowa tribes, who professes (and no doubt is in earnest) great friendship for the whites; he has about a dozen lodges, and they are principally old men, women, and children. He exercises great influence with his tribe, and it is thought will yet prevent many from joining the Cheyenne, as he is very eloquent and earnest in his appeals to them. He asked many questions as to where I came from and what was my business. I told him, through an interpreter, that the great general commanding in this country was much pleased with him, and that he was known far and wide as a great and good chief. The old man is mourning for a near relative, and has lately cut off one of his fingers, and burned his fine lodge, 19 fine robes, and a wagon, and killed 3 horses, besides destroying other favorite things.[14]

The Cheyenne disturbance, however, had excited the Kiowas' warring spirits, and Tohawson found he could not hold back his young men. Eayre's attack on the Cheyennes had primed the Kiowa war chiefs for action, and trouble soon erupted both at the Kansas forts and along the Santa Fe Trail. On the morning of July 17, a Sunday, portions of the Kiowa, Comanche, and Plains-Apache tribes came into Fort Larned and were issued provisions. All was peaceful, but that afternoon a fracas erupted that resulted in Satanta loosing an arrow that slightly grazed the arm of a Larned sentinel.[15]

This incident signaled a raid on a horse and mule herd grazing within a quarter mile of the post. Whooping warriors drove off 147 horses belonging to Lt. George S. Eayre and his Colorado Battery, who were recuperating at Larned. Along with the horses went 47 government mules, 60 horses and mules belonging to the post sutler and others, and several head of beef cattle. Simultaneously, a bridge over nearby Pawnee Fork was put to the torch.

Eayre was sent to attack the Kiowa village that was encamped three miles from the fort. Before he got halfway, however, five to six hundred Kiowa warriors appeared to block his path, and others took up positions in front of the village. Eayre returned to the post, and some sporadic firing took place during the rest of the day. On Monday the Larned garrison looked out to see several hundred warriors surrounding the fort.

There was no attack on Larned, but one did take place that same day on a wagon train just up the Santa Fe Trail three miles west of Fort Zarah. Two government trains, one of twenty-one wagons and another of nine, had joined at the Big Bend of the Arkansas before heading west for Fort Union, New Mexico. They had just departed from Fort Zarah, where 50 or 60 soldiers were stationed, when a large body of mounted Indians was seen approaching. Jerome Crow, wagon master of the larger train, estimated the number of warriors to be from 100 to 125. Crow later described the affair:

> Our trains then stretched out about half a mile. The Indians divided at the head of our trains and rode down on both sides of us. They stopped along our trains and commenced firing upon us with bows and arrows and guns. They killed ten men and wounded five in the two trains. They then commenced plundering, and took away all the wagon-sheets and other articles [including 10 pounds of tobacco, 56 pounds of coffee, 460 pounds of bacon, two of the wagons, and other sundry items] . . . and also destroyed one hundred and thirty-two sacks of Government flour by ripping open the sacks and throwing the flour on the ground, and carrying off the sacks. They also took away some of the flour.[16]

As James L. Riggs, the train's assistant wagon master, described the affair, it was not a bold attack. He was riding in advance of the trains when the Indians approached. They appeared friendly and shook hands

Ox train lumbers westward past the small picket outpost of Fort Zarah. Inman, *Old Santa Fe Trail*.

with the whites. Riggs gave tobacco to several of the tribesmen. They conversed for about five minutes before the Kiowas continued on in columns down both sides of the wagon train. When about midway down the half-mile-long train, the Indians suddenly began their attack. Two men who were scalped alive were taken to Fort Larned where they received medical care and eventually recovered.[17]

The attack was made in full view of troops at Fort Zarah. Capt. Oscar Dunlap later testified that he hurried to the scene with his company of Fifteenth Kansas Volunteer Cavalry, but the attackers had already fled. At the site, Dunlap found a dead horse he and his men had particularly admired the day before when the Indians had visited Fort Zarah. It had belonged, he said, to a Kiowa chief named Kicking Bird. A teamster claimed he had shot both Kicking Bird and the horse.[18]

A Larned officer wrote that the attack had been made by young boys, whose purpose was to draw the troops out while a larger force of warriors waited in the woods, ready to cut them off from their fort. He said the Arapahos were also involved in the attack.

On August 7 a Kiowa party led by Satanta fell on a Mexican train camped seven miles from Fort Lyon. One Mexican was killed, and the raiders carried off sugar, coffee, and other provisions.[19] The Kiowas then attacked a white homestead not far from Bent's Fort, killed a man, and set fire to the house. On that same day a Kiowa party appeared at Bent's place. Bent described the visit:

About 10 or 11 o'clock to-day four Kiowa Indians came in sight and finally came up. One of them was Satanta, or Sitting Bear, and one of them the Little Mountain, or Tohawson's son. They said that they were on a war party, and when they first left their camp that there was a very large party of them, and on the Cimarron they killed five whites, and the most of the party turned back from there. The Little Mountain's son says he was sent to me by his father to see if I could not make peace with the whites and them. . . . The Little Mountain's son appeared to be very anxious for peace, but it may all be a suck-in.[20]

Major Anthony reported from Larned that on August 19 Indians had attacked an American wagon train near Cimarron Springs, leaving behind ten badly mutilated corpses and running off all of the stock. Two days later a Mexican train was struck sixty miles west of Fort Larned at the Upper Crossing of the Cimarron. The raiders, 200 strong, were well armed and splendidly mounted. They killed a wagon master and carried off a great many head of stock. Two whites were murdered and scalped between Larned and Lyon, and numerous other depredations were reported. With the enlistment of many of his troops about to expire, Anthony saw little hope of providing adequate protection on the death-ridden trail.[21]

Brig. Gen. Samuel R. Curtis, commanding the Department of Kansas, attempted to obtain troops with which to fight the Indians by recruiting a unit of Kansas 100-day volunteers. He also placed Maj. Gen. James Blunt in command of the newly created District of the Upper Arkansas, which included Fort Lyon. In late September Blunt marched from Fort Larned at the head of a small army composed of Kansas 100-day volunteers and troops from Lyon under Major Anthony. Blunt's intention was to attack a warrior camp on the Pawnee Fork estimated to hold 1,500 fighting men. Anthony was sent ahead with two companies of First Colorado troops to attack the camp. The Indians saw Anthony coming, however, and attacked first. They surrounded the troops and had them pinned down when Blunt arrived. Blunt attacked and routed the Indians, killing at least nine of them.[22]

Although its victory was minor, Blunt's force drove the Kiowas south into the Territory. From there the warriors launched a massive raid against north Texas. The old animosities that existed between Texas and the tribes had not gone away; raiding in the former republic was still a prime activity of the Kiowa and Comanche war societies. With the Civil War having drawn away most militia manpower, the thinly scattered ranches and homesteads of north Texas were highly vulnerable to Indian raiding. On October 13, 1864, a 250-man Comanche and Kiowa war party made a massive assault on settlements along the Elm Creek tributary of the Brazos ten miles above Fort Belknap.[23]

Lt. N. Carson of the Texas Cavalry reported the attack on October 16, 1864. He said the Indians attacked the Elm Creek settlements on October 13. At the time, he and his company were camped thirteen miles west of Belknap. Leaving six men in camp, he and fourteen men rode in pursuit of the Indians. At Elm Creek he found what he estimated to be a party of 300 Indians, who had taken positions in a semicircle. Fifty yards from the Kiowas, Carson ordered his men into a line formation. Even as he did so, the Indians began firing and advancing on the troops. Carson described the action:

> I ordered my men to fall back. . . . The retreat was continued some one-quarter of a mile to McCoy's house, where two women were taken. . . . I gathered my men and horses that were at camp and crossed over to Fort Murray [Murrah], one mile and a half. The Indians followed in hot pursuit, came up to McCoy's house, destroyed and carried off everything that was in it, then advanced on the camp. . . . They took all the tents, blankets, and clothing that were left in camp, breaking up and destroying all the vessels belonging to the company. . . . As far as I have been able to gain information, there has been 11 citizens killed, 7 women and children carried off, eleven houses robbed. It is estimated that there were 350 or 400 on the raid. . . . Mr. Pealer [Franz Peveler], a citizen of Fort Murray [Murrah], got on the top of his house with his spy glass, counted 250 passing over the flats and by our camp, while another party passed north of the fort with a herd of horses.[24]

Among those victimized was the ranch home of forty-year-old Elizabeth Fitzpatrick, whose Union-supporting husband had been hanged for not supporting the Confederacy. The raiders killed two persons, looted and burned the house and other structures, and carried off Mrs. Fitzpatrick and six others. The war party also fell on a fortified ranch known as Bragg's Fort and homesteads along Elm Creek. Two men were killed, horses and stock were taken, and captives were carried off. One of the captives, eighteen-month-old Millie Durgan, would spend the remainder of her life among the Kiowas as the wife of a chief named Goombi.[25]

Even as the Kiowas were striking in Texas, a military effort to quell them and other prairie hostiles was being organized in New Mexico under one of the most famous men of the American West, Col. Christopher "Kit" Carson. Carson's 350 regular troops were supported by 72 friendly Utes and Apaches and a pair of twelve-pound mountain howitzers. Marching from Fort Bascom, New Mexico, on November 6, 1864, the expedition drove eastward along the north bank of the Canadian River onto the Llano Estacado.

On November 24 scouts discovered signs of a large Indian camp that

Lt. Col. (Bvt. Brig. Gen.) Kit Carson led his
New Mexico forces against the Kiowas at
Adobe Walls. Courtesy British Museum.

had been abandoned on Mule Creek. Carson ordered his cavalry ahead,
holding the infantry behind to guard the long baggage train. Carson's
advance surprised a large Indian village that proved to be Tohawson's
band of Kiowas. The frightened tribespeople abandoned their 150 lodges
and retreated along the Canadian beyond the remains of William Bent's
old Fort Adobe trading post. Now roofless and crumbling away, it had
become known as Adobe Walls.

The Kiowas found support in a large Comanche village of 350 lodges.
The combined warrior force, well mounted and stoutly armed, blunted
the cavalry charge with yelping countercharges of its own. Carson brought
up his artillery and drove the tribesmen out of firing range before falling
back himself to the protection of Adobe Walls.

"The principal number were Kiowas," Carson noted, "with a small
number of Comanches, Apaches, and Arapahoes, all of which were armed

with rifles, and I must say that they acted with more daring and bravery than I have ever before witnessed."[26]

The battle soon became stalemated. Carson contented himself with burning the Kiowa village, destroying lodges and provisions—dried meat, berries, buffalo robes, cooking utensils, gunpowder, and all the paraphernalia of a well-furnished Indian camp. Many whites believed Carson had been whipped by the Indians, and it is likely that the Kiowas and Comanches thought so as well.[27]

Kicking Bird, now around thirty years of age, was undoubtedly an active participant in the fight with Carson. Kicking Bird's cousin and close friend, thirty-three-year-old Stumbling Bear, also a noted Kiowa warrior, is known to have been a key figure in the battle.[28]

Two items of special interest found in the village were a buggy and a spring wagon. These were thought to belong to Tohawson, who was known among his people as "Wagon Old Man."[29] The wagon was presumed to be the one presented to him in 1859 by the quartermaster in Maj. John Sedgwick's command, which was then operating on the plains of Kansas and Colorado. Robert M. Peck, a trooper under Sedgwick, told the story:

> That summer [1859] we had been camping along the Arkansas river moving camp occasionally up or down the river, trying to keep Satank and his turbulent followers from beginning another outbreak. Old To'hau-sen frequently came to our camp. Lieutenant McIntyre wanted to get rid of this old ambulance, which he had long had on his hands, and which in some of its parts was nearly worn out. After inducing Major Sedgwick to have it condemned as unfit for service, Lieutenant McIntyre had his blacksmith fix it up a little and presented it to the old chief. McIntyre fitted a couple of sets of old harness to a pair of To'hau-sen's ponies and some of the soldiers break the animals to work in the ambulance. But when To'hau-sen tried to drive the team he could not learn to handle the lines. He took the reins off the harness and had a couple of Indian boys ride the horses, and they generally went at a gallop. The old chief seemed very proud of his ambulance.[30]

On the very day Kit Carson was engaging the Kiowas, Col. John M. Chivington was marching eastward along the Arkansas River to attack the Cheyennes at Sand Creek, Colorado. This action had been prefaced by a series of events. In response to a letter from William Bent, Cheyenne principal chief Black Kettle sent subchief One-Eye to Fort Lyon in August 1864 with a letter stating that the Cheyennes had conducted a council and were determined to make peace.[31]

Maj. Edward W. Wynkoop, then in command at Lyon, had been greatly impressed both with the Cheyenne peace initiative and with One-Eye's bravery in risking his life to deliver the letter. Wynkoop reacted by

Fort Lyon in 1864. Courtesy Denver Public Library Western Collection.

leading his Fort Lyon First Colorado troops far into the wilds of western Kansas to council with the Cheyennes. There he was able to persuade Black Kettle and six other Cheyenne and Arapaho chiefs to accompany him to Denver for talks with Governor Evans and Colonel Chivington.[32]

In the meeting at Denver's Camp Weld, Chivington repeated Evans's pledge that the Cheyennes and Arapahos should go to Lyon to be secure against attack by U.S. troops. Black Kettle and Arapaho chief Little Raven complied, taking their bands to Lyon even though most of the Cheyenne and Arapaho war elements remained cautiously away. Wynkoop, in the meantime, had been relieved of his Fort Lyon position by army officials who resented his peacemaking efforts. The new commanding officer, Major Anthony, concluded that he could not feed the Indians and advised them to camp on Sand Creek forty miles north of Lyon.

In Denver, Evans and Chivington had recruited their own regiment of 100-day volunteers as the Colorado Third Volunteer Cavalry. Seeing little action, it had jokingly come to be called the "Bloodless Third" around Denver. In November, with the recruitment period for the volunteers approaching its end and a hot political race under way, Chivington decided to conduct a strike against the Indians. His target was Black Kettle's band at Sand Creek.

Chivington led the Colorado Third south along the mountains through falling snow to the hamlet of Pueblo on the Arkansas. From there he turned along the river eastward to Fort Lyon to pick up the First Colorado units. Most Fort Lyon officers had served under Wynkoop and protested Chivington's proposed plans to attack the camp. They had been members of the peacemaking expedition to western Kansas and fully supported the actions of their former commander. Anthony, however, willingly joined his Colorado First troops with those of the Colorado Third for an overnight march almost due north to Sand Creek.

The consolidated force of around 700 mounted troops, supported by four twelve-pound howitzers, arrived at Sand Creek at daybreak on November 29, 1864. They found the sleeping Cheyenne village of 100 lodges clustered unsuspectingly on the flat north bank of the stream where it was turned easterly by a range of sand hills.

Chivington attacked immediately, one cavalry unit sweeping across the frozen creek to cut off the Cheyenne horse herd. Other troops were ordered to dismount and commence firing at the fleeing forms in the now panic-stricken camp. They were joined by the artillery, which lobbed shells into the camp. As Cheyenne women and children fled in terror, Chief Black Kettle raised an American flag to indicate that the camp was peaceful. Chief White Antelope walked forward into Sand Creek with his hands raised, only to be shot dead.[33]

Chivington now sent his cavalry charging through the camp and in pursuit of fleeing Indians. The chase and shooting continued through most of the morning and into the afternoon before the troops returned to loot the camp and take souvenir scalps. When it was finally over, seventy bodies lay dead on the massacre site. Black Kettle had somehow escaped, but several leading peace chiefs were victims.

Chivington's attack on the Cheyenne village at Sand Creek was a significant moment of history to the Indians of the Central Plains, the final proof to many tribespeople that the white man could not be trusted. Importantly, the tribal leadership of peace-minded chiefs such as Black Kettle and Tohawson was severely undermined.

The massacre had also aroused great controversy among white Americans, enhancing opposition to militarism and exerting a strong effect on U.S.-Indian relations and the fate of the Kiowas. A great debate arose among government officials and the public alike as to how best to deal with the prairie tribes—by force or by persuasion.

8
Contest of Chiefs

In the aftermath of Sand Creek, Jesse Leavenworth was appointed agent for the Kiowas, Prairie Apaches, and Comanches. Despite his military background and affiliation, Leavenworth was known derisively to most Kansans of the day as an "olive brancher." He was convinced that the difficulties with the prairie tribes could be worked out through peace treaties. To most whites on the frontier, that meant pacifying the very ones who committed depredations against them almost daily. It broached the long-standing and passionate argument in America between those who would eradicate the Indian and those who would show him Christian understanding and kindness.

To aid him in contacting and dealing with the Indians, Leavenworth wisely sought the services of Jesse Chisholm, the Cherokee frontiersman and trader who had a long history of association with the prairie tribes, including the Comanches and thus contact with the Kiowas. Chisholm had been a guide and interpreter with the Leavenworth-Dodge expedition in 1834 and had much experience with the tribes in western Indian Territory and Texas. When the Civil War erupted he was conducting his Indian trade from the site of present west Oklahoma City. In 1863 he moved to the mouth of the Little Arkansas, where Wichita, Kansas, now stands. The Wichita Indians and other destitute refugees from the Leased District had settled there following the Wichita agency attack in 1862.[1]

Chisholm was highly knowledgeable of the Plains tribes and was much respected by them. He had long played a major role in arbitrating

Jesse Leavenworth, a controversial figure as agent for the Plains tribes. Courtesy Archives and Manuscript Division, Oklahoma Historical Society.

matters with them for both the United States and the Cherokees, as well as the Republic of Texas. Early in 1864 he served as an interpreter and adviser to the Comanches and Kiowas in a council with a Union officer who had offered the Comanches and Kiowas a large amount of arms and goods if they would make war on the Confederate-allied tribes. Chisholm warned the Indians against accepting the offer, and the Comanche chiefs agreed with him.[2]

As the Civil War neared an end during the spring of 1865, the factions of the woodland tribes who had gone with the Confederacy began to realize the precariousness of their situation. The reeling South offered them no law and order, no protection, and very little subsistence. Not only did blatant outlawry rule in the Territory, but the tribes still feared the unruly prairie bands to their west. Texas, too, was greatly concerned about its northern frontier, which was ravaged regularly by Indian Territory raiders. Federal withholding of military protection for Texas following the war left the former Rebel state virtually unprotected from Indian attack.

To ease these situations, Southern officials led by Gen. James W. Throckmorton arranged a grand medicine lodge to be held at a site called Camp Napoleon near present Verden, Oklahoma. He and other commissioners met there on May 26, 1865, with chiefs of the Rebel-siding tribes of eastern Indian Territory and the prairie tribes in an effort to reestablish peace and friendship through a formal pact. Delegates from the Cherokees, Creeks, Choctaws, Chickasaws, Seminoles, Caddos, Osages, Arapahos, Cheyennes, Prairie Apaches, major bands of the Comanches, and Kiowas were present. They smoked the calumet, orated, and signed a formal agreement vowing that "The path of peace shall be opened from one Tribe or Band to another and kept open, and traveled in friendship." The Kiowa delegates were identified as chiefs Tatobeeher, Tahebecut, and Quinetohope, who are otherwise unknown to record.[3]

When the Rebel commissioners sought a promise that the Plains tribes would never cross the Red River into Texas again, the notion was unanimously rejected. The Plains tribes insisted that they should be able to follow the buffalo herds into Texas as always—not to mention for other reasons. In talks with the Kiowas and Comanches, however, Throckmorton succeeded in securing the release of some Texans captured in the Elm Creek raid.[4]

Tohawson, now very old, had remained on the Arkansas with Leavenworth. He told the agent the Kiowas had learned that the Osages were coming south and feared a trap. He was further alarmed when a half-blood from New Mexico informed him that as soon as the grass was up, troops were going to attack. The Kiowas sent spies to keep an eye on the military posts along the Santa Fe road.[5]

Chisholm reported to Leavenworth that a Mexican officer at the Camp Napoleon meeting had revealed that the warring whites had all made peace. The Kiowas and Apaches quickly decided against making any further war to the north. A band of Indians had recently killed four Mexicans on the Arkansas, however, and had stolen their stock. George Ransom, Chisholm's black helper, believed the perpetrators were Kicking Bird and his band.[6]

During that summer, Leavenworth again sent Chisholm into the Indian Territory to talk with the prairie tribes in an effort to form a treaty-making council. The frontiersman met with a band of eighty-one Kiowas and a few Arapahos and Apaches on the Chikaskia River in July. Tohawson, Satanta, and Kicking Bird represented the Kiowas. The chiefs said they were willing to make and keep peace if the soldiers would cease fighting them. They wanted Washington and all of the troops notified, however, so they would not be deceived like the Cheyennes had been at Sand Creek.[7]

In early August Maj. Gen. John B. Sanborn arrived at Fort Larned with a large military force. From there he sent word to the tribes of the region proposing an October 1 peace council.[8] In response, a large party of Kiowas and Apaches, headed by Tohawson and Poor Bear, respectively, went into camp at the mouth of the Little Arkansas. A delegation of Comanches under Ten Bears arrived soon after. Cheyenne chief Black Kettle, escorted by George Bent, half-blood son of William Bent, brought his eighty lodges from the Territory despite dire threats from the hostile Cheyenne Dog Soldiers.

In a preliminary meeting on August 15, chiefs Tohawson, Lone Wolf, Heap of Bears, Satanta, Kicking Bird, and Bear-Run-Over-a-Man (Stumbling Bear) met with Leavenworth and Sanborn. The chiefs promised to cease all raiding against settlements and Santa Fe Trail travelers. They also agreed in writing to meet again on October 4 to the south on Bluff Creek, although this site was later changed back to the Little Arkansas. The Comanches, Prairie Apaches, Cheyennes, and Arapahos made similar commitments.[9]

As planned, the U.S. peace commission arrived and met with the prairie chiefs at the mouth of the Little Arkansas on October 4. The seven commissioners were Sanborn, Brig. Gen. William S. Harney, Col. Kit Carson, William Bent, Jesse Leavenworth, Superintendent of Indian Affairs Thomas Murphy, and Judge James Steele. Discussions were held first, and a treaty was signed with the Cheyennes and Arapahos and then with the Prairie Apaches. Finally, on October 16, the commission met with the Kiowa and Comanche chiefs in council. Representing the Kiowas were Tohawson, Satank, Black Eagle, Lone Wolf, Kicking Bird, and Fishemore (or, inelegantly, Stinking Saddle Cloth). Satanta would be present at a later meeting.[10]

Sanborn outlined the government's wants: to halt attacks on U.S. citizens, to locate the Kiowas and Comanches on a reserve in western Indian Territory and west Texas, and to recover white captives held by the tribes. Tohawson was the first to respond. Like a good bargainer he demanded more than he expected to get.

> The Kiowas own from Fort Laramie and the north fork of the Platte to Texas, and have always owned it. That is all the branches, creeks, rivers and ponds that you see; all the deer and buffalo, wolves and turtles, all belong to him—were given to him by the Great Spirit. White men did not give it to him . . . the Great Father is always promising to do some-

thing for him, but never does anything. . . . I want to tell you again and again to throw away the soldiers, and I will get all badness out of my heart, so that we can all travel kindly together.[11]

Tohawson openly admitted that the Kiowas were holding white captives. He agreed to their return. Eagle Drinking of the Comanches pointed out that the Texans likewise held several Comanche children.

"The prisoners were taken at Van Dorn's fight at the Wichita mountains," he noted, "and are now being educated and don't wish to come back to the tribe, but the tribe wish to visit them."[12]

"Last winter, when they made treaty in Texas," Comanche chief Silver Brooch added, "I gave up five prisoners. . . . The Texans had some children of mine [as] prisoners and promised to give them up, but I have not got them yet."[13]

Kicking Bird, Satank, and a small party of Kiowas took out a wagon and after a time brought in five white captives: Mrs. Caroline McDaniel, twenty-six, of Fredericksburg, Texas; her one-year-old daughter, Rebecca Jane; her niece, three-year-old Dorcas Taylor; nephew James Taylor, age seven; and James Burrow, age seven, of Georgetown, Texas. Other Kiowa captives were in distant camps, held by a band that did not wish to make peace. It was hoped they would be turned over to Leavenworth later.[14]

Whites were not the only captives being held by the two tribes. A Texas man of African descent, possibly the well-known frontiersman Britt Johnson, appeared in the treaty camp to report that he had recently ransomed his wife and two children from the Comanches with seven ponies. Mrs. Fitzpatrick, who had been taken in the 1864 Elm Creek raid in Texas, and her four-year-old granddaughter were supposed to have been given up also, but the Indians refused.[15]

In late October Leavenworth and Chisholm rode south to the Kiowa and Comanche camps near Fort Arbuckle—an eleven-day trip. There Chisholm was able to rescue three more captives: Mrs. Elizabeth Sprague, Alice Almeda Taylor, and nine- or ten-year-old James Benson. Still with the Kiowas were Milla Jane Sprague, Mahala Louise Elizabeth McDaniels, and one boy whose name was unknown. The two mothers, Sprague and McDaniels, refused to believe their children were dead and vowed they would not return home until a search had been made.[16]

The Cheyennes and Arapahos had already signed their treaty and departed. Water was beginning to freeze at night in the treaty camp. The season was getting late, and the Comanches and Kiowas were anxious to return to their home camps. Sanborn accepted the five captives as evidence of the good intentions of the two tribes, and on October 24 the treaties were concluded and presents distributed.

The most notable aspect of this treaty with the Comanches and Kiowas was their assignment to a reservation that included a large portion of western Texas. Later, the State of Texas would object strenuously to this clause and eventually cause it to be nullified. The two tribes would thereby lose a vast area of what had once been their hunting grounds and would be confined instead to the southwestern corner of Indian Territory.

Signing the original treaty (in order, as given by the treaty document) were Queil-park, or Lone Wolf; Wah-toh-konk, or Black Eagle; Zip-ki-yah, or Big Bow; Sa-tan-ta, or White Bear; Ton-a-en-ko, or Kicking Eagle; Settem-ka-yah, or Bear-Run-Over-a-Man; Kaw-pe-ah, or Plumed Lance; To-hau-son, or Little Mountain; Sa-tank, or Sitting Bear; Pawnee, or Poor Man; and Ta-ki-bull, or Stinking Saddle Cloth.[17]

The latter was listed as chief of the Kiowa tribe. It would appear that he was at last temporarily replacing Tohawson who may have stepped aside because of impairment from advanced age. On May 1, 1866, Leavenworth reported to Colley from the Salt Fork of the Arkansas that both Tohawson of the Kiowas and Ha-yo-ko-nah (Over the Buttes) of the Comanches had died a short time earlier.[18]

The distribution of annuities was an issue of vital importance to the Kiowas and Comanches, and it would prove to be one of the main causes of failure of the treaty. Some Kiowa bands received annuity goods, and some did not. Both Kicking Bird and Satanta were among those incensed over the matter. Kicking Bird claimed he had sent word to Leavenworth at Fort Zarah during the winter of 1865–1866 that his stock was too poor for his people to come up from the Territory and claim their goods. He asked the agent to hold his share, and he would get them in the spring. But, he said, Leavenworth would not listen and either gave all the annu-ities to bands then present or sold them to other Indians.[19] In doing so, Kicking Bird said, Leavenworth punished the innocent along with those who had evil in their hearts.[20]

This dissatisfaction was intensified by other problems. Illicit whis-key dealing by whites among the tribes continued to be a severe influ-ence on the young warriors, often stimulating them to take up the war trail. This was abetted by the selling of arms to the Indians by Mexican traders on the Red River. It was said that for a revolver a tribesman would give ten or even twenty times its real value in horses and furs.[21] Settlers in north Texas suffered the most during the summer of 1866 as a result of this trade in whiskey and weapons.

In August of that year a Kiowa war party splashed across the Red River into Montague County, Texas, looking for prey. The Kiowas chanced upon the wagon of the James Box family. The settler and his wife and five

Fort Dodge, Kansas, once a center of action for the Kiowas. *Harper's Weekly,* May 25, 1867.

daughters were nearing their homestead on a five-day return journey after visiting his two brothers in Hopkins County.

Upon seeing the Indians, Box yelled to his oldest daughter to get his six-shooter for him. Almost at the same time, Box was hit in the chest by an arrow. He jerked out the arrow and tried to fight back. He took another arrow in the head and pulled it loose, but he was soon overwhelmed, killed, and scalped. Mrs. Box and her girls were yanked from the wagon, tied on horses, and carried off into captivity.[22]

This was one of the tragic incidents of the frontier. In September the commanding officer at Fort Dodge, Capt. Andrew Sheridan, learned that a Kiowa village camped nearby was holding four white women who had been captured in Texas. Sheridan dispatched Lt. G. A. Hesselberger with two soldiers and an interpreter to the village. They arrived at a very large encampment. A general alarm went up as they entered the village, and they were instantly surrounded by a swarm of armed tribesmen.

The four men were taken to a lodge and kept there for about two hours before being escorted to the lodge of Satanta. The chief admitted that two of the Box girls were in his camp. Mrs. Box, he said, was about 40 miles away and another child about 130 miles away. Satanta claimed ownership of the older girl, seventeen-year-old Margaret Box, and Stumbling Bear claimed thirteen-year-old Maizie Josephine. The Kiowa chief told Hesselberger that the only way he could get the girls was to buy

General Hancock and his staff interviewed Kicking Bird and Satanta at Fort Dodge. *Harper's Weekly*, May 25, 1867.

them. The officer suggested that Satanta go with him to Fort Dodge, where ransom could be arranged.

The chief agreed to do so, and with a number of his warriors he accompanied Hesselberger back to the post. There Sheridan put together a large amount of sundry articles, estimated at $1,026 in value, and loaded them into wagons. Hesselberger and eleven men escorted the Kiowas back to their camp, where the two girls were turned over. Eventually, Mrs. Box and another daughter would be rescued. Baby Laura, it was learned, had either died or been killed during the eleven-day horseback ride from Texas.[23]

Just who led the raid has never been determined. Satanta later charged that Kicking Bird was the leader. In an interview at Fort Zarah, however, Mrs. Box stated that the twenty-three-man war party was led by Satanta.[24] Satanta did not deny his own involvement when Leavenworth said he should get no rations because of it. Instead Satanta asked indignantly, "Stumbling Bear was in that raid, and why should he get so many goods?" No evidence has surfaced that Kicking Bird was ever known to hold captives. It is questionable whether either Satanta or Kicking Bird would have taken part in a war party led by the other. Maj. Gen. Winfield S.

Hancock, however, claimed Kicking Bird was identified by the eldest Box girl as one of the chiefs who killed her father.[25]

"We thought the Great Father would not be offended," Satanta observed, "for the Texans had gone out from among his people and become his enemies. You now tell us they have made peace and returned to the family."[26]

In the wake of Tohawson's death, an intense rivalry had begun to develop among several band chiefs for the principal Kiowa leadership. Satank was old, and, as Satanta expressed it, the Kiowas had thrown him away as a chief. Lone Wolf had not been able to secure the following needed to become head man. The contest for the top position had narrowed to the shrewd Satanta; war leader Lone Wolf; and the younger, equally capable Kicking Bird. Satanta and Kicking Bird were effective spokesmen as well as noted warriors, and both were heads of sizable bands. DeB. Randolph Keim, in reference to his 1868–1869 association with the Kiowas, wrote:

> Satanta, when I met him, was a man of about fifty years of age. He rose first through prowess on the war-path, and afterwards through skill in council and diplomacy. He had an intelligent face, and was large in frame, and of muscular development, exhibiting a tendency to obesity. Lately Satanta had found a threatening rival in Lone Wolf, the war-chief of the tribe.[27]

Kicking Bird had begun to catch the notice of white military officers when he met Gen. William T. Sherman at Fort Dodge in the fall of 1866. Despite Hancock's charge against the chief, Sherman wrote: "I know Kicking Bird very well; he is intelligent, and I consider full faith can be given to his statements."[28] At Fort Dodge, commanding officer Henry Douglas stated his opinion that Kicking Bird was the most reliable of all the Indians.[29]

George Bent indicated that the Kiowas, along with the Prairie Apaches, Cheyennes, and Arapahos, were in winter camps on Bluff Creek in southern Kansas during the winter of 1866–1867. At that time he had lodged with Kicking Bird and frontiersman Charles Rath with Satanta while they conducted trade with the tribes.[30]

During a visit to Fort Dodge, Kicking Bird complained bitterly to the commanding officer about the annuity situation. He said all the bad feelings in his tribe were caused by the injustice of their agent and that it required all his influence to prevent his men from going on the warpath. The Lakotas and Cheyennes, Kicking Bird insisted, had asked his permission to move south of the Arkansas River. Although his warriors wanted this, he had rejected the request for fear it would ignite trouble.

Still, he expected that when the grass came up in the spring, there would be war.[31]

He was correct. Even as the Lakotas and Cheyenne Dog Soldiers were attacking transportation and railroad-building crews in Kansas, the Kiowas struck in Texas. In early February 1867 Douglas reported from Fort Dodge that a Kiowa war party had recently returned from Texas with the scalps of seventeen black soldiers and one white man. They had also brought in 200 head of stolen horses. Other war parties were still out.[32]

Charges continued to sound against Leavenworth, already intensely disliked by the frontier military and the Kansas citizenry for his pacification of the tribes. Comanche interpreter Philip McCusker accused Leavenworth of paying large prices for captives, thus encouraging the Indians to hold out for higher prices. McCusker also charged that the agent was making away with a large portion of their goods. The Indians agreed strongly with McCusker and did not like Leavenworth.[33]

Sketch of Kicking Bird at Fort Dodge, spring 1867. *Harper's Weekly*, May 25, 1867.

Satanta appeared at Dodge on February 23 with a small entourage to complain against whites who had opened a new wagon route along the Smoky Hill River. Also, they were building a railroad, the Kansas Pacific, across the Indians' buffalo range in western Kansas. The white men were cutting wood and running off the buffalo, and their stock was grazing off the grass. Satanta, who claimed he was the great chief of the Kiowas and the most friendly of all, insisted that it had to stop.[34]

Satanta returned on March 23, this time accompanied by Satank. In a council with Douglas, he said that because the white men evidently thought he lied, he would let Satank do the talking.

"I have some good news to tell," Satank said, "and some bad news with it."[35]

He and his braves were willing to accept the road running through their country, he said, even though the white people were building homes and killing the Kiowas' buffalo and deer. The Cheyennes, Lakotas, and other northern tribes, however, were preparing to go to war. The Kiowas, he promised, would remain the white man's friend. Douglas was skeptical, saying the chiefs talked half peace and half war.

While Satanta and Satank took their bands off north to hunt, Kicking Bird visited Forts Zarah and Larned and then headed south to Bluff Creek. At Zarah he defended the Kiowas against charges they had been running off stock in Kansas, saying it was the Cheyennes who had been doing so.[36]

In visiting the Kansas posts, Kicking Bird may have been sizing up the military situation. Word was circulating among the Indian camps that forces under Gen. Winfield S. Hancock at Fort Riley, Kansas, were planning a big push against the tribes. Hancock's army, whose Seventh U.S. Cavalry was led by Lt. Col. George Armstrong Custer, arrived at Fort Larned in early April. Marching up the Pawnee Fork, Hancock threatened a large Cheyenne-Lakota encampment. After a near clash that featured a classic standoff between U.S. cavalry and a whooping line of bonneted and well-armed tribesmen, the Indians withdrew, abandoning their camp during the night and fleeing with their women and children. While Custer led his regiment after them on a futile chase, Hancock vacillated and then finally burned the deserted village.

Shortly thereafter, on April 23, 1867, Kicking Bird, Stumbling Bear, and a few others met Hancock at a camp near Fort Dodge for talks. During the meeting Hancock warned that the Kiowas should remain south of the Arkansas and avoid any involvement with the warring Cheyenne Dog Soldiers and Lakotas. He also asked for young Kiowa warriors to serve as scouts for him.[37]

The Man That Moves, Tohawson's half brother, spoke first. He advised the other Kiowas to heed Hancock's talk. Kicking Bird then took the floor, saying:

> Our great chief Te-haw-son, is dead. He was a great chief for the whites and the Indians. Whatever Te-haw-son said they kept in their hearts. Whatever Te-haw-son told them in council they remembered, and [when] they would go to the road he told them; that is, to be friendly to the whites. Te-haw-son always advised the nation to take the white man by the hand, and clear above the elbow. Kicking Bird advises the same.[38]

Leavenworth echoed this assessment of the deceased Kiowa chief in writing to the commissioner of Indian Affairs on May 1: "He died as he had lived, the friend to the white man . . . better men, white or red, are seldom found."[39]

It was apparent that Kicking Bird, then still in his early thirties, was already taking up the mantle of Tohawson as a peace leader of the Kiowas. To Hancock he stated the course he would choose for his people, declaring that the Kiowas, Comanches, and Prairie Apaches were all against war. They wanted their women and children to be able to sleep without fear and their men to hunt buffalo without fear of attack. The warring Lakotas and Northern Cheyennes (undoubtedly meaning the Dog Soldiers in Kansas as contrasted to the peace-minded band under Black Kettle), he said, were not welcome south of the Arkansas.

On the matter of his young men serving as scouts for Hancock, Kicking Bird revealed his diplomatic skills. That would be a subject for discussion in the spring, he said, when the government annuities were sent out. "We cannot give an answer until we consult our chiefs, Satanta, or White Bear, Heap of Bears, Lone Wolf, Black Bird, Sitting Bear, and Little Heart. We want to know what we are to do with the Cheyennes who have gone south [meaning Black Kettle's peace faction]."[40]

Hancock advised him to stay away from the Cheyennes until their situation was resolved. He then warned the Kiowas not to resist the whites, who were invincible, but to settle down and learn agriculture.

Kicking Bird took no umbrage at the officer's hard talk. "That is what Dohasan [Tohawson], our great Chief now dead, told us," he said agreeably.

The competition between Kicking Bird and Satanta for the head chief's position became even more apparent when the latter talked with Hancock on Big Coon Creek a few days later. Satanta's jealousy of Kicking Bird was evident. He told Hancock:

> Other chiefs of the Kiowas who rank below me have come in to look for rations and to look about, and their remarks are reported to Washing-

ton, but I don't think their hearts are good. . . . The Cheyennes, the
Arapahos, the Comanches, Kiowas, Apaches, and some Sioux all sent
to see me, for they know me to be the best man . . there are five different
bands of Kiowas—those of Lone Wolf, Heap of Bears, Timber Mountain, and Stumbling Bear, and they profess to be chiefs, although they
have but two or three lodges each.[41]

The omission of Kicking Bird's band as one of the five was obvious
even as Satanta made the other chiefs appear insignificant by denigrating
the number of their following. At the end of the council Satanta insisted
that Hancock give him a letter he could take back to his camp to show
that he had talked with the general. He also worked to impress Hancock
with his importance in the tribe, at the same time revealing something of
his intratribal relationships.

> You are a very big chief; but when I am away over to the Kiowas, then I
> am a big chief myself. Whenever a trader come[s] to my camp I treat him
> well, and do not do anything out of the way to him. When the Indians
> get a little liquor they get drunk, and fight sometimes, and sometimes
> they whip me, but when they get sober, they are all right, and I don't
> think anything about it.[42]

Leavenworth was present at the meeting along with William Bent;
correspondent Henry M. Stanley, later of Africa fame; and a host of
ranked officers. An observer felt the agent, his back badly bent and
beard silvered with age, was virtually a paralytic. Satanta challenged
the beleaguered Leavenworth to the point of embarrassment with pen-
etrating questions over his issuance of annuities. He implied strongly
that the agent had traded Indian goods for buffalo robes, furs, and
lariats. Finally, Hancock rescued the agent by cutting off Satanta's
interrogation.

Leavenworth defended himself by saying that he had orders from
Washington not to issue annuity goods until the Kiowas' captives were
returned without ransom and assurances had been offered that no further depredations would be committed.

During his long speech to Hancock, Satanta also made his personal
wishes known.

> I am a poor man, but I am not going to get angry and talk about it. I
> simply want to tell this to those officers here present. Such articles as the
> white man may throw away, we will pick up and brush off and use, and
> make out the best we can, and if you throw away any provisions we will
> use them also, and thus do the best we can. I see a great many officers
> around here with fine clothing, but I do not come here to beg, but I
> admire fine clothing.[43]

Satanta had made his point. At the end of the council, he was presented with a major-general's coat and yellow sash. To this impressive attire he would add his bugle to dangle at his side. There could be no doubt that Satanta had cleverly outmaneuvered Kicking Bird.

Satanta's reputation was further enhanced during the summer of 1867 by reports that he had led a large Kiowa raiding party that captured virtually all of the horse herd belonging to the cavalry unit grazing a mile east of Fort Dodge.[44] Although he was by no means shy about accepting the honor for such a signal event, Satanta denied that he had been involved in the theft. Evidence would eventually surface that the raid had been conducted by the Cheyennes and Arapahos.[45]

In the eyes of both the whites and other Indians, Satanta was now the dominant Kiowa figure to be reckoned with. There was another strong point in his favor. U.S. officials invariably played up to the most warlike and aggressive tribal leaders. There was much less need to pander the peacemakers.

9
Changing Homeland

The Treaty of the Little Arkansas in July 1865 did little to solve the problems of the Central Plains or to change the developing conflict relationship between the prairie tribes and the United States. It did have the effect, however, of opening the Indian country much more to white traders, first in southern Kansas and then in western Indian Territory. Following the treaty, wagons began arriving at the Little Arkansas loaded with goods to trade for Indian horses and buffalo hides.

Some traders made permanent residences along the Arkansas. One was Charlie Rath, who settled near Fort Zarah and conducted trade with the Indians in breech-loading carbines, revolvers, powder, lead, and percussion caps. At Fort Dodge, Major Douglas complained that the Indians would give ten or twenty times the value of a pistol in horses and furs. He said Rath had "armed several bands of Kiowas with Revolvers, and has completely overstocked them with Powder."[1]

Traders had also begun moving south of the Kansas border into the wilds of western Indian Territory. Prior to 1865 the presence of the white man there had been limited to a few advance traders such as Chisholm to the Wichita agency and to small garrisons at Forts Arbuckle and Cobb. The Wichita agency was no longer maintained by the Confederacy following the massacre of 1862, although Texas troops remained stationed at Fort Arbuckle. The trading post of William Shirley, established near the agency in 1859, was about the only white presence in the region during the war. The end of the war and the ensuing Little Arkansas treaty opened the door to renewed territorial intrusion by whites, both in the reactivation of two forts and in the eventual reestablishment of the Wichita agency.

The end of the war also brought into the Territory a bevy of Kansas traders, many connected with trading firms. James Mead, founder of Towanda, Kansas; William "Dutch Bill" Greiffenstein, soon to be a prime mover in the development of Wichita, Kansas; Charles W. Whitaker, a veteran frontiersman who for a time would operate a trading post on the Canadian River near present Oklahoma City; A. F. Greenway, brother to the agent for the Osages; and others were taking their wagons loaded with trade goods south to the Indian camps and doing a lucrative trade. Greenway claimed that while trading with the Kiowas and Comanches on the North Canadian, he heard Kicking Bird boast of stealing a horse and a mule of his on Big Turkey Creek in the Indian Territory during the summer of 1864.[2]

In November 1866 the *Emporia* (Kansas) *News*[3] reported that a train of heavily loaded wagons from the Canadian River had just delivered a load of furs to Leavenworth. Whitaker, who was licensed as a trader among the Kiowas and Comanches, arrived at Leavenworth City from the Territory with 1,600 robes and a large amount of other peltry in May 1867. He was back again that fall with another load. As Kicking Bird would later indicate, this trade was very valuable in keeping his people supplied with goods they sorely needed.[4]

Several of the traders were connected with the Leavenworth firm of E. W. Durfee, which had sole trading rights to the Territory's Leased District. A letter that appeared in the *Weekly Free Press* of Atkinson, Kansas, on March 16, 1867, stated that three hunters engaged in strychnining wolves on the Cimarron River had been attacked by a band of twenty Kiowas who stampeded their horses. It was claimed also that an unnamed Kiowa chief had recently visited Fort Dodge and threatened to "scalp the garrison" if the commanding officer did not evacuate the fort.[5]

On July 20, 1867, Cheyenne chief Black Kettle, along with George and Charlie Bent and a party of Cheyenne men and women, arrived at the mouth of the Little Arkansas to ask Leavenworth's advice on finding safety.[6] Black Kettle feared that with the Cheyenne Dog Soldiers warring in Kansas, he might again be mistakenly attacked by troops. Leavenworth advised the chief to go to his agent at Fort Larned, but Black Kettle shook his head. He said he feared to go there because some of his band were bad at heart; twenty-eight of them had gone on the warpath after Hancock burned the village at Pawnee Fork. Leavenworth then suggested that Black

Kettle go to the Leased District near old Fort Cobb and take with him the part of his band that wanted peace.[7]

The chief agreed to do so, but he and George Bent went only as far as Black Kettle's camp at the forks of the Beaver and Wolf Creeks in northwest Indian Territory. Likely, the Cheyenne principal chief wished to remain close to the site of a proposed new treaty council to be held at Medicine Lodge Creek in southern Kansas.

The government had been slow to arrange for the return of the western Indian Territory exiles to their homes following the war. Again it was a case of giving far more attention to the warring tribes than to the smaller, less aggressive Indians of the Leased District. During the war and for two years after, the severely impoverished and decimated bands of loyal Wichitas, Wacos, Tawakonis, Delawares, Ionies, Caddos, Absentee Shawnees, and Kichais had suffered severely from starvation and disease in the camps at the mouth of the Little Arkansas.

Finally, the government made arrangements for their removal back to their former homes in the Leased District. As plans were under way in July 1867, the tribes were struck by even more misfortune, as Indian agent Henry Shanklin reported:

A few days before the time of departure the cholera broke out with fearful violence among the Wichitas—eighteen deaths in five days. The Wacoes, Keechies, and Towacaires, although living in close proximity, were not affected for some days after this terrible disease made its appearance. The Absentee Shawnees, Caddoes and Delawares, living on Dry Creek, some ten miles distant, were in good health. A physician was sent for and directed to render all the aid he could to the afflicted. He reported the disease to be *cholera morbus,* caused by their eating green plums and melons, recommending their breaking up camps and moving immediately as the most effective means to restore them to health. The day following the Towacaires were sick, and it became apparent that a panic had spread among the bands afflicted—refusing to be moved at this time, giving as their reason, at this late hour, that the Great Spirit had given them strength to plant some corn in the spring, and if they neglected to gather it, would not give them strength to plant in the future. . . . The Absentee Shawnees, Caddoes, and Delawares had broke[n] camp, and made every preparation for removal.[8]

Also, during July 1867 Leavenworth dispatched Buffalo Bill Mathewson to go to the Territory and receive a herd of Texas cattle that had been purchased to feed the Kiowas and Comanches.[9] Mathewson met the herd at Chouteau Creek near present Purcell, Oklahoma. After sending 25 head on to be issued to the Comanches in the spring, Leavenworth arranged for the remaining 400 cows to be pastured along the Chouteau through the winter. On his return trip to Kansas Mathewson made a gruesome discovery. At Skeleton Creek near present Enid, Oklahoma, he witnessed the carcasses of Indian people lying "like rotten sheep" along the banks.[10]

These were the remains of fifty Shawnees and forty-seven Caddos who had perished on their journey to the Leased District. They had hoped to escape the dreaded cholera that had invaded the Little Arkansas settlements, but the disease struck them with dreadful fury on the trail. The living had no choice but to push on and leave their dead and dying behind.[11]

The trailing group of Wichitas, Wacos, Tawakonis, and Kichais suffered a different calamity. While camped on the Ninnescah River, they were hit by a prairie fire. Fanned by a strong northerly wind, the blaze destroyed 131 head of invaluable saddle horses, mares, and colts. Interpreter Philip McCusker, who traveled with the Indians for a time, observed:

> This is the worst thing that could have befallen these people as they depended entirely upon their horses for supplies of meat and buffalo robes. The government ration always was too small, and last winter with the aid of what buffalo they killed they would go two or three days every week with nothing to eat . . . really it was a pitiful sight to see the women & children, old men and old women trudging along on foot most of them barefooted and naked, and yet these people are the best disposed to the whites of any Indians in the south.[12]

Delaware frontiersman Black Beaver had been hired to assist special agent J. J. Chollar in returning the refugee tribes to their former agency. When Chollar became ill with cholera at the Canadian, Beaver took the Indians on to their destination. Once there, he was left in charge of the decimated tribespeople without help from the government until Wichita agent Henry Shanklin arrived in September.[13]

On October 1 Shanklin reported on the progress at the restored agency. The Shawnees and Delawares, he said, had industriously built fences and put in crops. Among the Wichitas and other tribes of the agency, the men were refusing to make "squaws of themselves"[14] and use the ploughs provided. The women and children, however, had planted and cultivated a surprising amount of ground.

A more serious problem involved the presence of the Kiowas and Comanches. Many members of the two tribes had never seen an agency and were still very wild, uncontrollable, and demanding. Shanklin observed:

> Their conduct was insolent, and humiliating to the last degree, helping themselves to everything that pleased their fancy without paying the least

attention to protests against it. . . . They remained long enough to almost ruin the entire crop of corn and beans planted by the Wichitas. Complaints were made daily that the fences were broken down and herds of ponies turned into the fields.[15]

The Kiowas and Comanches, on the other hand, resented the relocation of the peaceful tribes on what they had been told was now their reservation land. Hostile elements burned one of the Wichita agency buildings to the ground and demanded that no more trees be cut down to build houses.[16]

On September 4 Leavenworth, Indian superintendent Thomas Murphy, and a small party rode south from the Little Arkansas on the same trail by which Mathewson had just returned. Murphy's mission was to meet with the headmen of the Kiowas and Comanches and persuade them to attend still another treaty-making council.

Indian-white friction had continued on the Plains, particularly in western Kansas, where a stage route had been opened along the Smoky Hill to Denver and the Kansas-Pacific Railroad was constructing a rail line. During the spring and summer of 1867, raids by the Cheyenne Dog Soldiers under Tall Bull and Roman Nose and the Lakotas under Pawnee Killer had created havoc. With the inability of Hancock and Custer to subdue the hostiles, the government concluded that it was necessary to conduct another peacemaking venture with the prairie tribes.

Murphy and Leavenworth's fifteen-man party found the Kiowas and Comanches encamped on the Salt Fork of the Arkansas River in northern Indian Territory. McCusker was along to serve as interpreter; also present was a reporter for the *Chicago Tribune* who provided a detailed account of the meeting. Of the Kiowas, he wrote:

> The old head chief Ta-Haw-Son, or "Over the Buttes," who was present at the last treaty, died some time ago, and no one has as yet been elected to fill his place, owing to the multiplicity of candidates, none of whom could bring to bear any controlling influences to establish a claim; hence they remain without a Chief. At last "Medicine," a chief councillor, was elected, whose position is similar to that of our Vice President. He acted as spokesman for his tribe on this occasion; his name I was unable to obtain. He is father of the noted Satanta, or White Bear, who was absent.[17]

The attending chiefs included Black Eagle (Wah-o-Konh) and Stumbling Bear (Sit-Em-Keah), among others. Kicking Bird may have been present, although it was noted that the main portion of the tribe was about eighty miles away at the forks of Beaver and Wolf Creeks. The Kiowas seated themselves in their traditional circle and announced

Chief Stumbling Bear, cousin and close associate of
Kicking Bird. Courtesy Archives and Manuscript
Division, Oklahoma Historical Society.

through McCusker that they were ready to hear from their Great Father at Washington. Leavenworth told them that the president was
sending seven chiefs to talk with them and all of the Plains tribes at
the fall of the next moon (mid-October). The purpose of this visit
now was to determine where the meeting could be held. Leavenworth
suggested several sites, including Fort Larned and the Great Bend of the
Arkansas.

Elderly, bespectacled Ten Bears, who had been to Washington in
1863, rose to shake hands and speak for the Comanches. He said Larned
was a bad place. He liked the mouth of the Little Arkansas, a "straight
road" for his people.[18] But he did not like the idea of waiting so long; the
weather would be getting cold by the time they adjourned, he noted. He
said that last fall they had waited and waited for their goods until winter

Chief Ten Bears, leading Comanche peace advocate, made
two trips to Washington, D.C. Courtesy Smithsonian Institution.

set in. They had lost many horses and suffered much for it, but the
Comanches were still willing to meet the white chiefs.

When Ten Bears observed that the Kiowas had just as many good
horses as the Comanches, Kiowa chief Black Eagle answered that he did
not like Larned, but the Kiowas would go anywhere the Comanches
would. He said he was glad the Kiowas and Comanches had not been
forgotten. They had lost their own country and were now in one they
knew nothing of. But his people were carrying out their promises and
were ready to listen—they all had holes in their ears to do so and knew
what was right.

Satanta's father rose next. He said he spoke for his son. He and his
people had traveled far, and their horses' feet were sore. He wanted the
commissioners to meet them at the Salt Plains where the Timber Mountain

Fork (Medicine Lodge Creek) joins the Salt Fork; the Arkansas was a bad stream, he said, and his people did not like it.

Ten Bears argued against the Salt Plains site, saying the last time the Comanches camped there they lost many young men—presumably in a fight with the Osages. He wanted to move east of Timbered Mountain Fork, but he was willing to meet the white chiefs. Both tribes agreed that they would begin moving north toward Timbered Mountain Fork shortly and conduct their buffalo hunt on the way. Whites called that stream "Medicine Lodge Creek," taking its name from an abandoned Kiowa medicine lodge that stood on its banks. Eventually, that stream was chosen for the treaty council.

Before the Murphy party left the Salt Fork, Chief Iron Shirt and other Plains Apache chiefs arrived and expressed their desire to attend the new treaty council. Iron Shirt complained that the Cheyenne Dog Soldiers often came to his camps below the Arkansas to boast of their exploits and display the scalps they had taken. The Dog Soldiers taunted the young Plains Apache braves, calling them "squaws and cowards."

George Bent also arrived at the Salt Fork encampments from Black Kettle's camp on Wolf Creek. He said he had recently been threatened by the Dog Soldiers for trying to restrain the young men of Black Kettle's band from going to war. The Dog Soldiers had also said they would kill Black Kettle's horses if he attended the proposed peace treaty. Although the Cheyenne peace leader feared for his life, he bravely took his family and rode with Bent to the mouth of the Little Arkansas.

Still another significant change was taking place in the nature of Indian Territory. The great cattle drives from Texas to railheads in Kansas began during the summer of 1867. Texas drovers had previously been driving their longhorns to eastern Kansas and Missouri over the Shawnee Trail. But the fear of local herds becoming infected with Texas fever had brought both physical and political opposition from farmers and ranchers. As a result, the Kansas legislature passed a law permitting the Texas herds to pass through the state only west of Saline County.

This spurred entrepreneur Joseph G. McCoy to establish stock pens at Abilene, Kansas, thus pushing the trail herds into central Indian Territory. Their new route followed in part the natural path between present west Oklahoma City and Wichita that Jesse Chisholm had used for his trade wagons. It would soon became known as the Chisholm Cattle Trail. Leavenworth wrote from the Little Arkansas on September 2, 1867, that two herds of Texas cattle, around 1,500 head, had just arrived there.[19]

The flood of Texas beef across the Indian lands would bring in more white men, many of them aggressive Texans. The intrusion of huge cattle herds also disrupted the prairie habitat of the tribes. Clashes between the freewheeling Texas drovers and the hot-blooded tribesmen were inevitable.

The day of the trail herd would also spawn new communities on both the northern and southern borders of the Indian Territory. This advent of the white man's civilization would restrict more and more the great freedom so essential to Plains Indian life. Both sport and professional hunters were increasingly intruding into the Territory, decimating the vital game supply. New wagon routes were opening, and U.S. military dominance loomed ominously ahead. Soon the surveyors would come.

For the Plains tribes, all of these changes tendered the inevitable options of resistance or capitulation in the face of overwhelming forces. As they prepared once again to meet with the Great Father's representatives, some of the older and wiser chiefs such as Black Kettle and Ten Bears—and perhaps Kicking Bird as well—realized that militant opposition was futile. But the war factions of the tribes were still powerful internal forces that would not be held back simply by the white man's paper promises.

10

"I Have Been Made Poor"

If a single chief stood out at Medicine Lodge, it was Satanta. Kicking Bird was there, seated prominently in the council circle. But it was Satanta, decked in his new finery, who orated at length and effectively stated the wants and desires of the Kiowas. He also played well to the corps of eight or so newspaper specials—as newspaper reporters of the day were called— who attended the treaty council. They filled the pages of newspapers around the nation with items on Satanta, printed his speeches in full, and made him into something of an Indian country celebrity.

The Kiowa chief was at Fort Larned when the peace commission, its entourage, and military escort arrived there on October 9, 1867, on their way to the treaty grounds. He invaded the sutler's store, greeting, shaking hands, and hugging commissioners, officers, and reporters with equal fervor. Satanta quickly became the center of amazement and interest to the urban journalists who until recently had been sitting comfortably behind a copy desk.

William Fayel of the *Missouri Republican* described him as "a man of splendid physique, square, full face, and sagacious looking eyes, which, when injured have a vindictive expression. His head is large and massive, measuring twenty-three inches around the cranium, only one inch less than that of Daniel Webster."[1]

"He is now forty years of age, of plump figure," penned scribe George Brown of the *Cincinnati Commercial*, "with massive hair, black as the wing of the raven, and parted in the middle, falling down his neck, over his shoulders. His eyes are of sparkling brilliancy, though no one can ever catch them."[2]

H. J. Budd of the *Cincinnati Gazette* wrote: "He wears a bugle which he stole from a soldier whom he murdered. This he always carries with him, and blows with no inconsiderable degree of skill."[3] S. F. Hall of the *Chicago Tribune*, however, complained that "he tooted unnecessarily all night, and set wild echoes flying recklessly without regard to tune."[4]

While Satanta was getting an essentially laudatory press, Kicking Bird was being denounced by Budd as the villain of the Box affair. The scribe wrote, without source or evidence, that Kicking Bird had "killed the father, dashed the brains of an infant child out against a rock, made to stand on coals of fire a girl of eleven years, and ravished the mother and two older daughters, keeping them in captivity three months."[5]

Another, far more positive story regarding Kicking Bird at Medicine Lodge was later told by newspaperman Milton W. Reynolds, who took up the pseudonym "Kicking Bird" as a writer. Journalists of that day took up such names as Frontier, Otoe, Seminole, and the like. Reynolds chose Kicking Bird, supposedly because the Kiowa chief had saved his life by interceding in Reynolds's behalf when he was attacked by a hostile warrior at Medicine Lodge. Twenty years later Reynolds wrote: "I slept in the same tent with him [Kicking Bird]. He once saved my life and that of my friend Colonel Murphy (Superintendent of Indian Affairs)."[6]

Reynolds's daughter claimed her father was in an Indian skirmish and was about to be scalped when Kicking Bird interceded and saved his life.[7] No report by any of the other newspaper specials at the council mentioned the incident. A Reynolds contemporary stated: "It was at this council [Medicine Lodge that] Reynolds first met that good-natured, amiable Kiowa chief 'Kicking Bird.' They became friends and visited together much of the time. It was after this great Indian council that he took the name 'Kicking Bird' as his pen name."[8]

Satanta made another lasting impression as the commission train of thirty-five wagons, escorted by 150 Seventh Cavalry, 130 Infantry troops, Larned's eighteen-instrument post band, plus two Gatling guns made its way to the treaty site. Maj. Joel Elliott was in command of the Seventh Cavalry; Custer was at Fort Leavenworth facing a court-martial on charges of deserting his post at Fort Wallace and excessively abusing his men on a futile Indian-hunting expedition into western Kansas. Near Rattlesnake Creek a huge herd of buffalo was spotted. Joyously, a number of the sports-minded men attached to the commission party and military escort spurred their horses in pursuit. After killing several of the animals, the men cut out their tongues, leaving the carcasses where they fell. A furious

Satanta spurred his pony up beside that of peace commissioner William S. Harney.

"Has the white man become a child," Satanta was reported to have demanded, "that he should kill and not eat? When the red men slay game they do so that they may live, and not starve."[9]

Harney immediately ordered that the buffalo killing stop, and there was no more shooting. The peace expedition reached the treaty grounds on October 14 to find the crosspoles of 850 tepees peeking above the brush that lined the banks of Medicine Lodge Creek. The Kiowa, Comanche, Cheyenne, Arapaho, and Plains Apache tribespeople were estimated at 5,000 or more.[10]

A preliminary council was held on October 15. The tribesmen arrived early, exhibiting a multitude of cloth headdresses decorated with tin plates and hanging down their backs to the ground. This meeting merely set the stage for discussion of central issues on October 19. In the interim, testimony was taken from Edward W. Wynkoop, now agent for the Cheyennes and Arapahos. Wynkoop told the commission:

> After a treaty was made in 1865, some annuity goods were distributed to the Cheyennes and Sioux. They were bought of a firm in New York, and they were the most worthless things I ever saw. . . . The things consisted of goods entirely worthless to the Indians, such as shoes and boots, and not worth more than one-third of the $20,000 said to have been purchased and contained in this lot were there. The blankets, when opened, were thin, flimsy affairs, not worth more than one dollar apiece, and the barrels of sugar were not more than a third full.[11]

Reynolds, writing for the *Chicago Times,* described the setting:

> The great council with the five tribes of the plains convened today. The four sleeps have passed; the moon is full; and all but the Cheyennes are ready to have a "big talk." One band of the hostile Cheyennes arrives tonight, and the remainder of the nation will arrive tomorrow. The council is held in a cottonwood grove on the banks of the Medicine Lodge creek, 30 miles from the southern boundary of Kansas. The Kiowas and Comanches claim it as their country. A patch of brush is cleared away; a temporary covering is constructed for the commissioners and the council convenes. In the center of the semicircle sits Commissioner Taylor, president of the council. On his left Gen. Harney, Senator Henderson, and Gen. Sanborn; on his right, Gen. Augur, Gen. Terry, and Col. Tappan. The military gentlemen are in full uniform. The Indians call them war chiefs, and the others big chiefs of the big council at Washington. The Arapahos, Apaches, Comanches, and Kiowa, with full representatives, and a portion of the Cheyennes, sit on the ground in a semicircle facing the commission. Behind them are large numbers of Indians on horseback, with bows and arrows strung to their backs,

while a few of them have revolvers. In the rear of the commission sit the reporters, and peering over their shoulders are a large number of teamsters, stragglers, hangers-on, frontiersmen—a rather seamy looking set generally.[12]

Sitting in the front row of the semicircle of Indians were Kicking Bird and Fishemore; Arapahos Little Raven and Spotted Wolf; Cheyennes Heap of Birds, Black Kettle, and Spotted Elk; and Apache Poor Bear. Satanta had managed a camp chair on which he enthroned himself before all the others. Fishemore, identified as the Kiowas' council orator who spoke five languages, went down the line of commissioners shaking hands.[13]

Commissioner Taylor opened the council by saying that he and the others had come to make peace, correct any wrongs the tribes might be suffering, provide for schools and churches, and make it possible for them to select farming land. Schools, churches, and farms, however, were not what Satanta had come to talk about. He rose and took center stage, a formidable and striking figure in his general's uniform. "Gifted with natural eloquence," Henry M. Stanley wrote, "he compels attention."[14]

First, Satanta somewhat disingenuously insisted that since signing the treaty at the Little Arkansas he had not done any bad things: "I moved away from those disposed [Cheyennes] for war. . . . That peace I have never broken."[15] Some at the council may have questioned Satanta's

Satanta, seated at center, was a major player during the Medicine Lodge treaty council. *Frank Leslie's Illustrated Newspaper*, Nov. 16, 1867.

profession of innocence, but they had no doubts of his sincerity when he stated his love for the land and the prairie Indians' way of life:

> I have heard that you intend to settle us on a reservation near the mountains. I don't want to settle. I love to roam over the prairie. I feel free and happy, but when we settle down we grow pale and die. . . . A long time ago this land belonged to our fathers, but when I go up to the river I see camps of soldiers on the banks. These soldiers cut down my timber, they kill my buffalo, and when I see that my heart feels like bursting; I feel sorry.[16]

Ten Bears, who had once been to Washington to see the White Father, rose to speak. He said that if the Texans had kept out of the Comanches' country, there would have been no trouble. After brief talks by both the chiefs and commissioners, the council recessed until the following Monday. At nine o'clock that morning, the Kiowas and Comanches met at the commission tent to sign the treaty document that had been drawn up. Pending a reading of the pact, Satanta said again, "I don't want to settle down and live in houses . . . tell the Great Father what I say."[17]

Tosh-a-wah, peace chief of the Comanches, disagreed. He said he wanted the houses built that had been promised him and his band, and he wanted them built right away.

Like the other Kiowa chiefs, Kicking Bird was overshadowed at Medicine Lodge and became a secondary player in the council. But now he stepped forward to speak. He reminded the officials that he had signed a treaty two years before but had never received the annuities it promised. The commission was once again "getting up a great pile of papers," and it seemed the Kiowas would never get their goods.[18]

Kicking Bird also announced that he had a hunting pony to present to Commissioner Taylor, who earlier had said he wished to buy one. When Taylor tried to pay for the pony, Kicking Bird refused to accept any reward.[19] When he had finished speaking, however, he stood staring at one of the commissioners seated at a table. The man finally asked, "What do you want?"

Like Satanta, Kicking Bird was drawn to the white man's clothing. He pointed to the commissioner's high silk hat. The commissioner, thinking the Kiowa merely wished to look at the hat, handed it over. Kicking Bird, however, considered the item to be a gift. He put it on his head and walked off. The commissioner did not see fit to challenge him. Kicking Bird then dressed the hat with a streamer of red cloth that trailed him as he moved about the treaty grounds.[20]

After Kicking Bird had spoken, the chiefs began stepping up to make their mark on the treaty document. Signing for the Kiowas were Satanta, Satank, Black Eagle, Kicking Bird, Fishemore, Woman's Heart, Stum-

Tosh-a-wah, Comanche peace chief. Courtesy Western History Collection, University of Oklahoma.

bling Bear, One Bear, Crow, and Bear Lying Down.[21] A rain squall struck the camp the next day as the tribes were being issued treaty goods: blankets, coats, shawls, calico, shirts, hats, pants, plumes, cords, beads, needles, pins, thread, yarn, and bales of woolens. The tribespeople happily threw away their old clothes, donned the new ones, then loaded their new goods on their travois and departed.[22]

A memory account of the treaty council was given to W. S. Nye in 1937 by Joshua Given, the educated son of Satank. During the year of the Medicine Lodge Treaty, Given had joined Satanta and others in making a raid into Texas, where they captured young Mary Hamilton. The girl was adopted into the family of a noted warrior named Tan-goodle and his wife, Tope-kau-da. Given recounted:

> In the autumn of that year in which we made the raid we received word that all the tribes were supposed to assemble at Medicine Lodge, in

southern Kansas, where the people from Washington were going to give us some annuity goods. They were going to make a treaty with us, but we would not have assembled just for that. The reason we went there was that we were told that the soldiers were going to give us some free food.

It was a big gathering, and we had a fine time. A lot of speeches were made, which we did not understand. The interpreter [McCusker] kept mumbling something, but spoke only Comanche, and all of us did not know that language. Afterwards we learned that they were going to put us on a reservation near the Wichita mountains; we heard also that all white captives had to be given up. Tan-goodle and Tope-kau-da went off south on the prairie and hid their little white girl.[23]

Just how much of the agreement made in the white man's writing the chiefs had really understood is subject to question. But after the Kiowas had struck their camp and left for the Cimarron River, on the morning of October 24 Kiowa chief Satank, accompanied by a hundred or so warriors, returned to the commission camp. He indicated that he wished to speak to the commissioners. Satanta has often been called the "Orator of the Plains." It was this speech, however, described by some as "true eloquence," that some later accredited to Satanta. Reporter Brown, who was present, said it was Satank who made the speech, and its content proves this contention. Brown described the ancient warrior with his long, Mongolian-style whiskers as he stood wrapped in his blanket before the commissioners and looked steadily at each. McCusker interpreted as the old man spoke.

You, no doubt, are tired of the much talk of our people. Many of them have put themselves forward and filled you with their sayings. I have kept back and said nothing, not that I do not consider myself the principal chief of the Kiowa Nation. The Kiowas and Comanches have pledged their honor, and their word shall last until the whites break their contracts and invite the horrors of war. We do not break treaties. We make but few contracts, and remember them well. The whites make so many that they are liable to forget them. The white chief seems not to be able to govern his braves. He sometimes becomes angry when he sees the wrongs of his people, committed on the red men, and his voice becomes as loud as the roaring winds. But like the wind, it dies away, and leaves the sullen calm of unheeded oppression. . . . The white man once came to trade; he now comes as a soldier. He once put his trust in our friendship and wanted no shield but our fidelity. But now he builds forts and plants big guns on their walls. He once gave us arms and powder and bade us hunt the game. We then loved him for his confidence. . . . He now covers his face with the cloud of jealousy and anger and tells us to be gone, as an offended master speaks to his dog. . . . Look at this medal I wear. By wearing this, I have been made poor. Before, I was rich in horses and lodges. Today I am the poorest of all. When you

gave me this silver medal on my neck, you made me poor. . . . I shall soon
have to go the way of my fathers. But those who come after me will
remember this day. . . . You may not see me again, but remember Satank
as the white man's friend.[24]

By the Treaty of Medicine Lodge, the Kiowas and Comanches were
assigned a 6,000 square mile tract of land between the Red River and its
North Fork. There they would be supplied with an agency house, warehouse, school and teacher, church, farming implements and farm instructor,
miller, and physician. They would also annually be issued clothes (white
man's) and subsistence.

In return, the two tribes would settle on their reservation, offer no
opposition to railroad construction to the north, capture no women or
children, cease their killing of white men, and permit whites to hunt
south of the Arkansas. The treaty satisfied the current interests of the
United States; it was not what the Kiowas had wanted. Correspondent
Stanley held a cynical view of the treaty. He wrote:

> The treaty with the Kiowas was something of a tremendous "goak"—a
> very farce, which had the people seen upon the stage, they would have
> laughed their very eyes out. To make a treaty it requires two interested
> parties. Well, a treaty in due form was drawn up by that legal Senator,
> John B. Henderson of Missouri . . . and before being signed by the head
> men of the Kiowa nation, a few pleasing extracts were read by Henderson
> to be translated by the interpreter to Satanta and his mates. . . . The
> treaty purports to be a candid and tacit acknowledgment that the chief
> has given up all the land south of the Arkansas down to the southern
> boundary of Kansas to the whites. It is no such thing.[25]

Stanley unquestionably had a valid point. As events would ultimately
determine, however, the ensuing treaty with the Cheyennes would also
severely affect the fate of the Kiowas. The commissioners, weary of camp
life and growing short on supplies, fretted over the absence of the much-
feared Cheyennes, who were off nearby making their annual medicine
and taking their time about coming in to sign a treaty.

During this interim period a small party attached to the peace commission entourage rode to investigate the medicine lodge located on the
bank of Medicine Lodge Creek six miles from the council site. One of
the tourists was Brown of the *Cincinnati Commercial*, who described the
Kiowa religious structure for his readers:

> It is two hundred and ten feet in circumference and seventy feet in
> diameter. It is made of brush and trees which are arranged in the form
> of a circle. Trees which have crutches are selected and driven into the
> ground at a distance of about ten feet apart, in the circle. These form

the posts for the fence, which is made of brush. In the center of the circular house a huge post, thirty feet high, is driven into the ground. To this pole are connected, from the tops of the circular fence, other poles, and thus forming a roof for the inclosure.[26]

Attached to the walls, ceiling, and center pole were offerings of brass rings, beads, feathers, brightly painted gourds, children's moccasins, and other paraphernalia while the center pole featured a decorated buffalo skull. The visitors filled their pockets with souvenirs. On the way back to camp, however, they heard shooting and saw a mass of well-armed Cheyenne Dog Soldiers galloping forth to meet with the commissioners, the alarmed men threw their loot from the Kiowa sanctuary into Medicine Lodge Creek.[27]

Finally, the Cheyenne Dog Soldiers, led by Bull Bear, Buffalo Chief, and Tall Bull, rode into camp, whooping and brandishing their weapons in a great display of defiance. When the time came to sign the treaty, the Cheyennes disdainfully jammed their pens to the treaty with little comprehension of it, in much the same manner as Stanley had described of the Kiowas. It was the Dog Soldiers' understanding that by this treaty they would still be free to roam the buffalo range of the upper Republican and Smoky Hill Rivers. In little more than a year, the Cheyenne conflict with whites in Kansas would bring a U.S. military invasion and war to the Kiowas' homeland in the Indian Territory.

11

In the Shadow of the Sword

Stanley's prediction of failure for the Medicine Lodge pacts with the Plains tribes would be borne out by events during the year to follow. Cheyenne, Arapaho, and Lakota war parties continued to strike against railway points, migration routes, and advance Kansas settlements between the Platte and Arkansas Rivers. Also, Kiowa and Comanche raiders continued their incursions into north Texas, killing citizens, driving off stock, and carrying women and children captives back across the Red River.

In compliance with the treaty, Leavenworth reestablished the annuity distribution center for the Kiowas and Comanches at the site of the former Wichita agency on the south side of the Washita—an area known as Eureka Valley or Eureka Springs. Even as he was on his way there, he was met at Fort Gibson by a messenger from Fort Cobb with word that the Kiowas were also moving toward the post. Of the seven captives the tribe held, it was reported, five had died. Two small girls remained with them.[1]

Leavenworth and his clerk, S. T. Walkley, arrived at Eureka Springs on February 19, 1868. On April 23 the agent reported that on reaching the agency he learned that both Kiowa and Comanche war parties had been committing depredations. Leavenworth began work to free some of the numerous captives. From the Noconi Comanches he rescued an eleven- or twelve-year-old girl named Vina Mars and returned her to her family in Texas. He also won the release of a small boy who could not identify himself clearly. The agent also believed a black slave boy would soon be freed.[2]

Most of the Kiowa and Comanche bands were camped along the Washita River near old Fort Cobb. Satanta, however, was absent. Kicking Bird told the agent he thought Satanta had gone to Kansas, possibly to collect a ransom for a white girl. Leavenworth learned from others that the girl had been in Satanta's camp even as the Medicine Lodge council was in progress.

Kicking Bird was correct regarding Satanta's whereabouts. During July, Satanta's Kiowas gave up two white captives at Fort Larned—a four-year-old boy and a thirteen-year-old girl—to Fort Dodge trader John Tappan. Further, Cheyenne and Arapaho agent Wynkoop discovered a white girl, Melinda Ann Candle of Texas, in a Comanche camp. He was able to persuade her captors to give her up without ransom.[3]

At Eureka Valley Leavenworth soon discovered that the more captives he rescued, the more were taken prisoner.[4] Evidently, the final blow came with the January 1868 massacre of the Fitzpatrick family of Denton County, Texas. The 100-man party had been led by Kiowa chief Heap-of-Bears, a nonsignator of the Medicine Lodge pact. The raiders had killed eight people and had taken two women and eight children captive. One of the women escaped, and the other was left at the first night's camp. Tragically, however, six of the children died in captivity. Leavenworth finally managed to rescue six-year-old Melinda Alice Fitzpatrick and four-year-old Susan Fitzpatrick.[5]

During late March, a survey crew was chaining the boundary of the Seminole and Creek lands as determined by treaties in 1866. They were intercepted near Chisholm's post just west of present Oklahoma City by a party of Kiowa, Comanche, and Cheyenne warriors. The Indians warned them in dire terms to leave and not come back. The men returned to the Seminole agency, more than thankful to still have their scalps.[6]

On May 26 Leavenworth left his Wichita agency. Walkley charged that the agent deserted his post after being told the Kiowas were going to clean out the valley and kill everyone.[7] Whatever his reason for leaving, Leavenworth took the two Fitzpatrick girls with him to Washington, D.C. He placed the parentless girls in the Protestant Orphan Asylum while Congress voted $10,000 for their care, the money to be taken from the Kiowas' treaty settlement. The names of the two girls were changed to Helen and Heloise Lincoln.[8]

Leavenworth would never return to the agency. Walkley, left without instructions or much authority, took over as the acting agent. Before leaving, Leavenworth had made arrangements with contractor J. C. D.

Blackburn to supply the tribes with beef, flour, sugar, and coffee up to September 1.[9] The raiding into Texas by Comanche and Kiowas war parties continued through the summer, as Walkley reported:

> On or about June 10, 1868, a party, consisting of Cochetekas and Noconees [Comanches], returned from a raid in Montgomery County, Texas, bringing one scalp (that of a young man about 18 years of age,) and the three McElroy children; also a number of horses.
> On July 14, 1868, a party of Noconees returned from a raid on the Brazos river, bringing four scalps (those of an entire family whom they murdered), and a few horses.
> On September 2, 1868, a party consisting of Nocones, Pennetkeas, Wichitas, and others, came in from a raid on Red river, near a place called Spanish Fort, bringing eight scalps, (being those of one woman and seven men, whom they killed;) they also brought in a good many horses and mules.[10]

Walkley was able to recover the three McElroy children as well as Tom Bailey and Dick Freeman of Grayson County, Texas. One boy of fourteen, whose parents were dead, rejected rescue, preferring to remain with the Indians. Release of the McElroy children had been effected by Cheyenne Jenny, wife of Kansas trader William Greiffenstein who had recently opened a trading post near Fort Cobb. Cheyenne Jenny bargained her own ponies and money to purchase the children.[11] Some Comanche chiefs had likewise used their own horses and blankets for ransom of captured children from their young men. Also, the chiefs had sent after warriors who had slipped away at night to raid.[12]

During the summer of 1868 Kicking Bird headed a big buffalo hunt on the upper Washita. After a successful kill, the various bands met to hold their annual Sun Dance. A party of nearly 200 warriors was organized to conduct an incursion on their old enemies, the Utes of Colorado. The venture proved to be a disaster for the invaders. Stumbling Bear, a participant, said the big fight took place at Red River Spring, where the South Canadian crosses the New Mexico border.[13]

The Utes whipped the Kiowas badly, killing Chief Heap-of-Bears along with six of his men and capturing the sacred Taime idol, which Heap-of-Bears carried in a bag on his back. When the defeated warriors returned to their camps near Fort Larned, the tribe went into great mourning. The women slashed themselves, lopped off fingers, and wailed night and day in their tepees.

To relieve their people's misery, Kicking Bird and Stumbling Bear led a war party back to the battlefield to gather up the bones of the Kiowa dead and bury them. They found a circle stomped around the bones of Heap-of-Bears where the Utes had held a victory dance. Stumbling Bear claimed that on this trip he encountered a lone Ute, whom he killed and scalped in revenge.[14]

In August 1868 E. B. Dennison, Indian agent at Cimarron Springs, New Mexico, replied to an inquiry from Indian Bureau official Thomas Murphy at Fort Larned regarding the Taime idol. Dennison reported that the Utes did indeed hold a medicine idol of the Kiowas. They were very bitter toward the Kiowas and would make no peace with them. The Utes were interested in knowing, however, what consideration in horses the Kiowas would be willing to make. If they accepted the Kiowa offer, they would turn the Taime idol over to Dennison to handle. In no case, however, would they meet the Kiowas on a peace footing.[15]

From Kansas, agent Wynkoop reported that the Kiowas were very sad, saying that since they lost the medicine the Great Spirit was angry with them. Lightning had struck the lodge of Lone Wolf and killed three people. Later, lightning had killed another man and his horse near Fort Larned.[16]

In March 1868 Maj. Gen. Phil Sheridan arrived in Kansas to replace General Hancock in command of the District of the Missouri. This region included the military districts of New Mexico, Indian Territory, Kansas, Missouri, and the upper Arkansas in western Kansas and Colorado. During an inspection tour of the military posts along the Arkansas, Sheridan found a large encampment of Kiowas, Comanches, Arapahos, and Cheyennes waiting at Fort Dodge for their annuities. The chiefs requested an interview with Sheridan, but he refused to talk with them.[17]

A fight between the Kiowas and U.S. troops almost occurred near Fort Zarah in late May. A government wagon master came to the fort and reported that his train had been attacked by Kiowas and robbed of some flour, sugar, and coffee. A squad of cavalry and a detachment of infantry were sent to the Kiowa camp to demand restitution. As the troops approached, women and children in the camp plunged into the flooded Arkansas River to escape. Meanwhile, the warriors arranged themselves in a line of battle, ready to defend their families. At the sight of them, the wagon master became frightened and confessed that he had lied. He admitted that he had given the items freely to the Indians.[18]

Brig. Gen. Alfred Sully met with some Kiowas, Comanches, Apaches, Cheyennes, and Arapahos at Fort Larned during mid-July. He described the Kiowas and Comanches as impudent and defiant. They adamantly rejected the idea of living on a reservation.[19] Murphy reported to the Indian Bureau on August 5 that bands of hungry Kiowas and Comanches were stopping wagon trains on the Santa Fe Trail to obtain food.[20]

Gen. Phil Sheridan threatened to hang Satanta and Lone Wolf if the Kiowas did not come in to the reservation. *Frank Leslie's Illustrated Newspaper,* Sept. 7, 1867.

A large number of Kiowas and an estimated one-third of the Comanches remained on the Arkansas into September.[21] Sheridan held an interview with the two tribes at Larned, advising them to return to their reservation at Fort Cobb.[22] He had concluded that a punitive strike against the Cheyennes and Arapahos was necessary: "I am of the opinion that these Indians require to be soundly whipped, and the ringleaders in the present trouble hung, their ponies killed, and such destruction of their property as will make them very poor."[23]

Two efforts to punish the tribes during September 1868 were failures, however. Sully led a cumbersome expedition into northwest Indian Territory, only to find he was unable to engage the enemy effectively. Lured into sand dunes at the juncture of Beaver and Wolf Creeks by the false trails of stone-weighted Indian travois, his heavy wagons became mired. Also, his grain-fed cavalry horses were ineffective in chasing the fleeter Indian mounts. The Indian warriors constantly appeared atop hills just out of rifle range. Some made derisive gestures by spanking their buttocks at the troopers.[24]

A fifty-man band of scouts under Maj. George A. Forsyth that invaded eastern Colorado found entirely too much of the enemy. The Cheyennes under the famous Cheyenne war leader Roman Nose pinned down Forsyth and his men on Beecher's Island and nearly annihilated them even though Roman Nose was killed during a charge.

In the Territory, Walkley managed to hold the Indians at the agency until October 5 when Company M, Tenth Cavalry, and Company E, Sixth Infantry, were sent from Fort Arbuckle to reactivate Fort Cobb. This was done on orders of General Sheridan, who with Maj. Gen. William B. Hazen met with the Kiowas at Fort Larned on September 20. In an effort to separate the hostiles from among the tribes, Sheridan sent instructions for all friendly Indians to go to Fort Cobb in the Indian Territory for their rations. Hazen was directed to go to Cobb, provide for the Indians in the area, and try to keep them quiet.

In the meantime, Sherdian laid plans for a multipronged winter campaign against the Plains Indian stronghold in western Indian Territory. He would personally accompany the strike force of U.S. Seventh Cavalry under Custer, which would drive south from Kansas into the Territory. Another command would march southeastward from Fort Lyon, Colorado, through the Texas Panhandle and another eastward from Fort Bascom in New Mexico.

From Fort Gibson, Capt. Henry Alvord, Tenth Cavalry, was sent ahead to Cobb to handle matters until Hazen could get there. Through the use of scouts and friendly Indians, Alvord was able to stay informed on the movements of the tribes. Kicking Bird's band, he reported, had gone to the vicinity of the Antelope Hills to hold a buffalo hunt.[25]

Upon completion of the fall hunt, Kicking Bird and Little Heart moved their bands down the Washita toward Fort Cobb, joining camps of Kiowas, Comanches, Plains Apaches, Cheyennes, Arapahos, Wichitas, Caddos, and others along the river. Satanta and Satank had brought their people down from the Arkansas to join the huge winter camp.

The annuities for the tribes had not reached Cobb when Hazen arrived on November 8. Nonetheless, he sent out runners to call in the peaceful bands of the area. Some of the Indians were skeptical of such promises, as Comanche chief Moh-wee indicated: "I won't come in until the goods have arrived. I am not angry nor do I want to fight. I have been fooled too much by the whites. They sent for me five times and told me there was goods for me, but there wasn't; it was a lie."[26]

On November 26 Hazen reported that the Kiowas and Apaches had been in to Fort Cobb, taken ten days' rations, and returned to their camps thirty miles up the Washita.[27] Black Kettle's band of Cheyennes and Arapahos under Big Mouth were also in the area. The Cheyenne chief had led his band southward to the area of the Antelope Hills in an effort to keep his young men away from the Cheyenne raiding and troubles in Kansas. Like the Comanches, the Cheyennes and Arapahos remained aloof from Fort Cobb after half-blood George Bent warned them that Sheridan's plan was a trap. In late November, however, Black Kettle led a delegation of Cheyennes and Arapahos to Fort Cobb to ask Hazen for asylum. Hazen rejected their plea, saying: "I am sent here as a peace chief; all here is to be peace; but north of the Arkansas is General Sheridan, the great war chief, and I do not control him. . . . I am satisfied you want peace, that it has not been you, but your bad men, that have made the war, and I will do all I can for you to bring peace."[28]

Black Kettle and his chiefs returned to their village, which anchored the western end of the long chain of conical lodges along the Washita—

Custer erroneously claimed Kicking Bird fought against him at the Washita. Dunn, *Massacre of the Mountains.*

a happenstance situation that would result in a new tragedy for him and his band, one reminiscent of Sand Creek.

A winter storm swept through the region on November 23, leaving the country frozen under several inches of snow. The storm had caught a Kiowa war party from Black Eagle's band in the field on its return from an excursion against the Utes. The Kiowas crossed the Canadian River near the Indian Territory-Texas border west of the Antelope Hills, then swung southeastward to follow down the Washita to Black Kettle's village where they spent the night. Around the lodge fire they told the Cheyennes of seeing a large trail in the snow near the Antelope Hills headed toward the Washita. The Cheyennes, thinking it unlikely that troops would be out in such weather, scoffed at them.

It was the Kiowas' clear path through the snowfield that was discovered near the Texas Panhandle by a scouting detail of the Seventh Cavalry on November 26. A snowstorm had struck shortly after Camp Supply had been established at the juncture of Beaver and Wolf Creeks. Believing the snow would hold the Indians to their camps, Custer had marched southwestward up Wolf Creek even as the storm continued. The storm had abated as Custer turned his force of 800 Seventh Cavalry troops south to the Antelope Hills. Upon reaching the Canadian River, Custer

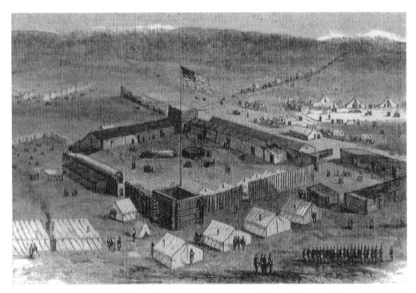

For a time Camp Supply, Indian Territory, was a Kiowa haunt. *Harper's Weekly,* Feb. 27, 1869.

dispatched a scouting party under Major Elliott up the stream to look for Indian signs.

Elliott's party soon discovered the Kiowa trail, which led south to the Washita River, and followed its course eastward.[29] Taking up the trail with a forced midnight march, Custer came upon Black Kettle's camp of fifty-one lodges in a bend of the Washita. Surrounding it, Custer waited for dawn to launch his attack. The ensuing charge routed the small camp. Cheyenne men and boys fought back the best they could as the women and children fled for safety. Black Kettle and his wife, both attempting to flee on his pony, were shot and killed in midstream of the icy Washita.

With the camp routed and fifty-three women and children captured, Custer spent most of the day burning the Cheyenne lodges and shooting over 800 horses and mules belonging to the Indians. Warriors from the camps downstream began to swarm the hills surrounding the demolished camp. Custer became concerned that he might be cut off from his baggage train parked near the Antelope Hills. Feinting a move eastward toward the encampments downriver until darkness covered his actions, Custer wheeled his command about and retreated back to the Canadian River. He departed without knowing the fate of Elliott and eighteen troopers who, in pursuing fleeing villagers, had been trapped and killed.

Custer later charged that Kicking Bird had taken part in the Washita fight by forming "a considerable portion of the hundreds who surrounded and killed Major Elliott and his party."[30] Alvord disputed this, however, saying that Kicking Bird and Little Heart had witnessed the fight but not as participants.[31] Army interpreter H. P. Jones agreed that "there were no Kiowas at the battle of the Washita, except a party of six or seven young men who were on their return from an expedition against the Utes or Navajos, and who happened to lodge with Black Kettle the night previous to the attack."[32]

After the battle, some of the Kiowas retreated to the sanctuary of Fort Cobb. The group included the bands of Satanta, Lone Wolf, and Black Eagle. Kicking Bird, however, joined the Cheyennes and Arapahos in reestablishing their camps on the North Fork of the Red River at the mouth of the Sweetwater. On December 1 a grand tribal council was held there. Kicking Bird and Little Heart, who said they had observed the Washita fight out of curiosity, attended the meeting and were asked to carry back the friendship of the hostiles to Black Eagle and others on the Washita.[33]

Black Eagle, third signatory at Medicine Lodge and apparently a leading Kiowa peace chief at this point, sent a "good talk" back to the Sweetwater camps. He said he would remain on the Washita and try to stop any military operation against the hostile Kiowa bands. But he asked that they not cause any trouble either to the north or in Texas and thereby bring trouble to the peaceful bands. He assured Hazen that he would keep the Kiowas on the Washita under control.[34]

Custer and the Seventh Cavalry returned to Camp Supply with the Cheyenne captives to receive the applause of Sheridan. With the Seventh Cavalry now joined in force by the late-arriving Nineteenth Kansas Volunteer Cavalry, Sheridan and Custer set out for Fort Cobb. En route the command camped near the Washita battle site, and on the morning of December 11 the two officers led an entourage on a visit to the battlefield. The bodies of a captured white woman, Mrs. Clara Blinn, and her small son were found. Downriver the corpses of Elliott and the other eighteen missing troopers were also discovered.

After the dead enlisted men had been buried, the bodies of Elliott, Mrs. Blinn, and her son were placed in a wagon for burial at Fort Arbuckle. The expedition then headed down the winding Washita toward Fort Cobb. On the morning of December 17 a courier from Cobb was brought to the column by Osage scouts who reported a body of Indians ahead. The courier carried a note from General Hazen that read in part: "All the camps this side of the point reported to have been reached are friendly, and have not been on the war-path this season. If this reaches you, it would be well to communicate at once with Satanta or Black Eagle, chiefs of the Kiowas, near where you are now, who will readily inform you of the position of the Cheyennes and Arapahoes, also of our camp."[35]

The command soon encountered a large body of well-armed warriors. Escorted by his staff, news correspondent DeB. Randolph Keim, and fifty scouts, Custer rode ahead to make contact. Signs were made between the two forces for a parley before Satanta and Lone Wolf finally rode forward.[36] By Keim's account, Satanta rode up to Custer and offered his hand. But Custer rejected it, saying "I never shake hands with any one unless I know him to be a friend."[37]

The two chiefs agreed to accompany the march to Fort Cobb and were joined by sixty other Kiowas. During the march, however, the warriors dropped away until only Satanta and Lone Wolf, riding at the head of the column, remained. When Satanta attempted to gallop off also, he was chased down. Custer ordered that both he and Lone Wolf be placed under guard, and upon reaching Fort Cobb both chiefs were placed in irons and held as hostages against the capitulation of their people. Tough-minded Sheridan threatened to hang them if their people did not come in.[38]

Two days later, Black Eagle and some other chiefs arrived with their bands, setting up their encampments near the fort. Kicking Bird was not among them. Possibly he was shying away from Sheridan and Custer, heeding the lessons of Sand Creek and Washita. Keim claimed he was depredating across the Red River into Texas.[39] Hazen, in his "Corrections" to Custer's book. *My life on the Plains,* insisted that Kicking Bird, "acknowledged the best and most reliable chief of the Kiowas," reported in to Fort Cobb several days after the Washita attack. This was verified by a letter from Custer to his wife, Libby, from Fort Cobb on December 19. Kicking Bird, he noted, had just arrived with word that the Kiowas were on their way to Fort Cobb.[40]

Even as these events with Sheridan and Custer were played out on the Washita, a clash between the Kiowas and U.S. troops took place on the North Fork of the Red River. On Christmas Day 1868 another arm of Sheridan's invasion force under Maj. A. W. Evans out of Fort Bascom, New Mexico, located a Comanche village encampment on the North Fork near where Dodge had first met the Kiowas in 1834. After overwhelming and destroying a Comanche village at the mouth of Devil's Canyon, Evans's command was harassed by bonneted warriors from the bluffs along the river. These were Kiowas under Woman's Heart (Man-yi-ten) who had come to support their Comanche allies. The action was inconclusive as Evans continued his march back to the north. That night the Indians burned the grass on the windward side of the command and at daybreak took shots at the troops.[41]

Sheridan continued to hold Satanta and Lone Wolf in irons as he transferred his base from Fort Cobb to the Medicine Bluff Creek, where in early January 1869 he established Camp Wichita, soon renamed Fort Sill. The Kiowa bands followed. Their chiefs went to Sheridan and argued for release of the two men, claiming the Kiowas were all in except one band they had thrown away.[42]

Sheridan also acted against civilians in the area whom he felt were an interference to the peaceful resettlement of the tribes. On January 26, 1869, he issued field orders directing the expulsion by February 15 of Dutch Bill Greiffenstein. He accused the trader of furnishing powder, lead, and food to the warring Indians, as well as buying 450 head of stolen Texas cattle from the Caddo Indians. Sheridan let it be known by word that if Greiffenstein did not depart immediately, he would be hanged. Walkley and two other men were likewise ejected for their part in the cattle transaction.[43]

On February 15 Sheridan held an interview with Satanta, Lone Wolf, and Comanche chief Horseback. Both Kiowas insisted they were ready to be peaceful and stop their raiding.

"Now I have taken the white man by the hand," Lone Wolf declared, "and it is strong, and our road will be white and pure and plain, until we are old men and die."

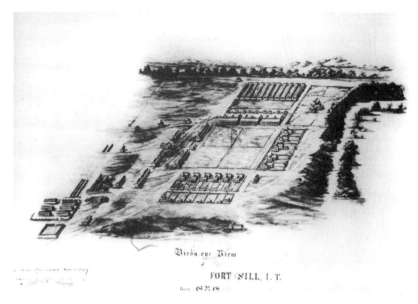

Fort Sill, Indian Territory, an agency for the Kiowas and Comanches. Courtesy Archives and Manuscript Division, Oklahoma Historical Society.

"Now my heart is glad," Satanta told Sheridan. "I have cut off fighting. I hope you and General Custer will cut off fighting."

"I am willing to do as you say," Horseback said quietly.[44]

Sheridan was not yet satisfied. He called still another conference with over fifty chiefs in full dress present.[45] Kicking Bird was at the circle in front of Sheridan's headquarters tent along with Black Eagle, Stumbling Bear, Timbered Mountain, and others. Sheridan came out of the tent and stood before them to make his pronouncement.

"Since the treaty at Medicine Lodge Creek," he told the chiefs, "in which you agreed to behave yourselves, you have committed a great many murders and robberies. . . . Satanta and Lone Wolf have promised to do everything in their power to keep their people here, and to prevent any of these crimes hereafter."[46]

If the chiefs were willing to do that, he concluded, he would issue their annuity goods and be on good terms with them. Kicking Bird joined the others in promising good behavior. Keim was greatly impressed: "The manner of some of the orators," he wrote, "was very striking. Tall and majestic in figure, with an air of boundless freedom, a grace of gesture, a flexibility of intonation, and harmony of expression, these savage warriors were the embodiment of dignity and elocutionary effect."[47]

Sheridan felt he had resolved the difficulty with the Kiowas and Comanches, at least within his department. He released Satanta and Lone Wolf from their bondage. After reviewing the troops at Fort Sill on February 23, he and Keim set off north for Kansas. Custer would follow with the Seventh Cavalry and Nineteenth Kansas in early March 1869, first scouring westward into the Texas Panhandle in search of the Cheyennes and two women captives they held. After a long march, he located Medicine Arrow's camp on the Sweetwater River and rescued the two women. He also captured three Cheyennes, taking them with him as prisoners to Camp Supply and on to Fort Hays, Kansas.

Fort Sill was now garrisoned by four companies of Tenth U.S. (Buffalo Soldier) Cavalry and two Sixth Infantry under the command of Col. Benjamin H. Grierson. A correspondent reported from there on March 18, 1869, that around 4,000 Indians were in the vicinity. In addition to Comanches, Apaches, Arapahos, and Caddos, the Kiowas were 700 strong under Satanta, Lone Wolf, Black Eagle, and Kicking Bird.[48]

Wichita agent Henry Shanklin wrote that the presence of several thousand Kiowas and Comanches had virtually halted work in the fields by the Wichitas and other Leased District tribes, who had to spend day and night guarding their stock.[49] A 1869 census listed the Kiowa bands as Satanta, with around 180 members; Kicking Bird, 180; Lone Wolf, 336; Black Eagle, 120; Timbered Mountain, 88; Tee-haus-an, 40; and Big Bow, 864, for a total of 1,808.[50]

Col. A. G. Boone, who had replaced Leavenworth, continued on for a time as agent for the Kiowas, Comanches, and Wichitas at Fort Sill. An important change was about to take place in U.S. Indian relations, however, and it would greatly impact the Kiowas and Kicking Bird.

12

As Would Have William Penn

When Ulysses S. Grant became president on March 4, 1869, the western Indian situation was in a crisis. In addition to Indian troubles south of the Platte River, the powerful Sioux were resisting the invasion of their country north of that stream. On December 21, 1866, a combined force of Sioux and Northern Cheyenne lured Capt. William J. Fetterman's command of eighty-one officers and men into a trap north of Fort Philip Kearny in Wyoming and wiped them out. The government had been forced to accede to Sioux demands and close both forts Phil Kearny and C. F. Smith.

Between the Platte and the Arkansas, the Cheyennes and Arapahos, with Sioux assistance, were still resisting U.S. presence in wagon commerce and migration, railroad expansion across Kansas, and the forward thrust of white settlements. Although Texas had divested itself of virtually all of its Indian population, the frontiers of the foundling state remained under persistent danger from tribal incursions.

The U.S. government was receiving severe criticism for its handling of the Indian tribes. Military abuses such as Col. John M. Chivington's massacre of Black Kettle's village at Sand Creek and Hancock's burning of the Cheyenne-Sioux village, along with thriving corruption among Indian agents and military post traders, had caused a rising wave of protest, particularly from religious organizations. Soon after taking office, Grant was persuaded to turn the management of the Plains tribes over to the Society of Friends, the Quakers. The humane and benevolent dealings with the Indians by their historical antecedent, William Penn, had been a success story of American colonial history. Grant ordered the U.S. Army under Gen. William T. Sherman to give full support to the Quakers in their work with the tribes.

Grant named Ely S. Parker, his former military aide-de-camp and a Quaker, commissioner of Indian Affairs. Quaker Enoch Hoag was appointed superintendent of the Central Superintendency with headquarters at Lawrence, Kansas. Brinton Darlington, an elderly Quaker, was assigned to establish a Cheyenne and Arapaho agency at Pond Creek, Indian Territory. Jonathan Richards, a Quaker from Philadelphia, went to the Wichita agency; and Quaker Lawrie Tatum, an Iowa farmer, became agent for the Kiowas and Comanches at Fort Sill.

Other Quakers enlisted as teachers, clerks, farmers, and carpenters and for other jobs at the Indian agencies. Virtually none of them had any experience in dealing with Indians, let alone with the unruly Plains tribes.

Quaker Vincent Colyer, secretary of the Board of Indian Commissioners, paid a visit to Fort Sill in March 1869. He found numerous Indians of various tribes, including Kiowas, camped in the area.

> The women and men were, some of them, half naked, and nearly all were in their native costume of blanket and buffalo robe, with bow and arrow, carbine, or revolvers. They were nearly all mounted on ponies and seemed awkward when dismounted. They are the finest riders in the world, and when seen moving about on their ponies and horses, with their bright-colored blankets, are the most picturesque people imaginable. The children are especially interesting, bright and intelligent looking.[1]

Agent Tatum arrived at Fort Sill during midsummer to take over the Kiowa-Comanche agency from Boone. He immediately busied himself with developing the agency. Boone had constructed an adobe warehouse to hold annuity goods. In fear that Cache Creek would flood, Tatum relocated the warehouse to a stone building on higher ground. In the fall he traveled to Chicago to purchase machinery for a sawmill, a shingle maker, and millstones for grinding corn. At the same time he hired ten men and four women, with two children, as employees of the agency.[2]

Tatum had seventy acres of land plowed and instructed the Wichitas and Caddos, who were planters by cultural habit, in the white man's method of farming. The buffalo-hunting Kiowas and Comanches were little interested in such activity. They were happy to follow their long tradition of enjoying the corn, melon, and other produce of the more sedentary tribes, at times through trade and at times through plunder.

Wichita village and crops. Courtesy and Manuscripts Division, Oklahoma Historical Society.

Although the Wichitas liked being near their ancestral home surrounding the Wichita Mountains, they were pleased that Tatum soon moved them and the Caddos back to the Wichita agency on the Washita under the supervision of Richards.

"The great danger and trouble is that when their crops are raised," an observer noted, "that the Cheyennes and Arapahoes, only forty miles north, and the Kiowas and Comanches, only thirty miles south, will raid in, and destroy and eat up their crops."[3]

Because of Sheridan's rough treatment of them at Fort Sill, many Kiowa and Comanche bands avoided the agency there for a time. Some went to Camp Supply for their annuities. John S. Simpson, Cheyenne interpreter at Camp Supply, reported in June 1869 that the Kiowas and Comanches were coming in slowly to that post.[4]

Few of the Plains bands were at Supply in August when members of a U.S. special Indian commission arrived there. The three commissioners conducted interviews at Supply with Arapaho chief Little Raven and Cheyenne chief Medicine Arrows before moving on to Fort Sill. There on August 20 the officials met in council with an assemblage of Kiowas, Comanches, Prairie Apaches, Wichitas, Wacos, Caddos, and Tawacaros. Satanta, Kicking Bird, Tohawson, Raven Lance, Stumbling Bear, Woman's Heart, and Timbered Mountain represented the Kiowas. Agent Tatum and Col. Benjamin H. Grierson, commander of Fort Sill, were present.[5]

The Quakers opened the council with a short prayer, with the chiefs rising respectfully to their feet. Commission chairman Felix R. Brunot announced that the president had sent them to hear what the Indians had to say and learn what might best be done for the mutual benefit of the whites and the Indians. He urged the tribes to submit peacefully to the authority of the United States, to give up their wandering and savage habits, adapt to farming and living in houses like the white man, and permit their children to be schooled. Satanta spoke for the Kiowas. He said:

> We have tried the white man's road and found it hard; we find nothing on it but a little corn, which hurts our teeth; no sugar; no coffee. But we want to walk in the white man's road. We want to have guns, breech-loading carbines, ammunition and caps. These are a part of the white man's road, and yet you want us to go back to making arrow-heads, which are used only by bad, foolish Indians, and have always been a mark of what was barbarous and evil.[6]

Comanche chiefs Milky Way (Es-sa-hab-et) and Shaking Hand (Mow-way) said they were ready to live in the houses that had been promised to the chiefs at Medicine Lodge. But Waco chief Buffalo Goad warned: "You ask the Kiowas and others to settle down, but they will not do it on the rations you give them."[7]

As a result of the council, the committee recommended an increase in the annuities to include various cooking utensils such as iron frying pans, tin cups, Dutch ovens, skillets, and kettles. It was also stoutly proposed that blankets and drill be substituted for the coats and pants that had usually been issued to the Indians; also cloth for leggings instead of the useless stockings.[8]

Meanwhile, Cheyenne-Arapaho agent Darlington and his son-in-law, J. R. Townsend, arrived at Pond Creek in northern Indian Territory during early August and began toiling under a torrid sun to erect an annuity storehouse. The Cheyennes and Arapahos refused to come there, however. Their ponies did not like the brackish water, and the herds were far too available to Osage and white horse thieves. As a result, Darlington decided to move his operations west to Camp Supply.

During August a Quaker delegation from Ohio composed of John Butler, Achilles Pugh, and Thomas H. Stanley arrived in the Territory to visit the tribes and encourage them to adopt "the habits of civilized and christianized society."[9] In Kansas they procured the piloting services of Dutch Bill Greiffenstein, who was further assigned by General Hazen to escort Darlington from Pond Creek to Supply. The men arrived at Fort Sill while the commission was conducting its talks with the tribes.

In a letter to the *Emporia News,* Stanley reported that Comanche chief Asahava, once a great war chief, had told the Kiowas that if they went on the warpath he would take the side of the Americans against them. Stanley noted also that the tribes were very unhappy over the stopage of their sugar and coffee rations.[10]

The commission's promise to make improvements in the annuity program failed to pacify the hungry Kiowa warriors. On January 15, 1870, Lt. Col. Anderson D. Nelson, commanding at Fort Supply, reported that a Texas herd driven by a trail boss named Jacob Hershfield and sixteen men plus some Caddo Indians had been intercepted on the eleventh by a body of Kiowa Indians under Satanta forty miles below the post on the North Canadian near present Seiling, Oklahoma. The drovers were robbed of supplies and money. Satanta's men stampeded the herd and then poured arrows into 150–200 head of the cattle merely for sport before Kicking Bird arrived and stopped the slaughter. Hershfield declared that Kicking Bird had saved the lives of himself and his men.[11]

On January 19 Maj. Meredith H. Kidd with four companies of Tenth Cavalry met the Kiowas twenty and a half miles below Supply. The Kiowas were reluctant to talk with Kidd, but Cheyenne chief Medicine Arrows, who was riding with Kidd's detachment, persuaded Kicking Bird to come forth. Other Kiowa chiefs followed. Kidd asked why the Kiowas had killed the cattle, which had been headed for Camp Supply to feed the Cheyennes and Arapahos. The Kiowas said the herders had told them the cattle were for them also, and they were hungry. Kidd advised them to go to their own agency at Fort Sill. He invited Kicking Bird to his tent to eat with him, and upon leaving the chief said he would take his advice. He added: "When we reach there I will get a paper from the agency and come to Camp Supply, and fix it all right about the cattle."[12]

At Camp Supply Nelson had contracted for two private citizens to cultivate a garden five miles west of the fort. Fresh vegetables were badly needed by troops on the frontier. When two of the men's horses were stolen, Nelson sent an officer and five men out to protect the garden. This evidently incited some of the young warriors, for on May 29, 1870, a party of Kiowas and Apaches attacked and drove off the guards. They ran their horses through the garden plot, destroying it. Nelson reported that a week later a large band of Kiowas and Apaches made a dash against Camp Supply, and a fight ensued for some time.[13]

The scalped, stripped, and arrow-spiked corpse of a teamster was found three miles south of Supply. The Kiowas were held to blame when detachments arriving at the post that same day reported seeing a Kiowa war party with fresh scalps and stolen stock on the road to Fort Dodge.

When an escort detachment stymied a war party that was threatening a wagon train on the Cimarron, the Kiowas proceeded to Bear Creek Mail Station south of Dodge. There, after receiving food, they shot and killed two men guarding the station corral and seriously wounded a sergeant.[14]

Simultaneous to the tour by the Quaker committee, a story appeared in the *Leavenworth Call* and was reprinted in April in the *Kansas Daily Tribune* of Lawrence. It read:

> Kicking Bird, chief of the Kiowas, came into Camp Supply the other day, and becoming drunk and disorderly, Lieut. Col. Nelson ordered him put in the guard house, but soon after ordered his release. Kicking Bird then went to the commanding officer and informed him that he was no longer the white man's friend. Shortly after, news came into Camp Supply that Kicking Bird had taken a herd of 250 cattle belonging to Carney & Fenlon, of this city. This well-known Kiowa chief then proposed to scalp the herders, but on the intervention of a friendly savage, they were allowed to come into the post unharmed. Major Kidd with four companies of the Tenth cavalry, started in pursuit, but as yet nothing has been learned of the result.[15]

On his return to Lawrence, however, Superintendent Hoag reported that the Quaker committee had thoroughly investigated the matter and found the facts to be (1) that Kicking Bird was not drunk, (2) that he issued no threats, (3) that only eight cattle were killed, and (4) the deeds were committed by hungry Indians in search of a meal.[16]

Having been instructed to find a new site for his Cheyenne and Arapaho agency, Darlington moved to a location on the North Canadian River near present El Reno, Oklahoma. It would eventually become known as the Darlington Agency. A committee of Quakers met with the prairie tribes there on March 13 and 14, 1870. The Kiowas were represented, although none of their leaders was identified in the council records as having spoken. Superintendent Hoag told the chiefs:

> Brothers, the first treaty ever made with the Indians was made two hundred years ago, towards the sun-rising, near Washington. The man who made that treaty was a good man. His name was William Penn. This treaty was never broken, but was kept as long as William Penn lived. He and his red brothers lived in peace. We are here today to walk in Wm. Penn's road. We want the Indians to be his children, and we want to be his children.[17]

E-sa-da-wa of the Wichitas, Tonah of the Caddos, Toshewa and Esahabbee of the Comanches, John White of the Shawnees, Full Chief of the Kaws, War Coopa of the Caddos, and Buffalo Goad of the Wacos all spoke, expressing their desire to live in peace with the white man and asking for assistance in adapting to farming. The Quakers promised their full support. After the council the committee divided, one group going on to Camp Supply to talk with the Cheyennes and Arapahos and the other to Fort Sill to meet with the other Kiowa and Comanche chiefs "who have given our country, especially the frontiers, so much trouble."[18]

Efforts by the Quakers during 1870 to induce the Kiowas and Comanches to lead a quiet life as reservation farmers did little to alter the old prairie style of existence. Both tribes had moved south from Camp Supply to their reservation, making their camps on Cache Creek and the Washita. Nelson had told them to do so because their annuities would be issued at Fort Sill. But the government was very slow in delivering the issue goods, and other treaty promises had gone unfulfilled.

"Little has been done for my people by the whites," Comanche war chief Esa-habbee told the Quakers, "and although I am a young man, I fear I shall grow old and gray waiting for these promises of the white man. . . . How many years will it be before the Indians on the Wachita [Washita] river have cattle, houses, and farming implements, which the white man has promised us?"[19]

Another factor strongly affecting tribal behavior was the relaxed discipline at Fort Sill. The mild-mannered Quakers were prone to be especially forgiving of Indian indiscretions. Sheridan and Custer were gone; and Grierson, a strong supporter of the Quaker program, soon gained a reputation for weakness with the tribes. A civilian visitor to Fort Sill expressed the opinion of militant frontier whites:

> Colonel Grierson, the commander of this post, is said to be an honest man, and has no stock in Government swindles. . . . But as a commander he is certainly inefficient. He is not only afraid of the Indians, but what is worse has let the Indians find it out; they treat him with most perfect contempt. "What?" said old Satank, "you 'fraid of Gierson? I no 'fraid of him. He no big chief—dare not do anything. I was bigger chief at ten years old—could do as I wanted to. I'd like to drive him and his smoked soldiers out."[20]

Such criticism rankled Grierson, who wrote to Tatum: "It seems that I am too much of a *Quaker* myself for a soldier and too much of a *peace man* to be left in charge of military affairs of this Reservation. Had I launched out and killed a few Indians, I would no doubt have been considered by certain parties successful."[21]

Grierson reported optimistically to superiors that the tribes, knowing the buffalo would soon be gone, were ready to have their lands broken and fenced.[22] This was far from the case, particularly for warriors who still hearkened to the chase, horse stealing, and raiding. Both the

Kiowas and Comanches left their reservation area and headed to the North Fork of the Red River country for their spring buffalo hunt in May 1870. These annual gatherings and the ensuing Sun Dances inevitably spawned war parties of young men eager for action and tribal reputation.[23]

Already, tribal entrepreneurs had been quietly eyeing the tantalizing horse and mule herds of both the agency and the Fort Sill military. On May 28 the Comanches raided Tatum's corral and herded off twenty-eight animals. A party led by White Horse was not to be outdone; on June 12 the Kiowas took seventy-three mules from the post quartermaster's corral.[24]

Quaker teacher Josiah Butler thought the raid, "a most insolent, daring and adroit feat," had resulted from Grierson's threat to send soldiers and forcibly bring the reluctant Indians in to the reservation. He wrote in his diary: "6th month, 22d, a man named Lukens was shot by the Indians about 200 yards from where we were sleeping. The firing waked us up and, by the time I was dressed, they carried him to our door. He had received a carbine shot through the back and was in a critical condition but he finally recovered. The same morning others, who were farther from us, were killed and scalped."[25]

Big Tree, a noted Kiowa raider, decided that he could top the post corral raid by stealing the entire Fort Sill horse herd. He had observed that the mounts were grazed daily on a field near the post, often tended by only two or three guards. Recruiting an eighty-man war party, Big Tree arranged for ten of the men to make the initial steal. He and the others would then drive the horses west to the wilds of the Staked Plains. One warrior of the advance force, however, could not resist the chance to shoot and scalp a man on the way, and Big Tree's great plan was ruined. Still, the Kiowas were not to be denied. One portion of them attacked a government wagon train camped near the agency while others were chasing horses out of the agency corral. A Mexican teamster was killed and a quartermaster employee wounded in the affair.[26]

Tatum was greatly disturbed by these events. Calling his Quaker staff together, he told them he understood the danger they faced and offered them the opportunity to leave. Everyone but schoolmaster Josiah Butler and his wife accepted and departed with the next bull train to the East. After consulting with Grierson, Tatum decided to withhold the Indians' rations pending the return of the stolen animals. But his Quaker's conscience, which trusted his fellow man, drove him to remove the soldier guard Grierson had placed over the annuity beef herd. The Indians then gleefully helped themselves.[27]

Big Tree was sent to prison at Huntsville, Texas, along with
Satanta. Courtesy Western History Collection, University of
Oklahoma.

The transition from Sheridan's severe military restraints to the
Quakers' benign peace policy had released the pent-up marauding urges
of the Kiowa warriors. A warring mood now dominated in the tribe, and
Kicking Bird's position as a peace advocate was beginning to tarnish his
reputation as a warrior, even though his daring and ability in battle were
well proven. Although there is no record of it, Stumbling Bear claimed
that even during the short time Hazen was agent, Kicking Bird had killed
and scalped five men.[28] Two of these could have been soldiers in Texas
whom Kicking Bird and Stumbling Bear waylaid while returning from a
dance at Jacksboro, Texas, in early 1867.[29]

But now Kicking Bird was being chided as a coward by the war
faction of the tribe. This attacked the very core of respect for his
chieftainship and was causing him to lose face with his people. Clearly,

he needed to regain the warrior prestige that had originally won him his office.

To do so, in June 1870 Kicking Bird led a sizable war party on a foray into Texas. Just who was responsible for some of the depredations reported that month, however, is not clear. On June 16 the herd of C. P. Hamilton was attacked north of the Red River by a party of about thirty Kiowas. Around 139 head of cattle were taken, along with 16 horses. Five drovers were mortally wounded. Eight days later the consolidated herds of W. R. Baker and F. C. Bulkley, on their way to supply the Fort Sill bands with fresh beef, were struck by ten or twelve Kiowas who drove off 205 of the longhorns.[30]

On July 9 Kicking Bird and his warriors crossed the Red River and stampeded a Kansas-bound herd in Montague County, Texas. They took several horses and mules, blankets, gold coin, and other property and disabled a yoke of oxen. Two drovers were killed, and one was captured.[31] From there, Kicking Bird swept into Jack County. He had laid down strict guidelines that no one was to leave the party to act on his own. Despite the orders, a few of his braves broke away and robbed a mail stage at Rock Station.

When news of this incident reached nearby Fort Richardson, a detachment of fifty-three Sixth Cavalry troopers under Capt. Curwen B. McClellan was sent forth. McClellan intercepted Kicking Bird in Baylor County west of present-day Seymour, Texas. The officer initiated a cavalry charge, but Kicking Bird quickly formed a defensive line and threw back the troops. The Kiowa chief then counterattacked aggressively, sending out a flanking movement to cut off and attack McClellan's men, who had dismounted to form a skirmish line. Heavy fire from the Kiowas drove the troops back farther. Kicking Bird, who rode at the lead of his men, is said to have impaled a cavalryman with his lance. Twelve of the troopers were wounded and three others were killed before Kicking Bird withdrew at sunset on July 12. In his report on the affair, McClellan applauded Kicking Bird's military tactics in the engagement.[32] Kiowa Old Man Horse gave his account of Kicking Bird's raid:

> There is a great assembly among the different bands where he [Kicking Bird] addressed the tribe and made suggestions as to what is to be done for the benefit of the tribe. His first step was to take the white man by the hand to make peace and take the advice of the great white father in Washington and make peace. When they [the war chiefs] reared up and opposed this plan, Kicking Bird said, "It is wrong to go on war path." But they wouldn't listen to him. So a great party went to Texas to raid and murder and came home to celebrate. Chiefs hostile to him said to him, "Kicking Bird, if you don't quit opposing us, we are going to kill

you." He said, "Alright go ahead." "Kicking Bird," they said, "you are nothing but a low-down unrecognized man, no longer a chief." Kicking Bird said, "It may be true, but I am trying to put you in a good road which will be a protection for the lives of the women and children."

Whenever they come from the war party and scalp dance, they criticize Kicking Bird, saying, "you stay so close to the whites you never go past Rainy Mountain Creek." . . . They put up a challenge thus: "We must test [you] out to see whether you are a coward. If you show cowardice in battle, we will kill you." Kicking Bird agreed. He said he wanted to be friends with whites and the army. He was very sorry, but he would accept the challenge.[33]

The war party consisted of eighty to a hundred men, all decked for war with their paint, medicine, and war bonnets and armed with bows, lances, and pistols. They rode south, and on a creek west of Seymour they met a troop of soldiers. The soldiers saw the Indians coming and dismounted, establishing a line of firing positions in the grass.

Kicking Bird was mounted on [a] solid iron-gray horse. He was armed with lance and shield. He made a talk before the band, [saying] you will recognize me now. They waited to see him [go] first. The firing started. He rode right through the soldiers and lanced one in the middle as they rose up from shooting position. Then he shouted, "See what I have done. Now let's see you do it." They were scared to. He was unharmed in the heavy shooting. Their mouths were shut. "Now," he said, "You join me [and] let's have peace. . . . I am going to quit now, are you satisfied? You can now do your part. I shouldn't have done it, but I had to satisfy you to take my advice." It was hard for him, a great burden. They still hated him, didn't get over it. They were jealous of him.[34]

Implausibly perhaps, but on his return to the reservation Kicking Bird became engaged in rounding up stolen stock agent Tatum was demanding before further rations would be issued. On August 7 Lone Wolf and other Kiowa leaders came into Fort Sill with their bands to obtain rations. Kicking Bird's band may have been among the group, since they brought with them twenty-seven of the seventy-three mules stolen from the quartermaster's corral.

Another band brought in Mrs. Gottleib Koozer and her five children who had been taken captive during a July 10 raid led by White Horse. Gottleib Koozer had been killed. Tatum refused to issue any goods until the captives were returned. He was eventually able to ransom the family, along with a boy named Martin Kilgore who was captured at the same time, for $100 each.[35] On August 18 the Kiowas arrived at the agency en masse and gave up seven Texas captives.[36]

In November 1870 Dr. William Nicholson, acting as a general agent for the Society of Friends, made an investigative tour of the Indian Territory agencies. From the Cheyenne and Arapaho agency, he and several companions, including Enoch Hoag and Brinton Darlington, traveled to the Wichita agency, arriving on November 26. They found that Richards was away on a trip to Lawrence, and the Indians of the agency were off on a buffalo hunt. Moving on to Fort Sill, they were welcomed by Tatum. Most of his charges were on the hunt also. Nicholson learned that the Indians' annuities, due by treaty on October 15, had not yet arrived. The goods had left Fort Harker, Kansas, by ox team only on November 7, and it would take about two months on the 350-mile road for them to reach Fort Sill. The agency commissary had been buying and borrowing sugar for months, and its stock of bacon was virtually exhausted.[37]

In his diary, Nicholson recorded the fact that Chief Little Heart, who reportedly had killed a Mexican at Camp Supply the previous summer, had recently died out on the prairie. The Quaker also heard an unconfirmed report of more Indian raids into Montague County, Texas, in December. A woman and three children had been killed, another woman wounded and scalped, and a boy slightly wounded. Three children in the house had been left unhurt. The perpetrators were not identified.

On November 29 the Quakers held a meeting with the Kiowas with Lone Wolf, Kicking Bird, Stumbling Bear, and Satanta present.[38] Lone Wolf, acting as the principal spokesman, complained that Nelson had driven the Kiowas away from Camp Supply. The chief said the Kiowas had gone there because they had been made sick by farming and wanted to try their old way of life again. Lone Wolf further complained that their annuities had not come. His women were naked and needed blankets, kettles, and many other items, while his men needed powder and lead with which to kill turkey, deer, and buffalo for food—and also to kill the Texans, who had killed many Kiowas. He was very disappointed that the Quakers were not big enough chiefs to bring them presents.

When invited to attend the first meeting of the general council of Indian Territory tribes at Okmulgee on December 5, Lone Wolf declared that neither the Kiowas nor the Plains Apaches would go. The white people would pay no attention to them, he insisted—all their words would fall to the ground.

Satanta joined in the demand for ammunition. When pressed to stop his warring with Texas, he replied—evidently with some sarcasm—that if the Great Father would move Texas farther off, he and his men would not raid there any more. Satanta wanted Camp Supply closed. He rejected the suggestion of going to Washington. First the Great Father would have to send some powder and lead so the Kiowas could defend themselves against the white people.

Nicholson estimated the Kiowa population at 1,896, the Prairie Apaches at 300, the Comanches at 3,742. A census dated December 31, 1870, listed sixteen bands. The eight Ag-chet or Cold-Weather Kiowa bands included Kicking Bird, 180; Satanta, 180; Running Bear, 60; Lone Wolf, 300; Timbered Mountain, 78; Black Eagle, 120; Little Mountain (Tohawson), 108; and Stumbling Bear, 60, for a total 1,086. Eight Quah-ha-das, or Buffalo Hunters, bands included Big Bow, 180; Heid-sik, 90; Eagle Heart, 78; Woman's Heart, 108; Little Mountain (Tohawson, Satanta's son), 78; Satank, 78; Buffalo Shank, 156; and Runaway Bear, 42—total 810.[39]

By the end of 1870 the schism between the peace-minded and the war-determined Kiowa leaders had become pronounced. The increased presence of both the U.S. military and the Quakers was bringing the issue closer and closer to determination for tribal leaders. Kicking Bird was clearly becoming the leading advocate for an accommodation with the United States and for moving toward peaceful coexistence. He was supported by Stumbling Bear and other peace-minded chiefs.

In opposition, however were war leaders such as Satanta, Lone Wolf, Big Tree, Maman-ti, and White Horse. These hostile war chiefs could offer good arguments for their behavior. Just look at the Wichitas, they said. That tribe had been the original occupant of the country from the Red River to the Arkansas when the whites arrived. Their horse herds were among the largest on the prairie. But they had never fought with the United States, and now they had virtually nothing. The Kiowas had fought back, and they had a 60 by 100-mile reservation.

"They [the Wichitas] say that when they obey their treaties," a visitor noted, "respect their agents, and live peaceably, the Government forgets them, and does much more for the wild tribes who are constantly raiding upon the whites."[40]

No one on the frontier could dispute the validity of their argument.

13

Manacles for Satanta

When Satanta suggested that the government move Texas if it wanted the Kiowas to stop their raiding, he was pointing to the peculiarity of Fort Sill's geographical situation. "The agency of the Kiowas and Comanches," an observer noted, "is undoubtedly the worst agency in the Indian Territory—just far enough from Texas to make raiding into that State easy for the Indians. The nearest settlement in Texas is only sixty miles away (Red River Station); the same distance from Red River Station to Fort Richardson, the nearest post in Texas."[1]

The northern border of postwar Texas was direly unprotected from Indian Territory raiding. A line of posts composed of Forts Richardson, Belknap, Griffin, and Phantom Hill now stretched across the path of Indian Territory invaders. These garrisons, however, were poorly manned and equipped and still relied in part on the Tonkawa scouts, a tribe others north of the Red River detested, charging that they practiced cannibalism.[2] To make matters even more difficult to control, Fort Sill was in a different military department than the Texas forts. Troops from Fort Sill were assigned jurisdiction north of the Red River and troops from Texas south of the river. Further, no mail route or other communication existed between Fort Sill and Texas. A curtain of obscurity thus sheltered and protected the actions of Kiowa and Comanche raiders in Texas from immediate attention in the Territory.

Mostly, the Kiowa warriors had held to their camps through the winter months of 1870. In January 1871, however, a party of Kiowa and

Cheyenne warriors under Big Bow, Eagle Heart, and Fast Bear invaded Young County, Texas, and massacred four black teamsters near Weatherford. Kicking Bird reported the matter to Tatum and offered for himself and his men to go with the troops to capture the guilty parties.[3]

Several other raids resulting in killings and robberies took place in this area directly south from Fort Sill in the weeks that followed.[4] The news of these actions eventually reached Tatum, who wrote to his Quaker superiors on March 11 that he suspected the Kiowa militants were determined to provoke a war.[5] Meanwhile, the tribes of eastern Indian Territory, who were meeting at the Creek settlement of Okmulgee, voted to hold a conference with the Kiowas to persuade them to settle down and live peacefully. Superintendent Enoch Hoag eagerly supported the idea and called a general council for the tribes of the region at the Wichita agency on April 24 "that these tribes may be drawn from their warring and raiding, to a more industrious, peaceful and happy life."[6]

Rainy weather delayed the council until April 29. On that day, however, thirteen tribes gathered in the shade of a grove of trees near the Wichita agency. These tribes included the woodland Cherokees, Creeks, Seminoles, Chickasaws, Shawnees, and Delawares and the Plains-inhabiting Caddo, Wichita, Comanche, Kiowa, Apache, Cheyenne, and Arapaho tribes.[7] Log seats lined the fifty-foot-diameter council circle, while blankets had been spread inside the ring for the leading members of each tribe and the Quaker agents. Kicking Bird represented the Kiowas.

James Vann, second chief of the Cherokees and council chairman, passed the traditional calumet among the inner circle. Each chief puffed at the two-foot stem of a large red stone pipe filled with ta-loneh, the Cherokee mixture of tobacco and sumac. Kicking Bird, one of the few chiefs who did not smoke, accepted the stem but did not puff at it. Tatum gratefully followed his example.

Each tribe spoke a different language, and it would be necessary for different interpreters to translate every speech for every tribe. Vann opened the meeting with a call to Indian brotherhood and unity. "The Cherokee is the oldest brother of the Indian tribes," he said. "To them is entrusted the white path and the key of peace. All nations should go hand in hand, and always have a good talk."[8]

This was followed by Micco Hutkee of the Creeks, who also spoke for peace among the tribes:

> Our forefathers told us that something white was coming up beneath the rising sun that would distress us. This represented the white man, who has distressed and impoverished us, and moved from towards the rising sun in the direction of the setting sun. Although we are apparently

of three races, the red, the white and the black, we were all created by the same Great Spirit, and should live in love and peace together.[9]

Vann held up a string of white beads and took it around the circle for all to touch it. He then presented it to Kicking Bird along with a small piece of tobacco wrapped in more white beads. Other chiefs were similarly rewarded.

The following day Cherokee principal chief William Ross opened the talks. The dignified, Princeton-educated tribesman dressed and looked far more white than Indian. He recognized that fact but insisted that "It is the heart, and not the color, that makes the man. I speak to you as an Indian. I feel as an Indian." Noting that those attending the council represented around 60,000 Indians, he declared that his people were now living quietly, were prospering on their land, and were not "fading away like the snow in the warm sun."[10]

Assadawa of the Wichitas rose to his feet to complain that his people were not getting their just rations—a charge Tatum denied—and that he had heard that a railroad was to be built through his country. Elderly, peace-minded Comanche chief Toshawi, or Silver Brooch, who had signed the treaties of the Little Arkansas and Medicine Lodge, declared that he had been the first of his tribe to make peace with the whites and had never broken it. "As a bright fire in the night," he said, "so have I been to the Indians of the plains."[11]

Kicking Bird then rose to speak. "I like the talk of yesterday pretty well," he said. "I cannot promise to accept it all at this time, but may in the future. You have often heard that the Kiowas were a bad and foolish people, which is true. The reason is our land has been taken from us, and we are not permitted to purchase ammunition. If you wish us to become a good people you must get Washington to do something for us, especially in furnishing us with guns and ammunition."[12]

After short speeches by a Chickasaw and a Shawnee, Ross invited the chiefs and agents to form a line, take one another's right hand, and with the left hand grasp the other's right arm at the shoulder, thus taking "the whole arm" in friendship.[13]

Kicking Bird's reservations about the peace-mindedness of the Kiowas was well-founded. The war faction of the tribe was noticeably absent from the meeting at the Wichita agency. After the council, both Tatum and Ross expressed fears that there would be much raiding during the coming summer, particularly in Texas.[14] Their concerns were soon borne out.

A major infraction occurred during May 1871 while General of the Army Sherman was making a personal inspection tour of frontier posts

General of the Army William T. Sherman narrowly missed two deadly confrontations with the Kiowas. Scharf, *History of St. Louis.*

in north Texas and the Indian Territory. On May 18 he along with two of his staff officers and Gen. Randolph B. Marcy left Fort Belknap in an army ambulance following the Butterfield stage route eastward. They were escorted by seventeen Tenth Cavalry buffalo soldiers, who rode in advance. Marcy, an original army explorer of North Texas and a keen observer, pointed out the remains of several ranches whose occupants had been either killed or driven out by Indian raids. Although the weather was turbulent, the land appeared peaceful as they passed along Salt Creek Prairie and nearby Cox Mountain, reaching Fort Richardson at sunset. The travelers had no suspicion that peering down on them from the summit of Cox Mountain as they passed were over 100 well-armed Kiowa and Comanche warriors.

Just who was the leader of the war party is disputed. Satanta later claimed the honor. Likely he was right, although some Kiowas said the party was really under the direction of Maman-ti.[15] Whichever, it was decided not to attack the small military entourage. The raiders would wait for a more rewarding target.

A new opportunity appeared at midafternoon in the form of a ten-wagon mule train moving slowly west from Weatherford, Texas, toward Fort Griffin. These wagons, belonging to the firm of Warren and Duposes, government contractors, were loaded with shelled and sacked corn. From high above on the hilltop, however, no one could tell what booty lay beneath the glistening canvas wagon tops. As far as the war party could tell, it was possible that the wagons were hauling guns and ammunition to the soldiers at Griffin.[16]

When wagonmaster Nathan S. Long saw the avalanche of horsemen swarming down the long slopes of the mountainside, he managed to form his wagons into a circle. This provided little defense against the intense carbine and revolver fire of the Kiowas. Long and four of his eleven men were killed in the initial charge, and the other seven made a run for a wooded area two miles away. Two of them were killed as they ran, and three others were wounded.

Fortunately for the five live teamsters, the warriors gave up chasing them to join in plundering the wagons. The principal prizes of the raid were the mules they cut from the traces and herded back north. One Kiowa warrior had been killed. The train survivors claimed Kiowa women were with the party and held their spare horses during the final charge on the wagons.[17]

Col. Ranald S. Mackenzie pursued the war party and mules with a force of Fourth Cavalry but lost the trail west of the North Fork of the Red River. Sherman, who learned of the attack when the survivors staggered into Fort Richardson, beefed up his escort and continued his inspection tour on north to Fort Sill. He arrived there on May 23 and immediately contacted agent Tatum to ask if any of his Indians had gone to Texas lately.[18]

At the time, Tatum could not answer the question. But four days later, on May 27, Kiowa bands began arriving at the post for rations. When some of the leading chiefs—Kicking Bird, Lone Wolf, Satanta, Big Tree, and Satank—came to the commissary for coffee and other rations, Tatum invited them to come to the council room. There he asked them if they knew about the wagon-train raid. Satanta, feeling secure from retribution under the new Quaker oversight, stepped forward to issue a litany of charges against Tatum and whites in general.

> I have been told that you have stolen a large portion of our annuity goods and given them to the Texans. I have repeatedly asked you for

arms and ammunition, which you have not furnished; and made many other requests, which have not been granted. You do not listen to my talk; and not only that, but the white people are preparing to build a railroad through our country, which will not be permitted. When General Custer was here two or three years ago, he arrested me and kept me in confinement for several days. But that is played out now. No more Indians are ever to be arrested.[19]

Having made these declarations, Satanta then vaingloriously stepped off into troublesome water:

On account of these grievances, I too, a short time ago, took about 100 of my warriors with the chiefs Satank, Eagle Heart, Big Bow, and Fast Bear, and went to Texas, where we found a mule train which we captured and killed 7 men. Three of our men got killed, but we are willing to call it even. If any other Indian comes here and claims the honor of leading the party, he will be lying about it, for I did it myself.[20]

Tatum was dumbfounded. Undoubtedly, he would have overlooked the brash charges, but it was impossible to ignore the confession of guilt regarding the wagon-train massacre. The agent immediately reported the matter to Sherman and Grierson, noting that all the Indians present at the time had verified Satanta's story. Going against the essence of Quaker policy, Tatum requested that Satanta along with Satank and Big Tree be arrested. Grierson agreed. First, however, he placed the entire garrison on alert.[21]

To effect the arrest, the chiefs were invited to attend a meeting on the front porch of Grierson's quarters. Sherman, Marcy, Grierson, and a number of staff officers assembled there. Satanta arrived ahead of the others and brashly repeated his claim of leading the wagon-train party. When he was told he was under arrest and would be tried for murder, however, the Kiowa tried to play down his involvement in the attack. Realizing he had gotten himself into deep trouble, he started for his horse. Grierson's orderly pulled a pistol and told Satanta to get back on the porch. The chief returned to his seat, at the same time saying he would rather be shot down like a warrior than be taken to prison.[22]

It was about then that Kicking Bird and Stumbling Bear, who had been notified that Satanta and other raid participants were to be arrested, arrived at the headquarters building on horseback. Seeing them approaching, Satanta excitedly urged them to hurry. The two chiefs shook hands with the officers, who patted them on the back and called them by name. Everyone took a seat on the porch except Sherman, who paced back and forth and did the talking. He wanted Kicking Bird to go back to the camps and tell the other chiefs to come forth. Satanta said he would go, but Sherman would not permit it. Kicking Bird untied his horse and rode back to the Kiowa camps. When he returned, ten other Kiowa chiefs, including Satank, were with him. They all took seats on the floor of the porch. Sherman spoke to Kicking Bird again: "Kicking Bird, the President has heard of you. He knows your name and has written about you. We are all depending on you."[23]

Sherman announced that he planned to arrest Satanta, Big Tree, Satank, and Black Eagle for their part in the wagon-train raid. Kicking Bird rose and through the interpreter made a plea for his fellow chiefs. He reminded the officers that he had worked to keep his men on the peace path and promised that he would see that the captured army mules were returned. Sherman answered that he appreciated what Kicking Bird had done but still insisted that the four Kiowas would be sent to prison.[24]

At the same time this conference was under way at Grierson's house, troops attempted to arrest Big Tree at the trader's store. The Kiowa escaped by diving through a window. He fled with bullets cutting the air about him, one creasing his head. He was finally captured, winded and ready to give up, and taken to join the others on the porch. Black Eagle, who witnessed Big Tree's arrest, quickly disappeared.[25]

Lone Wolf appeared on the drill grounds mounted on his horse. Kicking Bird waved for him to come forth. The Kiowa rode up to the porch and swung to the ground. Taking his blanket from his shoulders, he tied it around his waist. With bow and arrows in one hand and rifle in the other, he shoved his way through the line of soldiers in front of the building.

Lone Wolf handed the bow and arrows to Stumbling Bear, but he brandished the rifle while speaking excitedly in the Kiowa tongue that none of the whites could understand. Grierson grabbed the rifle barrel and, through interpreter Jones, attempted to calm the Kiowa. Lone Wolf's agitation subsided; but Stumbling Bear, now armed with the bow and arrows, became very perturbed. He turned to the other Kiowas.

"You see Kicking Bird talking to the whites?" he asked angrily. "He is a young man, but has good judgment. He has tried hard to keep you out of trouble, but you have paid no attention. See what trouble you have gotten us into. I haven't said anything up to now, but now I am going to be the first to die. I can look into your eyes and see that you are whipped. Every one of you is a chief, but you are acting like women."[26]

Stumbling Bear waited until the pacing Sherman was about to make a turn on the porch before he let his blanket fall and drew back the bow. One of the other chiefs yelled and grabbed his arm, causing the arrow to fly skyward. Lone Wolf attempted to bring his rifle to bear on Sherman, but Grierson leaped forward and wrestled him to the floor. Kicking Bird moved to separate the men, tripped, and fell on top of them. Somehow the men were untangled without a shot being fired.[27] Sherman described the scene in a letter to his son two days later:

> The guard[s] in front of the house, cocked their guns and aimed them, but we were all mixed up with the Indians, and to have fired at them, some of us would have been hit, besides what damage may have been done by the Indians, all of whom had guns, pistols, knives, bows and arrows. For a few minutes it looked as though a fight was inevitable, but after some moments we calmed them down and resumed our "talk."[28]

Another incident occurred on the post grounds when an officer and a squad of soldiers attempted to arrest a small group of Kiowas. The Indians ran to escape, and the soldiers fired, killing one of them.[29] Sherman gave credit to Kicking Bird for helping to prevent a major fight: "One of the warriors, Kicking Bird, whom I had known on the Arkansas some years ago, kept them [the Kiowas] quiet."[30]

He also indicated that Kicking Bird did all he could to save Satanta, offering to give up forty ponies and mules to be held until the wagon-train mules could be returned. Kicking Bird pleaded with Sherman not to send Satanta off until he could bring back his people. Upon learning of potential trouble, the Kiowas had instantly packed up and fled the post.

Satanta, Satank, and Big Tree were manacled and taken off to confinement in the post icehouse. Kicking Bird, Lone Wolf, and the other chiefs rode out to round up the bands that had fled during the melee. Sherman, scheduled to speak to the Okmulgee convention of the Five Civilized Nations, departed from Fort Sill on May 30.

Five days later Mackenzie arrived there to find that the Indians he had been chasing were under arrest. He was assigned to transport the three captives to Fort Richardson. On the morning of June 8, the shackled Kiowas were placed into two wagons loaded with shelled corn. A detachment of Fourth Cavalry waited in the saddle to provide escort.[31]

Satanta and Big Tree were submissive, but Satank was not. Although in handcuffs, the old warrior who had spoken so firmly for the Kiowas at Medicine Lodge could not accept his loss of freedom. He had vowed to kill someone in order to be killed himself. He had secreted a knife under his robe; but when they were being taken from their cell, Big Tree had grasped his hand and did not let go until they reached the wagons. Big Tree lifted Satank into a wagon by himself.[32]

Grierson had sent out word for all Indians to come and witness the departure of the prisoners. Although the order was not meant to include them, teacher Josiah Butler placed the children of the Caddo school in a

Kiowa war chief Satank (Set-ankeah, or Sitting Bear) vowed to die rather than go to prison. Courtesy Western History Collection, University of Oklahoma.

wagon under the care of Caddo chief George Washington and sent them to Fort Sill to observe the event. They were within speaking distance of Satank's wagon as it passed. Butler described what happened then:

> When Satank began to sing his death song, Washington dropped back out of reach of the bullets, but in plain sight. The two guards on the seat behind Satank, thinking of no danger, put their carbines in the bottom of the wagon. When about one mile from Fort Sill, Satank sat still, looking up for a few minutes—as Washington expressed it, "he spoke to God." He then pulled the shackles off his hand, tearing the skin with them, grabbed his knife and stabbed at the guards who, dodging, tumbled out of the wagon and escaped, though one of them was slightly wounded in the thigh. Satank then grabbed a carbine but, as there was some little fixture about it that he did not understand, he did not get to shoot. The soldiers fired on him at once, five or six balls entering his body and

causing immediate death. The Tonkawa scouts begged hard for his scalp, as he had killed some of their own people, but they were not allowed to take it. They then begged for a blanket with some of his blood on [it], which they were allowed to take. Satanta and Big Tree, in the other wagon, remained quiet. Satank's body was taken back to Fort Sill and buried; the other two Kiowas were taken on.[33]

Washington rode with the party for some distance to receive any message Satanta might have for the Kiowas. "Tell the Kiowas that I may never see any of them again," Satanta told the Caddo, "that I now wish them never to raid anymore into Texas or anywhere else."[34]

Satanta and Big Tree were tried in the Jack County courthouse at Jacksboro during July. Agent Tatum and Mackenzie were present in the packed courtroom as the defense attorney listed the wrongs done to the native tribes of America. The speech made little impression on the twelve Texans who sat on the two jury benches, revolvers strapped to their waists. The Texas district attorney responded with an oration that described Satanta as an "arch fiend of treachery and blood" and Big Tree as "the tiger-demon who tasted blood and loved it as his food."[35]

Such grandiloquent oratory was particularly misapplied toward Big Tree. For whatever crimes he may have committed, the Kiowa would later prove equal to the assessment of a journalist who met him in his home camp:

> As we passed one of the Kiowa lodges, a young man, seemingly about twenty-five or twenty-eight years old, came out to meet us with out-stretched arms. With the exception of Kicking Bird, he was the most pleasing Indian I met. He was very fair-skinned for an Indian, bright, intelligent-looking, with a frankness of manner rare among Indians. He was presented to me as Big Tree, a paroled Indian.[36]

The verdict against the pair was a foregone conclusion. The jury retired and spent only a few moments in angry talk and head shaking before returning to their benches. When asked if they had found the two tribesmen guilty of murder or not, the grizzled foreman replied loudly for all to hear: "We figger 'em guilty."[37]

The judge rendered a sentence of death by hanging. Satanta and Big Tree were taken off in their leg irons and handcuffs to Fort Richardson, where they were held for a time. On August 2, 1871, Texas governor Edmund Davis consented to the request of the federal government and commuted the sentence to life imprisonment in the state penitentiary at Huntsville, Texas.[38]

Sherman wrote to Sheridan: "Old Satank ought to have been shot long ago, and Big Tree is a young warrior, the successor of Faint [Little] Heart, who died last winter. The impudence of Satanta will satisfy you that the Kiowas need pretty much the lesson you gave Black Kettle and Little Raven. . . . Kicking Bird is about the only Kiowa that seems to understand their situation, but Lone Wolf ought to have been hung when you had him in hand."[39]

Kicking Bird and Lone Wolf were angry with Satanta for causing so much trouble. Grierson reported that Kicking Bird nonetheless was working hard to retrieve the captured mules and had promised to do all he could to prevent the Kiowas from committing further depredations. On August 11 Kicking Bird and Plains Apache chief Pacer brought thirty-eight mules and one horse into Fort Sill. Kicking Bird also reported to Tatum that the Kiowas had returned to the reservation, adding:

> We intend to cease raiding and depredations on the white people and hereafter follow the example of the Caddo Indians, who have long been

Big Tree and Satanta appear emaciated as inmates of the prison at Huntsville, Texas. Courtesy Archives Division, Texas State Library.

161

on the white man's road. As evidence of our good intentions we have brought in the mules as required of us. And now we want you to write a strong appeal to the officers at Washington for the release of Satanta and Big Tree, who we think have suffered enough, and then every thing will be right.[40]

Neither this nor the peace efforts of Kicking Bird would stem the depredations, however. A company of Tenth Cavalry was attacked west of the Wichita Mountains, and a trooper was killed. Two cattle herders were shot in the back and scalped within a mile of Fort Sill, it was believed by Kiowas. Kicking Bird sent a man to remain with some herders chopping wood near Fort Sill to prevent others of his young men from killing them.[41]

Tatum announced that Eagle Heart, Fast Bear, and Big Bear, who had been among the wagon-train raiders, would no longer be recognized as chiefs. Further, any chief who accompanied a raiding party would no longer be recognized by the U.S. government.[42] Kicking Bird, who would now be seen by government officials as the principal chief of the Kiowas, was asked to nominate successors for the deposed chiefs.

But the Kiowas were not the only problem. The Comanches and Cheyennes were still raiding and taking white captives. Tatum, going against Quaker policy, sought the help of the military in rescuing the Comanche-held captives. Grierson, leading his Tenth Cavalry buffalo soldiers, joined with Mackenzie's Fourth Cavalry regulars on Otter Creek during August 1871 to conduct a campaign against hostiles north of the Red River.

Although restricted from taking troops outside the reservation except on the hot pursuit of depredators, Grierson held rank over Mackenzie while in the Territory. Mackenzie deeply resented this, and the resulting estrangement between the two officers created a lapse of communication. Either Grierson never told Mackenzie of Kicking Bird's commitment to peace or Mackenzie chose to ignore it.

Mackenzie led his command on a scout to the Sweetwater, determined to punish Kicking Bird, who he erroneously believed was responsible for the wagon-train massacre at Salt Creek Prairie. Mackenzie and his men were so convinced that they were on the trail of the Kiowa leader that a Fourth Cavalry officer, Robert G. Carter, later published an account of the affair under the title *Pursuit of Kicking Bird: A Campaign in the Texas Badlands.*

Kicking Bird had indeed been camped on the Sweetwater in the Texas Panhandle outside the Kiowa reservation. Grierson, however, sent word by Fort Sill interpreter Horace Jones, warning the chief to move back east onto the reservation to avoid being attacked by Mackenzie.[43] With Kiowas on treaty-protected ground and his horses wearing out, Mackenzie had little choice but to retreat back to Fort Richardson in disgust. He and his men were convinced that they had been betrayed by Grierson as a tool of the "Indian Ring" that supposedly operated from the nation's capital.[44]

In September Kicking Bird reported to Cheyenne/Arapaho agent Darlington that a party of his Indians had passed through the Kiowa camps with twenty-two large mules they had taken in Texas.[45] Still, tribal raiders held largely to their lodges during the ensuing winter. The difficulties of 1871 had brought Kicking Bird into a position of top leadership. He was now recognized as the leading Kiowa peace chief not only by U.S. authorities but by a large portion of the Kiowa people as well. In the coming months he would play a major role not only in resisting the war element in his tribe but in setting a precedent for the formal schooling of Kiowa children.

14
Guest in Camp

In the early spring of 1871, Thomas Chester Battey, a Quaker who had been friends with agent Tatum in Iowa, accepted an assignment as a teacher among the Caddo Indians at the Wichita agency. Leaving his home and family on October 2, 1871, he headed south, hoping to catch a wagon train leaving Lawrence, Kansas, for the Indian Territory under wagon master J. J. Hoag. Delays caused him to miss the train at Lawrence, but he managed to overtake it at Emporia. Passing through the foundling cattle-trail towns of Newton, Wichita, and Caldwell, the wagon train pushed on southward for the new Cheyenne and Arapaho agency on the North Canadian River.

Battey now experienced the sights and trappings of the Indian Territory: huge Texas cattle herds pushing northward, prairie-dog villages, slinking coyotes, fleeting antelopes, grazing buffalo, wild turkeys, flocks of migrating geese, stands of blackjack oak, unbridged streams, and a fenceless countryside totally unbroken by the plow and seemingly uninhabited.

At the Cheyenne and Arapaho agency Battey continued his journey with an eight-wagon bull train that was headed to the Wichita agency. After camping one night near the home of Caddo chief George Washington near the main Canadian, Battey became impatient with the tediously slow train and disgusted with the teamsters' profanity. Although still twenty-three miles from his destination, he took his blankets, box of provisions, and satchel, left the train, and trudged ahead through scrubby

Quaker Thomas C. Battey accepted Kicking Bird's invitation to school his daughter. Courtesy National Archives.

sand hills and grassy valleys to the Wichita agency. He had no idea of the potential dangers that had lurked about him in the wilds of the Indian Territory.

Battey, who became known to the Indians as Thomissey (i.e., Thomas C.), first met Kicking Bird on February 18, 1872, when the Kiowa chief and his wife took dinner with him, Caddo chief Guadelupe, and two other tribesmen at the Wichita agency's Caddo school. At about the same time, the Quaker became acquainted with the famous and highly respected Delaware frontiersman Black Beaver. Beaver, who operated a large farm and lived in a good house near the agency, was a leading advocate for encouraging the prairie tribes to make peace and settle down. He was also a friend and counselor to Kicking Bird and other tribal peacemakers, as the Delaware indicated at one council: "A great many of you know me; every once in a while, since I built my house, my friend, Kicking Bird, comes to see me; when he comes he always asks, got any news for me? I always explain to my friend, nothing bad, all good."[1]

On the evening of March 30, Kicking Bird and his wife came with an interpreter to visit Battey again. It was a providential event for the Quaker teacher. On awakening that morning the thought had come to him: "What if thou shouldst have to go and sojourn in the Kiowa camps?"[2] The idea persisted through the day.

The Kicking Birds had a request. They wanted Thomissey to be a father—that is, a teacher—to their daughter Topen. Battey replied that if they wished to bring her to the Caddo school, he would treat her as one of his own children. Kicking Bird and his wife discussed the matter before Kicking Bird shook his head.

Kicking Bird's daughter Topen, the original Kiowa child to receive white schooling. Courtesy Center for American History, Texas University.

"We cannot leave her," he said. "We have lost five children; she is all we have. We cannot leave her here, but we want you to be a father to her, as you are to the children here."[3]

Battey asked if they meant they wanted him to go to their camp and live with them. Kicking Bird replied that yes, that would be good.

"If you come," he promised, "I will be your friend, and nobody shall do you any harm. My people will be your brothers."

Battey said he would have to think a great deal before deciding to come.

"You think, and when you make up your mind to come, let me know," Kicking Bird answered, "and my wife and I will come and get you, and you shall live in my lodge and be a father to the Kiowa children, as you are to the Caddoes."

Even with Kicking Bird's assurance of protection, it was a challenge for the Quaker to go live among what was reputed to be "a wild, depredating tribe."[4] Still, the Quaker could not escape the notion that the Lord had spoken to him. As it happened, he would have until the end of the year to consider the matter. Much would take place before then.

During February and March 1872, Cyrus Beede, a Quaker official representing Enoch Hoag in Lawrence, and J. R. Townsend, of the Cheyenne and Arapaho agency, toured the agencies of western Indian Territory. They had hopes that a delegation could be arranged for a visit to Washington, D.C. Hoag had requested that Kicking Bird and Lone Wolf be chosen to represent the Kiowas.[5]

On March 18 they visited a 200-lodge Cheyenne encampment on Wolf Creek between present-day Gage and Shattuck, Oklahoma, and on the twenty-first went to Little Raven's Arapaho camp seven miles northeast of Camp Supply. After a stop at the Wichita agency, they headed for Fort Sill to get supplies.[6]

On the third day out, the two men encountered a Kiowa party under Kicking Bird and Lone Wolf. After eating and talking with the chiefs, it was agreed that Kicking Bird would go on to the post and Lone Wolf would escort the Quakers to his camp. There Lone Wolf ordered his lodge cleared for use by the two white men. Big Bow (Zipkiyah, Zipkohera, or Zepko-eete), who was camped thirty miles away, was called to the camp for talks.

A virulent antiwhite Kiowa, Big Bow had also experienced his share of friction within the tribe itself. He had once stolen Satanta's wife. After staying in hiding for three months, he ventured into the agency with his band. Satanta had been there with his followers. Both groups were heavily armed, and a conflict appeared imminent. Comanche chief Horseback interceded, however, and arranged a truce whereby Big Bow presented Satanta with five ponies.[7]

In council with the Quakers, Lone Wolf spoke with eloquence and deep feeling for the return of Satanta, saying it would ensure peace forever with the white man no matter what new provocations might occur. Big Bow declared that he had been a very bad man, but now he was going to live peacefully. He would even send for his son, who was out on the warpath, to come home. Both chiefs, however, thought that surely the Americans would not mind if they raided into Mexico provided they left Texas alone. The Quakers were informed privately of an interesting fact: the young men of the tribe had considered taking the two of them captive to hold as hostages for the return of Satanta, but the chiefs had overruled them.

Kiowa and Comanche raiding picked up again during the spring and summer of 1872. During April Big Bow and White Horse led a party far south to the road between San Antonio and El Paso. On April 20 they attacked an unescorted wagon train resting at a lonely watering place known as Howard Wells. Seventeen Mexican teamsters were killed—some burned to death—the wagons looted and burned, and the mules taken. A Ninth Cavalry patrol from Fort Concho, Texas, discovered the carnage and set off in pursuit. They found the Kiowas in camp and attacked. White Horse was shot in the arm and Lone Wolf's son, Sitting-in-the-Saddle, in the knee. The Kiowas killed an officer and a trooper before they withdrew under the cover of darkness.[8]

On their return the party had another fight with a group of Texans near the Double Mountains. White Horse's youngest brother was killed. White Horse organized a revenge raid.[9] On June 9 he and his men came onto the house of Abel Lee on the Clear Fork of the Brazos. They shot and killed Lee as he read a newspaper outside his house, then invaded the house to murder and scalp Mrs. Lee. The four children ran in terror. Frances, fourteen, was killed with an arrow; but Susanna, seventeen, Millie, nine, and John, six, were captured and carried back to the Kiowas' camps north of the Red River.[10]

Tatum was distraught when he learned of the attack and demanded that the military arrest White Horse and the other perpetrators. But Enoch Hoag, who believed reports of the Lee massacre were exaggerated, rejected the request. He was looking to a new convention of the Five Civilized nations and prairie tribes in July in hopes of reforming the prairie raiders by friendly persuasion.[11]

Kicking Bird, meanwhile, was attempting to stop his warriors from raiding in the vicinity. He, along with two other Kiowa chiefs and three

Comanche chiefs, diverted them with an expedition against the Utes in Colorado. The party killed one Indian and a Mexican who was herding sheep. When he returned, Kicking Bird was greatly disturbed to learn that other Kiowas had been raiding around Fort Sill during his absence.[12]

Kiowa raiders had also been striking to the north into Kansas. During May, 121 government mules and other animals were taken from an infantry battalion on Bear Creek fifty miles south of Fort Dodge.[13] In Lawrence, Superintendent Hoag dispatched Cyrus Beede to return to the Territory and attempt to retrieve the stock. At the Cheyenne and Arapaho agency, Beede learned that a large medicine lodge celebration had recently been held by the prairie tribes.[14] The Kiowas had declared for war and invited the Cheyennes and Arapahos to join them. The two tribes declined. Cheyenne chief Grey Beard even managed to persuade the Kiowas to turn over some stolen mules to him so he could take them to Camp Supply.

Another grand council between the organized woodland tribes and the prairie tribes had been set for July 22 near old Fort Cobb. Beede arrived there on the twenty-third and, as the meeting got under way, began making a detailed transcript of the events, speeches, and interviews. In a talk with Comanche chief Horseback, Beede was told that Lone Wolf, Kicking Bird, and Stumbling Bear had been opposed to the raiding policy of the tribe. Big Bow, White Horse, and Woman's Heart were named as the tribe's war leaders.

The principal goal of the meeting was to persuade the Kiowas to adopt the path of peace. It was August 2, however, before Lone Wolf and White Horse made their appearance. When Beede had visited the Kiowa camps the previous March, Lone Wolf had emptied his lodge and made it available to the Quaker.[15] He now listed to Beede all the raids committed by the Kiowas since their last meeting.[16]

Lone Wolf admitted to numerous depredations by the Kiowas: to the theft of the government mules and horses near Fort Dodge; to taking thirty-eight mules and horses from William Shirley, trader at the Wichita agency; to the killing of a young would-be cowboy who was visiting Fort Sill from New York; to the White Horse–led wagon-train massacre; to taking sixty horses in Palo Pinto County, Texas; and to White Horse's murder of the Lee family in Texas.

White Horse, whose recent raiding had left his right arm broken by a bullet and wounds in many other parts of his body, also had a confession. When Tatum and interpreter Jones visited the Wichita agency last winter, White Horse and Big Bow had met them. The brothers had planned

Kicking Bird's brother, Son-of-the-Sun, or Sun Boy, visited
Washington, D.C. Courtesy Fort Sill Museum.

to follow them on the road and kill them and would have done so except
for the objections of a woman. White Horse expressed his opinion that
"it was no use to hold council with [the] old coffee chiefs, for they might
make peace."[17]

Lone Wolf; Woman's Heart; Kicking Bird's brother, Son of the Sun
(Pai-tälyi'), commonly known as Sun Boy;[18] White Horse; Running Bear;
and Black Eagle's brother were present to represent the Kiowas when the
meeting got under way at nine o'clock on August 3. By the time Kicking
Bird arrived that afternoon, several members of eastern tribes had already
made speeches pressing the Kiowas to give up their prisoners and stolen
animals. White officials had let it be known that if they did not do so, the
military was ready to come out after the tribe. Lone Wolf, speaking as the
principal chief of his tribe, now made his talk:

My friends, I am ready to do all that you ask me to do, but first I want you to take away all the soldiers from my country. I want to live just as you do. I want traders but no soldiers up and down these streams.

Kicking Bird and all these young men are of the same mind as myself. They left the buffalo and went on the white man's path; but those white men about Fort Sill used my people badly, and they went back to the buffalo.[19]

Lone Wolf and Kicking Bird joined Beede for lunch the following day. That afternoon Caddo chief George Washington advised the Kiowas to give up the captives and prisoners they held and then go to Washington as the white men wanted. Lone Wolf addressed the assembly again:

I will now make you a straight talk. You white men bring back Satanta, so we can see his face, and then we will return all the prisoners and mules, and go to Washington as you requested. Bring up Satanta, so I can see his face and I will return all the prisoners and all the mules, and go to Washington. Give up Satanta and I will give up myself and my whole tribe. Work hard for this, and have Satanta brought back quick. If I can't see Satanta's face, Washington cannot see mine. I am not a very nice man myself; but I have some young men I love, and want very much to see Satanta. This is all I have to say.[20]

Kicking Bird had not spoken during the meeting, but upon adjournment that day he came to Beede's tent again with interpreter Jones. Kicking Bird expressed his concern that Lone Wolf had not taken a wise course, saying "he [Lone Wolf] and the commission got the matter into a big smoke." He said that when the demand was made to give up the prisoners and mules, he had not spoken, but in his heart he said yes. He asked that he be given time to talk with his young men and get them thinking right. Beede promised to forward Kicking Bird's talk to Washington.

Beede met with Lone Wolf and Kicking Bird again at the Wichita agency on August 5. Both were worried about the Kiowas' situation, fearful of a military attack against them. Lone Wolf said he was willing to go to Washington with a delegation of his people. His son, however, still recovering from the potentially fatal wound he had received at Howard Wells, was confined at home. Lone Wolf did not want to leave him until he was well. Perhaps, he said, he would when cooler weather came.

Before parting, Kicking Bird asked Beede for a private interview that evening. At that time he requested that any hostile action against his people be delayed until he had time to counsel with his young people for the return of the captives and stock. He wanted to know how long he had to bring them in. Beede suggested that Kicking Bird make him a definite proposal to return the prisoners in a certain number of days.

Kicking Bird replied that the day was almost gone, and he had yet to go after his family at the Wichita camps. "In ten days after tomorrow," he said, "I will deliver the three prisoners in the hands of my people to the Wichita agency. I will not carry them to the Kiowa agency on account of Fort Sill; I am afraid to go there."[21]

Beede accepted the proposal and promised to do what he could to hold the soldiers back from attacking the Kiowas in the meantime. Two hours later Kicking Bird returned to the agency office and asked to see Beede. With no interpreter present, Kicking Bird pointed in the direction of the Kiowas' distant camps. "Ride, ride, ride," he said, "heap riding. Kicking Bird no tire, heap talk." Holding up his fingers and thumbs on both hands, he signified ten days. He then held up three more fingers to denote the three prisoners and made a motion to indicate that he would set them down at the Wichita agency. The two men shook hands, and Kicking Bird headed off on his mission.

Beede harbored doubt that Kicking Bird had the influence and power to carry out his promise over the wishes of the Kiowa militants. A correspondent from Fort Sill wrote on August 9 that "It is not understood that this concession on the part of Kicking Bird will make peace with the tribe, but it is looked upon rather as an earnest [indication] of his desire to sustain friendly relations with us."[22]

On August 19 Black Beaver wrote to Cherokee D. H. Ross to say that two days earlier Lone Wolf, Kicking Bird, and Big Bow had arrived at Beaver's home with Susanna Lee and Milly Lee. The Kiowas had promised that the girls' brother John, who was left sick in the camps, would be brought in within two weeks. According to Battey, Kicking Bird had purchased the captives personally with his own horses in order to win their freedom.[23]

The two girls were taken on to Fort Sill by Lone Wolf, Sun Boy, and seven other Kiowas, with Kicking Bird remaining at the Wichita agency. Lone Wolf told Tatum this was proof that the Kiowas were determined to follow the white man's road. Still, he claimed, a reward was due for bringing in the captives. He was given or promised none, but the Kiowas were fed and issued rations for fourteen days.[24]

Kicking Bird informed Beaver that the Kiowas had held a council and, in a tradition-breaking move, passed laws forbidding any of their young men from going to Texas. If any man under their control was known to commit any further depredations, he would be discarded forever. Lone Wolf, too, avowed that his people wanted peace and would cease their raiding unless the white people became foolish and did something to them. Tatum, however, still felt the Kiowas were beyond his control and had no confidence that their good behavior would last any longer than it took their horses to recover their flesh the coming spring.[25]

The commissioner of Indian Affairs, in the meantime, had appointed Capt. Henry Alvord and Prof. Edward Parrish of Pennsylvania to visit the prairie tribes and arrange for a delegation to go to Washington. While at Fort Sill, Parrish became ill with malaria and died at Tatum's home. He was buried in the post cemetery.[26]

Alvord continued on by himself, meeting with the various tribes. Few Kiowas except Sun Boy were present when Alvord met with the tribes six miles north of the Washita on Leeper Creek on September 6 and 7. Sun Boy said he had come in lieu of Kicking Bird, who was ill at home.

Alvord was particularly impressed with a speech by a Comanche chief "of fine physique, unmistakable talents, and great power." The chief told the assembly of tribes:

> I am your kinsman and friend, but I cannot in silence hear you throw upon the Kiowas, the Quahadas, and their associate Comanches, all the blame for depredations committed, claim innocence for yourselves, and promise the good behavior of your people. I see here but three tribes whose young men, at least, have not been present, and equally guilty with our people and the Kiowas, in more or less of the forays of the last two years, and they are the Arapahoes, the Caddoes, and the Delawares.[27]

Sun Boy told Alvord he was not authorized to speak for his people and that another council would be necessary to arrange a trip to Washington. Alvord arranged to meet with the Kiowas at the Washita again on September 19. Now present were Lone Wolf, Woman's Heart, Red Otter, Little Mountain, Sun Boy, Stumbling Bear, Sleeping Wolf, and Fast Bear. The Kiowas showed no interest in going to Washington until Alvord finally promised that Satanta and Big Tree would be brought from Huntsville, Texas, to meet with them during the trip.

Alvord's delegation consisted of thirty-seven men and eleven women of the Kiowas, Comanches, Apaches, Caddos, and Arapahos. On the night prior to departure, however, rumors swept the Indian camps that troops were threatening the Kiowa and Comanche camps to the west. As a result, many of the chiefs left during the night.

The peace delegation moved out from the Wichita agency in army wagons on September 20. Lone Wolf, Sun Boy, and Sleeping Wolf represented the Kiowas. Also with the group were Ten Bears of the Comanches, Pacer of the Apaches, Big Mouth of the Arapahos, and George Washington of the Caddos. Horace Jones, Philip McCusker, William Shirley, J. J. Strum, and Black Beaver went along as interpreters and aides.

It was a long, jolting six-day ride to Atoka, Indian Territory, and several important chiefs almost deserted. Alvord managed to keep the group together and on the twenty-sixth placed his charges aboard a special car of the Missouri, Kansas, and Texas Railroad. He was careful not to let the Kiowas know that Satanta and Big Tree, released from prison temporarily by the governor of Texas, had also arrived at Atoka and were camped nearby in custody of a company of U.S. cavalry. Alvord feared that if Lone Wolf met Satanta there, the Kiowas would not continue on to Washington. The cavalry kept the two prisoners out of sight until the others had departed and put them on a later train.

The delegation reached St. Louis on September 28. In a meeting at the Everett House the next day, the members of the delegation were seated on chairs around the large dining room with spectators against one wall and the commissioners and interpreters in the center. Enoch Hoag made a brief introductory talk, and then Alvord stepped forward to present Satanta and Big Tree. When the two men appeared, a long exclamation of joy sounded from the delegation. The Kiowas covered their faces with their hands, and tears streamed through their fingers. Satanta was the center of all attention. A St. Louis reporter described him: "He appeared to be a man in the very prime of life, with a well formed head, a broad but not high forehead, a strong jaw, brilliant black eyes, and complexion a shade darker than that of Big Tree. He had every appearance of a man of great daring and strength of will, and seemed to weigh about one hundred and sixty pounds."[28]

Satanta made a speech, avowing his friendship for Texas and his wish for his people not to raid in Texas anymore. He said if they remained peaceful, he would be freed. "I have left the bad road. I have not been a bad man, as you know. I always tried to make peace. Among all the chiefs of the plains, Satanta is second to none."[29]

Afterward, the Kiowa leader shook hands with the white officials and with the Indian men of the delegation. "When he came to the men of his own tribe, he embraced each of them, kissing them on the cheek while the tears streamed from their eyes. He shed no tear himself, however, although his feelings were deeply moved. His sister threw her arms about his neck and kissed him many times."[30]

Lone Wolf spoke to say that when he got to Washington he would swallow every word of the president and put them all in his heart. He vowed that the Kiowas would stop fighting and throw off the bad way.

The following day, at the invitation of the president of the St. Louis Transfer Company, the delegation was placed on trolleys and taken through the city to places of interest, among them the manu-

Satanta and Big Tree at a reunion with other Kiowas at
St. Louis. Courtesy British Museum.

facturing furnace at Carondelet. Alvord thought the Indians had been
greatly impressed and that much good would result from the visit. The
Kiowas were very disappointed, however, that Satanta and Big Tree were
not permitted to accompany them to Washington, as they believed had
been promised. Instead, the two prisoners were escorted in chains back
to Huntsville.

From St. Louis it was on to Cincinnati, where the tribespeople were
permitted a three-hour visit to the Annual Industrial Exposition. On
October 2 the delegation reached Washington, D.C. After being presented with silver peace medals, they were shown about the capital. On
the eleventh they were taken to meet with President Ulysses S. Grant in
the East Room of the White House. The chiefs were decked in full costume with painted faces and feathered headdresses, and each filed before
the president and shook his hand. Grant spoke briefly, encouraging them

to take up industrial pursuits and give up their roving life. The tribesmen made no talk themselves.[31]

In another meeting on October 22, Commissioner of Indian Affairs Francis A. Walker bruskly informed the delegation that Indians who did not behave would no longer receive rations. Further violators would be hunted down and killed by the troops. The chiefs, who had remained silent, were asked if they had anything to say. After conferring with others, one of the chiefs replied merely that they would not have left their homes if they did not intend to do well.[32]

In answer to their pleas for the release of Satanta and Big Tree, Walker told the Kiowas that under no circumstances would the government give up the prisoners.[33] Before the delegation left Washington, however, the commissioner relented and promised that if the Kiowas behaved, Satanta and Big Tree would be released the following March 1. It was a mistake. Walker had no authority to make such an offer; the two Kiowas were prisoners of the State of Texas, not the federal government. But the promise would not be forgotten or taken lightly by the Kiowa people.

The delegates were met at Fort Sill by Kicking Bird with nearly all the Kiowas and the Comanches under Shaking Hand. Some Kiowa warriors, it was reported, were still expressing defiance, but they had been outlawed even by their own chiefs.[34] The future of peace and war with the Kiowas, however, would hang dangerously in the balance on the commissioner's slender promise of Satanta's release.

During the delegation's absence, the torch of warfare on the Plains had been reignited. The rumors of an impending attack by U.S. forces that had circulated through the Indian camps before the chiefs departed had been well-founded. Mackenzie, marching north from Texas guided by Tonkawa scouts, struck a nonreservation Quahada Comanche camp under Mow-way scattered along McClellan Creek. This occurred on September 29—the very day the Kiowas were temporarily reunited with Satanta in St. Louis. Mackenzie killed 23 or more Indians and took 124 women and children prisoner. He also captured over 1,200 ponies, driving the immense herd with him for some distance back toward his supply camp. But that night the Comanches stampeded the herd and drove most of them off.[35]

15
The Great Kiowa Is Watching

Few outsiders developed a better knowledge of the early Kiowas, their culture, and their trials in adjusting to the new world of white influence than did Thomas Battey. History is well served indeed by the extensive narratives this brave and compassionate observer supplied in letters to *The Friend*, a Quaker publication in Philadelphia. The letters were later published by Battey as a book, *The Life and Adventures of a Quaker Among the Indians*. A more observant and fair witness to Kiowa life could not have been found.

Battey was absent from the Indian Territory from July 13 until October 15, 1872, making the long journey back to Iowa to see his wife and children. During this time he had decided that he would indeed go among the Kiowas. On October 28 Kicking Bird and seven other Kiowa chiefs arrived at the Fort Sill agency to return seventeen of the mules taken near Fort Dodge. Battey broached the matter of going with them to their camp and setting up a school for Kiowa children. All of the chiefs present were very much in favor of having the Quaker schoolteacher among them and offered to do all they could for him.

But Kicking Bird now expressed reservations. He said his wife, whom he had loved very much, had died recently. He did not feel he could care for Battey as he had promised earlier. Further, he had little confidence that the Kiowa young men were ready to settle down and follow the peace road being set by Washington. He suggested that Battey wait until Lone Wolf and the others returned home from Washington.[1]

When the delegation arrived back on November 21, the weak and exhausted Ten Bears was seriously ill. Battey served as his nurse in the agency office, but the fine old Comanche chief died on November 23. Kicking Bird along with Dangerous Eagle arrived at the agency again on December 1 to attend a meeting and obtain their annuity goods. Teacher Josiah Butler took his schoolchildren to observe the distribution.

"It was really a sight," he wrote, "to see so many strangely dressed and yet more strangely painted men, women, and children, with their herds of ponies and packs of dogs. When each chief got the share of annuity goods apportioned to his band, he had all put in a pile and then collected his band in a semi-circle around the pile, when all goods were divided."[2]

Kicking Bird eventually agreed to take Battey back with him to his camp, and Tatum supplied the teacher with a mule to ride and some rations. Moving at a fast clip until eight in the evening, the two men reached the camp of Kicking Bird's friend, Plains Apache chief Pacer. The village was swarming with snarling, threatening dogs. The men beat them back with sticks and made their way to Pacer's lodge, where they enjoyed a supper of boiled beef and biscuits and stayed the night. They arrived the next evening at Kicking Bird's camp of forty lodges situated on the wooded banks of a creek six to eight miles above the deserted Fort Cobb and thirty miles south of Fort Sill. There they were met by a throng of Kiowa children, nearly naked even in winter, who stared in wonderment at the strange sight of a white man.

Battey found that Kicking Bird's family now consisted of the chief, his mother, and his daughter Topen. In addition to Sun Boy, Kicking Bird had another brother named Ze'bile (Big Arrow), who invited Battey to share his lodge.[3] Kicking Bird spoke lovingly of his deceased wife. She had been a good woman, he said, who held much love and friendship for the white people. He had promised her that he would try to get his people to throw away their raiding and killing, vowing if they did not he would settle down at the agency and let them go their way.[4]

The Quaker soon discovered why death came often to the native people of the Plains. Men, women, and children had few clothes to protect them in winter. Often a blanket was their only protection in the outdoors, even during bitter cold when snow was on the ground. When illnesses such as pneumonia came, usually the only remedies were provided by tribeswomen who made mysterious hand movements over the sick person, accompanied by terrible moaning and howling.

The lack of food also was often a problem because of the failure of the government to provide the annuities it had promised by treaty. On

Kiowa-Apache chief Pacer, close friend of Kicking Bird.
Courtesy Western History Collection, University of Oklahoma.

one occasion, with the prairie badly snowbound and all of the beef eaten, Kicking Bird was forced to kill a mule to eat until the agency could be reached for rations. At another time, a young colt was butchered.[5]

Battey was joined at Kicking Bird's camp in February 1873 by Butler, who hitched a ride in a wagon from the agency. Butler was received hospitably by Kicking Bird, Ze'bile, and others and was fed breakfast at the lodge of Trotting Wolf, who "served as 'wit,' keeping all of us laughing with his talk and action."[6]

The following day, however, Butler's tent was invaded by Chief White Horse and several other Kiowas, who angrily demanded to know, "You Te-hah'-ny?" Butler had been seen taking notes near the Kiowa pony and mule herds and was suspected of being a Texan there to recover stolen stock. Butler was saved by a Mexican who identified him as a Quaker teacher.[7]

Although he immediately set about to learn the difficult Kiowa language, Battey at first had virtually no communication with the children he was to teach. When his charts, slates, and other teaching paraphernalia arrived, a tent was erected in the camp to serve as a school as well as a home for Battey. The first Kiowa classes opened on January 23, 1873, with twenty-two young scholars. Instruction was severely impeded, however, by curious onlookers who talked and laughed loudly as Battey attempted to put the youngsters through English enunciation drills.

Lucius Aitsan was a student under Battey. As an elderly man, he told of having been born on the head of the Canadian River in the Texas Panhandle where the Utes had once burned Tohawson's tepee. Lucius was the son of one of Satanta's four wives. He was nine years old when Battey came to the Kiowa camp. He told how the Quaker would show big pictures of various animals and fish, saying their names in English and having the Kiowa children repeat them as best they could. One day a woman came in and took her son away for fear that if he looked at Battey's pictures he would die like the Caddos. Lucius's mother removed him from the school as well.[8]

The problem had arisen when some of the Caddos, among whom Battey had taught earlier, told the Kiowas that the Quaker was a medicine man who had made their children sick and caused them to die. As a result, the Kiowas began holding their children away from the school. A couple of armed warriors were posted to keep an eye on Battey.

When Kicking Bird became aware of the situation, he called a meeting of the chiefs. After a long deliberation, a number of them came to Battey's tent. They were cheerful and smiling. Kicking Bird and Stumbling Bear took Battey to one side.

"Caddo talk no good," Stumbling Bear told him. "Thomis-sy good man."[9]

On one occasion a tribesman decked in war paint entered the school tent and threatened Battey with an uplifted war ax, cursing him in broken English. Battey bravely seized the intruder's arm and forced him out of the tent. It was not uncommon for young men to enter the school, laugh at the students, and abuse them until they left. Eventually, Battey was able to overcome the interference and get on with his instruction.[10] Still, Kicking Bird and other chiefs did not want Battey to go very far from camp. There were those around, they said, who would kill him for his clothes if they had the chance.[11]

Gradually, Battey became accepted. When the Kiowa village moved to the South Fork of Cache Creek, his tent and school equipment, which the agency had transported by wagon, were the first to be set up at the new site, and the Kiowa lodges were erected around it.

Kicking Bird's interest in schooling for the Kiowa children was reflected in a visit he made to the Caddo school in March 1873. Accompanied by daughter Topen, Battey, Dangerous Eagle, and others, he set out to see for himself "the purposes and good results of a school."[12]

The issue of freedom for Satanta and Big Tree, as had been promised by the commissioner of Indian Affairs, was very much on the minds of the Kiowas during the spring of 1873. Texas governor Edmund J. Davis, however, was strongly against freeing the men. He stated his expectations for such in a letter to the secretary of war:

> There will certainly be no peace on the frontier until the Indians are put on foot, disarmed, and kept under close surveillance. Anything short of this is a makeshift. If we propose to civilize them, this is the only way it can be done. After disarming and dismounting is accomplished, it will cost really less to preserve peace on the frontier than under the present system, even though the Government should have to feed and clothe all such Indians for a generation.[13]

Quaker officials were hopeful that President Grant would be able to persuade Davis on the matter. In early April Tatum wrote to a Texas citizen to point out that in line with their promises the Kiowas had turned in 164 head of horse and mules and 18 captives, all without ransom.[14]

Much of this had resulted from work among the tribes by Kicking Bird. In recognition of their deeds, the government sent silver medals to both Kicking Bird and Chief Horseback of the Comanches, who had also returned captives.[15]

Kicking Bird offered to attempt to rescue a white boy from the Apaches of New Mexico. He had seen the captive while visiting an Apache camp. The boy was believed to be the brother of another boy from Randall County, Texas, who had been rescued earlier. Kicking Bird agreed to make the long trip and talk with the Apache headmen. The Quaker authorities had full confidence in him. They said, however, that if there was any chance of trouble with other tribes, they preferred that he not go. Kicking Bird, who had good relations with the Pueblos of New Mexico, suggested that perhaps his brother-in-law Quoi-e-boi, "who is also a very good chief," go in his place.[16]

Tatum, too, was very much against freeing Satanta and Big Tree. He felt strongly that their release was a mistake and a repudiation of his policies. As a result, he resigned in March 1873. Kicking Bird paid tribute to Tatum in a short speech.

"I am sorry you are going to leave us," he said. "You have had a hard time trying to get us to behave. Now, as we have concluded to take your advice and follow the white man's road, we would like for you to remain.

No other agent has treated us with such uniform kindness that you have. When you leave you will be dead to us."[17]

During March 1873 Kicking Bird's village on Cache Creek was host to a group of their former enemies, the Pawnees of Nebraska, who often came south to visit their Wichita relatives. Wishing to escape the harassment of the Dakota tribes, the Pawnees were considering moving south permanently. First, however, it was necessary to feel out the other tribes in the Indian Territory, particularly those with whom they had made war in the past.[18]

Battey was in Kicking Bird's camp at the time and provided a detailed account of the tribal formalities involved in the meeting.

The Pawnees came on foot bearing a white flag, planted it a hundred yards from the Kiowa camp, and sat down in a line on either side of it facing the camp. After arrangements had been made in the village to receive the guests, Kicking Bird and his chiefs walked slowly forward with great dignity. They were followed by tribespeople of his band. Some of the older Kiowa women set up a high, shrill chant. The Pawnee chiefs rose and moved forward to meet and embrace the Kiowa chiefs, presenting some with shawls and blankets. After shaking hands all around, the Pawnees took seats on the ground.

> After this the Pawnees set up a weird song, during the continuance of which Kiowa fathers, each carrying a small child in his arms, bearing a piece of stick in its little hands, young girls, and occasionally a woman, would approach the Pawnees, and selecting some one, would present themselves before him holding out the stick. Thereupon he [the Pawnee] would arise, place his hands upon the donor's head in a reverential manner, as if blessing, pass them down the sides, following the arms, take the stick and sit down. Each stick thus given was a pledge from the giver to the receiver for a pony, to be given when the visitors are ready to return to their homes. Old men from time to time addressing the Kiowas, urged them to liberality, to show the largeness of their hearts—the warmth of their friendship—by giving ponies to these poor Pawnees who had come so far to see them and renew their friendship, and not allow them to go back on foot as they came. I know not how many ponies were pledged to them, but there must have been many.
>
> At the conclusion of the ceremony, the Pawnees arose in a body, ceased their singing, took up their flag, and a part following one Kiowa chief and a part another, accompanied them to their lodges to partake of their hospitality; the head chief, with four or five others, including the flag-bearer, accompanied Kicking Bird to his lodge, thus becoming his guest.[19]

Tatum was soon replaced as agent by another Quaker, James M. Haworth. According to an account in the Quaker weekly *Friends' Review*, his introduction to the agency was a new experience indeed.

Soon after J. H. came here, the Indians tried to intimidate him into giving them more than the government allowance of rations. When he refused they threatened to kill him, and came with their bows strung and looking so ominous that some of those around wished him at once to send to the fort for troops. He replied that he had come as the representative of a peace policy and was not going to overawe them. So he continued firm, gained the day, and they left him unharmed, though completely unnerved for a time by the tension of the intense excitement.[20]

Haworth, however, soon adopted a more lenient approach than Tatum's practices by removing the guards around the agency warehouse.

The issue of freeing Satanta and Big Tree overrode all other Kiowa-related matters during the spring of 1873. With the promised March 1 date having come and gone and no apparent willingness by Texas to comply, the Quakers and Kiowas alike felt the government had betrayed them. The Kiowas found it difficult to understand how the Texas chief was a bigger chief than Washington. On request of the secretary of the interior, Governor Davis finally gave in and agreed to release the two Kiowas, in hopes that doing so would finally stop the raiding into Texas. On March 28 Beede was sent to reassure the Kiowas and tell them the prisoners would be delivered to them on June 1.

Beede called a meeting of the leading Kiowa and Comanche chiefs at the Fort Sill agency on March 28. When pressed as to why the promised release had not been carried out, Beede said the White Father was at times discouraged over the honesty of the tribes because of their raiding. But now his heart had softened again and he was disposed to give up the prisoners.[21]

At the meeting forty-four Kiowa, Comanche, and Plains Apache chiefs—including Kicking Bird—signed a letter to the president of the United States pleading for the release of Satanta and Big Tree. Tatum noted that the message, which had clearly been drafted by one of the Quakers, had been carefully interpreted to the Indians in council before it was signed by every chief present. Haworth, Battey, and Black Beaver were among the witnesses. The letter read in part: "If our Great Father will do this, we solemnly promise in the presence of these witnesses, that with the assistance of the Great Spirit above, we will hereafter obey the wishes of our Great Father, as made known to us by his agents and messengers sent among us. We will go no more raiding into Texas, but will remain in our own lawful reservation."[22]

Lone Wolf promised Haworth that although the Kiowas were going to make medicine—that is, hold their Sun Dance—again in June, the chiefs had the young men under control. He said that if any got away, other Kiowas would follow them, kill their ponies, and make them walk home.[23]

The Kiowas proved their willingness to comply with their promises in early May when they were visited by three Cheyennes in their camps west of the Wichita Mountains. The Cheyennes wanted the Kiowas to join them on a raid. Kicking Bird, Stumbling Bear, and Quoi-e-boi met with the visitors in council and told them they would have no part of the raid. Battey reported that Kicking Bird told the Cheyennes that "the Kiowas wanted nothing to do with them while they were hostile to Washington" and sent them home.[24]

Further proof that the Kiowas were sincere came on the evening of May 15 when a Comanche raiding party on its way to Texas stopped by Kicking Bird's camp and invited the Kiowas to go along. The chiefs and head warriors held a council that night and came to a firm determination. If any Kiowa warrior joined the Comanches, they decreed, his war horses would be killed and his saddle, bridle, blankets, and lodges would be destroyed.[25] A few days later the Kiowas intercepted a band of raiders from another tribe and surrounded them. The Kiowas said they would give them four talks. If they still persisted, the Kiowas would kill their horses, tear their blankets, and let them go naked and afoot on the prairie. It was not a difficult choice for the would-be raiders to make.[26]

Battey was in the Kiowa camp on the North Fork of the Red River at the time of the Cheyenne visit. He returned to the Kiowa agency on May 21 after three days of hard travel. In a letter written to his wife before he left, he described the situation at the agency:

> From the number of lodges there must be 800, or 900 Kiowas in the camp, and several hundred Comanches and Apaches, camped close by. The weather continues so cool that the trees do not come out as usual, and so dry that the grass is very backward and slow in coming forward. The Buffalo is scarce here, though we get plenty to eat. There is an extensive bed of rock-salt a few miles from here, but I do not know that I shall see it, as Kicking Bird and the other chiefs are unwilling for me to go far out of camp while there are so many Indians around.[27]

The murder of Maj. Gen. E. R. S. Canby by the Modocs in northern California on April 11, 1873, shocked U.S. officials and brought a halt to U.S. plans to release Satanta and Big Tree. The secretary of the interior telegraphed Davis to hold up the release for the present. Davis wrote to Superintendent Hoag that he wished to wait until the Texas legislature adjourned on May 20, after which time he could visit Fort Sill himself.[28] Seeing that the June 1 date would not be met, Thomas Wistar of the Quaker executive committee arrived at the Fort Sill agency on May 30 to hold a council.

When the news of Canby's murder and cancellation of the release reached the agency on May 31, Battey immediately took it on himself to speak up for the Kiowas. That same day he wrote a letter to the commissioner of Indian Affairs expressing the interest of the tribe. The letter was eventually reprinted in the *New York Times* and other papers around the country. It detailed how the Kiowas had willingly given up the captives and stolen animals, suffered badly from hunger, refused to join in raiding parties when invited to do so, and rejected the Cheyennes' invitation to go to war. Battey described, too, how Kicking Bird and other chiefs had threatened not only their own warriors but a war party of another tribe in order to stop the raiding.[29]

By June the Kiowas were growing increasingly suspicious of and upset with the government over the Satanta–Big Tree issue. Word reached the agency that a plot had been conceived among some of the Kiowas to seize Haworth and Battey, hold them as hostages, and kill them if the two prisoners were not released. The Kiowas' frustration was made worse by threatening rumors that the soldiers were going to surround them and that they would have to give up their horses and arms. The hopes of both the Quakers and the Kiowas were enlivened, however, when in early June the federal government released the Quahada Comanche women and children who had been captured by Mackenzie the previous year and held at Fort Concho, Texas.[30]

Nine of the captives had died during the winter. Shortly before departing from Concho, five of the women had escaped and made it back the nearly 300 miles to their camps in the Indian Territory on their own, subsisting on roots and tortoises. The remaining 100 arrived at Fort Sill on June 10 under the escort of Capt. Robert McClermont. In making the march, McClermont and his 21 men were forced to evade a large force of armed Texans at Jacksboro who had gathered to prevent the return of the prisoners.[31]

High water of streams held Battey to the agency during the first two weeks of June. Kicking Bird sent a small party to bring him out, promising that if any of the Kiowas did him any wrong, he would personally escort him back to the agency.[32] It took three days of hard riding to reach Kicking Bird's camp 150 miles northwest of Fort Sill. There in a wide, beautiful valley, the entire Kiowa tribe had been joined for a great medicine dance by the Plains Apaches, 500 Comanches, plus a like number of Cheyennes, Arapahos, and other Indians.[33]

Over a hundred chiefs of these tribes gathered in council and were anxious to hear what Battey had to report concerning the status of Satanta and Big Tree. The Quaker was ushered to a seat beside Kicking Bird.

Little was said to him until he had eaten and the smoking of the pipe had begun. Then he was asked what news he brought from Washington. As a solitary white man in a far-off land among strangers, many of whom were hostile to whites, Battey felt very much alone. With almost suicidal courage, he managed to answer, "Bad news."[34]

The pipe continued to pass about in dead silence, every eye on the schoolteacher as Battey explained that Washington's (the Indians referred to "Woosinton",[35] meaning the government, as "he," a personal entity) heart had suddenly become hard and cold to all his red children because of the killing of General Canby. Washington had closed his hand on Satanta and Big Tree.

The chiefs did not understand; they had never heard of the Modocs. They only knew the White Father had broken his word. A heated discussion began, and Satanta's brother, Little Robe, jumped to his feet, gesturing wildly, and issued a violent harangue. The chief of his band quieted him, commenting to Battey in disgust, "He papoose."

But the excitement for war was high among the assemblage of chiefs. This meeting was likely the closest the Plains tribes would ever come to an organized, multitribal assault on the outside forces that were threatening their existence. According to Battey, it was argued that the tribes should continue with their dance and make war medicine. Then a force of 500 warriors would be divided into raiding parties of 15 to 20 men and sent to various white settlements in Kansas, Colorado, New Mexico, and Texas. The old men, women, and children would be secluded at a secret location in the middle of the Staked Plains, probably the Palo Duro Canyon. When the specified time came, the warriors would make simultaneous attacks all along the frontier.[36]

In the stormy debate that followed, Kicking Bird was openly criticized for his peace policy. Some war chiefs became so agitated that they broke tribal decorum and leaped to their feet to speak. The most agitated was Satanta's father, who demanded of Kicking Bird: "Why you no talk? Are you woman now—sit there and say nothing?"[37]

The insult was reflected on Kicking Bird's face, but he restrained his anger. With outer calm he replied that he would speak when the time came. But now he wanted to hear what Thomissey had to say. The pipe was passed to Battey. Taking a puff, he pulled his thoughts together the best he could and plunged forward. The Kiowas had kept their word, he said, while the White Father had broken his. But they should remain calm and not act rashly. He told them of the letter he had written in their behalf. Perhaps Washington would get over his anger, and his heart would grow warm to the Kiowas once more.

Kicking Bird then spoke in support of Battey, saying that angry people seldom act wisely or do the right thing. Nothing could be lost by waiting; there would be plenty of time to act later. Much to Battey's surprise, the council grew calm and orderly. The chiefs agreed to wait until they heard more from Washington.[38] Few people would ever know that Kicking Bird had personally prevented a major Indian outbreak.

For the remainder of June, the Kiowas were kept busy with their Sun Dance,[39] and after that the men were occupied with their buffalo hunt and the women with curing the meat, preparing skins, and making new lodges. Once the summer festivities were over, however, the Satanta–Big Tree issue resurfaced. The Kiowas still felt strongly that they were being betrayed. During July, Kicking Bird informed Haworth that it was becoming increasingly hard to control his young men. He was not certain he could do it much longer. Satanta's father was exerting a strong influence on the tribe, he said. On the other hand, Satanta's son Tehausen (or Tohawson), a young but good chief, would have a large influence if his father was released.[40]

Battey, too, was feeling the effects of the Satanta–Big Tree situation. On July 31 he wrote to Haworth to say he had been forced to close his school. Elders were withdrawing their children because of the government's failure to comply with its agreement. "Washington talk good," they said, "but does not do as he talk."[41]

Battey remained with Kicking Bird until August 1, when his health caused him to return to the agency. Soon after, on the advice of friends, he took leave for another visit to his family in Iowa. William Nicholson wrote from Lawrence on August 14 to say that Battey had stopped by on his way home. The schoolteacher was very ill with ulcers caused from drinking strong alkaline water, obtained by scooping holes in dry beds of streams during the excessively hot weather on the prairie, and from other dietary habits he had endured among the Indians.[42]

While he was in Iowa, Battey learned that on the request of the United States, Governor Davis had agreed to send Satanta and Big Tree to Fort Sill. A council would be held there regarding the potential release of the Kiowas. Battey's letter had been largely responsible for persuading Commissioner Smith to set the two prisoners free. In a letter to Haworth, Smith cited "the compliance of the Kiowas with their promises, their friendly attitude towards the government, their effort to restrain hostile Indians from raiding, &c., and their anxiety for the return of Satanta and Big Tree."[43]

Although still ill, Battey hastened back to the Kiowa-Comanche agency to attend the fateful meeting.

16
A Road We Cannot Travel

The possibility of the release of Satanta and Big Tree from prison drew much attention from the national press. In August 1873 the *New York Times* republished an article by a Houston journalist who had visited the pair at Huntsville. The journalist had written:

> Satanta is about fifty-three years of age, above the average height, and compactly built. His face wears a thoughtful rather than a treacherous look, and his large, keen eye has nothing of the devilish in it except when angered; then it flashes and burns into yours like a living coal. Big Tree, who is only a sort of second lieutenant to Satanta, and has no influence with the tribes, is a short, wiry, treacherous-looking savage, in whose coal-black eye gleams the desire to do deeds that chill the blood to think of. Strange to say, he is the most industrious of the two, and has actually learned the art of putting a cane-bottom in a chair. Satanta sits during the day in a different shop and chews tobacco, of which he is a passionate lover. At night they both occupy the same cell, No. 3, in the east building. They are cleanly in person and habits only by the usual coercion, and they are industrious by the same process. Big Tree, according to this rule, works all the time. He is employed in a shop in the third story, and it is curious to see him looking out of the window every now and then; curious to watch the emotions of his heart, readable in his face, as he peers into the woodland bordering the town. As a general thing these Indians are on good terms with those working and living with them, and although they have not settled down in the habits of the white man, they have learned some of his ways. Big Tree will do things on the sly, but Satanta does all he does do open and above board, and

when reprimanded plays ignorance and of course escapes. He often scolds Big Tree in vigorous Kiowa, and sometimes he whips him in real earnest. The Indian notion gives Big Tree no chance to fight back, and he takes it mutely. They are both in good health, though Satanta is less the robust Indian he was when first incarcerated.[1]

At the request of Commissioner Smith, Captain Henry Alvord wrote a lengthy analysis regarding the Kiowa situation prior to the release of Satanta. He argued that Satanta was the national leader of the tribe and that both Lone Wolf and Kicking Bird knew their reign would cease when Satanta was set free.[2] While Satanta was certainly a leading figure at the time, he was by no means the principal chief of all the Kiowas. And if Alvord meant to imply that the two chiefs opposed Satanta's release, he was also wrong. During the summer of 1873, both Lone Wolf and Kicking Bird did all they possibly could to keep their young men quiet and get the government to carry out its promise. Had new Kiowa depredations been committed in Texas, it is unlikely that Governor Davis or the United States would have permitted a parole for the prisoners under any circumstances.

Lt. Alexander W. Hoffman, Tenth Infantry, took charge of the pair at Huntsville on August 20 and escorted them by way of the M.K.T. railway to Muskogee, Indian Territory. There he turned them over to Lt. Charles G. Gordon, Sixth Cavalry, who took them by wagon to Fort Sill, where on September 5 they were lodged in the post guardhouse. Satanta was peaceful and friendly; Lone Wolf, Kicking Bird, and others were permitted to visit with him in his cell.[3]

Davis had approved the transfer of Satanta and Big Tree to Fort Sill only on condition that he would then conduct a council there with the Kiowas and secure a firm commitment to peace from the "horse Indians" bordering on Texas. Federal officials, including Commissioner Smith, felt Davis lacked experience dealing with Indians and resented this state intrusion into national Indian policy. They had no choice, however, but to let Davis take the lead. Davis and his party arrived at the post on October 3. The tribes, remembering the fracas on Grierson's porch, at first refused to meet inside the garrison, but the governor insisted and eventually prevailed.[4]

On October 6 the council gathered on the Fort Sill parade grounds. Davis and Smith, their aides, Hoag, and other Quaker officials were seated at a table facing the circle of chiefs from the various tribes of the Kiowa-Comanche and Wichita agencies. Principal among them were Lone Wolf and Kicking Bird of the Kiowas, Horseback of the Comanches, Pacer of the Plains Apaches, Buffalo Goad of the Wichitas, and Guadalupe of the

Caddos. Satanta and Big Tree, still wearing their striped prison clothes, were brought from the guardhouse and seated on a bench under heavy guard.

Davis opened the proceedings by noting that the lives of Satanta and Big Tree had been spared by the Texans, who wished to be at peace with the tribes. He had hardly begun his speech, however, when Satanta's father pushed forward to make an impassioned plea for the release of his son. "I am a poor old man," he said. "I want you to pity me and give up my son. The Indians love their children as much as the white people do theirs."[5]

Satanta was allowed to speak. "Whatever the white man thinks best," he proclaimed, "I want my people to do. Strip off these prison clothes, turn me over to my people, and they will keep their promise."[6]

Davis, who had not consulted with Smith on the matter, detailed the conditions under which he would release the two prisoners. Those experienced in Indian affairs knew that most of Davis's demands were totally unrealistic for the moment. The tribes would have to settle down on individual farms near the agency, raise crops, and tend hogs and cattle. Every camp would have a government man—to the Indians, a spy—to watch them and report their activities to their agent. Each tribal member would have to draw his own rations in person every three days and at that time answer to roll call. The warriors would be required to assist the army in tracking down other Indians who committed depredations. And, undoubtedly the condition most objectionable to every tribesman, the Indians would have to give up their riding stock and their arms.

Satanta and Big Tree, meanwhile, would be held in the Fort Sill guardhouse and, subject to the behavior of their tribe, would perhaps one day be released at the will of the governor. Even then, the pair would not be pardoned but would be subject to rearrest at any time.[7]

It is possible that the chiefs did not comprehend the full import of what Davis had said. They obviously did not understand the relationship between federal and state authority. The Kiowas, however, instinctively realized that this was no bargaining session where a consensus agreement would be reached. They had come to secure the release of Satanta and Big Tree, and the only way to achieve that end was to agree to whatever terms were laid before them. Both Lone Wolf and Kicking Bird made speeches acknowledging their subservience to Washington and willingness to comply with Davis's terms.

"I have been trying for a long time to keep peace between my people and the whites," Kicking Bird said, "but they are like boys; they sometimes do right and sometimes do not."[8]

Horseback, Pacer, Buffalo Goad, and others spoke in a similar vein. Despite their promises, however, Davis would still not release Satanta and Big Tree, and Smith backed his demands. The meeting adjourned, and the chiefs returned to their camps where anger and hostility soon took over. Kicking Bird was severely disillusioned. His heart, he said, was like a stone, with no soft spot in it. He had taken the white man by the hand as a friend, but the government had deceived the Kiowas. "Washington," he said in disgust, "is rotten."[9]

Some of the Kiowa war element met during the night and made plans to take the prisoners by force. When morning came, Kiowa warriors were posted with weapons beneath their blankets, ready to overcome the guards as they brought the prisoners forth, seize their tribesmen, and flee on fast mounts that stood saddled and ready nearby.

During the night, however, agent Haworth and Battey had worked hard to convince the governor and commissioner that if Satanta and Big Tree were not released, the frontier citizens of Texas would pay a heavy price.[10] Finally, an agreement was reached between Davis and Smith. The commissioner pledged that if the Kiowas raided into Texas, Satanta and Big Tree, or chiefs of equal rank, would be returned to prison and a roll-call check would be conducted to prevent warriors from slipping away from the reservation. The Comanches would be placed under similar restrictions and safeguards. Accordingly, a note was sent to the camps setting up a second meeting and promising that it would be more favorable than the first to the Indians.[11]

When the chiefs were assembled again the next morning, Davis appeared before them and made a short speech outlining the terms of his agreement with Smith. He also alluded to the Kiowas' having lived up to their promises by remaining peaceful during the summer. Davis then announced that he was releasing the two men without pardon to the custody of the other Kiowa chiefs. Satanta and Big Tree stepped forward and happily embraced the governor and all of the chiefs. But it was at the Kiowa camps following the meeting that the chiefs, their families, and the entire tribe celebrated their immense joy.[12]

Satanta, however, did not return to the tribe as a chief. Although still highly regarded by his people and commanding a following of warriors, he had been replaced as chief of his band while in prison by his son Tohawson. He apparently accepted this as a fact of life, he himself admitting to it.[13]

Commissioner Smith called his own meeting on the afternoon of October 8 to address the Comanche situation. Five Comanche warriors had recently made a raid into Texas and stolen a number of horses and mules. Smith demanded that the Comanches give up either the five guilty men or five others as hostages in their place. He also demanded that the Kiowas bring in five men to be held against the good behavior of Satanta and Big Tree. The chiefs, even if they wished to do so, were generally powerless to arrest their own warriors.

The tribesmen were shocked at Smith's ultimatums, and anger swept through the room. One by one, various chiefs rose to reject the idea of turning in their young men as prisoners. When Lone Wolf spoke, his voice quivered with emotion. He said the commissioner's road was too hard; his people could not follow it.

Smith foolishly accused the Kiowas of cowardice, adding to the Indians' furor. Cheevers, a Comanche chief whose band had long been quiet, charged that white renegades were causing much of the trouble and that they were the ones who should be arrested. He promised to bring in the stock that had been stolen and join with troops in capturing the white out- laws. Kicking Bird also spoke and helped to calm the meeting. In the end, Smith gave the tribes thirty days to comply or he would cut off their rations.[14]

Kicking Bird, fearing for Battey because the Comanches were con- vinced he was a spy, reluctantly permitted the Quaker to return with him to the Kiowa camp. The chief gave approval only when Stumbling Bear and Sun Boy agreed to share the responsibility for Battey's safety. Upon arrival at his camp on Rainy Mountain Creek three days from the agency, Kicking Bird sent word to Haworth that some Kiowa bands were moving northward toward the Antelope Hills. They hoped to kill buffalo and get hides for trade. He assured the agent they were trying to do as Washing- ton wished and would soon return to the reservation.[15]

The difficulty of transforming buffalo-hunting Indians into farmers was illustrated during the conference when Comanche chief Quirts Quip complained to Commissioner Smith that the government had not made him a house and cornfield as it had promised. Smith asked if his agent had not done anything for him. Quirts Quip admitted that the agent had made him a little cornfield last spring. He had come and sat down by it. But then a thunderstorm had come up right over the field. Everywhere else it was clear, but over his lodge and field the lightning flashed and thunder roared terribly. He decided there was bad medicine in the field. He left and never returned.[16]

Battey, still in ill health, returned to the agency during the last of November just as an ultimatum arrived by telegraph from Washington giving the Comanches ten days to bring in their five raiders or have their rations stopped. Fearing the edict might touch off a war with the Comanches, Haworth dispatched Battey and George Chisholm with a

Kiowa chief Lone Wolf tried to walk the peace path until the death of his son overcame him. Courtesy Western History Collection, University of Oklahoma.

letter to the Kiowas assuring them of his friendship and asking them to "keep on a good road" even though the Comanches were in trouble. He asked the Kiowas to come in close to the agency.[17]

Despite being struck by a snow and sleet storm, the two men reached Kicking Bird's camp and found that he and most of his chiefs were away on a buffalo hunt. Securing a guide, they rode on to the camp of Lone Wolf. Battey read Haworth's message to the chief and three others. Lone Wolf wanted to know about the Comanches' trouble. Battey explained that "Washington's heart had again become hard towards the Comanches." If they did not comply by bringing in the five men, there would be trouble with the soldiers. After listening carefully, Lone Wolf said this was such an important matter that he wished to think about it overnight. The next morning he had Battey take down his reply in writing.

"I want you to go to the officers at the fort," he said, "and tell them to throw away their bad words, so that my people will not be angry. I want to live friendly with everybody. I do not want to see any more war. . . . If those foolish young men have killed any of the people of Texas, they are dead. Some of those young men have been killed; they are dead. Let it all pass; do not let it make trouble among the living."[18]

Lone Wolf also brought up another matter. He told of a big council the Osages had called. Although he had not attended, the Kiowas, Comanches, Cheyennes, Arapahos, and Apaches were all there. The Osages wanted to unite the tribes—have one fire for them all. They also wanted the other tribes to join them in killing the white surveyors who were coming into the Indian Territory.

"They are our enemies," the Osages said. "They kill our buffalo, and we will kill them whenever we meet them on our land."[19]

Battey and Chisholm found Kicking Bird at his camp when they returned. Haworth's message was read to an assembly of the chiefs. On the issue of taking his band close to the agency, Kicking Bird pointed out that they had done so the previous fall on a request from Washington. Because of this his people were not able to garner any buffalo robes. Thus they were poor the whole year and could not purchase much-needed articles from the post trader.

Further, he said, the agent had not let him have his annuities when he was at the agency. Battey explained that the annuities for the Kiowas and Comanches had come packed together and had to be separated first. Could he get them now if he went in? Battey answered honestly that he did not know. Kicking Bird then addressed the issue of the Comanche trouble. His talk was recorded by Battey and eventually forwarded to the secretary of the interior. Although Kicking Bird, having just returned from meetings in the Comanche and Cheyenne camps, was in a belligerent mood, his speech was a heartfelt statement for the prairie Indian of the day:

This country, from the Arkansas to the Red river, was given by Washington to his red children, the Kiowas, Comanches, Osages, Wichitas, Cheyennes, Arapahoes, Apaches, and Caddoes. It was a country of peace. I now see white men in it making lines, setting up stones and sticks with marks on them. We do not know what it means, but [are] afraid it is not for our good. The Commissioner, by making one bad talk, has set all this country on fire. He has required a hard thing, which was not in the road our fathers travelled. It is a new road to us, and the Comanches cannot travel it—they cannot bring in the five men. If they attempt it, many women and children will be killed, and many men must die. It all rests on the commissioner.

This trouble will not affect the Comanches alone; it will spread through all these tribes, and become general. It is a new road to all the Indians of this country, and they will be affected by it.

I have taken the white people by the hand; they are my friends. The Comanches are my brothers. By and by, when I am riding on these prairies, and see the bones of the Comanches, or the skull of a white man lying on the ground, my heart will feel very sad, and I shall say, Why is this? It is because Mone-kome-haint ["Without a Pointing Finger"—the Kiowa name for the commissioner who was minus the forefinger of his right hand] made a road the Indians could not travel.

If Washington would put his soldiers all along on the frontiers, and kill every young man who goes across the line, we would cry for them, but it would be right. When they cross the line they take the chances of war. I do not want to see trouble in this land of peace; but I fear blood must flow, and my heart is sad.

The white man is strong, but he cannot destroy us all in one year; it will take him two or three, maybe four years; and then the world will turn to water or burn up. It is our mother, and cannot live when the Indians are all dead.[20]

Battey argued in response that the Comanches had done bad but that the Kiowas had nothing to do with the trouble: "If you love the Comanches—who, by getting on the bad road after Washington gave them back their women and children, made it such very hard work for you and your friends to get back Satanta and Big Tree—better than you love your wives and children, and so stay out and miss getting your annuities, the loss will be yours, and you cannot blame the agent for it."[21]

The schoolteacher's argument hit home with the Kiowa leader. Kicking Bird's entire demeanor changed, the anger fading from his face. He became calm and thoughtful and was silent for several moments. When he answered, his tone was calm and subdued.

"I know the Comanches have been raiding in Texas," Kicking Bird admitted, "and that they have done badly." Then he asked, "Had we better go in and get our annuities, or stay out?"[22]

Battey took the real essence of the question to be a choice between peace and war.

"The agent's heart is warm," he replied; "he does not want trouble to arise, but he is alone. Perhaps, if his Kiowa and Apache friends come in, they can help him to stop this trouble, even after it is begun, so that it will not amount to much."[23]

Battey's talk was well received by the chiefs. Kicking Bird agreed to take his band in to the agency. There it was learned that Washington officials had reconsidered the Comanche deadline and eased the crisis. Now the government demanded only that the Comanches return the stolen stock—as the tribe had first offered to do in the council with Davis.

But even as these developments were taking place during the last weeks of 1873, Kiowa hostiles were in action. During November a party of seven or more Kiowas under the leadership of Bird Chief observed three Englishmen conducting a wild turkey hunt at Cottonwood Falls on the North Canadian below Camp Supply. When teamster Jacob Dilsey was headed back to Camp Supply to deliver a load of turkeys and pick up fresh supplies, the Kiowas killed him and then burned his wagon with his body in it. Woman's Heart was said to have been a member of the group.[24]

Still another war party composed of twenty-one Comanche and nine Kiowa warriors was raiding into Mexico. Among these were a favorite son and a nephew of Lone Wolf. The warriors likely saw this as no violation of the agreement to cease raiding in Texas. Still, it was necessary to pass through that state, and they ultimately came in conflict with U.S. troops. After crossing the Rio Grande between Laredo and Eagle Pass, Texas, they struck the Mexican village of Olmos. There they killed fourteen Mexicans, captured two young boys, and herded away 150 horses and mules.[25]

Buoyed with this success, the party killed two U.S. citizens on the wagon road between San Antonio and Laredo, a clear violation of Kiowa vows to stop their raiding against Texas. Unfortunately for the raiders, one of the Mexican boys escaped and was found by a detachment of U.S. Fourth Cavalry under Lt. Charles L. Hudson, on a scout out of Fort Clark, Texas. Hudson caught up with the war party on December 7 near South Kickapoo Springs. In the fight that followed, nine of the Indians were killed and fifty animals recovered. Among the dead tribesmen was the son of Lone Wolf, Tau-ankia (Sitting-in-the-Saddle), who had recovered from the knee wound he suffered in 1872. Also killed was Gui-tan (Heart-of-a-Young-Wolf), the son of Red Otter, Lone Wolf's brother. Retrieving the bodies was impossible, and they were left unburied where they fell.

"To-day is a day of wailing [in] our camp," Battey wrote from Kicking Bird's camp; "news arriving of the death of two young Kiowa braves. . . . The camp resounded with the death wail, the war whoop and the song of mourning for the unreturning braves. This was revived at intervals for several days."[26]

When Lone Wolf learned of the deaths, he was far too deeply grieved and heartbroken to remember his recent words: "Some of the young men have been killed; they are dead. Let it all pass; do not let it make trouble

Tau-ankia, Lone Wolf's favorite son, was killed while on a raid into Texas. Courtesy Fort Sill Museum.

among the living." Now caught up by utter despair, he plunged deeply into mourning for his son. Philip McCusker reported from the Indian camps that in Plains Indian fashion, "Lone Wolf cut and carved himself frightfully and the old women vied with each other in cutting themselves, tearing their hair, and making all sort of extravagant demonstrations for his death. Lone Wolf burned his wagon, lodges, and all his effects . . . he also killed several horses." Other reports said he was living almost alone at some point near the Antelope Hills.[27]

For a time, Lone Wolf—who had twice been to Washington and had shaken hands with the White Father—had tried to walk the path of peace. But now his personal tragedy had shoved him back to the side of war. Once again he was a bitter enemy to the white people who had killed his son. With Lone Wolf indisposed and Satanta deposed, Kicking Bird was clearly the dominant chief of the Kiowas. He did not command the full and complete loyalty of all the Kiowa chiefs as had old Tohawson, although he clearly did of the majority. But in the days ahead, Indian officials and the military would look to him as the head chief of the tribe.

17

A Stone Thrown Away

Tribal conflicts with the U.S. Army and white civilians on the frontier began to increase in 1874. Around thirty Kiowas and Comanches were reportedly killed in various clashes with troops early in the year.[1] In February a surveyor was murdered by Indians—either Kiowas or Cheyennes, it was thought—along the Canadian River. The troubles of 1874 did not result from an organized or planned effort to overthrow white military power. Most acts against whites stemmed largely from the resentment over intrusion onto lands Indians had once controlled and over a vast array of injustices committed by both the government and private citizens on the frontier. Some infractions were conducted to avenge deaths within the tribe, out of hatred for whites, or as a continuance of the Plains warrior's penchant for action. At times, however, it was simply a case of murder for gain, as when Dilsey had been killed on the North Fork.[2]

During March, the grieving Lone Wolf began trying to recruit a party to go to Texas and recover the bones of his son and nephew. At one time he had talked of bringing his son's body to Fort Sill for burial with a cross over it, but his grief was too bitter to share with the white man. Word circulated that Lone Wolf planned to make a revenge raid when the grass next came. The Kiowas insisted that the trip would be peaceful and wanted orders sent to army posts not to attack.[3] When the military learned of Lone Wolf's party, however, patrols were sent out in an effort to intercept the band of Kiowas and Comanches. The troops were unsuccessful; but once he had retrieved his son's bones, Lone Wolf was forced to stash them in a rocky crevice of a mountainside because of military pursuit.[4]

The Kiowa chief and his party made it safely back to the reservation. But the matter was not finished. Upon finding his son's remains on the prairie, he had knelt and made a spiritual vow. One day he would take the life of a white man on the very spot where his son had died. Kicking Bird learned of this vow, and while on a visit to the agency he called Battey to one side. To kill a white man on that ground, the chief noted, Lone Wolf would first have to catch one. Kicking Bird suggested that Battey remain at the agency until there had been a chance to talk with Lone Wolf.[5]

In April Thomas Wister and James E. Rhoads of the Executive Committee of Friends, Cyrus Beede, and the local Quaker agents, making a tour of the agencies, arrived at the Fort Sill agency to meet with the Kiowas and Comanches. In his report of the visit, Beede described the scene as the tribes assembled to receive their rations.

> First came the men, who were armed with bow and arrow, revolver or rifle. Orders for live cattle were given to them, and they rode off to collect them and slaughter [them] for use. Then came the women on their ponies for the supplies of flour, sugar, coffee, baking soda, soap and tobacco. It was pleasant to behold the good humor which prevailed in the motley group. Women, children and ponies all mingled together, but none apparently interfering with each other. In one place could be seen a company of women seated in a circle around a heap of sugar. One being selected to distribute it, took a tin pan and measured to each one their portion. In another place, flour was distributed in like manner. All appeared to enjoy the work, laughing and chatting together. There was no fault-finding or complaining of unequal division, but all appeared confiding and satisfied. Then commenced the loading of the ponies. Bacon, flour, sugar, &c., being secured in various kinds of wraps, were skillfully attached to the saddle, and then the women mounted and trotted off. The children enjoyed the fun, running or crawling about among the ponies and provisions scattered over the ground.[6]

At noontime the Kiowa chiefs began arriving, with Satanta the first. Surrounded by a body of well-armed warriors, he had come in with much reluctance. Beede saw him as over six feet in height. His countenance was stern and hard, but he gave a big smile as he shook hands with the Quakers. Big Bow came soon after and then Kicking Bird, whom Beede identified as the head chief.[7] In all, over twenty chiefs and their bands were on the ground when the council met the following morning, April 11.

An 1874 Kiowa census, likely taken at this council, listed 23 bands that included Kicking Bird, (approximately) 110 persons; Satanta, 110;

Lone Wolf, 110; Big Bow, 100; Sun Boy, 95; Stumbling Bear, 80; Crow Neck, 80; Swan, 75; Red Otter, 65; Dangerous Eagle, 65; Headsick (Heidsik), 65; Woman's Heart, 65; Trailing Wolf, 65; Tohawson, 65; Feather Head, 65; Ermote, 65; Poor Buffalo, 65; Adigaquas, 65; Napawat, 65; Running Bear, 65; Euhoken, 65; Quiboile, 50; Double Vision, 50; for a total of 1,705 tribespeople.[8]

In an address Haworth read to the chiefs, the Kiowas were advised to live in peace, remain on their reservation, and stop their raiding into Texas. If they did not, it was emphasized strongly, Haworth might be removed and the tribes placed under the charge of the military. Other speakers urged them to send their children to school, cultivate their lands, and give up their unsettled life that encouraged raiding and brought them in contact with whiskey dealers who cheated and brought ruin to them.

Kicking Bird was the spokesman for the Kiowas. He said he liked the talk he had just heard. He felt confident that after a time his young men would learn to do what was right. Eventually, he said, they would plant corn, build houses, and send their children to school if the government would provide them with homes and schoolhouses and send the soldiers away. He had heard many talks from the white man, he pointed out, but the Indians never got anything from them. Nonetheless, he would try to keep his young men from raiding. If the government would give the Kiowas permission to go out and retrieve the bones of Lone Wolf's son, they would settle down and listen to what was said to them.[9]

Satanta then rose to speak. He had three parents, he declared. They were God, the Earth, and Washington (the government). If God was angry, the Kiowas would be destroyed. If the Earth got mad, they would perish. But if the government got mad, Satanta implied, it could do nothing as long as there were still plenty of buffalo—"They are medicine." The Indians did not want war, but the white man had spoiled their country. The council closed with the chiefs indicating that they supported the words of their head chief, Kicking Bird.[10]

The abdication from the road of peace to that of war by Lone Wolf was a severe blow to Kicking Bird, making his efforts at pacification all the more difficult and precarious. The year 1874 would severely test his resolve and ability as the Kiowas' leading peace advocate. Certainly, his concern for the welfare of the Kiowa women and children was not lessened by the addition to his family of two new wives, who were sisters, and an infant son known to whites as Little John.[11] There were other pressures as well. According to Battey, the Comanches very much wanted the Kiowas to join them in raiding against Texas.

Because Kicking Bird would not smoke the war pipe with them, the Comanches were constantly harassing him. On one occasion, they stole two of his best horses and one belonging to Topen. Two of the ponies were returned after Kicking Bird went to the Comanche camp and gave them a hard talk. Still, he was greatly upset that the Comanches trailed his band and camped nearby, their immense pony herds grazing off the grass around his camp area.[12]

He had other troubles. His friendship with the whites and the war chiefs' anger over it brought him into a dangerous confrontation with Woman's Heart. The incident occurred in late May 1874 when Kicking Bird brought his band on a routine visit to the agency to receive their annuity goods. On the evening of May 21 Kicking Bird dropped by the office of agent Haworth and engaged in a conversation with Haworth and Battey. The recent government issue of supplies to the tribe had been short. Haworth said he was concerned that this may have contributed to resentment against Kicking Bird among some of the Kiowas, and he was sorry they were angry with him.[13]

Kicking Bird replied that not all of the people were angry. A good number of the other chiefs and the majority of the tribe still supported him. He said, too, that his heart felt good because, as he had pushed them to do, the Comanches had brought in some of the horses and mules their young men had stolen recently. He had refused to smoke the war pipe with the Comanche chiefs, and now some of those leaders were ready to follow him and do right. Those chiefs were having the usual trouble, however, controlling their young warriors. Kicking Bird went on to say that he wanted to do right and lead the Kiowas on the right path. He was raising his daughter Topen to love the white man and to travel the white man's road. He wished to do the same with his new son, Little John.

As the three men were conversing, a Kiowa man was eavesdropping at the doorway. The man hurried to the Kiowa camp and told Chief Woman's Heart that Kicking Bird was at the agency telling lies against all the other Kiowa headmen. Woman's Heart, who had smoked the war pipe with the Comanches, was infuriated. He was a stout, seasoned war maker of middle age with a wide face, high forehead, and eaglelike eyes. Storming into Haworth's office, he accused Kicking Bird and Battey of portraying him and others as bad men. The young men, he declared, had thrown Kicking Bird away. Nothing the agent or Battey could say could disabuse the longtime war chief of what he had heard or calm his rage.

Woman's Heart left but returned to the agency the next morning at the head of a sizable body of Kiowa warriors. Sullen-faced, some trem-

Woman's Heart (Man-yi-ten) challenged Kicking Bird's friendship with whites. Courtesy Western History Collection, University of Oklahoma.

bling with anger and readiness to fight, they filed into Haworth's office. They strung their bows as they entered and laid three or four arrows across their laps as they squatted against the office wall. Others took pains to let the butts of their revolvers protrude from their tunics at the waist. The peril of the moment was etched in the tense, chalky faces of the agency clerks who quickly retreated to a distant room.

Soon after Woman's Heart and his men arrived, Kicking Bird, his brother Couquit, and Trotting Wolf rode up. Kicking Bird calmly stepped into the office at the lead of his companions. He looked slowly about the room, gazing into glowering faces that would not look back. As he seated himself, he noticeably made his own weapons readily available. He then asked that Haworth repeat their conversation of the night before and hold nothing back. Haworth did so. This was followed by a heated

Big Bow (Zepko-ette), a notorious raider before taking to the road of peace. Courtesy Western History
Collection, University of Oklahoma.

discussion between the agent and the chiefs, but the explosive situation
was eventually diffused.

On the heels of this affair, Kicking Bird received a grievous, although
unintended, insult from Haworth. The agent admitted that in making a
report to Washington he had cited Big Bow as "one of the most active
[Kiowa chiefs] in working for good."[14] He had based this comment on
Big Bow's talk during a recent visit to the agency. Big Bow had insisted then that he had thrown all his bad ways aside and claimed he
spoke for a large number of chiefs, although Lone Wolf was the big
chief.[15]

The Kiowas chose their own leaders, but government support of a
particular chief was, as Satanta had known, immensely important. Thus
the result of Haworth's accreditation of Big Bow was, it seemed, to elevate
him to the rank of leading Kiowa peace chief. Kicking Bird, who had

risked far more and worked much harder in support of the Quakers than anyone, felt grossly degraded and cast aside.[16]

Haworth had indeed committed a gross blunder. Big Bow had long been a leading hostile. Lieutenant Pratt classed Big Bow as "one of the foremost raiders along the frontiers of Texas and Kansas, and I had traced many acts of violence to him." Battey had expressed a similar opinion of Big Bow in his diary after an encounter with the Kiowa:

> Just at starting, this morning, an Indian rode up to me, asking me if I knew him. I at once recognized in him the notorious Kiowa raider Big Bow, who has, probably, killed and scalped more white people than any other living Kiowa; and who, with his brother raider, White Horse, has been for years the terror of the frontiers, not only Texas, but of Kansas, Colorado, and New Mexico. These two men, with small companies of their braves, have been continually going up and down, not as roaring lions, but prowling about in secret, seeking whom they might destroy; and woe to the white man, woman, or child, who fell in their way.[17]

Only recently, Big Bow had told scout Ben Clark, who had visited his camp of twenty-five lodges, that he wanted nothing more to do with the Fort Sill agency. They never gave him anything there, he said, and he feared he would be taken prisoner like Satanta and Big Tree for raids he had led.[18]

Deeply hurt over Haworth's admission, Kicking Bird left the agency office without speaking even to Battey. The teacher was much concerned and went looking for the chief. He found him at the post store with his family. Battey soon learned that the man who only moments before had unflinchingly faced down Woman's Heart and his men was now severely depressed. Kicking Bird said it appeared he had now been rejected both by his own people and by the government. Battey tried his best to lift his friend's spirits, insisting that if he would keep straightforward on the same road he had traveled so long, the Kiowas would yet hunt him up and say, "Kicking Bird is our chief."[19] Kicking Bird answered:

> I long ago took the white man by the hand, I have never let it go; I have held it with a firm and strong grasp, I have worked hard to bring my people on to the white man's road. Sometimes I have been compelled to work with my back towards the white people, so that they have not seen my face, and may have thought I was working against them, but I have worked with one heart and one object. I have looked ahead to the future, and have worked for the children of my people, to bring them into a position, that when they become men and women, they will take up with the white road. I have but two children of my own, but I have worked for the children of my people as though they had all been mine. Five years have I striven for this thing, and all these years Big Bow has

worked against me, to keep my people on the old bad road. When I have brought in and delivered up white captives to the agent, Big Bow has taken more. Now for a little while *he* has come on to the good road. The agent has taken him by the hand, and thrown me away, after my many years' labor. I am as a stone, broken and thrown away, one part thrown this way, and one part thrown that way. I am chief no more; but that is not what grieves me, I am grieved at the ruin of my people, they will go back to the old road.[20]

Kicking Bird sent his family off to their camp. He returned to the store, still despondent, and seated himself on the floor away from everyone. Soon white people in the store came to him in sympathy. On Battey's suggestion, they presented the chief with a woven coverlet as a token of their friendship. Battey insisted that neither he nor Haworth had thrown Kicking Bird away. This promise and the gift almost magically lifted Kicking Bird's spirits. The Kiowa rose from the floor and stood erect.

"I will now go to my camp," he said, "collect my band of people, and when I come again, you will know who is chief of the Kiowas."[21] When Battey next saw him, Kicking Bird was still fully in command as a Kiowa headman.

While many Kiowas chose to come in to the reservation, others were smoking the war pipe. Comanche-Kiowa raiding into Texas was only part of a general uprising of the prairie tribes. The Kiowas, Comanches, and Cheyennes each claimed the others were trying to talk their young men into going to war. In truth, each of the tribes had elements promoting war. The Osages, too, were active in the Territory. At times it was difficult to pinpoint the blame for atrocities, but clearly each of these tribes was involved in depredations. Every violation resonated within the Kiowa tribe and challenged Kicking Bird's efforts to lead his people down the path of peace.

There was reason enough for general animosity to Anglo-Americans over their invasion of tribal-assigned territory, the lost freedom of the prairie, poor and insufficient rations, and the mass slaughter of the all-important buffalo herds conducted by white professional hunters. Kicking Bird explained to Haworth just how important the buffalo was to the Indians and how they felt about the white man's decimation of the great herds.

The buffalo was the same to the Indians, he said, as money was to the white man. The buffalo *was* their money, their only resource with which to buy what they needed and did not receive from the government. They loved the buffalo just as the white man did his money. They felt just as bad when they saw the buffalo being killed as the white man did when his money was stolen. The buffalo, Kicking Bird said, was given to the Indians by the Great Father above, and it belonged to them.[22]

All of the major Plains tribes remained divided between the war-natured and the peace-minded. Visits to Washington, such as had taken place the previous year, were generally successful in persuading the chiefs of white invincibility. But that message often failed to transcend to the warrior body of the tribes. Battey gave an excellent example of the effect of those visits within the Kiowas.

When chiefs returned from the East to tell of the many sights they saw and the many white people they had witnessed, tribespeople at home often believed their leaders were under some sort of sorcerous spell. Not uncommonly, those who told of such unimaginable things were derided as silly-headed like "wolves running wild on the plains."[23]

One day Battey brought to the Kiowa camps some kaleidoscopic and stereoscopic views of the white man's cities, replete with images that bore out much of what Lone Wolf, Sun Boy, and others had been telling since they returned from Washington. The Kiowas were familiar with the scenes of the Colorado Rockies, but pictures of locomotives passing through deep cuts of the mountain brought expressions of wonderment. The viewers looked at pictures of Niagara Falls with open-mouthed awe.[24]

"What you think now?" Sun Boy exclaimed. "You think we all lie now? You think all chiefs who have been to Washington fools now?"[25]

But only a scant few of the prairie Indians saw the pictures, and few of the war-minded would have been influenced. It was in the air now among the warrior element to lash out against the restrictions of the reservation, seek bloody atonement for white injustices, and once again take openly to the war path.

18

Last Uprising

The emergence among the Comanches of Indian prophet Isa-tai (Rear End of a Wolf) occurred during the spring of 1874 and set the stage for a general revival of the war spirit among the prairie tribes. This came to a head when the Comanches held their first Sun Dance on the North Fork of the Red River in late June. The dance was also attended by Kiowas, Cheyennes, and others. There was talk at first of attacking the Tonkawas, the much-hated allies of the Texans whom the other tribes had long accused of cannibalism. But the Tonkawas were located near Fort Griffin, and that would mean a raid into Texas and a possible clash with U.S. troops.[1] An idea was put forth to attack Adobe Walls where a number of white buffalo hunters had located. A Kiowa party under Stone Wolf had killed and scalped two buffalo hunters named Dudley and Wallace fifteen miles southeast of the place on June 9.[2] Other hunters had been caught afield and attacked, and the idea of a mass assault on Adobe Walls and wiping out the buffalo killers appealed to many.

A makeshift group of dirt-roofed sod buildings had sprung up around the old trading post.[3] They embodied a trader's store, stables, blacksmith shop, and saloon. The population included twenty-eight men and one woman. The men, mostly hunters and all excellent marksmen, were well armed with long-range .50 caliber buffalo guns and Sharps rifles.

Led by the famous half-white Comanche chief Quanah Parker, the consolidated force of warriors launched its attack at the first light of dawn on June 27. It would have caught the settlement completely by surprise had it not been for the happenstance snapping of a roof support in Hanrahan's saloon during the night. This caused hunter Billy Dixon to rise early and spot the dark mass of advancing warriors. Thus fore-warned, the Adobe Walls occupants were able to blunt the initial attack, as well as others that followed during the day.

Although Indian sharpshooters picked off all of the Adobe Walls horses, mules, and oxen, the long range of the buffalo guns and accuracy of the hunters kept the Indians well at bay. Three Adobe Walls defenders died in the fracas, while seven Comanches and five Cheyennes were killed and a number of others were wounded. No Kiowas were killed. Arapahos present at the fight told McCusker that Isa-tai, who had been afraid to charge with the others, had his horse shot from under him and was rescued only with great difficulty. The Cheyennes had declared him a fraud and a coward. Satanta, Lone Wolf, Woman's Heart, and White Horse were said to have been among the Kiowas participating in the skirmish.[4]

The Cheyennes were also on the warpath elsewhere. On July 3 a Cheyenne party attacked a train under wagonmaster Patrick Hennessey on the road between the Cheyenne-Arapaho agency and Wichita, Kansas. They tied Hennessey to a wagon wheel, burned him to death, and killed his three drivers. Cheyenne-Arapaho agent John D. Miles discovered the gruesome scene while fleeing from his agency to Kansas. He reported the matter to Washington in a telegram from Osage City, Kansas.[5]

On July 8 Haworth also reported on the Adobe Walls fight, noting that for some time the white hunters had been slaughtering buffalo and leaving their bodies to rot on the prairie, "which has had a very bad influence upon the Indians, who regard them as sacred, or in their language 'Medicine,' the gift to them of the Great Spirit, and they do not expect to survive their extermination."[6] He added:

> The Kiowa Medicine dance has closed. An old man came in from Kicking Bird's band; he reported them divided in sentiment; the Cheyennes had been making very strong overtures to them; the majority of them were in favor of remaining loyal and friendly. I am expecting Kicking Bird, Sun Boy, Stumbling Bear, Satanta, and a number more chiefs in to-morrow or [the] next day. Kicking Bird sent me word I need not be uneasy about his half of the Kiowas; that they intended to do right whether the others did or not, and he did not want me to give them up and let my heart get tired, and quit, but stay and help those who wanted to do right; and he thought the others would soon get tired and be sorry for doing wrong.[7]

On July 11 Haworth reported the arrival of Kicking Bird with ten other Kiowa chiefs. Big Bow and Satanta, Kicking Bird said, were in favor of peace and would come in, but Lone Wolf and three or four other chiefs advocated joining the Cheyennes in a war against whites. Haworth insisted that Kicking Bird and Pacer were working earnestly to keep their people out of trouble.[8] This was supported by Napawat, the Kiowa high priest, who assured Haworth of his friendship and claimed the Kiowas would not go to war without his sanction.

Lone Wolf was still determined to retrieve his son's bones and avenge his death. After the Sun Dance he remained behind and began recruiting for a revenge raid into Texas. Because he had ridiculed the warriors who had gone off and left the bodies of his son and nephew, he had little luck enlisting followers. It was only when Maman-ti volunteered to lead the group that the war party began to form.

As the countryside burned in the sweltering heat of midsummer, Maman-ti led the group of around fifty Kiowas back to Cox Mountain from where he had launched his Wagon Box victory three years earlier. After chasing some cowboys back to the nearby headquarters of Loving Ranch, the war party spied a posse of twenty-five Texas Rangers intently following the trail of Comanches who had killed a cowboy the day before. The preoccupied rangers rode into a trap set by Maman-ti and found themselves pinned down in a shallow depression not far from a small creek.

The scorching July sun soon caused the rangers to suffer badly from thirst. That evening two of the men made a dash for a nearby creek to get water. They reached the stream and filled their canteens, but on the return trip they were charged by a squad of mounted Kiowas. One of the rangers managed to escape, but the other was caught and driven from his mount with a lance by Satanta's son Tohawson. Lone Wolf rode up and axed the man to death, finally gaining the gory revenge he wanted so badly. Another ranger died from wounds received in the fight, but the remainder eventually made it to the Loving Ranch house.[9]

These infractions, in addition to theft of stock, the murder of a cattle herder, and other depredations within close proximity to Fort Sill, provoked a reversal of thinking by official Washington. With the approval of Grant's secretary of the interior, Columbus Delano, the War Department issued orders reinstituting military control over those Indians considered hostile. Friendly and unfriendly Kiowas would be separated by instructing the former to establish their camps on Cache Creek and by making a formal enrollment of them preparatory to a campaign against the hostiles. Orders for this action reached Fort Sill on July 26, 1874.[10]

This overriding of the Quaker Indian peace policy greatly upset agent Haworth. It also disturbed the Kiowa chiefs, who resented the enrollment. Woman's Heart was particularly belligerent. He and his men waved their pistols and made threats against the peaceful Indians. Only Haworth's interference prevented his being jailed by the military.[11]

True to his word, Kicking Bird led three-fourths of the Kiowas back to their reservation at Fort Sill where he established what an officer termed a "city of refuge" for his people.[12] He advised Haworth to warn whites to be careful where they went, as they might be killed.[13] On August 17 the agent wrote that 250 lodges of Kiowas were camped on Cache Creek fifteen miles from the agency. The absent bands included those of Lone Wolf, Red Otter, Maman-ti, Tohawson, and Big Bow.[14]

With the Quaker policy faltering badly and pressure mounting to end the Indian depredations in Texas and elsewhere, Delano approved Sheridan's plan to conduct a multipronged military campaign into the Indian country to beat down the hostile prairie tribes and drive them to the reservation. Similar to the 1868 campaign, five columns would be sent into the field from different directions.

Lt. Col. Nelson Miles would march from Fort Dodge to Camp Supply and push on from there; Maj. William R. Price from Fort Union, New Mexico; Mackenzie from Fort Concho, Texas; Davidson from Fort Sill; and Lt. Col. George P. Buell from Fort Griffin, Texas. All of these units would converge on the hostiles' retreat along the upper Red River of southwestern Indian Territory and the Texas Panhandle. This offensive would become known as the Red River War.[15]

Originally, the operation was scheduled for the summer of 1874. A severe period of searing temperatures and drought gripped the Plains. In addition, the country was inundated with swarms of grasshoppers. It was decided to postpone field operations until cooler weather came in the fall. But even as preparations were under way, trouble erupted within the reservation area.

In late August, against instructions, Lone Wolf, Woman's Heart, Satanta, Poor Buffalo, and other chiefs took their bands to the Wichita agency at Anadarko. Reluctant to go to their Fort Sill agency, they hoped to get in on the August 22 ration-day issue of the Wichitas, Caddos, and other docile tribes. Also camped near the Wichita agency were friendly Penateka Comanches and a band of hostile Quahada Comanches under Chief Red Food. Nearly all the Kiowa leaders were there except Kicking Bird and allied bands, who remained on Cache Creek. Big Bow was away on a raiding expedition.

The intruders began looting the melon fields and corn cribs of the Wichita agency tribes and demanded that the agency provide them with beef and other rations. Agent Richards was away, but his alarmed assistant sent word to Fort Sill urging the authorities there to come and get their Indians. Davidson responded by marching to the Wichita agency with four troops of Tenth Cavalry buffalo soldiers.[16]

Davidson demanded that Red Food and his band surrender their weapons and become prisoners of war. Red Food was agreeable until Davidson's men attempted to collect not only guns and ammunition but also bows and arrows, which were normally excluded from surrender.

Spurred by taunts from Kiowas, Red Food suddenly gave his war whoop, leaped aboard his pony, and fled. The troops fired after him to no avail. Kiowas under Lone Wolf and Woman's Heart began shooting at the troops. A general melee resulted, with friendly chiefs trying desperately to separate their people from the mixed issue-day crowd.[17]

The remainder of the day was chaos. Parties of Kiowas and Comanches rampaged through the surrounding area, ravaging farms, burning property, and killing any white men they encountered. Other Indians mobbed and looted the store of trader William Shirley. Davidson and his men responded under great difficulty, not knowing which Indians were friendly and which were not. That evening Davidson ordered his men to burn Red Food's encampment of around eighty lodges.[18]

The hostiles reacted the next morning by setting fire to the prairie. The wind-driven blaze threatened the agency mill and other buildings, but the troops and others finally managed to save them. The Wichita schoolhouse five miles from the agency was burned to the ground, and numerous homes and lodges of agency Indians were looted and destroyed, their ponies, cattle, and other stock either stolen or killed. Several of Black Beaver's men were killed, including his white son-in-law.

More troops arrived from Fort Sill. By August 24 the warring Indians had fled, and the military had the situation under control. Kicking Bird, along with Sun Boy and other friendly chiefs such as Comanches Cheevers and Horseback and Pacer of the Apaches, rode to the agency to offer their assistance in quieting the disturbance.[19]

The outbreak at the Wichita agency only added to the complaints of the peaceful tribes in the area. Wichita chief Chestedadessa expressed the view of his people:

> The trouble and suffering was caused by the Kiowas and Comanches camping near our village, and by their bad conduct involving themselves in a war with the United States troops. Many innocent people were killed, and my people, fearing they would be involved in the war, fled from their homes, in their haste abandoning all their property but their houses. The Kiowas plundered our village, robbed us of all that we had, burnt our school house, destroyed our crops that we had gathered and laid by for winter use.[20]

Comanche chief Horseback cut his hair in mourning for his son. Courtesy Western History Collection, University of Oklahoma.

As a result of the Anadarko fight, the Kiowas, Comanches, and Kiowa-
Apaches effectively separated into the peaceful and hostile groups the
military wanted. The outlawed bands fled toward the Staked Plains west
of the Wichita Mountains. Some of the peaceful chiefs under Kicking
Bird also abandoned their camps at the agency and sought to hide out on
the prairie. Word was sent out for them to return. When they did not do
so, Kicking Bird went to Davidson and asked permission to send a runner out after five chiefs and their families near old Fort Cobb. Davidson
did so on September 5, noting in his report on the affair that "Kicking
Bird tried hard to save his tribe from just punishment, but the turbulent
spirits were too much for him."[21]

Six chiefs responded, bringing in 77 tribespeople who gave up
twenty-one Lehman rifles, eleven Spencer carbines, ten revolvers, and

twenty-seven bows and arrows. They had remained peaceful even though Lone Wolf had visited their camp and invited them to join his people.[22] Haworth estimated in September that Kicking Bird's 585 people represented "as much, or more, than four-fifths of the Kiowas, who were enrolled as friendly."[23]

Clearly, Kicking Bird had become the one chief whom the tribespeople and whites alike looked to for avoiding the scourge of war. Allied with and supporting his efforts toward peace were tribal leaders such as Stumbling Bear, Sun Boy, and others. The hostile chiefs, meanwhile, led the remainder of the Kiowas westward to the head of the Washita River in the Texas Panhandle. Their objective was to reach the seemingly safe haven of the Palo Duro Canyon. Their flight was interrupted, however, on September 9 when the Indians discovered a supply train on its way to meet the military expedition under Miles.

The Kiowa warriors quickly made their medicine, painted themselves for battle, and rushed out to attack the thirty-six-wagon train under the escort of thirteen Sixth Cavalry troops and fifty Fifth Infantry soldiers under Capt. Wyllys Lyman. When the Kiowas appeared, Lyman circled his wagons and successfully held off their charge.[24]

Unable to overrun the wagon train, the Kiowas laid siege to it. The standoff continued for four long days. During this time, word of the fight reached Kicking Bird at Fort Sill. He sent two messengers to the scene, advising the tribesmen to give up their attack on the train and come in to the reservation. The excitement of the battle was too much for the couriers; they joined in the fray.

Even as this siege was under way, on September 12 a large group of Kiowas and Comanches attacked a party of four soldiers and scouts Amos Chapman and Billy Dixon, who were on their way to Camp Supply with dispatches from Miles. The six men took refuge in a buffalo wallow and held the circling Indians at bay. One soldier was killed in the all-day fight, and scout Chapman was wounded in the leg, causing it to be amputated when the men finally reached Camp Supply.[25]

With their families hungry, their horses overworked, and the knowledge that other troops were active in the vicinity, the Kiowas eventually withdrew. Satanta, Woman's Heart, and Big Tree hid out in the Red Hills near present Geary, Oklahoma. Satanta soon decided that he wished to give himself up, but he did not wish to go to Fort Sill. Instead, he sent Big Tree in to the Cheyenne and Arapaho agency to arrange for him to surrender their twenty-four lodges to troops there.[26] On October 4 Satanta's party arrived at the Cheyenne agency with 145 tribespeople that included 37 warriors, 40 women, 66 children, and

2 old men. They surrendered thirteen rifles, nineteen bows, and four lances.

"I am tired of fighting," Satanta told Lt. Col. Thomas H. Neill, "and I do not want to fight any more. I came in here to give myself up and do as the white chief wishes. I want to cultivate a farm at the Cheyenne agency here. I do not like the agency at Fort Sill. I am half Arapahoe, half Kiowa, and I want to live near the Arapahoes."[27]

The famous Kiowa insisted that when the fighting started at the Wichita agency he had packed up and left and had taken no part in the fight. He later told Quaker Jonathan Richards that at the time of the fight he had gone to a Caddo village with Woman's Heart to get melons and found some whiskey there. He had been so drunk, he claimed, that he hardly knew what he had done.[28]

In any case, Neill was not impressed. He immediately put the Kiowa leaders in chains, and they were soon headed under escort for Fort Sill.[29] Commissioner Smith wrote to the secretary of the interior to say he felt Satanta had not been engaged in acts of violence while on parole. This plea, however, failed to persuade higher officials who were determined to punish the Kiowas for their hostilities. By approval of the president and on orders from General Sheridan, Satanta was turned over to Lt. Patrick Kelliher on November 5, 1874, to be escorted back to prison at Huntsville, Texas, by way of the railroad stop at Caddo, Indian Territory.[30]

The *Oklahoma Star* at Caddo noted the event, commenting: "Last Saturday Satanta passed through town in the charge of a U.S. officer, on his way to his old quarters in the Huntsville penitentiary, where it is hoped he will remain til the Lord takes a liking to him."[31]

Sheridan's campaign was launched when Miles led his Fort Supply columns down Wolf Creek into the Texas Panhandle during August. After a minor engagement at Adobe Walls, Miles's command was attacked by a large body of Cheyennes on the Canadian. His overwhelming firepower forced the Cheyennes to flee southward toward the Red River.[32]

The most damaging blow against the hostile elements, however, was struck by Mackenzie. The bulk of the warring Kiowas under Maman-ti and other chiefs had taken their families into the Palo Duro Canyon, pitching their camps in the bottom of the chasm. There they were joined by other bands of Comanches and Cheyennes.

The refugees felt secure within the towering walls of the gorge that they believed would provide ample protection from discovery and attack. Their sense of safety, however, was misleading. Mackenzie, following an Indian trail picked up by his Tonkawa scouts, discovered the Indian encampment on September 26. At dawn the following morning his troopers,

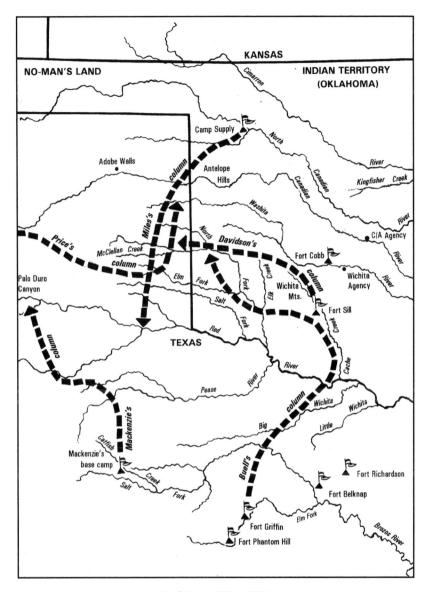

Red River War, 1874

leading their mounts, worked their way down the sides of the canyon. They had reached the canyon floor and reformed before they were discovered.[33]

Attacking down the canyon, Mackenzie and his men drove the over-whelmed tribespeople before them. The warriors fought from behind

221

boulders and cedar trees to delay the onslaught, but there was no chance to save anything. The Kiowas and other bands lost all of their invaluable, life-sustaining property: lodges, foodstuff, robes, clothes, camping paraphernalia, horses. Mackenzie captured 1,414 Indian ponies and mules. Remembering how the Quahadas had retaken their horses on the Sweetwater, he had 1,048 of the animals destroyed, some by gunfire and others, to conserve ammunition, by driving them off a cliff onto the floor of the Palo Duro.[34] A trooper later described the scene:

> All the forenoon the slaughter was continued, and until over one thousand ponies' dead bodies were scattered o'er the plains. Numbers of them were young and many very handsome, and it seemed the greatest pity to be compelled to kill them; but, taking everything into consideration, it was undoubtedly the wisest course to pursue; for it was the very worst blow that could be administered to the Indians, their ponies being their most valuable property.[35]

Buell, marching north from Fort Griffin, Texas, was also successful. On October 9 he burned several camps in present Greer County, Oklahoma. Buell reported the destruction of over 500 lodges and the capture of a large number of Indian mounts.

Woman's Heart, Bird Chief, Little Crow, White Wolf, Tabananica, and Red Food, all of whom surrendered to Maj. George W. Schofield at Elk Creek on October 21, were placed in chains in the basement of the post guardhouse and held there through the winter. Big Tree, who was not considered to have violated his parole, was confined in the post icehouse as a prisoner of war along with 117 other Kiowa and Comanche men and boys.[36]

On November 8 Lt. Frank D. Baldwin, on his way from the field to Camp Supply to pick up supplies for Miles, attacked a Cheyenne camp on McClellan Creek. Baldwin charged through the village with his cavalry and infantry troops in mule-drawn wagons. Most of the Cheyennes escaped, but the village was taken and destroyed. Two captive white girls, Julia and Nancy Germain, were rescued.[37] Still other engagements added to the loss of lodges, food supplies, robes, and horses for the Indians.

Price's Fort Union, New Mexico, command drove eastward across the Texas Panhandle searching for Indians. Crossing Miles's line of march, Price's unit finally located an Indian village on Gageby Creek. The occupants of the village escaped, but Price destroyed their lodges, food supply, and camp accouterments.

Davidson, held up by the Anadarko affair, did not take to the field until mid-October when he moved north to Chandler Creek and on to

Fort Cobb.[38] Riding with the troops were guides and scouts from other Plains tribes. In addition to five white scouts, Davidson's column, which left Fort Sill on October 21, 1874, was supported by over sixty members of the peaceful Plains tribes that included Wichitas, Pawnees, Tawakonis, Wacos, Kichais, Caddos, Delawares, Arapahos, and one Comanche under the command of Lieutenant Pratt.[39]

North of Fort Cobb in the Red Hills near present Geary, Davidson's Tenth Cavalry buffalo soldiers attacked and destroyed fifty Cheyenne lodges. The Cheyenne warriors fought a delaying action that permitted their people to scatter into the hills, but the band was forced to abandon pack animals that carried their camping equipment.[40]

During mid-November a driving sleet storm and bitter cold swept across the Plains, effectively ending the campaign. It caught Davidson's command on McClellan Creek of the Texas Panhandle and drove the frozen and hungry command back to Fort Sill. Another Fort Sill column of Tenth Cavalry under Major G. W. Schofield conducted a search to the north of the Cheyenne agency during the last three weeks of December 1874. During the operation twenty Cheyennes were captured on the head-waters of the Kingfisher Creek by Schofield—much to the chagrin of the Cheyenne agency military who felt Fort Sill troops had no business oper-ating in their area.[41]

There were other engagements between various arms of Sheridan's offensive and the now desperate bands of Kiowas, Comanches, Chey-ennes, Arapahos, and Kiowa-Apaches still on the prairies. When Indian camps were discovered, they were attacked, the inhabitants sent fleeing, and the villages torched. Not many Indians were killed, but those tribespeople who escaped were left without shelter, robes, or food and with very little clothing in the dead of winter. Further, their fighting men had precious little weaponry or ammunition with which to fight. Many had no choice but to make their way to Fort Sill or Darlington and turn themselves over to the authorities there.

Die-hard leaders such as Lone Wolf, Tohawson, and Maman-ti re-mained out, knowing that if they did come in they would surely be sent to prison the same as Satanta. Lone Wolf and six of his warriors were re-ported to be hiding somewhere between the Red Hills and the Antelope Hills.[42] Following the surrender of Double Vision and his small band on November 19, Kicking Bird estimated to Haworth that close to 300 Kiowa warriors were still out.[43]

On December 8, 1874, Gen. C. C. Augur reported that "Kicking Bird has given me names of four of his people now in the ice house who participated in murders in this vicinity last summer."[44]

Capt. Richard H. Pratt, a friend and admirer of Kicking Bird.
Miles, *Personal Recollections*. Courtesy Bison Books edition,
University of Nebraska Press.

Davidson placed Lieutenant Pratt in charge of the Indian prisoners
and assigned him the task of determining the crimes for which they
would be held liable.[45] He was ordered to review the records of the Kiowas'
most "turbulent" men and take testimony regarding their warring activities. Whites and Indians alike were called to testify. From these interviews Pratt prepared a list of potential candidates for imprisonment.

Final resolution of determining the guilt for most tribesmen was
reached following a trip to the Wichita and Cheyenne agencies Pratt
made in company of Capt. C. D. Emory, Judge Advocate of the military Department of Texas. Emory, who had come to Fort Sill for a
court-martial trial, had been asked to work up the cases of Indians
who had committed crimes within the past two years. "The cases that
first suggested themselves to me as most likely to be conducted to a

successful issue," he later reported to Mackenzie, "were the series of murders committed in August last, at the Wichita agency 35 miles from here."[46]

Emory conducted interviews with witnesses who included Black Beaver; Dr. J. J. Sturm, who resided between Fort Sill and the Wichita agency; interpreters and scouts Ben Clark and Romero; and other agency employees, as well as tribesmen. Chief Grey Beard, a noted Cheyenne war leader, told Emory and Pratt that two days before the Adobe Walls fight, Lone Wolf and Maman-ti had ridden into his camp on Gageby Creek with two bloody scalps, declaring that they belonged to two white men (buffalo hunters) they had just killed.

"I believe that a Commission would receive Indian testimony for what it is worth," Emory concluded in his report, "but it is hard to get and I can hardly say how reliable it is after it is gotten. As yet none have turned states evidence."[47]

For his part, Pratt concluded: "Much of the evidence, heretofore obtained, is confirmed, criminating Kiowa and Comanche prisoners now in the guard-house."[48]

One of the leading candidates for imprisonment was White Horse, a large, powerfully built man whose happy countenance belied his capacity for mayhem. He had been enrolled as a "friendly Indian" in August by Captain Sanderson on the basis of Kicking Bird's vouching that the twenty-seven-year-old warrior chief had not engaged in hostilities during 1874.

Pratt, however, was unwilling to overlook charges that White Horse had been involved in the wagon-train attack at Howard Wells, the Lee family massacre, and possibly the murder of the Koozers. Further, testimony from whites and—importantly—from Lone Wolf tied White Horse to the murder of two Mexicans on the Fort Sill–Wichita agency road.

This had occurred following an incident when White Horse and a party of Indians had gone to the house of Dr. J. J. Sturm and threatened to kill him. Sturm's life had been saved only through the intervention of Comanche chief Horseback and a messenger sent by Kicking Bird. The bodies of the dead Mexicans were found nearby soon after, and it was generally believed White Horse and his men had killed them.[49]

Pratt felt the young chief deserved a far worse fate than imprisonment and wanted him sent to Texas to be tried on the Koozer and Lee matters. At Davidson's request, Haworth sent word for Kicking Bird, Sun Boy, and White Horse to come see him. When the agent told White Horse he was to be arrested for his part in the murder and kidnapping of the Lee family, he consented peacefully. The three chiefs went with

Haworth to the officer's quarters where White Horse was placed under arrest.[50] Pratt had him placed in irons in solitary confinement to cure him, Pratt said, of the same "insolent, swaggering, braggadocio disposition" that had affected Maman-ti before he was similarly isolated for a time.[51]

A writer for the *Catholic World*, who happened to be at Fort Sill during this time, described a touching scene that occurred when White Horse's two mothers—his natural mother and an aunt—were permitted a brief reunion with him in the guardhouse.

> The mother rushed to her son, threw her arms around him, kissed him on both cheeks, while the tears rolled down her face; but she uttered not a word. The aunt kissed him in like manner. White Horse submitted to their embraces, but made no emotion of responding affection. He seemed a little nervous under their caresses. . . . They sat on a rough wooden bench, White Horse in the centre, his mother on his right, his aunt on the left, each holding one of his hands in both of hers. White Horse uttered no sound; no gesture betrayed any emotion, yet I thought I could detect a moistening of the eye. . . . I suppose I ought to be ashamed to say it; but the truth must be told, and I must confess that, villain as he was, I could not help feeling for him.[52]

Haworth interceded on behalf of White Horse, arguing that the Kiowa had remained at peace since the Adobe Walls fight. When Sanderson enrolled White Horse, the agent argued, the officer had promised that the Kiowa would not be held responsible for crimes committed prior to Adobe Walls.[53]

Haworth asked Hoag if the Kiowa were to be defended by council selected by the Interior Department or by the military court—or if there would be any trial at all.[54] This last option would prove to be the prisoners' fate.

19

Gone the Warriors

With limited holding capacity in both the guardhouse and the icehouse, Colonel Davidson issued orders for those Indians against whom no accusations had been found to be released and turned over to the custody of Kicking Bird, Dangerous Eagle, and Comanche chiefs Cheevers and Horseback.[1] As of January 1, 1875, forty-one Kiowas and thirty-eight Comanches remained confined in the post icehouse. Seven Kiowas and three Comanches were being held in the guardhouse in irons, four of whom were charged with murder.[2]

The coldest weather of the season struck on January 9, the temperature dropping to below zero readings. The prisoners shivered in their cells, but they were little worse off than the tribespeople in the camps. Most had suffered severe loss of property and personal belongings, as testified to by the report that 600 confiscated Indian ponies were sold at auction in Wichita in one day's time.[3]

Haworth opined that Kicking Bird had been nothing short of heroic in holding his people quietly on the reservation under such conditions. The chief had seen his once proud and abundant horse herd dwindle to a scant few, and some of those were in very poor condition. Still, he said, "he had come in to take the hand of Washington, and he intended that nothing should make him tired, or cause his heart to change."[4]

Davidson and Pratt looked to the Kiowa peace leader for help in arranging for the peaceful surrender of the militant Kiowa leaders. Kicking Bird had suggested an approach through Big Bow, whose band was off with a village of Comanches at the time of Mackenzie's attack at Palo Duro. When refugees from the canyon arrived at his camp to tell of their disaster, Big Bow had fled toward New Mexico. There many of the Kiowas' horses were stolen by a party of Mexican traders and Navajo Indians. Big Bow's situation now desperate, he and his band limped back to the west side of the Wichita Mountains and looked for an opportunity to surrender.[5]

Kicking Bird convinced Davidson that Big Bow knew where the other Kiowas were hiding and could help bring them in. Kicking Bird was permitted to send word to the fugitive chief with Davidson's promise of safe conduct if he would come to Fort Sill and confer about surrendering. Big Bow arrived there on January 27, 1875, with four men and twelve women and children and was allowed to go into camp without being arrested.[6]

Big Bow told of a big fight some Quahada and Noconie Comanches had engaged in with Texas soldiers (Texas Rangers) somewhere around San Antonio while returning from a raid into Mexico. Several of the Comanches, including Horseback's son, were killed. Horseback cut off his hair and went into mourning. Big Bow said also that the Kiowa bands still out were low on ammunition and anxious to surrender.

During a meeting in Davidson's office, Big Bow said he was willing to surrender at a certain date if he would be permitted to bring his people in to the post unmolested. Davidson agreed and promised that if the Kiowa did so, he would be absolved from all punishment.[7] After the chief had left to return to his band, Davidson prepared to lead a large command of cavalry troops and Indian scouts to accept Big Bow's surrender in the field.[8]

Pratt, however, suggested that such a show of force might cause Big Bow's people to panic and run away. He recommended that a smaller party be sent to bring Big Bow and his band to Fort Sill for a formal surrender. Davidson agreed, and Pratt organized a group that consisted of Kicking Bird, Phil McCusker, the medicine man Napawat, and sixteen Indian scouts. Forty miles west of the post, they were met by three of Big Bow's warriors who displayed a white flag of truce. An agreement was made to meet in camp near a mountain stream Pratt's party had just passed. The Kiowas joined them at the stream with their horses, mules, and travois, which were loaded with their lodges, camp utensils, and small children.

"I established my camp well to one side," Pratt wrote, "and soon the lodges were all up and the animals out to graze, and when all were ready, as the commanding officer's representative, I received the surrender of

Pratt's meeting with Big Bow, sketched by Kiowa artist Etahdeleuh (Boy Hunting) at the surrender of 72 lodges. Courtesy Yale Collection of Western Americana, Beinecke Rare Book and Manuscript Library.

all their war material and enumerated the guns, pistols, bows, arrows, quivers, spears, and shields. They were all brought by the owners and piled together on the ground near one of the wagons."[9]

The band was destitute, starved, and eager to be taken back to the agency. The Kiowa men were lined up so a census could be taken. This done, Pratt distributed bread, sugar, coffee, and other foodstuff he had brought for that purpose.[10]

Kicking Bird and Napawat went with Big Bow to his camp that evening. After his people had eaten their first good meal for some time, Big Bow told Pratt his people now felt happy and wished to hold a dance if they could. Pratt gave his approval and attended as a guest along with Kicking Bird, Napawat, and McCusker. When the drums started, however, the Kiowas displayed little enthusiasm for a celebration. They were finally energized when a young warrior began performing a wild dance with a knife. At one point when the dance was at a fever pitch, he leaned threateningly over Pratt with the knife, only to be pulled back by another dancer. Pratt felt he had had a very close call.[11]

After returning to Fort Sill, Kicking Bird was again called upon, this time to organize a party of 9 Indian scouts to accompany himself, Big Bow, and McCusker in going after the remaining Kiowas. The group was gone for some time, but finally on February 26 they arrived back at Fort Sill at the lead of a forlorn column of 250 Kiowas. Maman-ti, who had been located on the Salt Fork of the Red River along with Red Otter;

Tohawson; and Poor Buffalo were among those surrendering. Lone Wolf followed on February 18. These bands still had 475 horses and mules in their possession, but the people were badly impoverished and starved.[12] Lone Wolf, Red Otter, Maman-ti, and Poor Buffalo were placed in the guardhouse in irons.[13]

Gen. John Pope, commanding the Military Division of the Missouri at Fort Leavenworth, offered a plan to Washington whereby the captive hostiles of the Indian Territory would be placed under military guard on a reservation north of Leavenworth. His proposal was tentatively approved by the president, but cost factors eventually killed the plan. Pope also considered forming a military commission to try the Cheyenne prisoners at Fort Leavenworth. Fearing this would alarm the hostiles still out, however, he delayed the matter.[14]

Pope's plan was eventually dropped in favor of another place to incarcerate those involved in the uprising. Orders were issued by Secretary of War William W. Belknap for commanders at Darlington and Fort Sill to select those guilty of the most serious crimes and the so-called ringleaders. They would then be placed in chains and sent to far-off Fort Marion, Florida, where they would be imprisoned in the ancient Spanish-built fortress of Castillo de San Marcos. The famous Seminole leader Osceola had been held there for a time after his capture in Florida.

Not all is known of how Kicking Bird came to be involved in the selection of the Kiowa prisoners. As Pratt tells it, several hundred Indians were being held as prisoners at Fort Sill, and fifty of the leaders had been placed in irons. Davidson issued an order that divided the Indians into three classes—those against whom no crime or disturbance had been charged, those thought to have been involved in crimes but against whom there was no evidence, and those who were known to be guilty of having committed notorious acts against whites.[15]

Beyond the main perpetrators it was difficult to choose which ones would be used as examples. Davidson grew tired of tribesmen appealing to him on the matter, and he turned the problem over to Pratt to handle. Pratt claimed, however, that when he approached Kicking Bird as leader of the friendly Kiowas, the chief refused to help, saying he would deal only with the commanding officer of the post. Pratt reported this to Davidson, and the general suggested a ploy.

First, Pratt should find out who among the Kiowas was yearning to take over Kicking Bird's position as chief. That person would be called in and told that since he is a leading Kiowa figure, he had been chosen to help find out who had been guilty of depredating. He would then be told that if he would be willing to point them out, the military would provide some bread, beef, coffee, and sugar so he could hold a special feast to talk the matter over with other leaders. At the same time, Pratt would be polite but distant with Kicking Bird.

Inquiring about, Pratt selected Dangerous Eagle, the brother of Big Tree, as the man to approach. Haworth had earlier recommended him as a "good man." On the same day the Anadarko fight took place—August 21, 1874—the agent had written a note giving Dangerous Eagle permission to go to the Wichita agency and persuade other Kiowas to join Kicking Bird on the Little Washita.[16] On January 9, 1875, Davidson listed Dangerous Eagle along with Kicking Bird and Comanche chiefs Cheevers and Horseback as those who could be placed over the peaceful tribesmen against whom no charges had been made.[17]

Dangerous Eagle, according to Pratt, was ready and eager to pick out the Kiowa offenders when Pratt offered the special rations. The Kiowa had already supplied a good deal of information when Kicking Bird came to Pratt and said he had decided he would help.

"The conclusion of the matter," Pratt wrote later, "was that from these and other sources we found out who led and who were in each of the several parties of Kiowas who had been most active in hostility along the frontier during several years past."[18]

In addition to the four main chiefs—Lone Wolf, Woman's Heart, White Horse, and Maman-ti—the prisoners included minor chiefs Double Vision and Bird Chief, thirteen Kiowa warriors, and eight Kiowa warriors of Mexican descent, some of whom had been with the tribe for many years. It was only as a result of Kicking Bird's efforts in his behalf that Big Bow was not sent to Fort Marion. Satanta's son Tohawson was originally scheduled for inclusion but was also dropped from the list.[19]

Whether Kicking Bird had become involved in the selection of the Kiowa prisoners out of a wish to defend or advance his role as the leading peace chief or because he had concluded it would be far better for all if he took on the chore himself is a question that will never be firmly decided. On this matter, Kiowa historian Hugh Corwin wrote: "It has always seemed to the writer, very unfair, that the army authorities should have placed on Kicking Bird, the task of picking those of his tribe that were to be sent to prison in Florida. . . . However, such was his task, and he performed it, as he had many others, the best he could."[20]

Comanche chief Toshawah had little sympathy for the militants. "The soldiers have arrested and put in irons the worst of the men among the Kiowas and Comanches," he observed. "I hear these men are to be taken away and punished for wrongs they have done the white man and the

White Horse (Tsain-tainte), accused of several fron-
tier murders, was sent to prison at Fort Marion.
Courtesy Western History Collection, University of
Oklahoma.

Indian. While my people are sorry they were so foolish, still they have no
one but themselves to blame."[21]

In the end, twenty-seven Kiowa men, nine Comanches, and one
Caddo were selected from Fort Sill for imprisonment in Florida. The
army issued specific charges against each of them. Lone Wolf, age fifty-
five, was charged with killing two buffalo hunters near Adobe Walls in
early 1874 and with leading an attack in which three surveyors were
murdered. Woman's Heart, age unknown, was accused of taking part in
the Lyman's wagon-train attack, for an assault on frontiersman Amos
Chapman and party, and for the murder of a man below Fort Supply.
White Horse, age thirty, was charged with various crimes, including the
attacks on the Lee and Koozer families and on a mail stage west of Fort

Concho, Texas. Numerous charges were issued against Maman-ti as well, including the murder of a white woman and child in revenge for the deaths of two of his men who were killed during a raid.[22]

Twenty-two-year-old Wohaw, or Beef, was accused of participating in the murders of three men, including Jacob Dilsey on the North Canadian below Fort Supply. Bird Chief (also known as Bird Medicine or Bad Eye), age forty-three, was also charged in the Dilsey killing, along with the murders of three other men in Barbour County, Kansas. Sixty-two-year-old Double Vision was said to have held the bridle of Romero's horse, restraining it, as others murdered Earnest Modest. Bear in the Clouds (Sa-a-qui-a-da), forty-eight, was also implicated in the affair, having tended horses as his friends hacked Modest to death.[23]

The other Kiowa prisoners were charged with participating or being present during various attacks, many but not all involving killings or direct participation in them. Eight of the men—Ankle, age twenty-eight; High Forehead, twenty-five; Boy Hunting, or Etahdeleuh, twenty-one; Toothless, forty-five; Old Man, thirty-eight; Kicking, twenty-seven; Bull (or Buffalo) with Holes in His Ears, forty-five; and Pedro, forty-eight—were Mexican captives who had been raised among the Kiowas and had become warriors.

On April 3, 1875, orders were issued for Capt. Clarence Mauck to march the next day, taking the Fort Sill prisoners to Fort Leavenworth by way of the Wichita agency, the Cheyenne agency, and Wichita, Kansas. At the Cheyenne agency he was to pick up the Cheyenne prisoners. The orders were canceled the following day, possibly because the Cheyenne prisoners were not yet in chains.[24]

As the chaining was being undertaken on April 6, a Cheyenne brave who bolted from the blacksmith shop was shot and killed. This set off a general uprising by the Cheyennes, and a battle ensued in the nearby sand hills between Cheyenne warriors and military troops. The Cheyennes lost six men, and nineteen soldiers were wounded, four mortally.[25] Mauck hurried from Fort Sill with four companies of Fourth Cavalry to protect the agency.[26] The Cheyennes were eventually rounded up and readied for their journey of exile.

On April 23 thirty-three Cheyenne prisoners and two Arapahos, all in irons, were placed in four large government wagons. One of them was a Cheyenne woman named Mochi, or Calf Woman, whose family had been killed at Sand Creek in 1864. She was accused of taking part in the massacre of the Germain family in western Kansas in September 1874. Under escort of a company of cavalry the Cheyennes were taken to Fort Sill, arriving there on April 26.[27]

On April 27 Mackenzie, who had replaced Davidson in command at Fort Sill two weeks earlier, issued orders for the immediate transfer of the Cheyenne agency and Fort Sill prisoners to Fort Leavenworth. Capt. Theodore J. Wint with Company L, Fourth Cavalry; Lt. William J. Kyle with Company I, Eleventh Infantry; and Lt. W. H. Wheeler, Company C, Eleventh Infantry, would proceed with the prisoners to Pauls Valley, thence to the railroad depot at Caddo. There Wint was to turn the prisoners over to Lieutenant Kyle who, with Wheeler and the two infantry companies, would take the Indians by train to Fort Leavenworth.

Pratt, whose company was being transferred to the Concho military camp near the Cheyenne agency, addressed a letter to Sheridan on April 26. He offered his opinion that while certain leaders of the tribes should be tried and punished, he felt many of the young men were merely following orders and, as such, were not so culpable. Efforts to reform these young men, he suggested, should be made before they were returned to their tribes.[28]

In a private letter to Gen. Phil Sheridan, Pratt requested that he be given charge of the prisoners upon their leaving Fort Leavenworth for Fort Marion. He cited his familiarity with the leading Cheyennes from having served at Camp Supply during 1872 and 1873 and his recent experience in investigating the Kiowa and Comanche perpetrators. "I have been down here eight years," he wrote, "and am hungry for a change."[29]

Sheridan gave his approval, and Pratt was assigned to accompany the prisoners to Fort Leavenworth. On the morning of April 28 twenty-seven Kiowas, along with nine Comanches and one Caddo—added to the thirty-three Cheyennes and two Arapahos for a total of seventy-two prisoners—were marched from their icehouse prison and loaded aboard bow-canopied army ambulances into which beds of hay had been laid. Each wagon was drawn by two mule teams with a soldier-teamster astride one of the four animals. Soldiers of Company D, U.S. Fourth Cavalry, held their mounts at the ready, while Companies C and I of the Eleventh Infantry rested nearby.

Nine Indians were placed in each wagon, five seated on one side and four on the other, legs interlocking, with their backs against the wagon sideboards. A long, heavy chain was run between the legs above the ankle iron of each prisoner, extending from one end of each wagon to the other where it was fastened with large iron clasps. The backs of the prisoners' heads made dark rows beneath the rolled-up canopies.[30]

The relatives and friends of the warriors came to the wagons to say their farewells. As ordered, the soldiers did not interfere. Finally, Wint

Etahdeleuh depicts the Fort Sill prisoners being loaded into wagons for Fort Marion. Courtesy Yale Collection of Western Americana, Beinecke Rare Book and Manuscript Library.

raised his arm and gave a sharp command. The troops of Fourth Cavalry wheeled smartly into their position at the advance and rear of the wagons, and the infantry, bayoneted rifles at their shoulders, formed a line of march on either side against the possibility of an attempt to rescue the captives. Wint issued the command to move out, and the fifteen-wagon convoy headed off on its six-day, 165-mile journey to the Missouri-Kansas-Texas Railroad stop at Caddo, Indian Territory.

As the wagons rattled eastward out of the quadrangle, a forlorn wailing began among the Indian women, muffled at first then rising higher and higher—a uniquely eerie sound to the ears of the military and agency personnel who watched from the post's buildings.[31]

During the march, camps were made each night close to streams with running water. Two army wagons were parked just far enough apart to allow the prisoners a sleeping area. The Indians were chained to the wagons but were permitted to leave, still shackled and under guard, for toilet purposes.

At Caddo the prisoners were placed aboard three coaches of a special five-coach MKT train headed for Fort Leavenworth, Kansas, en route for St. Augustine. The two rear cars accommodated officers and men of the sixty-man escort. Guards were posted on the front and rear platforms of the cars carrying the captives.[32] Lone Wolf was the only one of the tribesmen who had ever ridden on a railroad train. The others watched from the car windows with excited curiosity as the train started off; but as it gathered speed and the telegraph poles rushed by, some pulled their blankets over their heads in fright.[33]

The prisoner train had been eagerly anticipated in Leavenworth, and its arrival on May 8 was greeted by a large, cheering crowd of spectators as it stopped briefly in town before sidetracking to nearby Fort Leavenworth. There the manacled prisoners were loaded aboard wagons, ten to each vehicle, and taken to the post guardhouse. Cheyenne Bird Chief and another tribesman who were ill were placed in an army ambulance.[34]

There had been some talk of holding court-martial hearings for the prisoners at Fort Leavenworth. Pratt reviewed the cases of the Kiowas and Comanches with Gen. Nelson A. Miles, commanding at Fort Leavenworth, but nothing more was done to give the prisoners a hearing. Further, communication was limited as the only interpreter was frontiersman Romero (often called as Romeo), whose tribal language included only the Cheyenne tongue. On May 11 orders arrived directing Pratt to take the prisoners by train to Fort Marion at St. Augustine, Florida. He did so, following a route through St. Louis, Louisville, Nashville, Atlanta, and Jacksonville.[35]

Even as these events were unfolding during the spring of 1875, another development of consequence was under way. With many Kiowa headmen now looking favorably to the path of formal education for Kiowa children set by Kicking Bird and Battey, Haworth had secured a building on the Fort Sill post to serve as the first school for the Kiowa, Comanche, and Apache children of his agency. The school opened on February 15, 1875, with twenty-seven children enrolled and A. J. Standing as principal. Haworth appointed two chiefs from each of the tribes—Pacer and Black Hawk of the Apaches, Quirts Quip and Cheevers of the Comanches, and Napawat and Dangerous Eagle of the Kiowas—to serve as a board of education. "They were as much pleased," Haworth reported, "as many white people, when first elected."[36]

Soon forty-four Kiowa and Comanche children—twenty-seven boys and seventeen girls—had been enrolled in the small schoolhouse. One of them was Joshua, son of the old warrior Satank. In March Haworth reported:

> The attendance continues *perfect*, which is very creditable to both parents and children, inasmuch as the camps are near the school-house. It will be noted that none of these Indians have ever before allowed any of their children to go to school, but since they are closely confined by the military near to the Agency, they are quite willing to let the Agent have as many of their children as he can provide for. . . . This is a new business for the Kiowa, and most of the Comanche.[37]

Already, few remembered the day when Thomissey Battey had set bravely off for the remote Kiowa camps to hold the first classes for Topen and other Kiowa children, the only white man within a hundred miles and surrounded by belligerent tribesmen.

20
Poison, Prayer, or Pulmonary Emboli?

A small party of visitors arrived at Fort Sill during January 1875 to "see of the Indians while opportunity offered." The guests wished to meet the principal men of the tribes, and they were invited to attend a council being held at Davidson's office relative to bringing in some Cheyennes believed to have fled to southern New Mexico. While there, they met Kicking Bird and were very favorably impressed, as indicated by a member of the group whose article "A Day Among the Kiowas and Comanches" appeared in the September 1876 issue of *Catholic World*. The author wrote of Kicking Bird:

> He was a fine-looking Indian and had as winning a countenance as I have looked upon anywhere. The expression of his eyes was remarkably soft and pleasing. There was a quiet, natural dignity in his manners, tempered by great natural grace. I was taken by his appearance from the first, and shook hands with him with pleasure and sincerity. . . . He was somewhat above middle height, richly but not gaudily dressed.[1]

After the Cheyenne matter was concluded, the meeting droned on as "every chief except Kicking Bird had some private 'axe to grind'—something to ask for."[2] With this process continuing, the visitors left and went to the Kiowa camp, where they were invited into Kicking Bird's lodge. They found it to be a large, roomy tepee of twenty-four poles. Behind it, covered by a tarpaulin, was a buggy Kicking Bird had obtained for his family's use. His adaptation to the white man's ways was even more apparent when the visitors later encountered Kicking Bird mounted on a large cream-colored mule: "We stopped, shook hands with him, and chatted a little. The interpreter joked him about riding a mule. Kicking Bird laughed, and said that as he was going to live hereafter like a white man, like a white man he should ride a mule."[3]

Inside Kicking Bird's lodge the tourists met Kicking Bird's young, attractive wife (the writer mentions only one wife). She wore a profusion of beads over her colorful blanket, and her cheeks were brightly painted with vermillion. Also present was Little John, Kicking Bird's ten-month-old son, who was just beginning to walk.

> He took wonderfully to us. He would try to walk across the lodge to each of us in turn, failing at every other step, and getting up again with a loud crow of determination. Then he would toddle from one to the other holding by our boot-tops as we stood in a circle around him, and being jumped as high as arms would admit of by each in turn, to his intense delight and the great enjoyment of his mother.[4]

On the afternoon of May 3, 1875, agent Haworth was returning from inspecting the Kiowas' newly planted fields of corn, beans, and watermelons near the post when he was met by a messenger bearing an urgent call for him to hurry to the Kiowa camp. He arrived there to witness a scene such as he had never seen before. Terrible wailing resounded throughout the camp. Women sat by their lodges rocking and moaning, their faces and bodies scarified and blood streaming down from the wounds. Kicking Bird, Haworth was told, had died![5]

By their custom, the Kiowas buried their dead immediately. Although it had been less than an hour since his death, Kicking Bird's body had already been wrapped for burial. Haworth later wrote:

> They unbound him for me to see, loosed his right hand that I might take it in mine and bid him farewell, by them considered a very solemn and secret act only allowed for those who are known to be friends. I stood gazing into the face of my dead Indian friend and held his hand in mine, while around me hundreds of his kindred and friends were mourning.[6]

The Kiowas acceded to Haworth's wish to bury Kicking Bird in the style of the white man with a Christian burial. They permitted the Quaker to take the chief's body and hold it overnight in an agency building under guard while a walnut coffin was prepared. By an earlier arrangement between Tatum and Grierson, a section of the post graveyard had been assigned to the agency. Remembering this, Haworth went to speak with Mackenzie. Post interpreter Horace Jones argued that Kicking Bird should be buried military style with uniformed soldiers firing volleys over his grave. Mackenzie agreed and said he would order out the post band.

But Haworth resisted. He told Mackenzie he appreciated the offer, but as a member of a religious sect he felt he should honor Kicking Bird's request to give him a Christian burial just as he would his own brother. After Haworth had departed, Jones called in Sun Boy, Heidsick, and two other chiefs and tried to persuade them to accept the military funeral. They refused, saying Haworth was Kicking Bird's brother and could bury him as he saw fit. The agent described the interment in a letter to Enoch Hoag:

> The funeral procession consisted of seven or eight wagons, containing the near relatives of [the] deceased, and persons connected with the agency. All the chiefs, and a large number of others on horse back, the first of the kind that has ever taken place in this country, and was indeed a solemn occasion. After the funeral, most of the chiefs met in impromptu council at the Agency, making several very good speeches, referring feelingly to the merits of the departed; and asked me to write to Washington, and tell him that Kicking Bird was dead, that he was a good man, and a firm friend to the whites, that the Kiowas would not throw away his talks to them, but keep on the same good road.[7]

Ordinarily, the Kiowas would have killed all of Kicking Bird's horses. Haworth told them he did not want any of the animals killed, and he took charge of two big white mules Kicking Bird had usually driven. After a few days he exacted a promise that they would not be killed and returned them. He learned later, however, that two horses had been destroyed.

A couple of days after the funeral, Stumbling Bear and Kicking Bird's brothers invited Haworth to come to their camp. He did so, and the men had a long talk and a "good cry" together. The Kiowas presented Haworth with one of the finest mounts remaining in Kicking Bird's herd as a token of their kind feelings for him. When he expressed fear that the tribespeople might resent him riding the horse, the Kiowa leaders insisted it would make them glad. They said they would feel bad if he neglected the horse and permitted him to become poor and to look bad.

Kicking Bird's death made the wire services, the *Leavenworth Daily Times* reporting:

> Kicking Bird, Chief of the Kiowas, died at Fort Sill, on the 3d inst., and was buried in the cemetery of the post yesterday by the Indian agent, Mr. Howarth [Haworth]. He died very suddenly.
>
> There is a subscription going around among the officers and civilians to raise money enough to place a monument upon his grave. Upwards of $80 have already been raised. The Kiowas lost their best friend in the death of Kicking Bird.[8]

With his death occurring so soon after the departure of the Fort Marion prisoners, whites speculated that Kicking Bird had been poisoned by his tribal enemies. Such was indicated in the monthly report of Dr. Gwin, the post surgeon, which stated: "Kicking Bird, one of the principal chiefs of the Kiowas, died suddenly May 4, supposed to have been poisoned by strychnia, probably through jealousy or anger of some of his tribe."[9]

This speculation, apparently unsupported by any actual examination into the matter, has been relied upon by virtually all writers on the subject. The commissioner of Indian Affairs even wired Haworth from New York, instructing Haworth to look into Kicking Bird's death and whether he had been poisoned. The agent did so, interviewing Kicking Bird's wife and the Kiowa chiefs at length. On May 27 he wrote to Commissioner E. P. Smith.

> I have very carefully examined into the matter and diligently sought information to throw light upon it. He [Kicking Bird] was sick during the night before his death, his wife says [he] was up several times. On the morning of the day he died, some of his people called at his lodge to get him to go with them to the school house. He said he did not feel well enough and declined to go; he generally called upon the Agency Physician in case of a sickness for himself or family but on this instance did not send for him. His own people made medicine for him after their own peculiar notions. He complained of pain in the heart, said it felt like some one was tearing it out. A little before noon he went to the creek, the water of which was quite cool, and took a bath. Soon after coming out [he] was taken worse and died about one o'clock and thirty minutes. His wife said he was not away from his lodge to eat anything the day previous or on the day of his death. I have talked to the chiefs about it, asking them what I should tell Washington was the cause of his death. They say they think it was something the matter with his heart, and do not think any of their people caused his death.[10]

The physician's report was incorrect in stating that Kicking Bird died on May 4 rather than on the afternoon of May 3. This error is evidently the source for those who have since made the same mistake. Further, no autopsy was done; thus there was no medical examination or factual foundation to indicate the presence of strychnine or any other poison. That Kicking Bird was poisoned by a vindictive tribesman was then and remains a much-accepted speculation.

The medical officer went on to state the prevailing white opinion of Kicking Bird: "Kicking Bird was far above any of his own nation, or of the Comanches, in general intelligence; of fine physique and had prepossessing countenance. He had been, to a great extent, relied upon in [determining] what Indians of those surrendering were most guilty of out-rages and murders within the last few years."[11]

Another explanation of Kicking Bird's death quickly circulated among the Kiowas, who had and still have their own ideas on the matter. While on his way to Florida, it was said, Maman-ti had placed a hex of death on Kicking Bird for his role in naming those who would be sent to prison. In *Carbine and Lance* Nye gives this version:

> The Kiowas attribute the death of Kicking Bird to a different cause than did the hospital authorities. They say that the second night after the prisoners left Fort Sill on their way to Florida, they were having a coun-cil. Eagle Chief, a noted medicine man, passed the pipe to the Great Owl Prophet Maman-ti and said, "Do-ha-te, pray that Kicking Bird may die right away." Maman-ti puffed the pipe thoughtfully for a few moments. Then he replied: "It would be a terrible thing to do. The laws of my medicine forbid the killing of one of our own people. My own life would be forfeited if I thus used my power. But I will do it. In four days, a little after sunup, Kicking Bird will suddenly die. But you must realize that I will pay for it." A few days later the Indians en route to Florida heard that Kicking Bird had passed away, and soon after they reached the end of their journey the Do-ha-te too was dead.[12]

At least two facts are known to be incorrect here. Kicking Bird died at around one o'clock in the afternoon, not in the morning. And Maman-ti lived until July 29, his death coming nearly three months after leaving Fort Sill. The insertion of dialogue into this rendition makes it suspect that Nye embellished his account, which relied on distant memory. His notebooks, which are held at the Fort Sill museum, offer the version of Old Man Horse, who believed Kicking Bird was appointed by God to lead the Kiowa tribe and that his death was caused by a medicine man. It was, the old Kiowa said, a witch murder.

> The day the prisoners left for Florida, the medicine man Maman-ti (Sky Walker) said to Kicking Bird: "You think you are going to live a long time on account of what you have done to us, but I tell you that you do not have long to live. Your life will be cut short."
>
> Maman-ti prophesied that Kicking Bird would die within 3 days in the middle of the morning. They proceeded to pray him to death— smoked a pipe, etc. Sure enough Kicking Bird died at the time proph-esied, suddenly, and without warning. He died in his lodge along the little branch west of Cache Creek.[13]

Maman-ti's time of incarceration at Fort Marion was long enough to support another cause of his own death. Pratt, who escorted the prisoners to Florida and remained there in charge over them, felt the heat and humidity and the close confinement within the walls of the old Spanish fort caused several of the prairie Indians, including Maman-ti, to perish within a few months.[14]

Parker McKenzie, noted Kiowa linguist, expressed the doubts of most Kiowas when he noted that the Kiowas knew nothing of poison: "They *knew* it was Mamanty's magical power that eliminated Kicking Bird."[15]

Nye also gave personal credence to the notion that Kicking Bird may have been hexed to death. In a letter to author Fred Grove, he wrote:

> I think he was prayed to death; and those who dismiss such things as superstition simply do not understand primitive peoples. Neither do they understand psychiatry. I am sure that there are modern doctors who would admit the possibility of such an occurrence. At any rate, I have seen it in Hawaii, and I know of several well-authenticated cases among the Kiowas. Authenticated by the Indians, that is. Of course the Quaker agents and possibly the military post commander, would scout such ideas.[16]

Indeed, it is difficult to avoid connecting these two signal events of Kicking Bird's fate: the departure of the prisoners and his demise. The two events are welded together by their proximity, which in itself breeds speculation and suspicion. The incomplete facts of his death, however, neither prove nor disprove a connection.

The story commonly told and seemingly accepted by virtually all writers on the subject has it that Kicking Bird had just finished a cup of coffee one morning when he fell over dead. Some say someone among his own people poisoned him; others suggest it may have been one of his new wives or some white person at the fort who stood to gain from the chief's death.

Trader Neal Evans, according to Nye, claimed in his reminiscences that he and Capt. Clarence Mauck visited Kicking Bird in his lodge on Cache Creek, three miles south of Fort Sill, the evening before his death. He said the chief was physically well but depressed. Evans, writing in retrospect, gives the coffee-after-breakfast theory and incorrectly states that his visit was made on the evening of May 3, at which time Kicking Bird was already dead.[17]

While much speculation has been issued on the subject of Kicking Bird's death, virtually no inquiry into the matter has been made. Testimony does exist regarding the matter that has long been overlooked by writers on the subject. This body of evidence involves letters agent Haworth wrote immediately after Kicking Bird's death. Although far from conclusive, the letters throw new light on the matter. One letter to Enoch Hoag on May 4, 1875, states:

I have the sad intelligence to communicate of the death of Kicking Bird. He died yesterday, after a few hours illness. I did not learn of this sickness until I heard of his death. I am not aware of the exact nature of the disease, of which he died. He was conscious of this situation, telling those around him that he was going to die, told them that he had worked hard for them to maintain peace, and friendship with the white people, that he had given his hand to the white people, had taken a firm hold of theirs, and died holding on to the white man's hand. Told them they must listen to what I said, and not get tired [of] doing right. Though a savage, raised up under the clouds of dark heathenism & superstition, his mind and heart had so far yielded to the civilizing influence, that I believe I can in truth say, he died a "noble man." As soon as I learned of his death, I went to camp, found almost the entire camp wailing, and mourning his death.[18]

Haworth added more in a letter to Cheyenne and Arapaho agent John D. Miles nine days later.

Kicking Bird's death was very sudden. I am not yet prepared to say by what means it took place. I guess its suddenness was the cause of the suspicion that he was poisoned. His wife says he was sick during the night. Up several times—he told someone that his heart felt just like someone had hold of it pulling it out. On the morning [of the day] he died some of the people went to his Lodge to [ask] him to go with them to the school house—he said he was feeling badly and would wait awhile. And as their custom is for almost all diseases he went into the creek and bathed. When he came out of the water he felt better for a while—he died about—past one Oclk P M.[19]

The precise cause of Kicking Bird's death will never be proven to the satisfaction of all. Nye's suggestion that the psychological effect of being hexed may have caused Kicking Bird's death requires that he had learned what happened among the prisoners on the trail—which is very unlikely. The long-existing belief in curses and other supernatural action, however, is impossible to disprove. The hexing of Kicking Bird will continue to serve as an explanation for many people who look to answers beyond modern scientific experience.

That he was poisoned also remains a possibility that cannot be disproved without exhumation of his body. Certainly, Kicking Bird had enemies. Mayhem was an ongoing fact of life on the frontier—men killed one another almost as easily as they do today—so the murder of a controversial Kiowa chief would not have been exceptional.

But one other explanation of his death merits consideration. "His illness was very brief," observed a writer in the Quaker journal *Friends' Review*, "so as to suggest poisoning at first, but it now appears that he died of disease of the heart."[20]

According to Haworth the other chiefs, who likely included his cousin and close friend Stumbling Bear, suggested that something may have been wrong with his heart. In our modern age we well know that heart attacks, or pulmonary embolisms, are a common cause of death, even among men Kicking Bird's age. His own description of how it felt as though someone had a hold on his heart and was pulling it out of his chest would appeal to the curse theorist. Although far less attractive as a speculation, this description also fits that of modern medical science as someone having a heart attack. Undoubtedly, the matter will forever dangle in history unresolved and argumentive, leaving people to determine for themselves what to believe.

The use of a coffin for Kicking Bird was reported as "the first instance in the history of the Kiowa tribe in which one of its chiefs was so buried,"[21] although Yellow Wolf's burial in Washington's Congressional Cemetery in 1863 had actually been the first. Kicking Bird's bows and arrows, war shield, carbine, silver-mounted pistols, and a roll of currency were reportedly buried with him at a spot now known as "Chief's Knoll" in the Fort Sill cemetery.[22]

Haworth recommended that the monument carry an inscription noting that it marked the last resting place of a great chief who died as an advocate of law and order.

> I believe the trials and tribulations through which he passed in trying to save his people, entitles his memory to such respect, and would show his people, that the Government appreciated his labors; a white man who could honorably place himself in so exalted a position before his people, as Kicking Bird did before his, would be called a great man, and such he was.[23]

Haworth's proposal for a gravestone was approved by the new commissioner of Indian Affairs, H. R. Clum.[24] Eventually, a concrete crypt with an iron door was placed over Kicking Bird's grave. In front of it stands a white, round-top marble tombstone in a style common to the graveyard. It carries the erroneous date of May 4, 1875. Close by is the grave of Stumbling Bear and that of Black Beaver, the famous Delaware tribesman who also led the way down the path of peace for his people and for other tribes. Nearby are the gravesites of Satanta and Satank, among other noted Indian personalities of that day.

It was probably Haworth who penned the unsigned tribute to Kicking Bird in the May 29, 1875, issue of *Friends' Review*:

> He was one of the leading chiefs of the Kiowas, and, doubtless won his position, as almost all chiefs of his people have done, by prowess in war

Kicking Bird's tomb atop the cemetery at Fort Sill, Oklahoma, with Black Beaver's tombstone in the foreground. Author photo.

and forays, and by the superior mental powers which gave a man the command of others . . . he showed his comprehensive view of events by desiring the education of his children in the white man's way. . . . During the agitation preceding the late Indian war, he resisted all attempts to induce him to join the hostile party, and helped to retain a large proportion of his tribe at peace. The course cost him almost all that Indians value—loss of warlike fame, and of wealth by the stealing of many of his ponies.[25]

It is understandable that today some Kiowas find it far more satisfying to look back on Satanta, Lone Wolf, or Maman-ti as symbols of Kiowa resistance to the white man than on Kicking Bird, Stumbling Bear, and other peace chiefs who bowed to the upheaval of tribal existence. Those who believe in the enlightenment of humankind through formal education and the need for peace as a means of resolving societal differences must, however, consider the merit of Kicking Bird's leadership. It is in recognition of this leadership that a bust of Kicking Bird stands in the National Hall of Fame for Famous American Indians at Anadarko, Oklahoma. Perhaps the most apt tribute was paid him by a writer who met him just before his death: "Poor Kicking Bird! He had given his gorgeous war-bonnet to a veteran officer of the army as a token that he had left the

Kicking Bird's bust in the American Indian Hall
of Fame, Anadarko, Oklahoma. Author photo.

war-path for ever. He proposed to teach his children the white man's
language and the white man's peaceful arts. He fell a martyr to his fidelity
to the government."[26]

Epilogue

Kicking Bird went to his grave a controversial figure of U.S. and Native American history, and he remains so today. Bitterness against him for aiding the military in choosing those to be sent to prison at Fort Marion still exists. In Kicking Bird's defense, however, it can be argued that without its peace leaders—Tohawson, Yellow Wolf, Stumbling Bear, and Kicking Bird in particular—the tribe may have warred itself into near extinction. Through his support of formal schooling and promotion of peaceful coexistence with the outside world, Kicking Bird helped lead his people into the modern age with their tribal identity firmly intact. Unfortunately, however, the trust these men placed in the United States reaped ill rewards for the Kiowas.

The picture Beede had painted in January 1874 of the Kiowas being generously supplied by the government and Satanta's boisterous confidence that the buffalo would last forever were far from reality in 1875. The tribes were already having a difficult time on the hunt. The attack on Adobe Walls had not only failed to halt professional hunting but had helped to open the gates even wider to intrusion on the buffalo grounds by white hunters. Not only was the buffalo becoming scarce, but as a military officer reported, "white hunters have carried themselves very insultingly to the Indians, evidently with a design to provoke them to the committal of crime."[1]

Other whites were causing problems for both the Indians and the Fort Sill military. It was reported on the morning of May 31 that ten

Kiowa scouts and three soldiers had ridden out of Fort Sill in pursuit of eight white men who had escaped from the post guardhouse. The men were charged with stealing cattle and selling whiskey.[2]

Loss of the buffalo was particularly tragic for the tribes because Indian annuities provided by the Treaty of Medicine Lodge had been reckoned only to supplement the normal subsistence of their hunting.[3] Two factors drastically altered the validity of this thinking. Not only were the buffalo becoming scarce, but the annuities supplied by government contractors were pathetically inferior. When interviewed on the subject in January 1875, Haworth was asked if it were true that the Indians on his reservation had been without bread for several weeks. He replied:

> It is. The freight contractors have failed to deliver the flour. I cannot issue what I have not. To make up for the lack of flour, I issue four pounds of beef to each Indian daily.
>
> It is charged that the beef is poor. Is this charge true?
>
> It is. What can I do? Like a quartermaster or commissary, I can issue only what I have on hand. If I had not this beef, the Indians would have nothing to eat. I cannot throw it back on the contractor's hands, and wait for a better quality of meat; for while I was waiting the Indians would starve or leave the reservation to find subsistence where they could.[4]

Even as the St. Augustine prisoners were departing on April 30, 1875, Lt. Col. John P. Hatch reported from Fort Sill on the matter:

> Frequent complaints having been made by the Indians encamped near this post that they are suffering badly from hunger, I have made an investigation, and find the complaints well founded. The following is the ration allowed by the Indian Department: Beef, three pounds gross, on the hoof, one day in fifteen; three-quarters of a pound of bacon is issued in lieu of beef; flour or bread, one-quarter pound to the hundred rations; four pounds of coffee, eight pounds of sugar, one pound of salt, one pound of soap and one-half pound of tobacco. This ration was established when the Indians could partly support themselves by hunting. With no other help it is barely enough to prevent hunger. It is not, however, all issued.
>
> There is at the agency no flour, and not over one third the authorized amount has been issued during the present fiscal year. There is no sugar, and not over two-thirds of the regular issue has been made during that time. The beef lately issued has been shamefully bad. It is so poor that the gross is altogether out of proportion to the weight. The acting Indian agent, Howard [Haworth], acknowledges that the beef lately issued was unfit for food. The condition of affairs at the Wichita agency is worse than this here. There has been no flour for a long time. The agent is absent, and the Indians are killing and eating their horses.[5]

When Mackenzie took command of Fort Sill in April, he sent Dr. J. J. Sturm with a small party of reservation Comanches out to the Staked Plains to seek a surrender of the Quahada Comanches. Under the leadership of a rising young chief named Quanah Parker, the half-blood son of captive Cynthia Ann Parker, the Quahadas eventually accepted their fate and made their way to Fort Sill. There they were stripped of their arms and horses.[6] Like Kicking Bird, Quanah would later be sorely criticized for his fraternal relations with whites.

Mackenzie quickly moved to destroy the warring capacity of the Kiowas, Comanches, and Plains Apaches. When all of the various bands had finally surrendered, they had turned over around 3,500 horses and mules. Eight hundred of these animals were shot, while others were distributed among friendly Indian scouts or sold for the benefit of the tribes. Mackenzie used the nearly $22,000 that was collected to buy sheep and goats on the idea of converting them to the pastoral habits of the Navajo.[7] The roving nomads of the Plains did not take to the life of herders and stock tenders, and the experiment failed.

The essential conflict of existence faced by the Kiowas and others was succinctly illustrated in a painting by Kiowa St. Augustine prisoner Wohaw. An Indian man stands between two sets of images. On the one side are the buffalo, tepee, and prairie. On the other side are the domesticated cow, the white man's schoolhouse, and cultivated fields. The man offers the sacred pipe equally to both as they breathe out to him. Above him the emblems of the sun, the moon, and a flaming meteor of the heavens serve as witnesses to his great dilemma.[8]

In April 1878 the St. Augustine prisoners other than those who had gone to the school founded by Pratt at Carlisle, Pennsylvania, arrived at Wichita, Kansas, on their way back to the Indian Territory. The thirty-five men, two women, and two children were greeted by Dutch Bill Greiffenstein, the former Indian trader who was now the mayor of Wichita. The *Wichita Eagle* reported:

> These sturdy chieftains liked to have eaten our chief executive up in their joy at seeing one they had known in the long years agone. They hugged him and shook him up in such an earnest manner that for a brief space we thought we would not only be compelled to attend a funeral but hold another "blue ribbon" election for Mayor. All the Indians were in uniforms, such as are worn by United States soldiers, and were a remarkably fine looking set of men. Many of them spoke English quite well. During their stay at St. Augustine they were regularly drilled and treated as soldiers by Captain Pratt, of the Tenth Cavalry.[9]

Satanta lived three years and five months past Kicking Bird's death. He had first attempted suicide in December 1876 by hanging himself at Huntsville, Texas. Newspapers of the day reported: "He secured a small rope, and, fastening one end to a scantling, tied the other end around his neck, and was caught dangling, with his feet about twenty-four inches from the ground, but was cut down before life was extinct."[10]

Satanta found a more foolproof method on October 10, 1878. This time he jumped headlong from a second-story balcony onto the prison courtyard and successfully killed himself. He was buried in the prison graveyard, but his body was eventually returned to Fort Sill and interred in the post cemetery. One of his sons became a member of the Indian police; another enlisted in the Seventh Cavalry.[11]

Big Bow was granted amnesty for his past deeds by the United States and later served well as a sergeant in the Indian Scouts at Fort Sill. After this service he spent the remainder of his life peacefully on the reservation, dying around 1900.[12]

Following the imprisonment of his fellow Kiowas, Big Tree settled into reservation life at Fort Sill. For a number of years he operated a supply train that ran between Wichita, Kansas, and Anadarko. He eventually took up farming on an allotment near Mountain View and married a Kiowa woman. After converting to Christianity, Big Tree served for thirty years as a deacon at the Rainy Mountain Indian Mission. He died at Fort Sill on November 13, 1929.[13]

Upon Kicking Bird's death, Stumbling Bear took up the mantle of peace advocacy for the Kiowas. He founded a Kiowa settlement along Canyon Creek on the northern boundary of present Comanche county. There in 1877 the government constructed permanent homes for Stumbling Bear and nine other chiefs. Nearby Stumbling Bear Pass is named for him. Virginia Stumbling Bear, Stumbling Bear's daughter who was educated at Carlisle Institute, was the first interpreter at the Methodist Missionary at Anadarko.[14]

Stumbling Bear visited Washington, D.C., as a delegate for his tribe. In 1890 he hosted ethnologist James Mooney of the Smithsonian Institution and provided much of the information in Mooney's *Calendar History of the Kiowas*. In his later years Stumbling Bear became blind and crippled, and he died on March 14, 1903. He was buried in an unmarked grave, but in 1963 his remains were reburied beside the tomb of Kicking Bird on Chief's Knoll at Fort Sill.[15]

Lone Wolf, who had twice been to Washington to talk peace, was in bad health when he was released from Fort Marion in May 1878. He died a year later and was buried in an unmarked grave on the slopes of Mount

Scott. The town of Lone Wolf, Oklahoma, bears his name. His son, also named Lone Wolf, became a prominent Kiowa leader.[16]

Woman's Heart survived his imprisonment at Fort Marion, being released on April 18, 1877. While there he was observed by Harriet Beecher Stowe, who wrote: "It is said he wears the little moccasin of one of his children tied around his neck, and that he seems at times to suffer from homesickness."[17] Captain Pratt told her of a time he had observed the Kiowa as he was returning from a bath. Woman's Heart had paused to kneel down on a little elevation, raise his hands to the heavens, and pray with great fervor for some time.

Satank's son Tau-koi-te was sent to Carlisle and took up the name of Joshua Given. Ultimately, he became an ordained Presbyterian minister and a progressive leader among the Kiowas, although he still found it difficult to break through the cultural barrier of the old tribal system.[18] Linda D. Smalling wrote of him: "Joshua Givens opted for the survival of his people. He reasoned that the most productive way for him to help the Kiowa people survive was to acquire the education that would allow him to gain support in political and religious circles."[19]

The government also built a home in the Mount Scott area for Sun Boy, who died in 1888. A Kiowa named Kicking Bird also built a house there for himself. This could hardly have been Little John, who was born in 1874. It is possible that this Kicking Bird took his name and descendance from a sister of Chief Kicking Bird, as was sometimes the practice among the Kiowas.[20] A Rev. Kickingbird, a Kiowa, became a local preacher for the new church built in 1894 across Medicine Creek north of Mount Scott.[21] Sadly, much like Ahyokah, the famous daughter of Sequoyah, Topin has faded from the pages of recorded history. Whether she died young, married early like most other Kiowa girls, or went on to receive fuller schooling is unknown. The ultimate fate of Kicking Bird's son, Little John, is likewise unknown.

Records show that a twelve-year-old boy named Ernest Kickingbird was a student in Methvin Institute at Anadarko in 1898. He had a younger sister, seven-year-old Belle. An old Indian who visited the school played up to Ernest and asked him for Belle. Ernest agreed, but when the old man went to their father to claim the girl he was flatly refused.[22]

In 1877 Thomas Battey, whose accounts of life among the Kiowas were first published in *The Friend* of Philadelphia during 1873–1875, returned to Fort Sill and the Kiowa-Comanche School from where he reported on December 10 that 72 students were enrolled—49 boys and 23 girls. Battey wrote:

The girls take turns of a week at a time in the dining room, kitchen and wash room, ironing, bed-making, &c., and about an hour is devoted to sewing every evening. The boys also prepare the wood for the institution, working in companies a week about. They are intelligent, and mostly contented—readily adapt themselves to the required changes on coming from camp . . . it is a great satisfaction to see these wild tribes, to whom I went five years ago at the peril of my life, so peacefully settled and their children in school and learning the simple lessons of Christianity.[23]

Other teachers who followed Battey among the Kiowas were critical of his work. Ida Moore noted that "as to the school, as is generally understood the term, it did not seem to amount to much."[24] Another commented on the difficulty he met in getting the attention of the young Kiowas in his tent school. These comments, however, overlook Battey's courage in breaking the old curtain of tribal resentment to formal schooling at a time when most Kiowas were still strongly hostile. Battey himself felt he had achieved more good by working in the Kiowa camps than he ever could have in the classroom building, and those who followed him were beneficiaries both of his original efforts and of Kicking Bird's forward-looking resolve.

It was to the credit of both men that schooling of their children became so popular among the Kiowas that some parents offered to pay for the privilege. One chief was said to have offered a pony for the chance to enter his child in the school.[25]

Battey left the Kiowas for good in 1878 when the Quakers were removed as Indian guardians. In 1875 he published his *Life and Adventures of a Quaker Among the Indians*. After his wife, Lucinda, died in 1887, he moved to Ohio and married again. He died of cancer at Middleton, Ohio, in 1897.[26]

During 1878 the Kiowa-Comanche agency was moved from Fort Sill and consolidated with the Wichita agency at a new site named Anadarko. A new schoolhouse for the two tribes was built near the Wichita agency.[27]

James Haworth was replaced as the Kiowa-Comanche agent by P. B. Hunt on April 1, 1876.[28] Despite his health problems, Haworth extended his work in the Indian service, first as an Indian agent at large, working with the Sioux, Pawnees, Utes, Pi Utes, and Nez Perces. In 1882 he was appointed inspector of Indian schools and supervised plans for schools in the Dakotas, Wyoming, and Indian Territory—among them the Chilocco Industrial School. He died on March 12, 1885, in an Albuquerque, New Mexico, hotel and was buried at his hometown of Olathe, Kansas.[29]

With a tribal enrollment of well over 6,000, the Kiowas of Oklahoma exist today as a distinct and viable people. Their pride in warriorship is undiminished, and their young men and women have served with great distinction in America's wars. In peacetime pursuits they have excelled as highly skilled artists and craftsmen. Drawings by Koba, White Horse, Etahdleuh, and other prisoners at St. Augustine called national attention to the unique talent of the Kiowas and other Native Americans to express themselves through artistic imagery.

Tribal members of following generations have built upon this reputation to achieve international recognition as artists, sculptors, writers, musicians, and dancers. Other Kiowas are educating themselves at colleges and universities and entering into the professional fields of American life. Undoubtedly, Kicking Bird would have felt rewarded for his original efforts to provide formal schooling for Topin by the statement in a modern brochure issued by the Kiowa-operated Southern Plains Indian Museum and Crafts Center at Anadarko, Oklahoma. It has stated as its creed: "With the education of young Kiowa tribal members lies the prospect of a bright future of accomplishments and advances for the tribe."[30]

Appendix

Following are four Kiowa tales that appeared over the years in the Daily Oklahoman. In many ways they may be more revealing of early-day Kiowa life than a straight rendition of events taken from historical record. Having been written in an earlier period, these accounts of Kiowa warfare contain some insensitive language and perspectives. It would be corruptive, however, to alter the writers' telling, and these narratives offer a valid copy of the original works. —STAN HOIG

THE DEATH OF NAH-GOEY
by Capt. W. S. Nye
(© Oklahoma Publishing Company
from *The Daily Oklahoman*, October 10, 1937)

Jimmy Wolf-Tail (Gui-tone, or Que-tone), an 80-year-old Kiowa who lives near Meers, north of Mount Sheridan, tells the story of the killing of Nah-goey, chief of the Kogui band of the Kiowa tribe. He had the tale direct from his grandfather, An-zah-te (Buffalo Udder), and it is an authentic part of the tribal history. An-zah-te himself was an interesting character, once, a prominent chief and medicine man. He must have been born prior to 1800, and thus heard from his own parent of the days when the Kiowas lived in the Yellowstone country and used dogs instead of horses as a means of transport. Jimmy Wolf-tail owns a Kiowa pictograph calendar which was made by Hau-vah-te, one of the Indians present at Fort Sill in 1871 when Stumbling Bear tried to shoot General Sherman.

There have been a number of these calendars in the tribe; they record the principal event which occurred each winter and summer, thus making it possible to place the date of events with reasonable accuracy. Jimmy's calendar shows the year in which "the stars fell," which, according to the Smithsonian ethnologist James Mooney, was in 1833, when there was a notable shower of meteors visible all over the western plains.

Having identified this year on the Hau-vah-te pictograph, it is easy for one to determine that the calendar year began in 1827, which antedates by five years any Kiowa calendar seen by Mooney. The event portrayed for 1827 on the Hau-vah-te calendar signifies that An-zah-te received a special memorial pipe from a visiting delegation sent by some other tribe, possibly Wichitas. In the language of the interpreter George Hunt, who also interpreted for Mooney in 1895, this meant that An-zah-te was "made a prince." Evidently this was some special, little-known (to the whites) ceremony of the Plains Indians, which may be compared, imperfectly, to our own custom of receiving honorary degrees from universities.

Or more aptly, it may be likened to the British custom of being knighted, for the recipient of the pipe was expected to make rich presents—horses, robes, and the like to the visiting delegation that bestowed the honor. From this it may be inferred that An-zah-te was not only a noted warrior, but also a wealthy fellow; paupers were not made "princes." The Plains Indians frequently exhibited an astonishing materialistic viewpoint in these transactions.

Gui-tone says that his grandfather, An-zah-te, was a chief of the highest type, one of those who were permitted to wear leggings fringed with scalp hair. He rode a pure white war pony and wore at all times a scarlet cape. Thus he was easily distinguished in battle, both by friend and foe. The Pawnees, at that time an enemy of the Kiowas, knew him well and respected him; they even had a name for him: Sat-tai.

Once when the Kiowas were fighting the Sah-kee-bo (Pawnees), An-zah-te advanced toward the enemy holding a shield fringed with prairie chicken feathers. This unusual decoration seems to have given him some sort of miraculous power, for when he ducked and hid in the grass, the Pawnees were wholly unable to hit him with their arrows. After this display of magic he was recognized as a greater chief than before.

Five years later An-zah-te's rising star set abruptly. He disgraced himself at the massacre of Beheading mountain in 1833 when the Osages cut off the heads of the Kiowas. This occurred at the western exit of Cutthroat gap, at the northwestern corner of the Wichita mountain wild life reserve. An-zah-te was in the camp that morning when the Osages attacked, but he fled without making any attempt to defend himself or his several wives. It was not of vital importance, thought the Kiowas, though scarcely praiseworthy or decent, that he should abandon his women to the slaughter. They did consider, however, that he should have had enough nerve to rescue his "outfit"—his shield and other war parapher-nalia. For those offenses An-zah-te was reduced to the ranks. He lost face completely. He became a soul in torment.

The following year, the winter of 1834, An-zah-te joined a war party—probably for the purpose of redeeming himself in the eyes of his tribes-men. Thus he became a member of the ill-fated Kogui raid into Mexico, and witnessed the death of Nah-goey.

The Kiowas had established their camp on the Washita river. While they were at this location a prominent chief named Nah-goey recruited a party of his own band, the Koguis, to go on a raid against the No-water people, that is the Mexicans, of Chihuahua. Two non-Kogui men who had married into this popular subdivision of the Kiowa tribe, joined the expedition: An-zah-te and Tau-kan-ta-le (Antelope Drive Boy).

The latter was a young medicine man whose duty it was to take charge of antelope drives; he also was an amateur prophet. Altogether there were about 20 who joined Nah-goey. They made elaborate prepara-tions for the trip, for it was dangerous, and might last for two years. It was essential that such a raid be led by a man who knew the landmarks and waterholes, one who was experienced and resourceful. Nah-goey was such a man.

On the second day of the journey the Kiowas came to the Red River which, swollen from recent rains, was unfordable. They were forced to swim their horses across, a dangerous feat and one which required cour-age as well as skill. Also they had to construct little "swimming boats" or coracles, made of willow frames covered with buffalo hides. These were used for ferrying across the grandmother god and special equipment, which pertained to this ancient medicine idol.

In spite of all precautions, one of the medicine pouches got wet. The Indians were aghast. This was a highly unpropitious omen. After consid-erable consultation among themselves they decided that a sweat lodge should be erected and earnest prayers offered to the grandmother god.

Nah-goey did not approve of this delay; he was anxious to push on south. But the others raised such a clamor that he consented to wait while saplings were cut and bent into the little frame of the lodge, and stones heated red hot to make the steam. While the devotees were pull-ing a robe over the lodge it caught fire from the hot stones beneath, and was badly scorched before the flames could be extinguished. This was worse and more of it. Most of the Kiowas were so alarmed that they proposed that the trip be given up.

This did not suit Nah-goey. He was made of sterner stuff. All these bad luck signs, he said, meant simply bad luck for the enemy—good luck for the Kiowas. He expressed such fine scorn of their fears and talked so long and good that finally they agreed to continue on the journey, but they were uneasy.

These misgivings were increased a thousand fold a few days later; as they rode along the edge of the Staked Plains a bear appeared in the trail in front of them. Everyone knew that the grandmother god taboo was strong concerning anything to do with bears.

The Kiowas reined in their horses and contemplated the shaggy beast with great dismay. The bear stood up on his hind legs, then got down on all fours and approached the Indians. He repeated this bold performance and seemed to be motioning to the Kiowas to go back. A third time he stood erect, and again approached. Finally, a fourth time (four is the magic number in all Kiowa supernatural manifestations) the animal distinctly waved his paw in a sign for the Kiowas to return to their villages.

This should have been enough for anyone. But the perverse Nah-goey insisted that it was a sign that they would win from their enemies. The bear then ran straight away from them.

"Hah!" cried the leader triumphantly. "That is the way our enemies will run from us."

So strong was his personality that the others were constrained to stay with the expedition, though there was considerable muttering as they rode along. They could not help but wonder what all these unusual signs portended.

The antelope medicine man, Tau-kan-ta-le, made strenuous efforts to find out. Each night he slept apart from the band, trying to get a vision which would signify the situation. But not a dream came to him. He was not very experienced as a soothsayer, and Nah-goey kept assuring everyone that all would be well with the Koguis.

They went on. A vast flock of crows passed overhead, streaming north and crying raucously as they went. The warriors thought that this must have some significance. Nah-goey agreed. "It is a signal that we will put on the black paint of victory on our return from the raid," he insisted. At length a tremendous scourge of flies came upon them, lasting several days. This was most unnatural—far out in the wilderness in an arid locality. Nah-goey was supremely optimistic, as ever. "Even the flies tell us of good luck to come," he informed them. But the others were profoundly apprehensive; someone suggested that it was more likely that soon the crows and flies would be feasting on their dead bodies.

The days passed. Spring was nearly at hand, and they were far down toward the southern edge of the Staked Plains, nearing the Mexican settlements beyond the Little Rio Grande (Pecos). Nah-goey said, "Which of you young men are willing to scare the crows away?" Which was the Indian way of calling for volunteers to act as rear guards. While it was customary for traveling bands of Indians to employ advance scouts or guards, they were even more careful to post rear guards, since they felt that an enemy was most likely to find them by following their trail. The rear scouts or guards, as well as the advance guards, were usually apprentice warriors or others who were not recognized as being of first rank in the tribe.

This was not because these posts were not important, for they were; but because they involved hardship, discomfort, and often danger, and were lonely posts besides. The Indians preferred to avoid these things, if possible, and were always willing that someone else perform guard duty. So in this case it was the two non-Koguis who volunteered, Tau-kan-ta-le for rear scout, and the disgraced An-zah-te for advance scout.

It was agreed that they would meet at some rendezvous outside the camp each night, and then report to the leader, Nah-goey. So they parted, An-zah-te riding ahead, and Tau-kan-ta-le turning back to observe from a distance the old camp site which they had vacated that morning.

It was a custom among the Kiowas that when a messenger approached the main body from scouting duty, bearing tidings of great importance, such as notification that the enemy had been sighted, the medicine men and chiefs received him with a special ceremony. First they would build a little altar of buffalo chips, then stand in the rear of it chanting while the messenger approached, circling his horse. The messenger halted at a respectful distance; the principal chief went up to him, plucked a wisp of straw from the ground, and thrust it in the messenger's hair. Then the messenger gave his information.

So on this occasion when the two scouts met at the rendezvous shortly before dark, they went through this same ceremony, in a spirit of fun this time, for they were close friends and no one was watching them.

"I saw nothing today, brother," said An-zah-te. "What did you see?"

"I went back along the trail," Tau-kan-ta-le replied, "and laid down behind some rocks at a distance from our old camp ground. All I saw was a lizard playing on the hot sand in front of me, and a buzzard wheeling in the clear blue sky. Then toward midafternoon I saw something moving on the hills far to the rear. In the shimmering heat I could not tell what it was, but it seemed that two men rode down through the mesquite and examined our camp site. After a time they turned back, and were joined by a much larger group who also came forward and appeared to be studying the ground where we slept last night. I have hurried forward to tell our leader."

So they went to where the main body was bivouacked under little wickiups made of bark and brush. Nah-goey came out of his hut and listened carefully to Tau-kan-ta-le's report. The others gathered around to hear the news.

"At this time of year many people are often fooled by large herds of elk," Nah-goey remarked, grasping Tau-kan-ta-le by the arm and pinching his skin cruelly. This was a test to see if the messenger was telling the truth; if he squealed with pain he was supposed to be a liar.

Tau-kan-ta-le did not shout, but nevertheless Nah-goey kept pinching him and criticizing him and doubting his story, while the other members of the band stood about grinning. Tau-kan-ta-le felt that he was being treated poorly, but he stoutly repeated that he had seen a great many men at the old camp site. Then he remembered how far he had been from the place, and how the heat waves made the objects look queer and uncertain.

"Maybe they were elks, at that" he said, doubtfully.

Nah-goey grunted. "Be sure of what you see next time," he said.

On the following morning the two non-Koguis again volunteered for scout duty. They felt that they were on trial. Nah-goey again impressed on them the necessity for verifying what they saw, and not turning to any false alarms. When the main band had gone ahead, Tau-kan-ta-le selected a position on the high ground at a distance from the camp and took post there.

Toward evening he observed again what he had seen on the previous day, with this exception: the main body of strangers was not preceded by two scouts. This time he saw plainly the sunlight glinting on weapons, red coats on the enemy, and heard faintly the clank of metal as saber and lance jostled stirrups. He did not wait to see more, and slipped away and rode rapidly to the rendezvous. Greatly alarmed, the two scouts rode to report to Nah-goey.

"Hah!" sneered the chief. "More elk!?" And he pinched the hapless Tau-kan-ta-le severely. The latter took it hard this time. "No doubt you are all-wise, Nah-goey," he said. "I am a young man, and not very experienced. I suppose that elks wear red coats and carry lances."

But Nah-goey was unimpressed. He was still wrapped in the sense of his infallibility. The following day the Indians lolled in bed late, as if they were safe on the Washita among their own people. They took life much as they found it; there were no trains to catch, no jobs to go to. If they did not feel like moving, they stayed where they were. Finally they prepared to resume the march.

"Who is going to volunteer for scout duty today?" called Nah-goey.

Tau-kan-ta-le whispered to An-zah-te that he personally did not care for it, as he had not been believed on the two preceding days. However, he felt that he would have to volunteer. He was in a spot. He knew that the enemy was following. He felt sure that they would attack on this particular day; and when this happened he would much prefer to be out in front, away from what looked like sure disaster, in view of the large number of the enemy which he had observed. However, if this did occur, then the Kiowas would say that he must have known that the attack was going to take place, and that that was the reason that he had gone on ahead, failing to volunteer for rear guard. "But there is no reason why you should not act as advance scout. Do it, and I hope that you will avoid this danger," he added to An-zah-te.

And so the advance guard moved out. Three or four others joined An-zah-te this day, for the leader felt that since they were nearing the enemy country, it was best to strengthen the advance guard. The advance guard rode on ahead, up the slope of a mountain which the Kiowas call Black-ice mountain, apparently somewhere north of Paso del Norte (El Paso). When they reached the summit they halted to look back. There far below in the valley they could see their comrades leisurely catching up their hobbled horses, packing the pouches carried on the saddles.

An-zah-te could even see Tau-kan-ta-le sitting disconsolately on a rock, some distance away, waiting until the main body had gone before taking up his lonely vigil near the camp site. Then, of a sudden, the watchers on the mountainside saw a large group of red-coated Mexican lancers ride out of a gulch in rear of the unsuspecting Indians, and break into a gallop as they charged the camp. They watched helplessly, unable to warn their friends, who could not have heard them no matter how loud they might have shouted.

Now the Koguis were aware of their peril. The advance scouts could see them running toward the mountain. Nah-goey and Tau-kan-ta-le were not with them. The chief was nearest the Mexicans, standing still in the path, with his bow drawn. Tau-kan-ta-le was a little distance behind him. The enemy dispatched a few who rushed up to Nah-goey; the rest passed on by him in pursuit of the others. The scene was obscured by a cloud of dust raised by the galloping horses. Scarcely a minute later it was all over. The men on the mountain side could see the red coats standing around in groups looking at the bodies of the Kiowas.

They waited until the Mexicans had gone. Then they made their way cautiously back to count the bodies of their friends, to make sure that all were accounted for when they took the sad news home to the tribe. As they neared the scene of the massacre they saw a crippled figure hobbling toward them, using his bow for a crutch. It was Tau-kan-ta-le. He was badly hurt, but would live. They washed his wounds and made him lie down in the shade of a bush. When he was able, he told them what had happened. When Nah-goey realized that the enemy was sure to catch them he told his men to flee. "I will stay here," he had said.

"When a cow is run all day, then butchered, its meat is soft and no good," were his last words. "It is obvious that I am going to be butchered and thrown to the enemy's dogs. But I will not run and make my meat soft. I want it to be good and sound when the enemy dogs sink their teeth in it!" A few moments later the lancers had run him through. He had not been prudent; he had been stubbornly reckless. But the Kiowas say that he was the bravest of the brave, ever cool and calm, no matter what the danger. The Koguis lost a great leader. The survivors stood there crying for him and for the others. Already the crows and flies were feasting on their bodies.

THE LOST SHIELD
Capt. W. S. Nye

(© Oklahoma Publishing Company
from *Daily Oklahoman*, November 28, 1937)

Several years ago there died at Fort Sill a Kiowa Indian named Iseeo. A protege of the late Major General H. L. Scott, this Indian was noted chiefly as the last active member of the detachment of United States Indian scouts at the post. Scott credited him with contributing much toward maintaining peace with the Indians during the turbulent times in 1891. It was not generally known that the name Iseeo was a hereditary one, which had been held by a succession of warriors in the Kiowa tribe. An uncle of the Fort Sill Iseeo was a renowned chief during the middle of the last century. Andrew Stumbling Bear, son of old Chief Stumbling Bear, tells a story of this earlier Iseeo which forms a portion of the history of the Kiowas.

In the late fall of 1853 the Kiowas were camped in what is now northern Oklahoma, near the site of Fort Supply. Iseeo and Tsain-hay-te (Big Horse), the father of the noted chief Kicking Bird, recruited a war party to raid in Old Mexico. In those days the Kiowas and Comanches did not hesitate to extend their forays far down into the country below the Rio Grande.

GENERAL PERSHING
AND I-SEE-O,
FORT SILL, OKLA.

Kiowa scout I-see-o congratulated by General Pershing for his WWI service. Courtesy Western History Collection, University of Oklahoma.

Chihuahua was their favorite raiding ground; they would establish a
raid headquarters in the high mountains overlooking the plains, and
descend from there to steal captives and stock from the haciendas. Kiowa
women state today that they can recall that their men would be gone for
two or three years on these raids, that they would take with them as many
as 20 pairs of moccasins apiece, all of which would be worn out before
they returned.

The Indians say that sometimes they went so far south that they saw
little men in the trees who had long tails (monkeys). This seems almost
incredible, but it well established that they did penetrate Mexico as far as
Durango, usually entering the country on foot, and returning to their
home on the Oklahoma plains with large bands of horses and mules
which they had stolen from the Mexicans.

Iseeo in 1853 was chief and an on-de. The Kiowa tribe used to be
divided into several castes, the highest of which, the top aristocracy, was
called on-de. A man became an on-de not so much by birth as by warlike
accomplishments, especially by those displays of individual valor which
constituted the approved ritual of Indian warfare. The prairie Indian
went to war mostly to win personal renown, and, while he liked to win

battles as much as anyone, the principal thing was to make sure that the proprieties of warfare were observed.

One of these customs was that no warrior should desert his war shield. The war shield was his medicine, his personal idol, his guarantee of safety and success. When not in use in battle, the shield was mounted on a special tripod outside the tepee. The Kiowas had a well-defined system of heraldry; each warrior had his war shield decorated and painted in accordance with this system. Iseeo's shield was painted sky blue with large red polka dots.

As was sometimes the custom, Iseeo took with him on this raid into Mexico his wife. It was her duty to cook his meat and take care of his horses, and she would have been extremely ashamed of herself not to have this honor. The girl was unusually handsome, and consequently Iseeo was quite jealous of her. For this reason he whipped her several times soundly, just to let her know that no foolishness would be tolerated while his back was turned. The girl's uncle, old Bait-sop-te, curiously enough resented this.

"Here we are on a raid," he complained. "Iseeo had no business bringing this girl in the first place. And now he is making trouble with her. He is only a poor, slim boy. I don't think he has any right to be called an on-de, or to be a chief."

Iseeo said nothing. But the others could see that he was irked by these remarks.

Soon the Kiowas started across the No-water Country (Chihuahua) against the Red-clothing People (Mexican lancers). They came to a great rancho where thousands of cattle grazed through the sparse shrub. They slaughtered several beeves, and were preparing to eat when they saw a party of red-coated soldiers coming along their trail. Now there would be some fun! It was only a very small troop of Mexicans, whereas the Indian war party was a powerful one, having many Kiowas and in addition a number of Comanches and Cheyennes. The Indians leisurely took position behind some rocks at the foot of a range of timbered hills and waited until the red coats came within bow-shot range. Few of the Indians possessed firearms.

But suddenly the Mexicans deployed. They looked much more numerous spread out than when they were in compact column. Many of the Kiowas promptly lost their lust for battle and retired hastily up the hill.

Not so Stumbling Bear and two lesser warriors. Stumbling Bear had been in many a fight, and he did not run unless forced to do so. But in the excitement he did not notice that many of his comrades had deserted him. The Mexicans did not see this either, or perhaps they suspected a trap. At any rate they advanced warily, leading their horses on foot, and shooting at the Indians with pistols. Stumbling Bear heard his friends calling to him from behind, far up the hill. Then he realized that he was unsupported. He and his two companions broke and ran up the slope, closely followed by the Mexicans.

Some of the Mexicans mounted. But their horses were impeded by the rocks. The three Indians slowed the pursuit by pausing now and then to fire to the rear. One of the three, a Cheyenne, paused too long. His old muzzle loader misfired. Red coats galloped up and thrust him through several times with their lances.

In a few moments Stumbling Bear and the other survivor were completely winded. They slowed to a staggering walk. It appeared that they would be overtaken by the Mexicans. Just then Iseeo came running down the hill toward them. He went on past and charged the Mexicans single-handed. The latter, thinking that he was leading the expected ambush counter-attack, turned and commenced to retreat. But one of their bullets struck Iseeo in the pit of the stomach. It did not penetrate several thicknesses of sheeting which Iseeo had wound about his middle, but it knocked the wind out of him.

The Kiowa unwound Iseeo's sheet. In the folds next to his belly was a flattened lead slug. The chief was only bruised. In a moment he sat up and saw the Mexicans running away, far down the valley. Then his gaze fell on old Bait-sop-te. The latter was seated on a rock, combing his sweat-drenched hair.

"Ah hah!" cried Iseeo. "So I'm not a chief? I guess you saw what kind of a man I am!" He grasped Bait-sop-te by the hair, twisted him to his knees and knuckled the old man's eyes severely. "You're a woman yourself!" he snorted, flinging Bait-sop-te sprawling.

The Indians rested for a time, then continued south. About sunset they approached a town on the outskirts of which were grazing many horses, tended by two peons. Iseeo and Big Horse rode up and shot down these two Mexicans, while the other Indians drove the animals into a corral. The leaders then discussed what they should do next. Big Horse thought that they ought to gather up the captured horses and start north with them before the garrison of the town should become aware of their presence.

But Iseeo, emboldened by his recent successes, wanted to actually enter the town, perhaps steal more stock, and at any rate stir up some devilment. He had little fear of the Mexicans. He was accustomed to see them run from him. Therefore he told Big Horse to return with the majority of the band to the place where they had killed the beeves, and wait there until he should come. Hone-zeptal and Au-an-todal volunteered to accompany him on his private foray into the ciudad.

It was almost dark. Near the corral Iseeo and his comrades could see the naked bodies of the fallen Mexicans gleaming faintly white through the dusk. Iseeo rode over and idly stuck his lance into one of them. The miserable fellow was not dead; he was only playing 'possum. He gave a horrible scream. This frightened Iseeo's horse, throwing the Indian to the ground on his head. It did not hurt him seriously, but he emitted a yelp. The main party of Indians riding away, laughed heartily at Iseeo's mishap.

Iseeo and his two companions rode toward the ciudad. They could hear a military band playing softly, not far away. The townsfolk were having their customary evening concert and promenade in the plaza. Presently the Indians came to the rock wall which enclosed the village; they tied their horses and climbed over to the inside. They were tired. Iseeo's head throbbed from the bump he had received. They sat down to rest, with their backs against the wall. Iseeo unslung his shield and commenced to rub his bruised poll. Soon all three of them were dozing in the quiet evening air.

But around the top of the wall was a sentry beat. Soon the sentinel came along, walking slowly. He saw the three strange figures slouched in the shadow of the wall, stopped to peer in indecision. Just as he was about to challenge, an officer of the guard approached with a small patrol. The sentry pointed out what he saw.

As the Mexicans conferred in low tones, the Indians were aroused. They sprang to their feet. There was a blinding flash as the sentry fired his piece. The Kiowas vaulted over the wall and fled, not stopping to untie their horses. They dashed blindly into a cactus fence, but did not feel the angry thorns. On through they floundered, struggled across a plowed field in the gathering darkness, and fell into an irrigation ditch. They scrambled up the bank and paused to listen for their enemy.

Not far away horses were running. Shrill orders were being given in Spanish. There was a great deal of dashing to and fro.

Suddenly Iseeo gave a cry of anguish.

"I've left my shield," he moaned. This was an appalling disaster.

"I'm going back after it!" cried Iseeo.

The other seized him. "No, you are not. We all will be wiped out if you try it. Come on, let's get out of here!"

The soldiers were in front of them by now, dashing here and there like beagles. The Kiowas had to drag Iseeo away. He dug his heels in the ground, insisting that he was going back after his shield.

"Be quiet!" hissed Hone-zeptal. "You can't do it. We'll make up a story when we get back, saying that you lost the shield when you were thrown from your horse at the corral, and that you didn't notice that it was missing."

They jumped into a steep, rocky ravine. Soldiers' voices were coming from every direction. The fugitives crawled under a rock, where there was a shallow cave screened by a rank growth of weeds. All the time they had to keep a tight hold on Iseeo.

It was black in the gorge. The Mexicans had scattered out, and were feeling their way through the canyon. Several of them rode right past the hiding place. When all had gone, the Indians slipped out and started to run. Soon they had left the tumult of the search far behind them.

All night long they traveled on foot. At daylight, weary and forlorn, they came to the rendezvous. The rest of the Indians were eating breakfast. The trio struggled up to the camp fire of Iseeo's kinsman, Stumbling Bear.

"Why, what is this?" asked Stumbling Bear in astonishment. "You went after more horses, yet you return without even your own mounts!"

The other chiefs and braves gathered to hear the story. Their faces were expressionless, but their sharp eyes did not fail to note that Iseeo's shield was missing.

"We got a large bunch of horses," explained Hone-zeptal, blandly. "But they got tired. We had to leave them behind. And, as you see, poor Iseeo lost his shield in the darkness when the horse threw him, and didn't notice it until just now."

The Kiowas snorted. "A fine story!" they said.

Iseeo sat apart, silent and troubled. The affair worried him intolerably. He wished that they had agreed to tell the truth. But it was too late now.

The band journeyed north for several nights. Finally they stopped to kill some cattle for food. Iseeo walked up on a knoll. He stood alone on a low bluff overlooking the camp. All at once a great cry was wrenched from his heart.

"I've disgraced myself. I left my shield. I ran from the enemy. Ai-ee! Ai-ee!"

Old Bait-sop-te heard the wail. His eyes narrowed.

"Everyone come here! Listen to Iseeo," he called.

The other Indians came running, and listened coldly while the conscience-stricken young chief poured out the whole miserable story.

"I have no sympathy for you," snarled Bait-sop-te, when it was finished. "I always knew that you were that kind of man. You are no chief. You are lower than a dog. You are no on-de!"

The others nodded solemnly. In formal conclave they voted Iseeo out of his chieftainship, reduced him also to the lowest caste of the tribe.

But Iseeo felt better for having confessed.

When the expedition returned to the main camp of the Kiowas, the whole tribe was informed of Iseeo's disgrace. For a year no one but his father would talk to him. Old friends did not recognize him when they met face to face. Finally Iseeo kept to his tepee, venturing out only under cover of darkness.

His father attempted to cheer him. "I will see the medicine man," he said. "He will help us."

Later he returned bringing a rabbit-skin cap, topped with a white eagle feather. "It is a cap like that worn by the Tai-me priest at the sun dance," he explained. "The next time the Kiowas have a fight with the enemy, you must wear it. It will bring you so much bravery that the chiefs will reinstate you."

Iseeo promised to do his best.

It was not long before he had his chance. They were on another expedition; the enemy was following them, possibly Mexicans again, a whole troop of soldiers, accompanied by a little brass cannon drawn by mules. The Kiowas made ready to fight. It was a rocky country, suitable for defense. They took position behind a little creek. The enemy came up on the other side and deployed in plain view. The Indians saw them tie their horses together in the shelter of a hollow, and came forward to lie down behind a rock breastwork which ran parallel to the creek.

The firing became general. A number of the Indians mounted their ponies and prepared to make individual charges. It was their way of displaying their bravery.

But who is this? It is that disgraced Iseeo on a white horse! On his head was the medicine cap, making him invulnerable, giving strength to his heart. His blanket was hooked over his shoulders like a red military cape. His body was naked, and painted light blue with great scarlet splashes to match the shield which he had lost. The white feather in his cap nodded in the slanting rays of the mid-morning sun. His only weapon was a long polished lance.

Iseeo ran his horse toward the enemy. The firing had slackened, but it picked up at once as Iseeo came into the open. He galloped across the entire length of the firing line, then returned unhurt to the gully. Immediately he repeated the performance, this time at a slow trot, and much nearer the enemy.

This was too much for the chiefs of the Kiowas. No such low, unrecognized dog could best them in a show of courage. That night Tohawson came forth and circled even closer to the enemy than had Iseeo. But before he regained the shelter of the gulch he saw Iseeo following him, cutting much closer to the firing line than he had. Iseeo was not hit. He rested for a moment. No one seemed to be anxious to duplicate his feat, much less better it.

Iseeo looked around at the hesitating brave, then gathered his reins and dashed straight forward to the enemy. They saw his horse rearing and plunging in the very midst of the smoke and stabbing flashes. But he came back untouched.

Stumbling Bear was getting ready to make a charge. Iseeo dismounted. "I have no shield," he shouted. "I am not allowed to carry a bow and arrows. Only a lance. I will even leave my special war pony behind. I will go on foot. But I'm going forward again!"

He and Stumbling Bear dashed forward at the same time.

"Somebody catch my son," shrilled Iseeo's father. "Save him!"

Several Kiowas snatched at Iseeo as he ran past them, but were able only to catch the empty quiver on his back. Iseeo tore himself loose and ran on. The other warriors were fired by his example. The whole mass of Kiowas charged. But Iseeo did not know that they were coming. He thought he was alone except for Stumbling Bear. The painted horde rushed the enemy breastwork. The cannon roared. Overhead flew a solid shot. Dust spurted up between the Indians and where the bullets were striking.

Iseeo was still a little ahead when the Indians reached the firing line. The soldiers stood up to receive the impact. In the middle of their line was a baldheaded man, evidently their commander. He and Iseeo thrust at each other simultaneously. The enemy tumbled over backward, his back broken by Iseeo's spear. Iseeo was hit also, in the knee. He went down, as the enemy fired almost in his face.

But the red coats could not stand the shock. They fled down the reverse slope, with the howling Kiowas at their backs. The air was filled with the white streaks of pursuing arrows. The Mexicans were in utter confusion, knocking each other down in their efforts to escape. Those who were not overtaken reached a creek, where they jumped into a pool of deep water. The Indians surrounded the hole. They poured hundreds of arrows into the struggling, bloody mass. Soon there was nothing but a tangle of floating bodies. The stream ran scarlet.

Presently the shooting died down. Not one enemy remained alive. The Indians lay on the ground and panted.

Stumbling Bear tried to cut the mules loose from the cannon. He saw a crowd of Kiowas gathered off to one side, ministering to one of the wounded warriors. It was Iseeo. At first they thought he was dead, but he was only stunned, though badly hurt. His face was black from powder burns. The Indians were licking and sucking the powder grains from his face and eyes. The buffalo medicine men were prancing around whining and shaking their buffalo-hoof rattles.

The Kiowas stripped the red uniforms from their vanquished enemy and dressed themselves in the resplendent coats. Then they went to where the Mexican horses were tied, caught them, and mounted. When they arrived back at their old position they found one man shot through the temples with a spent bullet. His eyes were hanging out on his cheeks. It was Half-sto-te. He was dead.

The Indians rode on in formation to imitate the Mexicans. While crossing a flat country they saw two Mexicans on a hill signaling to them. They waved back. The Mexicans came down, thinking they were friends. Too late they realized their mistake. The Kiowas killed them with con-siderable pleasure and collected the scalps. Presently they encountered another Mexican, whom they fooled in the same manner, with a fatal ending for the Mexican. It was a most successful expedition.

Eventually they returned to their own country on the Arkansas river. Iseeo was blind. And he had a wound in the knee which later caused his death. But at the time of the triumphant return he did not care. He was a chief once more. He was an on-de. Although he had no further use for a war shield, his friends made a new one for him.

THE MOUNTAIN ROUTE
by Capt. W. S. Nye
as told to him by I-see-o

(© Oklahoma Publishing Company
from *The Daily Oklahoman*, January 30, 1938)

Sometimes young Indian boys went to raids with the older men. They were allowed to guard the spare horses, saddles, and other impedi-ments, which the warriors always cached at their raid headquarters, prior to descending on the settlements. Indians who were too young had to secure permission from their fathers to go on such expeditions, for the older warriors did not care to be bothered with boys unless they were relieved of responsibility for their safe return.

It was under these conditions that in 1861 a warrior named Hone-zep-tai (On-top-of-a-gun) took two boys named Set-koi-k'e and Tape-ai-tian with him on a raid into Mexico. Tape-ai-tian, then about 13 years old, was an older brother of the famous scout I-see-o who served at Fort Sill for so many years. Set-koi-k'e was perhaps a year older. Hone-zep-tai, the leader, was an experienced raider; it was his plan to join the Comanches in their lucrative raids into Chihuahua.

The three Kiowas left their tribal camps on the banks of the Arkansas river and drifted south along the edge of the Staked Plains. After many days of travel they crossed the Pau-aidle-san or Little Rio Grande (the Pecos); not finding the Comanches, they continued across the deserts into Mexico. It was a long, dangerous trip, but Hone-zep-tai had been there before and knew the location of every landmark and knew the location of every waterhole along the route usually followed by war parties. He and his comrades rode toward the purple heights of the Sierra Madre mountains, where they expected to make their headquarters.

They were grateful to leave the heat of the lowlands and climb up among the cool pines where there were sparkling springs of water and where a refreshing breeze blew constantly. Far below them was the grassy plain of Chihuahua, with an occasional clump of mesquite. They also observed extensive ranchos with oases surrounded by high adobe walls. In the distance was a village consisting of a few flat-topped adobe huts, and here and there a more pretentious casa with plastered facade tinted sky blue or pink—all clustered around a lofty old church.

Hone-zep-tai was sure that the Comanches had established their base of operations in these mountains. He made a brief search and presently he located them. The Comanches proved to be so hospitable that the three Kiowas remained with them for two years. During this time they made it a practice to descend stealthily on the Mexican settlements, steal a few head of stock, then drive the animals swiftly back to the mountain hideout before the Mexicans could organize a pursuit. When the captured herd became unwieldy on account of its size, the Indians would return to Texas, where they turned the booty over to the Indians who had been left in charge of the "pool." Then the raiders returned to Mexico for more stock.

By spring of 1853 Hone-zep-tai and the two boys had obtained so many horses and mules that they decided to return to their own people. They realized that if they remained away from home much longer their relatives would give them up for dead. Hone-zep-tai wanted to travel to the Arkansas river by a new route. He was an unusually restless nomad, a true explorer. It was his theory that he could follow the Rocky Mountains north to near the source of the Arkansas river, somewhere in Colorado he thought, thence follow the stream east until he came to the Kiowa camps. This route would avoid the desert and the arid Staked Plains, and possibly would be less dangerous because it would avoid Texas, where rangers would be apt to make an inconvenient appearance, and also

Kansas, where there were United States troops. At any rate it was something novel, and he wanted to try it.

Probably no small part of his motive lay in a desire to have some experiences which no other Kiowa had been through, so as to have tall tales to tell when he returned to the tribal campfires. It was not difficult for him to persuade the two boys to agree to this plan. They were too inexperienced to appreciate properly the probable hardship which lay ahead of them. Trusting implicitly in their leader, they anticipated only a pleasant and interesting series of adventures.

They told the Comanches to hold their share of the stock, that they would either come to the Pecos for it later in the year, or that some of their kinfolk would do so. Then they made preparations for the long journey north. They killed a few stolen beeves, jerked the meat, tanned the hides, and made extra pairs of moccasins. They selected the hardiest horses to ride and to be used as pack animals. But they did not care to be burdened with a large remuda.

At first the explorers traveled slowly, and by easy stages, so as to harden themselves and their horses for the rough trip which they suspected lay ahead. As the summer wore on, and the mountain ridges still stretched far away to the north they knew that they would have to push ahead faster if they were to finish the trip before winter set in. But the country was becoming more and more rugged, and their ponies were developing tender feet from continual contact with sharp rocks instead of the prairie sod to which they had become accustomed.

Finally, one after another, the animals began to give evidence of complete exhaustion. The Indians were forced to shoot them and butcher them for food. Eventually they were reduced to but one mount apiece, and these were failing rapidly owing to the scarcity of food and the hard going. The Indians had been moving constantly north, keeping along the eastern edge of the mountain region in order to avoid the fierce Utes and Navajos who lived farther west. By the time that all their horses except the three they were riding had been killed they were far north, probably somewhere in the vicinity of Raton Pass.

One day they looked far down in the canyon below them and saw a wagon train toiling along a narrow road. A body of men who appeared to be soldiers were riding as escorts. This may have been one of the convoys of gold or silver from the mines in New Mexico, destined for the United States mints in the east. (Large shipments of bullion were passing over the Santa Fe Trail during the Civil War to assist the federal government in meeting the expenses of the war.) At once Hone-zep-tai began making plans to raid this train at night in order to secure fresh horses. He had no idea what the train carried, and he was not interested in finding out, for he realized full well that three tired Indians could accomplish nothing elaborate against so strong a party.

Toward evening the Kiowas saw the white men halt the wagons and form them into a circle for the night camp. Here was the chance they had been waiting for. Before it became too dark to see the trail they began to pick their way down the mountainside. As they got deeper into the pass they noticed that some of the streams flowed east from this point, others west. This was very curious, something they had never seen before. At the foot of the peak they found a beautiful little creek lined with timber. There they tied their weary animals, then on foot they commenced to sneak down the creek bed to where they thought that the white men had pastured their horse herd.

It was entirely dark by the time they arrived opposite the camp, but they were able to make their way quietly on account of the dim light of the dying camp fires, reflected from the surrounding pine trees. While the Indians were crouching below the bank of the stream, a man approached from the direction of the camp, carrying a musket on his shoulder. Just as they decided he must have seen one of them, he turned and walked slowly away in the direction from which he had come. They realized that he was a sentry walking a regular beat. They conferred in low tones and determined to kill him when he approached on his next round. They strung their bows and waited, tense with excitement.

Suddenly Hone-zep-tai whispered, "Here he comes!"

The Kiowas ran silently toward the soldier, loosing a shower of arrows as they ran. The man gave a great cry and discharged his piece. Almost instantly the little valley was lighted up by the fire of 50 guns. The canyons reverberated with the sound, which was practically continuous. Later, in discussing the affair, the Indians decided that the white men must have seen them on the mountainside during the afternoon, possibly through field glasses, and were on the alert for an Indian attack.

At any rate the Kiowas fled in confusion. But when they reached the timber the two younger Indians paused; both discovered that their leader was not with them. They looked back hastily. He was not in sight. They stared at each other in dismay. Hone-zep-tai must have been struck down by that first volley! But the bullets were still flying overhead, so they resumed their flight, fearful that they too would be hit. Presently they came to a safer place, sheltered by a low spur in the mountain. They stopped again and called to Hone-zep-tai. The only answer was an angry increase in gunfire. The two boys began to weep. They were sure that their leader was dead.

Soon they reached the place where they had tethered their horses. There stood Hone-zep-tai's pony, saddled and bridled just as the leader had left him a short time before. The boys' lamentations broke out with renewed vigor. They untied their mounts, including Hone-sep-tai's, and commenced to climb the mountainside. As they made their way through the darkness, brush, and trees they could hear the shooting still going on in the valley, growing fainter now as the jumpy white men continued to "repel" a supposed Indian attack. By midnight the Kiowa boys reached the top of the mountain, where they sat down among the boulders and waited for daylight to come.

In the morning they could see the white men preparing to break camp, the blue smoke from their camp fires rising straight in the quiet morning air. The Kiowas knew that their enemies were eating breakfast. They gnawed on the few remaining bits of dried beef which they carried in their saddle bags and watched dismally while the train formed in column and marched slowly east. Toward sunset the boys felt that it was safe to go down to search for Hone-zep-tai's body.

Far below they saw a flock of crows circling, and knew that he must be there somewhere near the deserted camp. However, the darkness of the night brought back their fears. They thought that the enemy was waiting for them in ambush, or that other and more dire things lurked in the darkness. They turned and retreated hastily up the mountainside. Here they remained for three days, trying unsuccessfully to gather the courage sufficiently to descend into the pass.

"What shall we do?" they asked. "Shall we go on, or shall we turn back?" They doubted their ability to find the head waters of the Arkansas, or to distinguish it from any of the other streams which rose in these mountains. They feared lest they perish in this hostile region far from their tribe. Reluctantly they decided to return to Mexico; from there they felt they could find their way home even though it involved crossing the No-water country without a guide. It was a hard decision to make, to take such a round-about route, but they saw it as the lesser of two evils, preferring the known to the unknown.

Sadly, they killed Hone-zep-tai's pony and butchered it for the long journey. Then they turned their faces south once more. Their hearts were full of foreboding. Winter was close at hand, it would be fatal to stay in the north until the cold overtook them. They were uncertain as to the route and worried lest they be unable to find sufficient water along the way.

After a week or so their horses, being in a pitiable condition, gave out and had to be shot. They cured the meat, but were unable to pack most of it, and realized that they must brace themselves to short rations so as to use their supplies as long as possible. They were able to kill some game, but not much, for their bows were made for shooting buffalo at short range, not deer at long range. There were no buffalo in the mountain ranges, and little game of any kind.

The youths did not dare go down to the lowlands, even though they sometimes saw settlements and ranches with grazing cattle. Like the wise wolves, they knew that the hand of every man was set against them and that they would be killed on sight.

Even their clothing was rotting and falling from them. Their moccasins had worn through and they were forced to walk barefooted through the sharp rocks. Mounted or "horse" Indians that they were, this form of locomotion was not merely unpleasant but it was an actual hardship. Before long their feet were cut and their flesh torn by briars and cactus thorns, and they were in a scary condition.

Eventually they came to an exceptionally rugged part of the mountains, a region which was bleak and dry. They had been without water all day. Toward mid-afternoon Set-koi-k'e, the older boy, went eastward in search of water. Tape-ai-tian waited for him until the evening shadows blackened in the canyons; then he became fearful that something had happened to his companion. He felt that he ought to go in search of him, but hesitated to do so lest they miss one another in the darkness. The chill of night descended on the mountain top.

At length Tape-ai-tian arose and began to grope his way forward along the ridge running to the east. Now and then he stopped to call feebly. There was no reply except weird echoes thrown back from the sides of the mountain. The Kiowa youth stopped, afraid to go farther because of the danger of falling over a cliff. In the meantime, Set-koi-k'e was searching for him. Both were lost. And they passed each other in the darkness, on opposite sides of the ridge.

In some way the horrible night was relieved. But when daylight came they were little better off. They kept up the search, but were only able to struggle along, weakened by thirst, hunger, and panic. Finally, on the third day, when he had almost given up hope, Tape-ai-tian saw Set-koi-k'e at a distance. He called hoarsely but the other did not look his way. Tape-ai-tian tried to run in that direction, but his legs failed him, and the other boy had turned away. Then Set-koi-k'e turned around and saw the younger boy. They limped painfully toward each other. It was a joyous reunion, with much weeping and embracing. The boys felt that, having overcome such hardships during the last few days, nothing worse could be in store for them, provided they stayed together. And so with a better spirit they resumed their journey southward. Early in the winter they arrived back at their old headquarters in the Sierra Madre mountains.

Looking around, they found the deserted campsite of the Comanches. There was no sign that the Indians had been there recently. In a clearing in the woods they saw an old broken-down burro, feeding peacefully. They shot the animal and butchered him for food. While they were cooking the meat they saw something moving in the timber on the opposite side of the meadow. At once they concealed themselves in the high grass. A group of strange Indians had been attracted by the smoke of their fire. The leader of this band rode forward to investigate. The Kiowas recognized him as a Comanche, but they did not know him; however, they knew that he was a member of a friendly tribe, so they came out of their hiding place and gestured to him.

The Comanche was shocked by the appearance of the two young men. They looked like animals, with their naked, lacerated bodies, their hair unkempt and matted with dirt and briars, and their eyes bloodshot from lack of sleep and from hardship. Plains Indians were accustomed to keeping themselves well clothed and neatly groomed, especially the hair. They considered it shameful to be seen in a disreputable condition.

"Who are you?" the Comanche called.

"Kiowas," they answered.

The Comanche chief embraced them and cried over them.

"Stay here until I can collect some clothing for you," he said. Then he returned to his party, borrowed several garments, a comb, and a small looking glass. No self-respecting Comanche ever set forth on a trip without these necessary toilet articles. When the Kiowas had made themselves presentable he took them to join his companions. They would have lost great face to have appeared in their original destitute condition.

A great welcome was prepared, and a fine feast, at the Comanche camp fire that night. The Kiowas related the entire story of their misfortunes, while the Comanches listened sympathetically. The Comanche chief then told them that he was going on the final raid of the season, and that he would be glad to have them accompany him, after which they would all go home together. The Kiowas were glad to accept. The Comanche chief was a kind-hearted fellow and, although the Kiowas were not very successful in the raid, he gave them some horses, and took them north with them.

Weeks later, they reached their camps on the Arkansas river. It was a sad duty to report the death of Hone-zep-tai, but the survivors were proud to be able to tell what hardships they had overcome in making their way back. I-see-o said that when his brother had left home he was a boy, but that when he returned he was a man.

WHEN THEY CUT OFF THEIR HEADS
by Alvin Rucker
As told by Alukah, Keeper of the Taime

(© Oklahoma Publishing Company
from *The Daily Oklahoman*, May 26, 1929)

The Kiowas were camped on Rainy Mountain creek, in our own country. All the young men were away on hunting expeditions and on war parties against the Utes. Only the women and children and old men and the chief, Island Man, were left in camp. In the afternoon before the day of the beheading, a woman and her son were out looking for a stray pony. The boy whispered to his mother that he saw a person passing forth behind a rock. The mother told him to pay no more attention, as the person would notice he had been discovered. They caught the pony and in doing so got a look at the person and saw that he was not a member of the Kiowas tribe.

They didn't let on, but when they got into camp, they told about the spy they had seen. The old men laughed loud and made fun and said that was just the way of women, they were always seeing spies when it was nothing but their sweethearts peeping at them. The next morning the boy went to a low hill to get his shield from a tree where he had left it over night so that the rising sun would shine on it and bless it. While he was on the low hill he saw the Osages coming. He called out to the people that the enemies were approaching. The Osages were afoot and had been creeping up. When the boy called out the warning the Osages knew they had been discovered and they stood up, rushed upon the village and began killing the women and children. Island Man, the Kiowa chief, who was in the camp at the time, cried out to the women and children, "to the rocks! to the rocks!" The women and children who had not been hurt rushed up the rocky side of [the] nearest mountain and got to the top. The Osages stopped to cut off the heads of those they had killed, and then shot arrow after arrow at the people on the mountain. As they could not afford to shoot all their arrows away, they undertook to rush up the mountain and get to the women and children on top. The women and children rolled and threw rock down on the Osages and kept them from coming up. The Osages then gathered up the heads they had cut off and put them in brass buckets which were in camp, and took some of the buckets to the highest mountain nearby, leaving the other buckets of heads setting around on the camp ground. They set fire to the tepees and most of the village was burned. When the Osages made their rush upon the village, the wife of the taime keeper put her baby on her back and rushed to the taime pole to get the taime. While she was unfastening it she and her baby were killed and the taime carried off. One mother put her baby on her back, and dragged an older daughter by the hand. An Osage grabbed the older daughter loose. While he was trying to cut her head off, the mother beat him off with rock and rescued her daughter who had a small gash on her head. A boy named Sitting-on-a-Tree was rescued by his father who seized and held him with his teeth while he fired arrows to keep off the pursuers, and taking him up again to run. After the Osages went away the Kiowas sent up smoke signals to ring in the warriors and hunters who were away at the time and to reassemble the Kiowa women and children who had fled across the prairies. When the men came in they went to the top of the high hill and found the baskets of heads setting all around the brow of the hill.

The Kiowas refused to make peace until they recovered their sun god, the taime, which the Osages at the time would not surrender. A meeting of the two tribes was arranged, during which the taime was to be restored. The meeting of the two tribes was to be on the Cimarron river. All the Kiowas went to the designated place and stopped when they came in sight of the Osage village. The Kiowas sent men forward and so did the Osages. After much talk the Kiowas agreed to give a pinto pony for the sun god. The Osages said all right and sent for the god and the Kiowas sent for the ponies. When the ponies were brought up, the Osages said that the pinto pony alone would be sufficient. The Kiowas paid over the pinto pony and the Osages surrendered the sun god. As soon as the Kiowas got the sun god into their possession they sent runners back to the Kiowa camp with the news and a great celebration followed.

Notes

CofIA–Commissioner of Indian Affairs
HofR–U.S. House of Representatives
KSHS–Kansas State Historical Society
NA–National Archives
OHS/AM–Oklahoma Historical Society, Archives and Manuscript Division
OU/WHC–University of Oklahoma, Western History Collection
UCO/OkC–University of Central Oklahoma, Oklahoma Collection

PROLOGUE

1. Mooney, "Calendar History," 216.
2. Kickingbird, *Tene Angopte*, 4.
3. Vail, *A Memorial*, 42.
4. Richardson, *Law and Status*, 30-31.
5. Corwin, *Kiowa Indians*, 110-111.
6. Pratt, *Battlefield and Classroom*, 40-41.
7. Nye, *Bad Medicine*, 131.
8. Trial of Satanta and Big Tree papers, microfilm AK, OHS/AM.
9. Marriott, *Ten Grandmothers*, 134-141.
10. Pratt, *Battlefield and Classroom*, 102.
11. *The Friend* 48 (Aug. 7, 1875): 401. Little is known of Big Horse other than that he was still conducting raids into Mexico as late as 1853. See "The Lost Shield" in the Appendix.

CHAPTER 1

1. Nye, *Carbine*, 233; Special Order 86, Fort Sill, April 27, 1875, Fort Sill Record Books (Bound), NA.

2. Nye, *Carbine*, 233.
3. Ibid., 234.
4. Ibid.
5. Kicking Bird's death occurred on the afternoon of May 3, 1875, not May 4 as most writers and historians have said and as his tombstone at Fort Sill reads. Haworth to Smith, May 27, 1875, Ltrs. Recd., Kiowa Agency, NA.
6. Butler, "A Day Among the Kiowas and Comanches," 837.
7. Ashabranner, *A Strange and Distant Shore*, 22. Seminole leader Osceola had been held prisoner in the Spanish castle for a time.
8. A person who met him just before his death estimated him to be about "thirty-five years old." "A Day Among the Kiowas and Comanches," 841.
9. Gilstrap, citing Elsie Clews Parsons, *Kiowa Tales* 22: 11, 13, 15.
10. *The Friend* 48 (Aug. 14, 1875): 410–411.
11. Ibid.
12. Still another variation of the Great Kiowa account, which reflects some degree of white influence, was published in a Quaker publication: "The Kiowas and Apaches have interesting traditions respecting the Creation and Deluge. The former worship a spirit whom they call the Great Kiowa, whose visible manifestation is in the Pleiades. He made the world; then he put animals upon it, and lastly man. He struck a tree and men and women came out. They were not rightly formed, so he struck it again, and others came who were. Men displeased the Great Kiowa, and he swallowed them with a flood of water. One man was saved. He looked very lonely, so the Great Kiowa took compassion on him, cut him in two, and of the two halves made man and woman. It was a different spirit who made the white man. They believe in future rewards and punishments, but their heaven is quite as little spiritual as the one described so minutely in 'Gates Ajar.' The earth is their mother, and when the last Kiowa is gone it will burn up with grief." *Friends' Review* 30 (Dec. 2, 1876): 243–244.
13. Butler, "Pioneer School Teaching," 496.
14. Mooney, *Calendar History*, 154.
15. Ibid., 153; Northcutt, "Leadership Among the Kiowa," 15.
16. Rucker, "Taime," *Daily Oklahoman*, May 26, 1929.
17. Campbell, "Down Among the Red Men," 624.
18. Mayhall, *Kiowas*, 9.
19. Mishkin, *Rank and Warfare*, 14; McCoy, *Kiowa Memories*, 2.
20. Mooney, *Calendar History*, 154.
21. des Montaignes, *The Plains*, 127, 131.
22. *The Friend* 48 (Aug. 7, 1875): 401–402.
23. Battey, *Life and Adventures*, 322–323.
24. Hyde, *Pawnee Indians*, 145. This latter group is said to have formed when the Kiowas were joined by a migrating band of Apaches in western Montana. Time-Life Editors, *The Buffalo Hunters*, 21.
25. *Daily Missouri Republican*, Nov. 10, 1851.
26. Mooney, *Calendar History*, 157; Northcutt, "Leadership Among the Kiowa," 16.
27. Time-Life Editors, *The Buffalo Hunters*, 45.

28. The presence of the Kiowas in the region was indicated by French trader Jean Baptiste Truteau in 1795. Canadian trader Charles MacKenzie was present at the Missouri River villages in June 1805 when the Crows of the Rocky Mountains arrived to trade. The visitors came on horses with most of the men riding bareback and the women on saddles made of woven cottonwood limbs. Children above age six were able horsemen; younger ones were lashed to their saddles. Around 2,000 animals, including spare mounts and those pulling travois loaded with camp equipage, gave the appearance of a small army. The Crows pitched their conical leather tents, more than 300 of them, a short distance from their hosts' dome-shaped brush-and-mud huts. The buckskin-clad warriors, many fancily decked with beads and silver trinkets, halted in a circle on the high ground behind the village where their chief addressed them. Then with the energy of a Cossack cavalry they came war-whooping at full speed into the village, exhibiting their great dexterity as horsemen and flaunting their bows and arrows, lances, and shields. MacKenzie, "The Mississouri Indians," 344-346.
29. Hyde, *Red Cloud's Folks*, 23.
30. Mishkin, *Rank and Warfare*, 7.
31. Gilstrap, "Sayt-aym k'ee-ah" 1: 5.
32. Keim, *Sheridan's Troopers*, 1830-1884.
33. John, "An Earlier Chapter," 381.
34. Ibid.
35. Northcutt, "Leadership Among the Kiowa," 17.
36. John, "An Earlier Chapter," 381.
37. *Annual Report, CofIA, 1848*, 136-138.
38. Gilstrap, "Say-aym k'ee-ah" 1: 15-16. Charles Apekaum, who relates the tale, states that the medal was placed in the hands of his nephew, Scott Tonemah.
39. Ibid., 389-391.

CHAPTER 2

1. Mooney, *Calendar History*, 158-160; Ronda, *Lewis and Clark Among the Indians*, 48, 67. Canadian trader Alexander Henry in *New Light on the Early History*, 354-359, provides good descriptions of the trade activities and goods on the Upper Missouri during this period. White buffalo hides, which carried special superstitious value, and grizzly bear skins were highly regarded items. Nasatir, ed., *Before Lewis and Clark*.
2. Lewis and Clark, *History*, 20-21.
3. Pike, *Expeditions*, 449, 846.
4. Ibid., 468, 757. Donald Jackson, ed. and anno. of *The Journals of Zebulon Montgomery Pike*, 59-60, n. 11, states that Purcell, accompanied by two French-men, had earlier been twice captured on the South Platte by the Kiowas before escaping. Purcell may have been the first white American to discover gold in Colorado.
5. Pike, *Expeditions* 2: 743-745.
6. Mooney, *Calendar History*, 167-168.

7. Ibid., 168–169. Mooney surmises that the tribe may have been hit similarly in 1801. Still another smallpox epidemic struck the northern tribes during the 1830s.

8. Twaites, ed., *James's Account of S. H. Long's Expedition*, 157–160.

9. James, *Account of an Expedition* 2: 156.

10. Mooney, *Calendar History*, 136.

11. James, *Account of an Expedition* 2: 60–61. Expedition chronicler Bell indicated that the man was eloping with another man's wife and that the horse they led had been stolen. When Long purchased the horse, the woman had to make a new packsaddle, which she did with great dexterity from a small cottonwood tree. James, *Account of an Expedition* 2: 62.

12. Mooney, *Calendar History*, 136.

13. James, *Account of an Expedition* 2: 103.

14. Ibid., 101–102.

15. Ibid., 113.

16. Ibid., 177.

17. Ibid., 185–186, 216.

18. Ibid., 193–194.

19. Fowler, *Journal*, 68.

20. James, *Three Years*, 169–172.

21. Doyle, "The Kiowa and Comanche Reservation," *National Tribune*, Aug. 1, 1901.

22. Reid and Gannon, eds., "Journal of the Atkinson-O'Fallon Expedition," 23; "Atkinson's 1825 Expedition up the Missouri," American State Papers, Indian Affairs 2: 607.

23. Hafen and Rister, *Western America*, 255.

24. *American State Papers, Military Affairs* 4: 277–280.

25. Berlandier, *Indians of Texas*, 108, 134–135.

26. *Missionary Herald* 29 (1833): 369; *Niles' Register* 44 (March 23, 1833), 51; Foreman, *Pioneer Days*, 103–104; Gregg, *Commerce*, 253–255.

27. Chouteau to Stambaugh, *Arkansas Advocate*, Aug. 21, 1833, cited by Foreman, *Advancing the Frontier*, 119.

28. *Missionary Herald* 29 (1833): 369; Foreman, *Advancing the Frontier*, 118; Mooney, "Calendar History of Kiowas," *Bureau of Ethnology Report, 1895–96*, pt. 1, 257–259. A ceremony of reconciliation conducted by the Kiowas and Osages is depicted in a painting by Kiowa artist Etahdleuh. Petersen, *Plains Indian Art*, 143, Plate 33. According to Alukah, the Taime was returned to the Kiowas by the Osages at a meeting on the Cimarron River in northeast Blaine County in either late 1834 or early 1835. See the Appendix account by Rucker in this volume. Kicking Bird's older cousin Stumbling Bear, who was born about 1830, was one of the infants who miraculously escaped death at Cutthroat Gap. Griswold, "Chief Stumbling Bear," 474.

29. Report of the Secretary of War, *American State Papers, Military Affairs*, V, 170.

30. Catlin, *Letters and Notes* 2: 72–75.

31. Wheelock, "Dodge Report," 73–93.

32. Evans, "Journal of Hugh Evans," 192.

33. Wheelock, "Dodge Report," 83–85.
34. Evans, "Journal of Hugh Evans," 203–204.
35. Wheelock, "Dodge Report," 88. The Anglicized name for Tiche-toche-cha was not revealed in any of the accounts of the expedition or the ensuing council at Fort Gibson. It could be speculated, however, that allowing for diversity in translation, he was the same chief who would sign a treaty agreement for the Kiowas at Fort Gibson three years later. That chief was listed as Ta-ka-to-couche, or the Black Bird. Kappler, comp. and ed., *Indian Treaties*, 489–491.
36. Wheelock, "Dodge Report," 88.
37. *Arkansas Advocate*, Oct. 31, 1834, possibly written by Capt. Matthew Duncan of the First Dragoons.
38. *Sen. Ex. Doc. No. 1*, 23rd Cong., 2d sess., 89.
39. Ibid.
40. Catlin, *North American Indians* 2: 74.
41. Wheelock, "Dodge Report," 84.
42. Evans, "Journal of Hugh Evans," 212.
43. *Daily National Intelligencer*, Oct. 23, 1834. A letter in the *Arkansas Gazette*, Sept. 16, 1834, reported from Fort Gibson: "The celebrated artist George Catlin, Esq., who, you are aware, accompanied the Dragoons had a severe attack of fever on the prairie, but has returned with the command, and is now convalescent. He succeeded in painting the portraits of several of the principal Comanche chiefs, at their camp, and is about painting the chiefs and warriors of the Kioway and Towayash Delegations here; but his indisposition prevented his obtaining and gratifying us with views and sketches of the Towayash or Pawnee villages, and the picturesque and beautiful country adjacent."
44. Wheelock, "Journal of Proceedings," 59.
45. Ibid.; Evans, "Journal of Hugh Evans," 112.
46. Wheelock, "Journal of Proceedings," 59.
47. Ibid., 66.
48. *Arkansas Advocate*, Oct. 31, 1834.
49. Mooney, *Calendar History*, 171.

CHAPTER 3

1. Petersen, *Plains Indian Art*, 75, citing Lady Duffus Hardy, *Down South*, 168.
2. Battey, *Life and Adventures*, 329–330.
3. Marriott, *Ten Grandmothers*, 95–97.
4. Ibid., 56–57; Northcutt, "Leadership Among the Kiowa," 36–37.
5. Pratt, *Battlefield and Classroom*, 95.
6. Butler, "A Day Among the Kiowas and Comanches," 841.
7. Arbuckle to Mason, May 18, 1835, Fort Gibson Ltr. Book, 1834–1836, NA; Mason to Arbuckle, July 2, 3, 1835, Ltrs. Recd., AGO (Main Series), NA. Reports from Camp Mason appear in the *Daily National Intelligencer*, Aug. 7, 21, Sept. 2, 23, 1835; and in the *Army and Navy Chronicles*, Aug. 27, Sept. 3, 17, Oct. 1, 8, 22, 1835.

8. Foreman, ed., "Journal of Proceedings," 394.
9. Jones, ed., "Diary," 288–289; Mason to Arbuckle, Ltrs. Recd; Fort Gibson, July 2, 3, 8, 1835; Foreman, ed., "Journal of Proceedings," 406.
10. Mason to Arbuckle, July 8, 1835, Ltrs. Recd., AGO (Main Series), NA.
11. Foreman, ed., "Journal of Proceedings," 406.
12. Jones, ed., "Diary," 287.
13. Ibid., 288; Foreman, ed., "Journal of Proceedings," 409–410.
14. Van Zandt, "History of Camp Holmes," 319; Foreman, Pioneer Days, 223–225.
15. Estep, "Alexander le Grand," 176.
16. Ltr. P. L. Chouteau, April 20, 1836, in Arkansas Gazette, July 19, 1836; Foreman, Advancing the Frontier, 148.
17. Daily National Intelligencer, May 7, 1836.
18. Ibid., June 10, 1836.
19. P. L. Chouteau to Armstrong, Feb. 1, 1837, Ltrs. Recd., Western Suptcy., NA. Box C-32, Cass Collection, OU/WHC.
20. Chouteau to Armstrong, May 22, 1837, Ltrs. Recd., Western Suptcy., NA. Box C-32, Cass Collection, OU/WHC.
21. Kappler, comp. and ed., Indian Treaties, 489–491.
22. Chouteau to Harris, Dec. 10, 1837, Item 36, Cass Collection, OU/WHC.
23. Daily National Intelligencer, May 17, 1837.
24. Cass to Poinsett, Sept. 8, 1837, Item 30, Cass Collection, OU/WHC.
25. A. P. Chouteau Ltrs., Nov. 25, Dec. 8, 1837, May 1, 1838, Ltrs. Recd., Western Suptcy., NA.
26. P. L. Chouteau to Armstrong, May 22, 1837, Item 26, Cass Collection, OU/WHC.
27. Blaine, Pawnee Passage, 57.
28. Hyde, Pawnee Indians, 273.
29. Irving, Indian Sketches, 124.
30. Ibid., 135.
31. Grinnell, "Bent's Old Fort" (brochure), 42.
32. Grinnell, Fighting Cheyennes, 46–48.
33. Grinnell, "Bent's Old Fort" (brochure), 42.
34. Daily National Intelligencer, April 16, 1839.

CHAPTER 4

1. Nye, Carbine and Lance, 12. Mayhall, The Kiowas, 14, states that Tohawson succeeded the deposed A'date following the Osage massacre of the Kiowa village in 1833. Records of the Dodge visit and the ensuing council at Fort Gibson clearly indicate, however, that Tiche-toche-cha was the head chief in 1834. Likely this was the same man as Ta-ka-to-couche, head chief and leading signer of the Treaty of 1837.
2. Abert, Journal, 46.
3. Colley to Evans, Dec. 30, 1862, Ltrs. Recd., Upper Ark. Agency, NA.
4. Annual Report of CofIA, 1865, 714.
5. Gregg, Commerce of the Prairies, 109–111.

6. Armstrong ltr., June 8, 1839, Foreman Transcripts, I, OHS/AM.
7. Statement of goods and provisions furnished Comanches and Kiowas who lately visited Choctaw Agency on way to Washington, Ltrs. Recd., Western Suptcy., 1842-1843, NA; George Chisholm to Gov. P. M. Butler, Jan. 29, 1843, Ltrs. Recd., Western Suptcy., 1842-1843, NA.
8. Armstrong ltr., June 8, 1839, Foreman Transcripts, I, OHS/AM; Statement of Goods, etc., Foreman Transcripts, I, OHS/AM.
9. Grinnell, *Fighting Cheyennes*, 64-69.
10. Five years later, in 1845, a Cheyenne presented a painted lodge to Tohawson as an act of personal friendship. Other paintings were added as the lodge was passed down. The robe was eventually procured by the Smithsonian Office of Anthropology. It is reproduced in full color in Petersen, *Plains Indian Art*, 85.
11. Webb, *Texas Rangers*, 45-46; Fehrenbach, *Comanches*, 325-329; Wallace and Hoebel, *The Comanches*, 294.
12. Kendall, *Narrative*, 207-208.
13. Ibid., 212-214.
14. Gardner, ed., *Brothers on the Santa Fe and Chihuahua Trails*, 22.
15. Abert, *Journal*, 39-40; des Montaignes, *The Plains*, 119.
16. Abert, *Journal*, 39-40.
17. Ibid.
18. des Montaignes, *The Plains*, 114, 119-120.
19. Ibid., 113.
20. Barde, *"Billy" Dixon*, 174-175; *Kansas Daily Tribune*, Aug. 9, 1874.
21. des Montaignes, *The Plains*, 112, n. 6.
22. Ibid., 136-137.
23. Abert, *Journal*, 40, 46.
24. Ibid., 47.
25. des Montaignes, *The Plains*, 130-131.
26. Mayhall, *Kiowas*, 89-90.

CHAPTER 5

1. Marriott, *Ten Grandmothers*, 102; Northcutt, "Leadership Among the Kiowa," 37; Ewers, *The Horse*, 10, n. 10.
2. Abert, *Journal*, 47.
3. Ibid., 30; Nye, *Bad Medicine*, 114-117.
4. des Montaignes, *The Plains*, 126-127.
5. Mishkin, "Rank and Warfare," 39.
6. Northcutt, "Leadership Among the Kiowa," 38.
7. Mishkin, *Rank and Warfare*, 27-29.
8. Northcutt, "Leadership Among the Kiowa," 35.
9. *Report of Messrs. Butler and Lewis*, 13.
10. Duval to Medill, July 18, 1846, Ltrs. Recd., Seminole Agency, M-234, VA.
11. *Annual Report of CofIA, 1847*, 901.
12. Ibid., 244.
13. Gilpin to Jones, Aug. 1, 1848, *HofR Ex. Doc. 1*, 30 Cong., 1st sess., 136-140.

14. Ibid.
15. Fitzpatrick to Supt. of IA, ibid., 472.
16. Artist Richard H. Kern was a visitor at this time also. Although annoyed in camp by the tribesmen, he noted on November 10: "The Kiowas and our party raised camp together, Having traded meat, &c, and moved on pell mell together. It was a queer compound of civilization and barbarism—traveling in company." Grant, *When Old Trails Were New*, 125.
17. *Daily National Intelligencer*, Feb. 26, 1849,
18. Berthrong, *Southern Cheyennes*, 112–113.
19. *HofR Ex. Doc. 45*, 31st Cong., 2d sess., 27–28.
20. Barry, *Beginning of the West*, 873–874, citing Dr. A. M. Heslep ltrs. in *New York Weekly Tribune*, July 8, Aug. 4, 11, Sept. 1, 1849.
21. *Fort Smith Herald*, Sept. 5, 1849, Foreman Collection, Edwards' Trading Post file, OHS/AM.
22. *Arkansas Intelligencer*, July 14, 1849.
23. Grinnell, "Bent's Old Fort" (brochure), 20–21.
24. Barry, *Beginning of the West*, 873, citing St. Louis *Daily Union*, Aug. 16, 1849.
25. *New York Tribune*, May 19, 1851; *Daily National Intelligencer*, May 7, 1851.
26. Berthrong, *Southern Cheyennes*, 116.
27. *Transactions*, Nebraska State Historical Society 3: 292–294.
28. Hallock, "Siege of Fort Atkinson," 638–648.
29. Lowe, *Five Years a Dragoon*, 131.
30. Fröbel, *Seven Years' Travel*, 266–273. A fifty-man company from Santa Fe arrived at St. Louis in late August and reported seeing 300 lodges of Kiowas and Comanches on the trail at Rabbit Creek. The Indians were friendly and did not interrupt the travelers. *Daily National Intelligencer*, Sept. 11, 1852.
31. Nye, "The Lost Shield."
32. Kappler, comp. and ed., *Indian Treaties*, 600–602.
33. *Annual Report of CofIA, 1853*, 364–365.
34. *Sen. Ex. Doc. 78*, 33rd Cong., 2d sess., 26. Traveling with the Gunnison caravan was David Meriwether, on his way to become territorial governer of New Mexico. In his memoirs he tells of a merchant train on the Aubrey Cutoff of the Santa Fe Trail that was surrounded by the Kiowas who wanted the return of two Mexican girls who had escaped from them and taken refuge in the train. Meriwether, *My Life in the Mountains*, 152–153.
35. *Daily Missouri Republican*, Dec. 4, 1853.
36. *Sen. Ex. Doc. 78*, 33rd Cong., 2d sess., 31–33.
37. Ibid., 32.
38. Möllhausen, *Diary of a Journey*, 219.
39. *Annual Report of CofIA, 1854*, 89.
40. Grinnell, *Fighting Cheyennes*, 102–103.

CHAPTER 6

1. *Annual Report of CofIA, 1854*, 298–299.
2. Ibid., 299.
3. Whitfield to Supt. of IA, Aug. 1, 1855, Ltrs. Recd., Upper Ark. Agency, NA.

4. Whitfield to Supt. of IA, Aug. 15, 1855, ibid.
5. *Annual Report of CofIA, 1855*, 179.
6. Miller to Supt. of IA, Aug. 29, 1856, Ltrs. Recd., Upper Ark. Agency, NA.
7. *Annual Report of CofIA, 1857*, 143-144.
8. Miller to Supt. of IA, Oct. 28, 1857, Ltrs. Recd., Upper Ark. Agency, NA.
9. *Annual Report of CofIA, 1857*, 147.
10. *Annual Report of CofIA, 1856*, 174-175.
11. *Annual Report of CofIA, 1857*, 550.
12. Miller, "Surveying the Southern Boundary Line," 124-125.
13. Ibid., 131.
14. McKisick to Pulliam, April 15, 1858, Ltrs. Recd., Western Suptcy., NA.
15. Ford to Runnels, May 22, 1858, *HofR Ex. Doc. 27*, 35th Cong., 2d sess., 19; *Daily National Intelligencer*, June 10, 1858.
16. *Annual Report of CofIA, 1858*, 450.
17. Miller to Supt. of IA, July 20, 1858, Ltrs. Recd., Upper Ark. Agency, NA.
18. Ibid., 451.
19. Thoburn, "Indian Fight in Clarke County," 314-329.
20. Brice, *Reminiscences*, 12.
21. Ibid., 18-19.
22. Bent to CofIA, March 17, 1860, Ltrs. Recd., Upper Ark. Agency, NA.
23. Root, "Extracts From Diary of Captain Wolf," 204-205.
24. *Annual Report of CofIA, 1859*, 507.
25. Rector to Greenwood, May 3, 1860, Ltrs. Recd., Western Suptcy., NA.
26. Capt. Samuel D. Sturgis was in Kansas with a command from Fort Cobb at the same time. He reportedly crossed Sedgwick's trail on the Smoky Hill. Ibid., 206-209.
27. Root, ed., "Extracts From Diary," 207-208.
28. Robert Morris Peck, then a lieutenant, wrote a detailed account of this engagement that appeared in the Aug. 1, 1901, issue of the *National Tribune*. He mentions Tohawson as the head chief, Satank as the Kiowas' war chief, and Satanta as a subordinate chief. He makes no mention of Kicking Bird.
29. Barry, "Richardson's Letters," 54.
30. *Annual Report of CofIA, 1860*, 452.
31. Report, June 10, 1860, Ltrs. Recd., Southern Suptcy., M-640, NA; *Daily National Intelligencer*, Aug. 25, 1860.
32. Otis to CofIA, Aug. 17, 1861, Ltrs. Recd., Upper Ark. Agency, NA.
33. Articles of agreement, Sept. 6, 1861, Ltrs. Recd., Upper Ark. Agency, NA.
34. Yellow Wolf's Kiowa name is given as O-com-o-cost on his grave marker in the Congressional Cemetery, Washington, D.C.
35. Smith, *Frontier Defense*, 34.
36. *Message of President [CSA] and Report of Albert Pike*, 23.
37. Abel, *American Indian as Participant*, 64-65.
38. Pike to Hindman, July 3, 1862, *Official Records* 1 (8): 958.
39. *Official Records* 4 (2): 352-357.
40. Colley to Evans, June 30, 1862, Ltrs. Recd., Upper Ark. Agency, NA.
41. Colley to CofIA, Aug. 11, 1862, Ltrs. Recd., Upper Ark. Agency, NA.
42. Colley to Evans, Dec. 30, 1862, Ltrs. Recd., Upper Ark. Agency, NA.

43. *Annual Report of CofIA, 1863*, 239–257.
44. *Washington Evening Star*, April 6, 1863.
45. Ibid., March 27, 1863.
46. Ibid.; *Daily National Intelligencer*, March 28, 1863.
47. *New York Times*, April 6, 1863.
48. Ibid.
49. Ibid., April 8, 11, 13, 1863.
50. Ibid., April 13, 1863.

CHAPTER 7

1. *Annual Report of CofIA, 1863*, 376–377.
2. *Official Records* 1 (22-2): 316–317.
3. Ibid., 339–340.
4. Ibid., 400–401.
5. *Annual Report of CofIA, 1863*, 247–248.
6. Ibid., 540–541.
7. Ketcham to Evans, April 4, 1864, *Annual Report of CofIA, 1864*, 401–402.
8. Ketcham to Dole, April 10, 1864, ibid., 402.
9. *Official Records* 1 (34-4): 403.
10. In his report Eayre claimed falsely that he was attacked first. Ibid., 1 (24): 935.
11. Ibid., 1 (34-4): 149–150.
12. Hoig, *Sand Creek Massacre*, 30.
13. *Official Records* 1 (41-1): 964.
14. Ibid., 1 (34-4): 402–404.
15. *Leavenworth Daily Conservative*, July 21, 1864.
16. *HofR Ex. Doc. 62*, 42d Cong., 3d sess., 3–4.
17. Ibid., 5–6.
18. Ibid.
19. *Official Records* 1 (41-2): 735.
20. Ibid., 1 (41-1): 231-232. This is probably the same incident as the one reported by Major Anthony on August 23, 1864. Ibid., 1 (42): 926.
21. Ibid., 1 (41-2): 827, 926–927; (41-4): 319–322.
22. Curtis to Halleck, Oct. 7, 1864, ibid., 1 (41-3): 693.
23. Richardson, *Northwest Texas*, 246–248; Mayhall, *Indian Wars of Texas*, 124–125.
24. *Official Records* 1 (41-1): 885–886.
25. Details of the raid are provided in Cashion, *A Texas Frontier*, 66–67. W. S. Nye told of another white girl, Mary Hamleton, who lived her life among the Kiowas. Taken captive from her Tarrant County, Texas, home in the spring of 1867 at the age of five, she was given the name To-goam and was married to a Mexican captive. She died in 1924. Nye, "What Happened to Mary Hamleton?" *Daily Oklahoman*, Oct. 24, 1937.
26. *Official Records* 1 (41-1): 939–942; see also Pettis, *Kit Carson's Fight*.
27. R. Doolittle, May 31, 1865, *Official Records* 1 (48-2): 868–869.
28. Dockstader, *Great North American Indians*, 281.

29. Gilstrap, *Salt-aym k'ee-ah* 1, 41.
30. Grinnell, "Bent's Old Fort" (brochure), 16. Leavenworth said a Comanche chief had requested a small wagon such as Tohawson had until Carson burned it and the chief's lodge in 1864. Leavenworth to Cooley, Sept. 21, 1866, Ltrs. Recd., Kiowa Agency, NA.
31. Hoig, *Sand Creek Massacre*, 97–98.
32. Ibid., 91–128.
33. For a more detailed account, see ibid.

CHAPTER 8

1. For more on Chisholm, see Hoig, *Jesse Chisholm*.
2. Chapey-a-ne-Chis to Creek headmen, Feb. 21, 1865, Dale, "Additional Letters," 140–142.
3. Lewis, "Camp Napoleon," 162. Heap-of-Bears, a latter-day Kiowa subchief, said Tahebecut was his father.
4. Smith, *Frontier Defense*, 143.
5. Leavenworth to Ford, May 30, 1865, *Official Records* 1 (48-2): 687–688.
6. Leavenworth to Ford, June 27, 1865, ibid., 1009; Tibbits to Ford, June 28, 1865, ibid., 1021.
7. Chisholm to Leavenworth, July 15, 1865, Ltrs. Recd., Kiowa Agency, NA.
8. To-haw-son et al., Aug. 15, 1865, *Official Records* 1 (48-1): 362–363.
9. Agreement, Leavenworth and Sanborn with Indians, Aug. 15, 1865, Ltrs. Recd., Kiowa Agency, NA; *Annual Report of CofIA, 1865*, 394–395.
10. *Annual Report of CofIA, 1866*, 712.
11. Ibid., 714–715.
12. Ibid., 717.
13. Ibid., 719.
14. Ibid., 718; Pope to Harlan, Aug. 21, 1865, Ltrs. Recd., Kiowa Agency, NA.
15. "Diary of Samuel A. Kingman," *Kansas Historical Quarterly* 1 (Nov. 1932): 447.
16. Leavenworth to Cooley, Nov. 9, 30, 1865; Feb. 7, 1866; Ltrs. Recd., Kiowa Agency, NA.
17. Kappler, comp. and ed., *Indian Treaties*, 892–895.
18. Leavenworth to Colley, May 1, 1866, Ltrs. Recd., Kiowa Agency, NA.
19. *HofR Ex. Doc. 240*, 41st Cong., 2d sess., 47.
20. Monahan, "Kiowa-Federal Relations," 482.
21. *HofR Ex. Doc. 240*, 41st Cong., 2d sess., 47.
22. Statement of Mrs. Box, *Sen. Ex. Doc. 13*, 40th Cong., 1st sess., 100. See also *New York Times*, Nov. 8, 1866.
23. Report of Capt. Andrew Sheridan, Oct. 1, 1866, Ltrs. Recd., Kiowa Agency, NA; Report of Lt. G. A. Hesselberger, Sept. 29, 1866, Ltrs. Recd., Kiowa Agency, NA.
24. Bogy and Irwin to CofIA, Nov. 12, 1866, Ltrs. Recd., Kiowa Agency, NA; Jones, *Medicine Lodge*, 97.
25. Special Report on Box raid, *Sen. Ex. Doc. 13*, 40th Cong., 1st sess., 54. Custer, who met and talked with Mrs. Box and the eldest daughter immedi-

ately after their release at Fort Dodge, said it was Satanta who led the raid. *My Life on the Plains,* 59–62.

26. *New York Times,* Nov. 4, 1867.
27. Keim, *Sheridan's Troopers,* 185.
28. *Sen. Ex. Doc. 13,* 40th Cong., 1st sess., 54.
29. *HofR Ex. Doc. 240,* 41st Cong., 2d sess., 48.
30. Hyde, *George Bent,* 267.
31. *HofR Ex. Doc. 13,* 40th Cong., 1st sess., 54.
32. Douglas to Asbury, Hq. Records, Fort Dodge, Feb. 7, 1867, M989, NA.
33. McCusker to CofIA, June 5, 1868, Ltrs Recd., Kiowa Agency, NA.
34. Douglas to Mitchell, Feb. 13, 1867, Hq. Records, Fort Dodge, M989, NA.
35. Douglas to McKeever, March 24, 1867, Hq. Records, Fort Dodge, NA.
36. *HofR Ex. Doc. 240,* 41st Cong., 2d sess., 50.
37. Ibid., 102.
38. Ibid.
39. Leavenworth to Cooley, May 1, 1866, Ltrs. Recd., Kiowa Agency, NA.
40. Ibid., 102–103.
41. Ibid., 119–120.
42. Ibid.
43. *HofR Ex. Doc. 240,* 41st Cong., 2d sess., 121.
44. Douglas to McKeever, June 14, 1867, Fort Dodge Letterbook, RG 98, NA.
45. Monahan, "Kiowa-Federal Relations," 491.

CHAPTER 9

1. Douglas to McKeever, Jan. 13, 1867, Ltrs. Recd., Fort Dodge, NA.
2. Claim against Kiowas, Ltrs. Recd., Kiowa Agency (Reel 375, M-234), NA.
3. Nov. 24, 1866.
4. *Leavenworth Conservative,* May 13, 1867.
5. "By Paths of Kansas History," 154.
6. Leavenworth to Mix, Aug. 18, 1867, Ltrs. Recd., Kiowa Agency, NA.
7. Leavenworth to Taylor, July 24, 1867, ibid.
8. *Annual Report of CofIA, 1867,* 322.
9. Mathewson, a former scout who had once run a trading post on Cow Creek near present Wichita, Kansas, claimed he had had a personal encounter with Satanta there. By Mathewson's account, when the Kiowa chief threatened to kill him, the frontiersman had knocked him down with his pistol and severely whipped him. Mathewson also claimed that after being warned of an impending attack by Satanta, "the most valorous in battle and the most generous in peace of that warlike tribe, he and five men had held off 700 Indians for three days during July 1864 before repulsing them." *Portrait and Biographical Album,* 171. Neither of these stories has been otherwise validated.
10. *Leavenworth Daily Conservative,* Sept. 27, 1867.
11. Shanklin to Wortham, Sept. 1, 1867, *Annual Report of CofIA, 1867,* 321–323.
12. McCusker to Murphy, Nov. 15, 1867, Ltrs. Recd., Wichita Agency, NA.
13. Foreman, "Black Beaver," 281; Buntin, "Removal of the Wichitas," 72.
14. *Annual Report of CofIA, 1868,* 287.

15. Ibid.
16. Wright, "A History of Fort Cobb," 62.
17. *Chicago Tribune*, Sept. 30, Oct. 18, 1867.
18. Ibid.
19. Leavenworth to CofIA, Sept. 2, 1867, Ltrs. Recd., Kiowa Agency, NA.

CHAPTER 10

1. *Missouri Republican*, Oct. 18, 1867.
2. *Cincinnati Commercial*, Oct. 21, 1867.
3. *Cincinnati Gazette*, Oct. 24, 1867.
4. *Chicago Tribune*, Oct. 22, 1867.
5. *Cincinnati Gazette*, Oct. 24, 1867.
6. Thoburn, *A History*, 859.
7. Susan G. Reynolds interview, Indian-Pioneer Papers, OHS/AM.
8. *Edmond Sun*, Jan. 23, 1936. The name of Kicking Bird has been used as various place names in Edmond.
9. *New York Times*, Oct. 26, 1867.
10. Ibid.
11. *Cincinnati Commercial*, Oct. 24, 1867.
12. *Chicago Times*, Oct. 29, 1867.
13. Stanley, *My Early Travels*, 230-232.
14. Ibid.
15. *New York Times*, Oct. 30, 1867.
16. Ibid.
17. *Kansas Weekly Tribune*, Nov. 31, 1867.
18. Ibid.
19. Jones, *Medicine Lodge*, 146.
20. Taylor, "Medicine Lodge Peace Council," *Chronicles of Oklahoma* 2 (Nov.-Dec. 1924): 110-111.
21. Kappler, comp. and ed., *Indian Treaties*, 984.
22. *Leslie's Illustrated Newspaper*, Nov. 23, 1867.
23. Nye, "What Happened to Mary Hamleton?" *Daily Oklahoman*, Oct. 24, 1937.
24. *Cincinnati Gazette*, Nov. 4, 1867; *New York Times*, Nov. 4, 1867.
25. *Kansas Weekly Tribune*, Nov. 14, 1867.
26. *Cincinnati Commercial*, Nov. 4, 1867.
27. Jones, *Medicine Lodge*, 162-163.

CHAPTER 11

1. McCusker to Leavenworth, April 23, 1868, Ltrs. Recd., Kiowa Agency, NA.
2. *Sen. Ex. Doc. 60*, 40th Cong., 2d sess., 3. The Comanches at the same time were being victimized by the Navajos of New Mexico who stole 200 horses in a raid. The Comanches caught up with the Navajos, killed three of them, and retook the stolen animals. Shanklin to CofIA, June 15, 1868, Ltrs. Recd., Wichita Agency, NA.
3. Murphy to Taylor, Aug. 6, 1868; Wynkoop to Murphy, Aug. 4, 1868; Tappan to Murphy, July 20, 1868; Ltrs. Recd., Central Suptcy., OIA, NA.

4. McCusker to CofIA, June 5, 1868, Ltrs. Recd., Kiowa Agency, NA.
5. Walkley to Leavenworth, April 23, 1868, Ltrs. Recd., Kiowa Agency, NA; Foreman, "Leavenworth," 26-27. It is not known if this Fitzpatrick family was related to Mrs. Fitzpatrick, who was captured in the Elm Creek raid of 1865.
6. Robinson to Reynolds, March 31, 1868, Ltrs. Recd., Kiowa Agency, NA.
7. S. T. Walkley ltr., Ltrs. Recd., Kiowa Agency (Roll 376, frame 0188), NA.
8. *Congressional Globe*, 41st Cong., 2d sess., April 22, 1870, 2906-2907.
9. *Sen. Ex. Doc. 18*, pt. 3, 40th Cong., 3d sess., 18.
10. Ibid., 18-19.
11. Ibid., 19.
12. Ibid.
13. Nye, *Bad Medicine*, 148-149.
14. Mooney, "Calendar History," 322-325.
15. Dennison to Murphy, Aug. 30, 1868, Ltrs. Recd., Kiowa Agency, NA. In a conversation with Sheridan, Satanta said the Kiowas were "looking strongly for that medicine" and would make a lasting peace to get it back. Nye, *Carbine and Lance*, 93.
16. Murphy to Mix, Sept. 21, 1868, Ltrs. Recd., Kiowa Agency, NA.
17. Sheridan to Sherman, *Annual Report of Sec. of War, 1868*, Sept. 26, 1868, 10.
18. Murphy to Taylor, July 29, 1868, Ltrs. Sent, OIA, NA.
19. Ibid.
20. Murphy to Taylor, Aug. 5, 1868, Ltrs. Recd., Central Suptcy., 1868-1869, M-234, NA.
21. *Annual Report of CofIA, 1868*, 75.
22. *Annual Report of Sec. of War, 1868*, 17.
23. Ibid., 12.
24. Godfrey, "Some Reminiscences," 425.
25. Hazen report, June 30, 1869, *Annual Report of CofIA, 1869*, 388-391.
26. *Sen. Ex. Doc. 18*, pt. 3, 40th Cong., 3d sess., 23-24.
27. Hazen ltr., Nov. 26, 1868, Papers of Generals Sherman and Sheridan, Rister Collection, OU/WHC.
28. Alvord report, *Sen. Ex. Doc. 18*, pt. 3, 40th Cong., 3d sess., 22-23.
29. McCusker to Murphy, Dec. 3, 1868, ibid., 33.
30. *HofR Ex. Doc. 240*, 41st Cong., 2d sess., 160.
31. Alvord, Dec. 7, 1868, ibid. 151.
32. W. B. Hazen, "Some Corrections," 316.
33. Alvord Report, Dec. 7, 1868, Ltrs. Recd., AGO (Main Series) (M619, Roll 642), NA. Sheridan later read this as an act of hostility on the part of the two chiefs. Sheridan to Nichols, Dec. 24, 1868, Ltrs. Recd., AGO (Main Series) (M619, Roll 642), NA.
34. *HofR Ex. Doc. 240*, 41st. Cong., 2d sess., 151-152.
35. *Sen. Ex. Doc. 40*, 40th Cong., 3d sess., 6.
36. Keim, *Sheridan's Troopers*, 156. Charles Schreyvogel's famous painting of this meeting includes four chiefs intended as Satanta, Kicking Bird, Lone Wolf, and Little Heart. *Kansas Historical Quarterly* 19: 228.
37. Keim, *Sheridan's Troopers*, 136-137.

38. Custer, *My Life on the Plains*, 300–304. During their captivity at Fort Cobb, both Satanta and Lone Wolf painted buffalo robes depicting their exploits against the Utes and Navajos. These were purchased by Keim at the price of a pound of vermillion. Ibid., 223–224.
39. Keim, *Sheridan's Troopers*, 162.
40. Custer, *Following the Guidon*, 46; Custer, *My Life on the Plains*, 390.
41. *Army and Navy Journal*, Feb. 12, Mar. 13, 1869; Rister, ed., "Evans' Christmas Day Indian Fight," 281–301.
42. Nye, *Carbine and Lance*, 89.
43. *Leavenworth Daily Conservative*, Feb. 25, 1869.
44. Nye, *Carbine and Lance*, 90–91; see also Keim, *Sheridan's Troopers*, 275–276.
45. Council Held at Medicine Bluff Creek, Feb. 15, 1869, Sherman-Sheridan Papers, OU/WHC.
46. Nye, *Carbine and Lance*, 92.
47. Keim, *Sheridan's Troopers*, 276.
48. *Cavalry Journal*, April 24, 1869.
49. Shanklin to Wortham, May 30, 1868, Ltrs. Recd., Wichita Agency, NA.
50. Microfilm KA-1, Kiowa Census Records, OHS/AM.

CHAPTER 12

1. *Annual Report of CofIA, 1869*, 523.
2. Tatum, *Red Brothers*, 28–31.
3. *Kansas Daily Tribune*, Feb. 10, 1871.
4. Ibid., June 17, 1869.
5. *Annual Report of CofIA, 1869*, 502. The commission consisted of Felix R. Brunot, Nathan Brolop, and Col. William W. E. Dodge. Charles Findlay served as secretary.
6. Ibid., 503–504.
7. Ibid.
8. Ibid., 61.
9. *Emporia News*, Aug. 20, 1869.
10. Ibid., Sept. 10, 1869.
11. Lt. Col. A. D. Nelson to AAG, Jan. 15, 1870, Ltrs. Recd., Records of Fort Hays, Kansas, 1866–1869 (T-713, Roll 1), NA; Leckie, *Unlikely Warriors*, 171, citing Jacob Hershfield to Lt. John Sullivan, Jan. 11, 1870, Selected Ltrs. Recd., Tenth Cavalry. See also Carriker, *Fort Supply*, 42–43.
12. M. H. Kidd to J. K. Sullivan, Jan. 19, 1870, Fort Supply Ltrs. Recd., NA.
13. *HofR Ex. Doc. 123*, 41st Cong., 3d sess., 1–6.
14. Carriker, *Fort Supply*, 49–50.
15. *Kansas Daily Tribune*, April 2, 1870.
16. Ibid.
17. Ibid., April 12, 1870.
18. Ibid., April 13, 1870.
19. Ibid., April 12, 1870.
20. Ibid., Feb. 16, 1871.

21. Grierson to Tatum, Sept. 30, 1869, Kiowa Agency Papers, Military Relations, OHS/AM.
22. Nye, *Carbine and Lance*, 106.
23. Berthrong, *Southern Cheyennes*, 62–65.
24. Tatum, *Red Brothers*, 33.
25. Butler, "Pioneer School Teaching," 493.
26. Tatum, *Red Brothers*, 34–35.
27. Ibid., 35.
28. *The Friend* 48 (Aug. 7, 1875): 401.
29. Nye interview with Andrew Stumbling Bear and Charles Ape-Kaum, Jan. 1935, Nye notebook 15, Fort Sill Museum.
30. *HofR Report 2885*, 49th Cong., 1st sess., 1–3.
31. *HofR Report 1135*, 48th Cong., 1st sess., 4–5.
32. Nye, *Carbine and Lance*, 112–113. Corwin states that the scar on Stumbling Bear's face was caused by a soldier's bullet during this fight. "Fifty Years," 192.
33. Interview with Old Man Horse, May 12, 1934, W. S. Nye Notebook 2, Fort Sill Museum.
34. Ibid.
35. Tatum, *Red Brothers*, 38–44.
36. Butler, "Pioneer School Teaching," 494.
37. William Nicholson, "A Tour of Indian Agencies," *Kansas Historical Quarterly* 3, 4 (Nov. 1934): 351.
38. Ibid., 350–352. Stumbling Bear was listed as Tumbling Bird.
39. Microfilm KA-1, Kiowa Census Records, OHS/AM.
40. *Kansas Daily Tribune*, Feb. 10, 1871.

CHAPTER 13

1. *Kansas Daily Tribune*, Feb. 10, 1871.
2. Cashion, *A Texas Frontier*, 150–154.
3. Tatum ltr., Feb. 3, 1871, Ltrs. Recd., Kiowa Agency, NA.
4. Nye, *Carbine and Lance*, 123–124.
5. Tatum, *Red Brothers*, 107.
6. *Cherokee Advocate*, April 1, 1871.
7. Tatum, *Red Brothers*, 108–109.
8. Ibid., 110–111.
9. Ibid.
10. Ibid., 112.
11. Ibid.
12. Ibid., 114.
13. Ibid., 114–115.
14. Ibid.; *Kansas Daily Tribune*, June 7, 1871.
15. Nye, *Carbine and Lance*, 127.
16. Carter, *Massacre of Salt Creek Prairie*, 32–35; Nye, *Carbine and Lance*, 124–131.
17. J. K. Mizner report, May 20, 1871, Ltrs. Recd., Kiowa Agency, NA; W. T. Sherman report, May 28, 1871, Ltrs. Recd., Kiowa Agency, NA; Sherman to Wood, May 19, 1871, Ltrs. Recd., AGO (Main Series), M-666, Roll 10.

While a prisoner at St. Augustine, White Horse produced a painting that showed both himself and his wife, mounted, on their way to battle and leading his war horse to conserve its strength for combat. See Petersen, *Plains Indian Art*, Color Plate 3.

18. Tatum, *Red Brothers*, 116; Sherman ltr., May 24, 1871, Ltrs. Recd., Kiowa Agency, NA.
19. Sherman report, May 28, 1871, Ltrs. Recd., AGO (Main Series), M-666, Roll 10, NA; Tatum to Nicholson, May 30, 1871, *Friends' Review* 24 (July 1, 1871): 707-708.
20. Ibid.
21. Sherman to Townsend, May 28, 1871, Ltrs. Recd., AGO (Main Series), M-666, Roll 10, NA.
22. Sherman to Sheridan, May 29, 1871, Ltrs. Recd. AGO (Main Series), M-666, Roll 4, NA.
23. Nye interview with Andrew Stumbling Bear and Charles Ape-Kaum, Jan. 1935, Nye Notebook 15, Fort Sill Museum.
24. Rister, "Documents," 22-23. An account of this entire affair, written by Tatum in 1896, appears in Mooney, "Calendar History," 331.
25. Nye, *Carbine and Lance*, 140; Pratt, *Battlefield and Classroom*, 45-46; Pratt, "Some Indian Experiences," 210-211; Tatum, *Red Brothers*, 118.
26. Andrew Stumbling Bear and Charles Ape-Kaum interview, Nye Notebook 15, Fort Sill Museum.
27. Leckie, *Unlikely Warriors*, 187-189; Pratt, *Battlefield and Classroom*, 44-45.
28. Merrill, "General Sherman's Letter," 129.
29. Ibid.
30. Ibid.
31. Carter, *Massacre of Salt Creek Prairie*, 40-42.
32. Grierson to AAG, Dept. Mo., June 9, 1871, Ltrs. Recd., AGO (Main Series), M-666, Roll 10, NA.
33. Butler, "Pioneer School Teaching," 506-507.
34. Grierson ltr., June 9, 1871, Ltrs. Recd., AGO (Main Series), M-666, Roll 10, NA.
35. Carter, *Massacre of Salt Creek Prairie*, 45-47; Wharton, *Satanta*, 181.
36. Butler, "A Day Among the Kiowas and Comanches," 842-843.
37. Carter, *Massacre of Salt Creek Prairie*, 47.
38. Special Order 185, Dept. Texas, San Antonio, Sept. 12, 1871, Ltrs. Recd., AGO (Main Series), M-666, Roll 10, NA.
39. Sherman to Sheridan, May 29, 1871, ibid.
40. Tatum ltr., Aug. 12, 1871, ibid.
41. Tatum ltr., Sept. 23, 1871, Ltrs. Recd., Kiowa Agency, NA.
42. Grierson ltrs., June 9, Aug. 12, 1871, Ltrs Recd. Kiowa Agency, NA.
43. Nye, *Carbine and Lance*, 149.
44. Carter, *Pursuit of Kicking Bird*, 41-44.
45. Cheyenne/Arapaho Letterbook, Sept. 16, 1871.

CHAPTER 14

1. *Kansas Daily Tribune*, Aug. 27, 1872.

2. *The Friend* 48 (July 3, 1875): 362–363.
3. Ibid.
4. Ibid. (July 17, 1875): 377–378.
5. Hoag to Beede, Feb. 1, 1872, Cheyenne Agency File, OHS/AM.
6. Beede to Garrett, March 16, 1872, *Friends' Review* 25 (April 6, 1872): 518.
7. Butler, "Pioneer School Teaching," 495–496.
8. Report of Col. Merrill, April 29, 1872, *New York Times*, May 18, 1872.
9. *Annual Report of CofIA, 1872*, 247–248; *Kansas Daily Tribune*, Aug. 24, 1872.
10. *Annual Report of CofIA, 1872*, 247–248.
11. Ibid.
12. Tatum, June 22, 1872, Ltrs. Recd., Kiowa Agency, NA.
13. Hoag to Davidson, May 30, 1872, Special File, Div./Mo., RG-393, NA; *Army and Navy Journal*, Aug. 31, 1872.
14. *Kansas Daily Tribune*, Aug. 23, 1872. It was at this medicine dance in 1872 that the Kiowa medicine man No Shoes made medicine for rain. That afternoon there came a sudden electrical storm with severe lightning and thunder and heavy rainfall. Two Cheyenne women and several ponies were killed by lightning. No Shoes felt very bad that his medicine had been so strong. He apologized to his people, saying he was still young but as he grew older he would learn to control his medicine better. His explanation was accepted, but he was afterward known as "Dangerous Big Medicine Man." *The Friend*, Feb. 26, 1876, 219.
15. Beede, March 11, 1872, Ltrs. Recd., Kiowa Agency, NA.
16. *Kansas Daily Tribune*, Aug. 24, 1872.
17. *The Friend*, Sept. 14, 1872, 29.
18. Only recently, after some Mexican whiskey had been smuggled into camp, Sun Boy had become involved in a drunken brawl with a Kiowa named Bird Bow and killed the man with an arrow. He eventually became one of the last prominent chiefs of the Kiowas, dying in the fall of 1888. Mooney, "Calendar History," 221, 335.
19. *The Friend* (Sept. 21, 1872): 35.
20. *Kansas Daily Tribune*, Aug. 27, 1872.
21. Ibid.
22. *Army and Navy Journal*, Aug. 31, 1872.
23. *Cherokee Advocate*, Aug. 31, 1872; *Annual Report of CofIA, 1872*, 247–248; Report of Commission, Sept. 10, 1872, Ltrs. Recd., Kiowa Agency, NA; *The Friend* 49 (Sept. 25, 1875): 42.
24. Schofield to AAG, Dept. Texas, Aug. 19, 1872, Ltrs. Recd., AGO (Main Series), M-666, Roll 60, NA.
25. Tatum, Sept. 1, 1872, *Annual Report of CofIA, 1872*, 248.
26. *Friends' Review* 26 (Sept. 28, 1872): 84.
27. Alvord Report, Oct. 10, 1872, *Annual Report of CofIA, 1872*, 130.
28. *St. Louis Post Dispatch*, Sept. 30, 1872.
29. Ibid.
30. Ibid.
31. *Washington Evening Star*, Oct. 11, 1872.
32. *New York Times*, Oct. 12, 23, 1872; *Friends' Review* 26 (Nov. 2, 1872): 166.

33. *Washington Evening Star,* Oct. 23, 1872.
34. *Friends' Review* 26 (Dec. 7, 1872): 245.
35. Ltrs. Recd., AGO (Main Series), M-666, Roll 60, NA; *Army and Navy Journal,* Nov. 11, 16, 1872; *Washington Evening Star,* Oct. 17, 1872.

CHAPTER 15

1. Battey, *Life and Adventures,* 86-92.
2. Butler, "Pioneer School Teaching," 519.
3. *The Friend* 48 (July 31, 1875): 394-395. Mooney states that Sun Boy had a brother named Ä'to-t'aiñ, or White Cowbird. "Calendar History," 338.
4. *The Friend* 48 (Aug. 14, 1875): 410-411.
5. Ibid., 49 (Aug. 21, 1875): 2-3.
6. Butler, "Pioneer School Teaching," 523.
7. Ibid., 524-525.
8. Crawford, *Kiowa,* 35; Corwin, *Kiowa Indians,* 187.
9. *The Friend* 49 (Aug. 21, 1875): 2-3.
10. Ibid.
11. *The Friend* 46 (June 14, 1873): 342.
12. Butler, "Pioneer School Teaching," 527.
13. Davis to Delano, May 12, 1873, *New York Times,* May 26, 1873.
14. Ibid., April 5, 21, 1873.
15. Love to Clum, April 18, 1873, Ltrs. Recd., Kiowa Agency, NA.
16. Haworth to Hoag, May 14, 1873, Ltrs. Recd., Kiowa Agency, NA. The Kiowa Calendars refer to the winter of 1872-1873 as the "Winter that the Pueblos came," reflecting a visit during which the Pueblos and Mexicans traded the Indians bread and eagle feathers for horses and buffalo robes. Mooney, "Calendar History," 336.
17. Corwin, "Fifty Years," 126.
18. Mooney, "Calendar History," 333-335.
19. *The Friend* 49 (Sept. 4, 1875): 19.
20. *Friends' Review* 30 (Nov. 25, 1876): 231.
21. Beede report, April 4, 1873, Ltrs. Recd., Kiowa Agency, NA.
22. Plea to president by Comanche, Kiowa, and Apache chiefs; March 28, 1873, Ltrs. Recd., Kiowa Agency, NA; *New York Times,* April 20, 1873.
23. Haworth to Beede, May 8, 1873, Ltrs. Recd., Kiowa Agency, NA.
24. *The Friend* 46 (June 14, 1873): 342.
25. Ibid., 49 (Oct. 2, 1875): 59-60.
26. Ibid.
27. Ibid., 46 (June 14, 1873): 342.
28. *New York Times,* April 21, 1873.
29. Ibid., June 18, 1872; *The Friend* 49 (Oct. 2, 1875): 49.
30. Nye, *Carbine and Lance,* 166.
31. *The Friend* 49 (Oct. 2, 1875): 50. McClermont placed two of his men in irons for having abused the prisoners.
32. Haworth to Hoag, July 31, 1873, Ltrs. Recd., Kiowa Agency, NA.
33. *The Friend* 49 (Oct. 9, 1875): 62-63.

34. Ibid., 351.
35. Alice Marriott in introduction to Battey, *Life and Adventures*, xiv.
36. Ibid., 352–353.
37. Ibid., 353.
38. Ibid., 350–355.
39. Battey gives a detailed description of the 1873 Sun Dance in *The Friend* 49 (Oct. 9, 1875): 62–66. During the dance a Kiowa warrior stole the wife of another. The angry husband responded by killing seven of the seducer's horses, a normal tribal-accepted penalty. When the husband threatened to kill the man, however, the Kiowa Dog Soldiers stepped forth and stopped him. Mooney, "Calendar History," 337.
40. Haworth to Hoag, July 21, 1873, Ltrs. Recd., Kiowa Agency, NA.
41. Battey to Haworth, July 31, 1873, Ltrs. Recd., Kiowa Agency, NA.
42. *Friends' Review* 27 (Aug. 30, 1873): 28.
43. *The Friend* 49 (Oct. 2, 1875): 49–50.

CHAPTER 16

1. *New York Times*, Aug. 12, 1873.
2. Alvord to Smith, Sept. 20, 1873, Ltrs. Recd., Kiowa Agency, NA.
3. A. W. Hoffman report, Aug. 26, 1873, Ltrs. Recd., Kiowa Agency, NA; Haworth to Hoag, Sept. 8, 1873, Ltrs. Recd., Kiowa Agency, NA.
4. *New York Times*, Oct. 8, 1873.
5. Proceedings of Fort Sill Indian Council, Oct. 6, 1873, Ltrs. Recd., Kiowa Agency, NA.
6. Ibid.
7. Smith to Delano, Oct. 7, 1873, ibid.; *The Friend* 49 (Nov. 16, 1875): 89.
8. Winfrey and Day, *Indian Papers of Texas, 1860–1916*, 4, 354–355.
9. *The Friend* 49 (Nov. 16, 1875): 89.
10. Ibid.
11. Ibid.
12. Ibid. The Kiowa calendars mark this significant event by entitling the winter of 1873–1874 the "Winter of Satanta's Return." Mooney, *Calendar History*, 337.
13. *Friends' Review* 27 (June 21, 1874): 717.
14. *The Friend* 49 (Nov. 16, 1875): 89.
15. Haworth to Smith, Nov. 14, 1873, Ltrs. Recd., Kiowa Agency, NA.
16. *The Friend* 49 (Feb. 26, 1876): 219.
17. Ibid. (Nov. 20, 1875): 105–106.
18. Ibid.
19. Ibid.
20. Ibid. (Nov. 27, 1875): 115.
21. Ibid.
22. Ibid.
23. Ibid., 116.
24. Emory to Mackenzie, Mar. 30, 1875, Ltrs. Recd., Dept. of Mo. Five members of the party were among those sent to Fort Marion.

25. Nye, *Carbine and Lace*, 182–184.
26. *The Friend* 49 (Dec. 7, 1875): 137.
27. McCusker to E. P. Smith, Jan. 19, 1874, Ltrs. Recd., Kiowa Agency, NA; Haworth to Hoag, July 21, 1874, Ltrs. Recd., Kiowa Agency, NA.

CHAPTER 17

1. *Record of Engagements With Hostile Indians*, 1874, 44–49; Nye, *Carbine and Lance*, 187.
2. Clarke to Brooke, Jan. 22, Feb. 17, 1874, Ltrs. Recd., Fort Supply, NA.
3. Haworth to Hoag, April 13, 1874, Ltrs. Recd., Kiowa Agency, NA; Rhoads to Hoag, April 13, 1874, Ltrs. Recd., Kiowa Agency, NA.
4. Nye, *Carbine and Lance*, 188–189.
5. Battey, *Life and Adventures*, 306–307.
6. *Friends' Review* 27 (June 27, 1874): 716.
7. Ibid.
8. Microfilm KA-1, Kiowa Census Records, OHS/AM.
9. *Friends' Review* 27 (June 27, 1874): 717.
10. Ibid.
11. Battey, *Life and Adventures*, 291, 297; Pratt, *Battlefield and Classroom*, 93, 102.
12. Battey, *Life and Adventures*, 277, 284; Geo. W. Fox ltr., May 20, 1874, Ltrs. Recd., Kiowa Agency, NA.
13. *The Friend* 49 (Jan. 29, 1876): 286–294.
14. Haworth to Hoag, May 25, 1874, Ltrs. Recd., Kiowa Agency, NA.
15. Haworth to Hoag, May 9, 1874, Ltrs. Recd., Kiowa Agency, NA.
16. Battey, *Life and Adventures*, 293–294.
17. *The Friend* 49 (Sept. 25, 1875): 42. During January 1874 White Horse was involved in a plot to seize both Haworth and Battey, hie them off to the prairie, and hold them as hostages for the release of Satanta and Big Tree. Haworth, however, was forewarned by an Apache man. When White Horse and his four companions arrived, Haworth fed them and treated them with such kindness that they could not carry out the deed. The Kiowas reported back to the tribe that the agent's medicine was too strong. Battey, *Life and Adventures*, 250–252.
18. Clarke to Brooke, Feb. 17, 1874, Ltrs. Recd., Fort Supply, NA; Pratt, *Battlefield and Classroom*, 93.
19. Battey, *Life and Adventures*, 295.
20. *The Friend* 49 (Feb. 5, 1876): 194.
21. Battey, *Life and Adventures*, 299.
22. Haworth to Hoag, June 6, 1874, Ltrs. Recd., Kiowa Agency, NA.
23. Battey, *Life and Adventures*, 258.
24. *Friends' Review* 27 (June 17, 1874): 716.
25. Ibid., 258.

CHAPTER 18

1. Haworth to Hoag, May 25, 1874, Ltrs. Recd., Kiowa Agency (M234), NA.
2. Carriker, *Fort Supply*, 88.

3. Lt. C. J. Farnsworth of the Eighth Cavalry Regiment visited the site on September 23, 1874, and described Adobe Walls as comprising two 20 by 50 ft. buildings and another 15 by 20 ft., with stabling for 40 horses and a 200 by 300 ft. corral. Farnsworth report, Sept. 28, 1874, Ltrs. Recd., AGO (Main Series), NA.

4. McCusker to Jones, July 2, 1874; Barde, *"Billy" Dixon*, 196-219; Neeley, *The Last Comanche Chief*, 82-101; Nye, *Carbine and Lance*, 189-191; *Annual Report of CofIA, 1874*, 220.

5. *Kansas Daily Tribune*, July 8, 1874. Battey, whose health had finally forced his retirement from work among the Kiowas, had hoped to join the train on its return to Kansas.

6. *Friends' Review* 27 (July 25, 1874): 781.

7. Ibid., 782.

8. Haworth to Hoag, July 11, 1874, Ltrs. Recd., Kiowa Agency (M234), NA.

9. Nye, *Carbine and Lance*, 192-200.

10. Griswold, "Old Fort Sill," 11; Wooster, *Military and United States Indian Policy*, 152-153.

11. Davidson to AAG, Dept. Texas, Aug. 10, 1874, Ltrs. Recd., Kiowa Agency (M234), NA.

12. Lawson to Post Adj., Aug. 7, 1874, Pratt Papers.

13. Haworth to Smith, Aug. 11, 1874, Ltrs. Recd., Kiowa Agency (M234), NA; *Annual Report of CofIA, 1874*, 220.

14. Haworth to Smith, Aug. 11, 17, 26, 1874, Ltrs. Recd., Kiowa Agency (M234), NA.

15. Berthrong, *Southern Cheyennes*, 390-393.

16. Davidson to AAG, Dept. Texas, Aug. 26, 1874, Ltrs. Recd. by AG, 1874-1875, NA; *Annual Report of CofIA, 1874*, 220-221; Nye, *Carbine and Lance*, 205-210. The sanity of Davidson, who had once suffered sun stroke, was questioned by fellow officers. Wooster, *Military and United States Indian Policy*, 157.

17. Report of Davidson, Aug. 27, 1874, Ltrs. Recd., Wichita Agency (M234), NA; *Army and Navy Journal*, Sept. 5, 1874, 56.

18. Report of F. Grinnell, M.D., Aug. 25, 1874, *The Friend* 48 (Sept. 12, 1874): 29-30.

19. Ibid.

20. *Journal of the Sixth Annual Session of the General Council of the Indian Territory, 1875*, 29.

21. Davidson Ltr., Sept. 5, 1874, Military Affairs, Kiowa Agency Records, OHS/AM; Davidson report, Aug. 27, 1874, Ltrs. Recd., Wichita Agency (M234), NA.

22. Anderson to AAG, Dept. Texas, Sept. 25, 1874, U.S. Army Military Records, 1874-1875, microfilm, UCO/OkC.

23. Ibid.; *Annual Report of CofIA, 1874*, 221; Nye, *Carbine and Lance*, 210.

24. Miles to Pope, Sept. 17, 1874, Ltrs. Recd. by AG, 1874-1875, UCO/OkC; Nye, *Carbine and Lance*, 215-218.

25. Miles to AG, Dept. Mo., Sept. 24, 1874, in Miles, *Personal Recollections*, 173-174.

26. Neill to Pope, Oct. 2, 1874, Ltrs. Recd., AG (M666, Roll 159), NA.

27. Neill to AAG, Dept. Mo., Oct. 4, 1874, ibid.

28. *Friends' Review* 28 (Nov, 7, 1874): 188.

29. Haworth to Smith, Nov. 7, 1874, Ltrs. Recd., AG (RG393), NA; Neill report, Oct. 2, 1874, Ltrs. Recd., AG (RG393), NA.

30. Smith to Sec. of Interior, Nov. 9, 1874, ibid.; Haworth to Smith, Nov. 7, 1874, ibid.

31. *Oklahoma Star*, Nov. 13, 1874.

32. *Record of Engagements With Hostile Indians, 1874*, 46-49.

33. Carter, *On the Border*, 488-493.

34. Taylor to AAG, Nov. 7, 1874, Ltrs. Recd., AG (M666, Roll 159), NA.

35. Carter, "Scouting on the 'Staked Plains,'" 532.

36. Post Guard Reports, 1874-1875, Fort Sill Museum.

37. The family is often mistakenly identified as "German." The story told by the two girls of how the Georgia family of eight was attacked and massacred on the Smoky Hill River thirty miles east of Fort Wallace, Kansas, on September 11, 1874, and their ensuing experience of capture was printed in numerous newspapers, including the *Leavenworth Daily Times*, March 11, 17, 1875, and the *Emporia News*, March 26, 1875. Members of the family included John and Lydia Germain; Rebecca, 21; Stephen, 19; Catherine, 17; Johanna, 15; Julia, 7; and Nancy, 5. All but the four youngest girls, who were captured and eventually rescued, were killed during the attack.

38. In preparing for the march, Davidson's Pawnee and Wichita scouts confiscated a large portion of Kicking Bird's horse herd to replace disabled animals. Richards to Sheridan, Oct. 10, 1874, Special File, Dept. Mo. (RG393), NA.

39. Pratt to AAG, Nov. 29, 1874, Ltrs. Recd., Fort Supply, UCO/OkC. The Cheyennes were particularly incensed at the Wichitas and affiliated bands over their assistance to the army. McCusker to Smith, Sept. 5, 1875, Ltrs. Recd., Central Suptcy., OIA (M234, Roll 66), NA.

40. Davidson to Augur, Nov. 23, 1874, Ltrs. Recd., AG (M666, Roll 159), NA.

41. Topographical Sketch of Schofield March, Ltrs. Recd., AG (M666, Roll 160), NA; Haworth to Smith, Jan. 1, 1875, Records Central Suptcy. (M856, Roll 62), NA.

42. Pope to Sheridan, Nov. 3, 1874, Ltrs. Recd., Div. of Mil. Rec., 1874-1875 (RG-393), NA.

43. Haworth to Smith, Nov. 14, 17, 1874, Ltrs. Recd., Kiowa Agency (M234, Roll 379), NA.

44. Augur to Sheridan, Dec. 8, 1874, Div. of AG, Special File, Div. of Mil. Rec., 1874-1875 (RG 393), NA.

45. Davidson to Pratt, Dec. 14, 1874, Pratt Papers; Special Order 16, Dec. 16, 1874, Fort Sill Records (bound), Vol. 1 of 3, NA; Pratt to Sheridan, April 26, 1875, Ltrs. Recd., AG (M666, Reel 164), NA.

46. Emory to Mackenzie, March 30, 1875, Pratt Papers.

47. Ibid.

48. Pratt to Davidson, Ltrs. Recd., Dept. Mo. (RG393, Box 18), NA.

49. Petersen, *Plains Indian Art*, 117; Pratt, *Battlefield and Classroom*, 104-105.

50. Haworth to Smith, Jan. 1, 1875, Records Central Suptcy. (M856, Roll 62), NA.
51. Petersen, *Plains Indian Art*, 117; Pratt. *Battlefield and Classroom*, 148.
52. Butler, "A Day Among the Kiowas and Comanches," 839-840.
53. Haworth to Smith, Jan. 1, 1875, Ltrs. Recd., Central Suptcy. (M234, Roll 66), NA.
54. *The Friend* 49 (Feb. 19, 1876): 212-213.

CHAPTER 19

1. Davidson to Haworth, Jan. 9, 1875, Ltrs. Recd., Kiowa Agency, NA.
2. Haworth to Smith, Jan. 1, 1875, Records Central Suptcy., NA. According to the Post Guard Book, Woman's Heart and Bird Chief were joined in the guardhouse by Comanche chiefs White Wolf, Tabananika, Little Crow, and Red Food on October 31 and by Deemquat and Sun Boy on November 29. Little Crow and Red Food, who died soon after, were released in December. White Horse, Double Vision, Whow-haw, Poo-ki, and Chief Killer (a Cheyenne) were added. Post Guard Book, Fort Sill; Griswold, "Old Fort Sill," 13.
3. *Leavenworth Daily Times*, March 14, 1875.
4. Haworth to Smith, Jan. 1, 1875, Records Central Suptcy., NA.
5. Nye, *Carbine and Lance*, 224-225.
6. Haworth to Hoag, Jan. 30, 1875, Records Central Suptcy., NA.
7. Pratt, *Battlefield and Classroom*, 94.
8. Haworth to Smith, Feb. 20, 1875, Records Central Suptcy., NA.
9. Ibid., 95.
10. Pratt, *Battlefield and Classroom*, 95-97.
11. Haworth, Jan. 27, 30, 1875, Ltrs. Recd., Kiowa Agency, NA; Pratt, *Battlefield and Classroom*, 95-97.
12. Haworth, March 27, 1875, Ltrs. Recd., Kiowa Agency, NA; Nye, *Carbine and Lance*, 230-231; Pratt, *Battlefield and Classroom*, 141-143.
13. Haworth to Hoag, Feb. 27, 1875, Records Central Suptcy., NA.
14. Sheridan to Pope, March 1, 1875, Ltrs. Recd., Special File, Dept. Mo., NA; Pope to Drum, Feb. 15, 1875, Ltrs. Recd., Special File, Dept. Mo., NA; *Leavenworth Daily Times*, March 5, 12, 1875.
15. Pratt, *Battlefield and Classroom*, 91-92.
16. Haworth ltr., Chiefs file, Kiowa Agency, OHS/AM.
17. Davidson to Haworth, Jan. 9, 1875, ibid.
18. Pratt, *Battlefield and Classroom*, 92-93.
19. Mooney, "Calendar History," 215-216. The Kiowa prisoner list and charges as provided in Pratt list, June 4, 1875, Ltrs. Recd., OIA; Pratt list, June 4, 1875, Ltrs. Recd., AGO; and Pratt, *Battlefield and Classroom*, 141-143, read as follows:
Woman's Heart, chief—ringleader/murder
Bird Chief (Ta-na-ti, Bird Medicine, Bad Eye)—leader, murder
White Horse (Isa-tah), chief—ringleader/murder
Wo-haw (Beef), warrior—murder
Ah-ke-ah (Pah-o-ka, Coming to the Grove), warrior—murder

Double Vision (So-gau-se), subchief—ringleader/murder

Sa-a-qui-a-da (Bear in the Clouds), leader—ringleader/murder

Lone Wolf (E-si-sim-ers), chief—ringleader/murder

Zo-tom (Biter), warrior—murder

Mah-mante (Swan, Man Who Walks Above Ground), chief—ringleader/
    murder

On-ko-eht (Ankle), Mexican/warrior—murder/theft

O-bet-toint (High Forehead), Mexican/warrior—murder

E-tah-dle-uh (Boy), Mexican/warrior—murder

Zo-po-he (Toothless), Mexican/warrior—murder

Tsah-dle-tha (White Goose), warrior—murder

Zone-ke-uh (Teeth), warrior—murder

Beah-ko (Old Man), Mexican/warrior—robbery/theft

To-un-ke-uh (Good Talk), warrior—theft/murder

Ko-lah (Wild Horse), warrior—theft

Ih-pa-yah (Straightening an Arrow), warrior—theft

Maw-ko-peh (Flat Nose), warrior—theft

Aw-lih (Wise), warrior—murder/robbery/theft

Ko-ho (Kicking, Club Foot), Mexican/warrior—murder/robbery/theft

To-o-sape (Bull With Holes in his Ears), Mexican/warrior—theft

Tsait-kope-ta (Bear Mountain), warrior—robbery/theft/murder

Pedro, Mexican/warrior—robbery/theft

Co-a-bote-ta (Sun), warrior—murder

20. Corwin, *Kiowa Indians*, 104.
21. *Journal of the Sixth Annual Session of the General Council of the Indian Territory,
    1875*, 69.
22. Pratt, *Battlefield and Classroom*, 141–143.
23. Ibid.
24. Special Order 65, April 3, 1875, Fort Sill Records (Bound), NA; Special
    Order 66, April 4, 1875, Fort Sill Records (Bound), NA.
25. Berthrong, *Southern Cheyennes*, 401–402; *Wichita Eagle*, April 15, 1875.
26. Special Order 69, April 7, 1875, Fort Sill Records (Bound), NA.
27. List of Cheyenne and Arapaho prisoners, RG393, Box 20, NA; *Wichita
    Eagle*, May 6, 1875; Pratt, *Battlefield and Classroom*, 105. It was often re-
    ported that Mochi killed Mrs. Germain with a blow to the head with a war
    ax, but according to Catherine Germain's account it was her father, already
    seriously wounded and scalped, who received the death blow. *Emporia News*,
    March 26, 1875.
28. Pratt to Sheridan, April 26, 1875, Ltrs. Recd., AGO, NA. A slightly altered
    version of the letter is given in Pratt, *Battlefield and Classroom*, 106–107.
29. Pratt to Sheridan, April 26, 1875, Ltrs. Recd., AGO (Main Series), NA.
30. Two drawings by Etahdleuh show the prisoners being taken from the ice-
    house and loaded aboard the wagons, providing graphic illustration to Spe-
    cial Order 86, Fort Sill, April 27, 1875, Fort Sill Record Books (Bound),
    NA. See Pratt Papers, Etahdleuh sketches 8 and 9. Another (unnumbered)
    depicts the prisoners arriving at Caddo. See also *Leavenworth Daily Times*,
    April 30, 1875.

31. Pratt, *Battlefield and Classroom*, 107–108.
32. *Leavenworth Daily Times*, May 9, 1875.
33. Pratt, *Battlefield and Classroom*, 109.
34. *Leavenworth Daily Times*, May 9, 1875.
35. Pratt, *Battlefield and Classroom*, 108–115.
36. Haworth to Smith, Feb. 15, 1875, Records Central Suptcy., NA.
37. *Friends' Review* 28 (May 15, 1875): 619.

CHAPTER 20

1. Butler, "A Day Among the Kiowas and Comanches," 841.
2. Ibid.
3. Ibid., 847.
4. Ibid., 842.
5. Haworth to Smith, May 5, 1875, Ltrs. Recd., Central Suptcy. (M-234, Roll 60), NA.
6. Haworth to Beede, May 16, 1875, ibid.
7. Haworth to Hoag, May 4, 1875, Ltrs. Recd., Kiowa Agency (M234, Roll 380), NA.
8. *Leavenworth Daily Times*, May 13, 1875.
9. Record of Medical History of Fort Sill, Indian Territory, Feb. 1873 through May 1875, Fort Sill Museum, 66–67.
10. Haworth to Smith, May 27, 1875, Records Central Suptcy. (M856, Reel 62), NA.
11. Ibid.
12. Nye, *Carbine and Lance*, 234.
13. Nye interview with Old Man Horse, May 12, 1934, Nye Notebook 2, Fort Sill Museum.
14. Mayhall, *Kiowas*, 254; Pratt, *Battlefield and Classroom*, 97, 143; Nye, *Carbine and Lance*, 234.
15. McKenzie to Ashabranner, July 24, 1994, personal copy.
16. Nye to Grove, Oct. 22, 1956, personal copy.
17. Nye, *Carbine and Lance*, 233. Other records may exist, but the copy of Neal Evans's Reminiscences held by the Fort Sill Museum does not include the account cited by Nye.
18. Haworth to Hoag, May 4, 1875, Ltrs. Recd., Kiowa Agency (M234, Roll 380), NA.
19. Haworth to Miles, May 13, 1875, Kiowa Agency, Deaths file, OHS/AM.
20. *Friends' Review* 28 (May 29, 1875): 647.
21. Ibid.
22. Nye, *Carbine and Lance*, 234–235; Kickingbird, *Kicking Bird*, 10–11.
23. Haworth to Smith, May 27, 1875, Records Central Suptcy. (M856, Roll 62), NA.
24. Clum to Haworth, June 7, 1875, Kiowa Agency, Deaths file, OHS/AM.
25. *Friends' Review* 28 (May 29, 1875): 647–648.
26. Butler, "A Day Among the Kiowas," 848.

EPILOGUE

1. *Friends' Review* 51 (April 13, 1878): 273.
2. *The Vindicator*, June 5, 1875.
3. Nye, *Carbine and Lance*, 236.
4. Butler, "A Day Among the Kiowas and Comanches," 847.
5. *Leavenworth Daily Times*, May 4, 1875. As one of his last acts before departing from Fort Sill, Pratt wrote a long letter addressing the Indians' dire need. Pratt to Dunn, March 30, 1875, Pratt Papers.
6. Nye, *Carbine and Lance*, 235.
7. Mooney, "Calendar History," 214.
8. Petersen, *Plains Indian Art*, Color Plate 9, 91.
9. *Wichita Eagle*, April 25, 1878.
10. *Kansas Daily Tribune*, Dec. 23, 1876.
11. Nye, *Carbine and Lance*, 255-256.
12. Dockstader, *Great North American Indians*, 29.
13. Ibid., 33.
14. Corwin, *Kiowa Indians*, 185.
15. "Chief Stumbling Bear Pass," Notes and Documents, 472-476.
16. Dockstader, *Great North American Indians*, 155-156.
17. *Friends' Review* 30 (May 12, 1877): 621-622.
18. Szasz, *Between Indian and White Worlds*, 14-15.
19. Smalling, "From Satank to Joshua Givens," 35.
20. Corwin, *Kiowa Indians*, 111.
21. Corwin, "Fifty Years," 190. Rev. Kickingbird appears in a photo with five other Kiowas in Corwin, *Comanche and Kiowa Captives*, 165.
22. Methvin, *Andele*, 164.
23. *Friends' Review* 31 (April 13, 1878): 273.
24. Ellis, *To Change Them Forever*, 38.
25. Ibid., 39.
26. Battey, *Life and Adventures*, xvii.
27. *Friends' Review* 32 (Nov. 9, 1878): 202.
28. Buntin, "History of the Kiowa, Comanche, and Wichita Indian Agency," 52.
29. Vail, *A Memorial*, 110-167. Phil McCusker, who played an important role as an interpreter and intermediary between government officials and the Kiowas, Comanches, Cheyennes, and other Plains tribes, died in January 1885. While returning from Texas to the Wichita agency, he was forced to swim the Red River. He was found in a sitting position beside a tree, frozen to death, his horse unsaddled and tied nearby. He had tried unsuccessfully to build a fire. *Cheyenne Transporter*, Jan. 15, 1885.
30. "The Kiowa" (see Brochures in the Bibliography).

Bibliography

ARCHIVAL MATERIALS

Fort Sill Museum
  Fort Sill Record Books
  Nye, W. S., Notebooks
  Post Guard Reports, 1874–1875
  Record of Medical History of Fort Sill, Indian Territory
  Reminiscences of Neal Evans
Gilcrease Institute
  Cheyenne/Arapaho Letterbook, 1871–1873
Kansas Historical Society
  General Files—Kiowa Indians, Kicking Bird
  Hunnius, Adolph, Papers
  Kuhn, Henry, Collection
Oklahoma Historical Society
  Library
    Corwin, Hugh D. "Fifty Years With the Kiowas," unpublished manuscript,
      c. 1962
    Vertical files
  Archives/Manuscript Division
    Cheyenne Agency Papers
    Foreman, Grant, Collection
    Indian-Pioneer Papers
    Kiowa Agency Papers—Chiefs, Military Relations, Marriages, Interpreters,
      Traders, Census, Prisoners of War, Deaths File
    Letters Received, Kiowa Agency File
    Trial of Satanta and Big Tree Papers, microfilm KA37

University of Central Oklahoma
    Max Chambers Library
        "American Periodicals" microfilm series
        Newspaper microfilm collection
        "Western Americana" microfilm series
    Oklahoma Collection
        Fort Supply Letterbook, 1869–1870
        Robert C. Carriker notes re Fort Supply
        U.S. Army Military Records, 1874–1875 (RG-393)
University of Oklahoma
    Western History Collections
        "American Indian," National Archives microfilm series
        Berthrong, Donald, Collection
        Cass, Lewis, Collection
        Gilstrap, Lucille. "Sayt-aym k'ee-ah: Kiowa Chief and His People." Bound
            Manuscript. 3 vols. N.d., c. 1986
        Rister Collection, Sherman-Sheridan Papers
Yale University Beinecke Rare Book and Manuscript Library
    Richard Henry Pratt Papers
    Pratt Letterbook, November 1872–May 1875
    Drawings by Etahdleuh

ARTICLES

Barry, Louise. "Albert D. Richardson's Letters on the Pike's Peak Gold Region."
    Kansas Historical Quarterly 12 (Feb. 1943).
Buntin, Martha. "The Removal of the Wichitas From Butler County, Kansas, to
    the Present Agency." *Panhandle Plains Historical Review* 4 (1931).
Butler, G. "A Day Among the Kiowas and Comanches." *Catholic World* 23 (Sept.
    1876).
Butler, Josiah. "Pioneer School Teaching at the Comanche-Kiowa Agency School,
    1870–3." *Chronicles of Oklahoma* 6 (Dec. 1928).
"By Paths of Kansas History." *Kansas Historical Quarterly* 13 (May 1944).
Campbell, C. E. "Down Among the Red Men." *Kansas State Historical Collections,
    1926–28* 8 (Topeka, 1929).
Carter, Robert Goldthwaite. "Scouting on the 'Staked Plains' (Llano Estacado)
    With Mackenzie in 1874." *United Service* 13 (Oct.-Nov. 1885).
"Chief Stumbling Bear Pass." Notes and Documents. *Chronicles of Oklahoma* 45
    (Winter 1967).
Clapsaddle, David K. "Conflict and Commerce on the Santa Fe Trail: The Fort
    Riley–Fort Larned Road 1860–1867." *Kansas History* 16 (Summer 1993).
Corwin, Hugh D. "The Folsom Training School." *Chronicles of Oklahoma* 42
    (Spring 1964).
——. "Protestant Missionary Work Among the Kiowas." *Chronicles of Oklahoma*
    46 (Spring 1968).
Dale, E. E. "Additional Letters of General Stand Watie." *Chronicles of Oklahoma*
    1 (October 1921).

"Diary of Samuel A. Kingman at Indian Treaty of 1865." *Kansas Historical Quarterly* 1 (November 1932).

Doyle, Capt. W. E. "The Kiowa and Comanche Reservation." *National Tribune,* August 1, 1901.

Estep, Raymond. "The Military and Diplomatic Services of Alexander Le Grand for the Republic of Texas, 1836-1837." *Southwestern Historical Quarterly* 54 (Oct. 1950).

Evans, Hugh. "The Journal of Hugh Evans Covering the First and Second Campaigns of the United States Dragoon Regiment in 1834 and 1835," trans. by Fred S. Perrine, notes by Grant Foreman. *Chronicles of Oklahoma* 3 (Sept. 1925).

Ewers, John C. "Intertribal Warfare as the Precursor of Indian-White Warfare on the Northern Great Plains." *Western Historical Quarterly* 5 (Oct. 1975).

Foreman, Carolyn Thomas. "Black Beaver." *Chronicles of Oklahoma* 24 (Autumn 1946).

——. "Colonel Jesse Henry Leavenworth." *Chronicles of Oklahoma* 13 (Spring 1935).

——. "General Benjamin Henry Grierson." *Chronicles of Oklahoma* 24 (Summer 1946).

——. "General William Babcock Hazen." *Chronicles of Oklahoma* 20 (December 1942).

Foreman, Grant. "Historical Background of the Kiowa-Comanche Reservation." *Chronicles of Oklahoma* 19 (June 1941).

——, ed. "The Journal of the Proceedings of Our First Treaty With the Wild Indians, 1835." *Chronicles of Oklahoma* 14 (December 1936).

Garfield, Marvin H. "Defense of the Kansas Frontier." *Kansas Historical Quarterly* 1 (Aug. 1932).

Gill, Helen C. "The Establishment of Counties in Kansas." *Kansas State Historical Collections, 1903-1904* 8.

Godfrey, E. S. "Some Reminiscences." *Cavalry Journal* 36 (1927).

Griswold, Gillett. "Chief Stumbling Bear," in "Notes and Documents." *Chronicles of Oklahoma* 44 (Winter 1967).

——. "Old Fort Sill: The First Seven Years." *Chronicles of Oklahoma* 36 (Spring 1958).

——. "The Site of Camp Comanche, Dragoon Expedition of 1834." *Chronicles of Oklahoma* 63 (Fall 1995).

Grove, Fred. "Kicking Bird–Kiowa Martyr." *The West* (Aug. 1967).

Hallock, Charles. "The Siege of Fort Atkinson." *Harper's New Monthly Magazine* 15 (1857).

Hazen, W. H. "Some Corrections of 'Life on the Plains.'" *Chronicles of Oklahoma* 2 (Dec. 1925).

Jacob, Richard T. "Military Reminiscences of Captain Richard T. Jacob." *Chronicles of Oklahoma* 2 (March 1924).

John, Elizabeth A. H. "An Earlier Chapter of Kiowa History." *New Mexico Historical Review* 60 (October 1985).

——. "Nurturing the Peace: Spanish and Comanche Cooperation in the Early Nineteenth Century." *New Mexico Historical Review* 59 (October 1984).

Jones, Col. Harold W., ed. "The Diary of Assistant Surgeon Leonard Mcphail on His Journey to the Southwest in 1835." *Chronicles of Oklahoma* 18 (Sept. 1940).

Kroeker, Marvin. "Col. W. B. Hazen in the Indian Territory, 1868–69." *Chronicles of Oklahoma* 42 (Spring 1964).

Lewis, Anna. "Camp Napoleon." *Chronicles of Oklahoma* 9 (December 1931).

MacKenzie, Charles. "The Mississouri Indians: A Narrative of Four Trading Expeditions to the Mississouri 1804–1805–1806." *Les Bourgeois de la Compagnie du Nord-Ouest*, ed. by Louis R. Masson. Quebec: Impr. Generale A Cote, 1889–1890.

Merrill, James M. "General Sherman's Letter to His Son: A Visit to Fort Sill." *Chronicles of Oklahoma* 47 (Summer 1969).

Miller, Nyle H., ed. "Surveying the Southern Boundary Line of Kansas." *Kansas Historical Quarterly* 1 (Feb. 1932).

Monahan, Forrest D., Jr. "Kiowa-Federal Relations in Kansas, 1865–1868." *Chronicles of Oklahoma* 49 (Winter 1971-1972).

Mooney, James. "Calendar History of the Kiowa Indians." Bureau of American Ethnology, *Seventeenth Annual Report*, Part 1. Washington, D.C., 1898.

Nicholson, William. "A Tour of Indian Agencies in Kansas and the Indian Territory in 1870." *Kansas Historical Quarterly* 13 (November 1934).

Nye, Capt. W. S. "The Death of Nah-Goey." *Daily Oklahoman*, Oct. 10, 1937.

——. "The Lost Shield." *Daily Oklahoman*, Nov. 28, 1937.

——. "The Mountain Route." *Daily Oklahoman*, Jan. 30, 1838.

——. "Trapped in the Hueco Tanks." *Daily Oklahoman*, Jan. 16, 1938.

——. "What Happened to Mary Hamleton?" *Daily Oklahoman*, Oct. 24, 1937.

Peck, Robert Morris. "Rough Riding on the Plains." *National Tribune*, August 1, 1901.

Perry, Dan W. "The Kiowa's Defiance." *Chronicles of Oklahoma* 13 (March 1935).

Pratt, Richard H. "Some Indian Experiences." *Journal of United States Cavalry Association* 16 (October 1905).

Price, Catherine. "The Comanche Threat to Texas and New Mexico in the Eighteenth Century and the Development of Spanish Indian Policy." *Journal of the West* 2 (April 1985).

Reid, Russell, and Clell G. Gannon, eds. "Journal of the Atkinson-O'Fallon Expedition." *North Dakota Historical Quarterly* 4 (October 1929).

Rister, Carl Coke, ed. "Colonel A. W. Evans' Christmas Day Indian Fight (1868)." *Chronicles of Oklahoma* 16 (September 1938).

——. "Documents Relating to General W. T. Sherman's Southern Plains Indian Policy, 1871–1875." *Panhandle-Plains Historical Review* 9 (1936); 10 (1937).

Root, George A., ed. "Extracts From the Diary of Captain Lambert Bowman Wolf." *Kansas Historical Quarterly* 1 (May 1932).

Rucker, Alvin. "Taime." *Daily Oklahoman*, May 26, 1929.

Shamleffer, William F. "Merchandizing Sixty Years Ago." *Kansas State Historical Collections, 1923–1925* 16.

Steele, Aubrey L. "The Beginning of Quaker Administration of Indian Affairs in Oklahoma." *Chronicles of Oklahoma* 17 (Dec. 1939).

Steele, Mrs. J. Dorman. "The Indian Prisoners at Fort Marion." *National Teachers Monthly* 3.

Taft, Robert. "The Pictorial Record of the Old West." *Kansas Historical Quarterly* 19 (Aug. 1951).

Taylor, Alfred A. "The Medicine Lodge Peace Council." *Chronicles of Oklahoma* 2 (Nov.-Dec. 1924).

Taylor, Morris F. "Kicking Bird: A Chief of the Kiowas." *Kansas Historical Quarterly* 38 (Autumn 1972).

Thoburn, Joseph B. "Indian Fight in Clarke County in 1859." *Kansas State Historical Collections, 1911–1912* 12 (1912).

Van Zandt, Howard F. "The History of Camp Holmes and Chouteau's Trading Post." *Chronicles of Oklahoma* 8 (Sept. 1935).

Wellman, Paul I. "How Kicking Bird Chose Death and Dishonor Rather Than Break His Spoken Word." *Wichita Eagle,* Jan. 25, 1931.

Wright, Muriel. "A History of Fort Cobb." *Chronicles of Oklahoma* 34 (Spring 1956).

BOOKS

Abel, Annie Heloise. *The American Indian as a Participant in the Civil War.* Cleveland: Arthur H. Clark, 1919.

Ashabranner, Brent. *A Strange and Distant Shore.* New York: Dutton, 1996.

Barde, Frederick S. *Life and Adventures of "Billy" Dixon.* Guthrie: Co-operative Publishing, 1914.

Barry, Louise. *The Beginning of the West: Annals of the Kansas Gateway to the American West, 1540–1854.* Topeka: Kansas State Historical Society, 1972.

Battey, Thomas C. *The Life and Adventures of a Quaker Among the Indians.* Intro. by Alice Marriott. Norman: University of Oklahoma Press, 1968.

Before Lewis and Clark: Documents Illustrating the History of the Missouri, 1785–1804. Ed. and intro. by A. P. Nasatir. 2 vols. St. Louis: St. Louis Historical Document Foundation, 1952.

Belindo, John. *An Historical Chronology of the Kiowa Tribe.* Washington, D.C.: Institute for the Development of Indian Law, 1977.

Berlandier, Jean Louis. *The Indians of Texas in 1830.* Washington, D.C.: Smithsonian Institution Press, 1969.

Berthrong, Donald J. *The Southern Cheyennes.* Norman: University of Oklahoma Press, 1963.

Blaine, Martha Royce. *Pawnee Passage: 1870–1875.* Norman: University of Oklahoma Press, 1990.

Brice, James. *Reminiscences of Ten Years of Experience on the Western Plains.* Kansas City: James Brice, 1905.

Brown, John Henry. *Indian Wars and Pioneers of Texas.* Austin: L. E. Daniel, c. 1890.

Capps, Benjamin. *The Warren Wagontrain Raid.* New York: Dial Press, 1974.

Carriker, Robert C. *Fort Supply Indian Territory, Frontier Outpost on the Plains.* Norman: University of Oklahoma Press, 1970.

Carter, Robert Goldthwaite. *Massacre of Salt Creek Prairie and the Cow-Boy's Verdict.* Washington, D.C.: Gibson Bros., 1919.

——. *On the Border With Mackenzie.* Washington, D.C.: Eynor Printing, 1935.

———. *Pursuit of Kicking Bird: A Campaign in the Texas Badlands.* Washington, D.C.: Gibson Bros., 1920.

Cashion, Ty. *A Texas Frontier, the Clear Fork Country and Fort Griffin, 1849–1887.* Norman: University of Oklahoma Press, 1996.

Catlin, George. *Letters and Notes on the Manners, Customs, and Conditions of the North American Indians.* 2 vols. New York: Dover, 1973.

———. *North American Indians.* 2 vols. Edinburgh: Oliver and Boyd, 1926.

Chittenden, Hiram Martin. *The American Fur Trade of the Far West.* 2 vols. New York: Francis P. Harper, 1902.

Conover, George W. *Sixty Years in Southwest Oklahoma.* Anadarko: N. T. Plummer, 1927.

Corwin, Hugh D. *Comanche and Kiowa Captives in Oklahoma and Texas.* Guthrie: Cooperative Publishing, 1959.

———. *The Kiowa Indians and Life Stories.* Lawton: N.p., 1958.

Crawford, Isabel. *Kiowa, Story of a Blanket Indian Mission.* New York: Fleming H. Revell, 1915.

Custer, Elizabeth B. *Following the Guidon.* Norman: University of Oklahoma Press, 1966.

Custer, George Armstrong. *My Life on the Plains, or, Personal Experience With Indians.* Norman: University of Oklahoma Press, 1962.

Dockstader, Frederick J. *Great North American Indians.* New York: Van Nostrand, Reinhold, 1977.

Dodge, Richard Irving. *The Plains of the Great West and Their Inhabitants.* New York: G. P. Putnam's Sons, 1877.

Eastman, Edwin. *Seven Years Among the Comanches and Apaches.* Jersey City: C. Johnson, 1873.

Ellis, Clyde. *To Change Them Forever.* Norman: University of Oklahoma Press, 1996.

Ewers, John C. *The Horse in Blackfoot Indian Culture.* Washington, D.C.: Smithsonian Institution Press, 1980.

Fehrenbach, T. R. *Comanches, the Destruction of a People.* New York: Alfred A. Knopf, 1974.

Foreman, Grant. *Advancing the Frontier, 1830–1860.* Norman: University of Oklahoma Press, 1933.

———. *Indians and Pioneers.* New Haven: Yale University Press, 1930.

———. *Pioneer Days in the Early Southwest.* Cleveland: Arthur H. Clark, 1926.

Fowler, Jacob. *The Journal of Jacob Fowler.* Edited and notes by Elliott Coues. Minneapolis: Ross and Haines, 1965.

Fröbel, Julius. *Seven Years' Travel in Central America, Northern Mexico, and the Far West of the United States.* London: Richard Bentley, 1859.

Gardner, Mark L., ed. and annot. *Edward James Glasgow and William Henry Glasgow, Brothers on the Santa Fe and Chihuahua Trails.* Niwot: University Press of Colorado, 1993.

Garrard, Lewis H. *Wah-to-yah and the Taos Trail.* Norman: University of Oklahoma Press, 1955.

Grant, Blanche C. *When Old Trails Were New, the Story of Taos.* Chicago: Rio Grande Press, 1934.

Gregg, Josiah. *Commerce of the Prairies: or the Journal of a Santa Fe Trader*. Ed. by Max L. Moorhead. Norman: University of Oklahoma Press, 1954.

——. *The Fighting Cheyennes*. Norman: University of Oklahoma Press, 1956.

Hafen, Leroy, and Carl Cole Rister. *Western America, the Exploration, Settlement, and Development of the Region Beyond the Mississippi*. New York: Prentice-Hall, 1941.

Haley, James L. *The Buffalo War: The History of the Red River Indian Uprising of 1874*. New York: Doubleday, 1976.

Henry, Alexander. *New Light on the Early History of the Greater Northwest, the Manuscript Journal of Alexander Henry*. Ed. and commentary by Elliott Coues. 3 vols. New York: Francis P. Harper, 1897.

Hoig, Stan. *The Battle of the Washita*. New York: Doubleday, 1976.

——. *Jesse Chisholm, Ambassador of the Plains*. Niwot: University Press of Colorado, 1991.

——. *The Sand Creek Massacre*. Norman: University of Oklahoma Press, 1961.

——. *Tribal Wars of the Southern Plains*. Norman: University of Oklahoma Press, 1993.

Hyde, George E. *Life of George Bent, Written From His Letters*. Ed. by Savoie Lottinville. Norman: University of Oklahoma Press, 1968.

——. *The Pawnee Indians*. Norman: University of Oklahoma Press, 1951.

——. *Red Cloud's Folks*. Norman: University of Oklahoma Press, 1975.

Inman, Col. Henry. *The Old Santa Fe Trail*. Minneapolis: Ross and Haines, 1966 [1897].

Irving, John Treat, Jr. *Indian Sketches Taken During an Expedition to the Pawnee Tribes*. Ed. and annot. by John Francis McDermott. Norman: University of Oklahoma Press, 1955.

James, Edwin. *Account of an Expedition From Pittsburgh to the Rocky Mountains*. 2 vols. Ann Arbor: University Microfilms, 1966.

——. *James's Account of the S. H. Long Expedition, 1819-20*. 4 vols. in *Early Western Travels, 1748-1846*. Ed. Reuben Gold Thwaites. Cleveland: Arthur H. Clark, 1905.

James, Gen. Thomas. *Three Years Among the Mexicans and the Indians*. Chicago: Rio Grande Press, 1962.

Jones, Douglas C. *The Treaty of Medicine Lodge*. Norman: University of Oklahoma Press, 1966.

Journal of the Sixth Annual Session of the General Council of the Indian Territory Composed of Delegates Duly Selected From the Indian Tribes Legally Resident Therein. Lawrence: Republican Journal Steam Printing, 1875.

Kappler, Charles J., ed. *Indian Treaties*. New York: Interland Publishing, 1972.

Keim, DeB. Randolph. *Sheridan's Troopers on the Borders: A Winter Campaign on the Plains*. Philadelphia: David McKay, 1885.

Kendall, George Wilkins. *Narrative of the Texan Santa Fe Expedition, 1844*. New York: Harper and Bros., 1844.

Kickingbird, Robin, and Kirke Kickingbird. *Tene Angopte, Kicking Bird, 1835–May 4, 1875*. Oklahoma City: N.p., 1994.

Leckie, William H., and Shirley A. Leckie. *Unlikely Warriors: General Benjamin H. Grierson and His Family*. Norman: University of Oklahoma Press, 1984.

Lewis, Meriwether, and William Clark. *History of the Expedition Under the Command of Lewis and Clark*. Ed. by Elliott Coues. 4 vols. New York: F. P. Harper, 1893.

Lowe, Perceval. *Five Years a Dragoon*. Kansas City: Franklin Hudson Publishing, 1906.

Malinowski, Sharon, ed. *Notable Native Americans*. New York: Gale Research, 1995.

Manypenny, George W. *Our Indian Wards*. Cincinnati: Robert Clarke, 1880.

Marriott, Alice. *Kiowa Years, a Study in Culture Impact*. New York: Macmillan, 1968.

——. *The Ten Grandmothers*. Norman: University of Oklahoma Press, 1945.

Mayhall, Mildred P. *Indian Wars of Texas*. Waco: Texian Press, 1965.

——. *The Kiowas*. Norman: University of Oklahoma Press, 1962.

McCoy, Ronald. *Kiowa Memories, Images From Indian Territory*. Santa Fe: Morning Star Galley, 1987.

Meriwether, David. *My Life in the Mountains and on the Plains*. Norman: University of Oklahoma Press, 1965.

Methvin, Rev. J. J. *Andele or, the Mexican-Kiowa Captive*. Louisville: Pentecostal Herald Press, 1899.

Mishkin, Bernard. *Rank and Warfare Among the Plains Indians*. Monograph No. 3 of American Ethnological Society. Seattle: University of Washington Press, 1940.

Möllhausen, Baldwin. *Diary of a Journey From the Mississippi to the Coasts of the Pacific With a U.S. Government Expedition*. London: Longman, Brown, Green, Longman and Roberts, 1858.

Montaignes, François des (Isaac Cooper). *The Plains, Being No Less Than a Collection of Veracious Memoranda Taken During the Expedition of Exploration in the Year 1845*. Ed. and intro. by Nancy Apert Mower and Don Russell. Norman: University of Oklahoma Press, 1972.

Mooney, James. *Calendar History of the Kiowa Indians*. Washington, D.C.: Smithsonian Institution Press, 1979.

Neeley, Bill. *The Last Comanche Chief, the Life and Times of Quanah Parker*. New York: John Wiley and Sons, 1995.

Nye, Wilbur Sturtevant. *Bad Medicine & Good, Tales of the Kiowas*. Norman: University of Oklahoma Press, 1962.

——. *Carbine and Lance, the Story of Old Fort Sill*. Norman: University of Oklahoma Press, 1974 [1937].

——. *Plains Indian Raiders*. Norman: University of Oklahoma Press, 1968.

Petersen, Karen Daniels. *Plains Indian Art From Fort Marion*. Norman: University of Oklahoma Press, 1971.

Pettis, George Henry. *Kit Carson's Fight With the Comanche and Kiowa Indians at the Adobe Walls on the Canadian River, November 25th, 1864*. Providence: S. S. Rider, 1878.

Pike, Zebulon M. *The Journals and Letters of Zebulon Montgomery Pike, With Letters and Related Documents*. Ed. and annot. by Donald Jackson. 2 vols. Norman: University of Oklahoma Press, 1966.

Portrait and Biographical Album, Sedgwick County, Kansas. Chicago: Chapman Bros., 1888.

Pratt, Richard Henry. *Battlefield and Classroom: Four Decades With the American Indian, 1867–1904.* Ed. by Robert M. Utley. New Haven: Yale University Press, 1966.

Richardson, Jane. *Law and Status Among the Kiowa Indians.* Seattle: University of Washington Press, 1940.

Richardson, Rupert Norval. *The Frontier of Northwest Texas, 1846 to 1876.* Glendale: Arthur H. Clark, 1963.

Robinson, Charles M., III. *Bad Hand, a Biography of General Ranald S. Mackenzie.* Austin: State House Press, 1993.

———. *The Indian Trial: The Complete Story of the Warren Train Massacre and the Fall of the Kiowa Nation.* Spokane: Arthur H. Clark, 1997.

Ronda, James P. *Lewis and Clark Among the Indians.* Lincoln: University of Nebraska Press, 1984.

Smith, David Paul. *Frontier Defense in the Civil War: Texas Rangers and Rebels.* College Station: Texas A&M University Press, 1992.

Stanley, Francis. *Satanta and the Kiowas.* Borger, Texas: Jim Hess Printers, 1968.

Stanley, Henry M. *My Early Travels and Adventures in America and Asia.* 2 vols. New York: Charles Scribner's Sons, 1905.

Szasz, Margaret Connell. *Between Indian and White Worlds, the Cultural Broker.* Norman: University of Oklahoma Press, 1994.

Tatum, Lawrie. *Our Red Brothers and the Peace Policy of President Ulysses S. Grant.* Lincoln: University of Nebraska Press, 1970.

Thoburn, Joseph B., and Muriel H. Wright. *Oklahoma, a History of the State and Its People.* New York: Lewis Historical Publishing: New York, 1929.

Time-Life Editors. *The Buffalo Hunters. The American Indian Series.* Alexandria, Virginia: Time-Life, 1993.

Vail, Rev. Albert Lenox, prep. *A Memorial of James M. Haworth, Superintendent of U.S. Indian Schools.* Kansas City: N. H. Farey, 1866.

Voget, Fred W. *The Shoshoni-Crow Sun Dance.* Norman: University of Oklahoma Press, 1984.

Wallace, Ernest, and E. Adamson Hoebel. *The Comanches, Lords of the South Plains.* Norman: University of Oklahoma Press, 1952.

Webb, Walter Prescott. *The Texas Rangers.* Austin: University of Texas Press, 1965.

Wharton, Clarence. *Satanta, the Great Chief of the Kiowas and His People.* Dallas: Banks, Upshaw, 1935.

Winfrey, Dorman H., and James M. Day, eds. *The Indian Papers of Texas, 1825–1916.* 5 vols. Austin: Pemberton Press, 1966.

Wooster, Robert. *The Military and United States Indian Policy, 1865–1903.* New Haven: Yale University Press, 1988.

Wunder, John W. *The Kiowas.* New York: Chelsea House, 1989.

Young, Otis E. *The First Military Escort on the Santa Fe Trail, 1829.* Glendale: Arthur H. Clark, 1952.

BROCHURES

Grinnell, George Bird. "Bent's Old Fort and Its Builders." N.d.

"The Kiowa" (Southern Plains Indian Museum and Arts Center, Anadarko). Washington, D.C.: GPO, 1994.

GOVERNMENT DOCUMENTS—PUBLISHED

Abert, J. W. *Report of an Expedition Led by Lieut. Abert on the Upper Arkansas and Through the Country of the Comanche Indians, in the Fall of the Year 1845, Journal of Lieutenant J. W, Abert, From Bent's Fort to St. Louis in 1845.* Senate Document No. 438, 29th Cong., 1st sess. (1846).

Alvord, Henry E. *Report of Special Commissioners to Visit the Kiowas and Comanches, Arrapahoes, and Cheyennes, Caddoes, Wichitas, and Affiliated Bands.* Washington, D.C.: GPO, 1872.

American State Papers, Indian Affairs, 2.

American State Papers, Military Affairs, 4.

Annual Report of Commissioner of Indian Affairs, 1847–1874.

Annual Report of the Secretary of War, 1868–70.

The Chivington Massacre. Reports of the Committees, 39th Cong., 2d sess. Washington, D.C.: GPO, 1867.

Compilation of the Official Records of the War of the Union and Confederate Armies, War of the Rebellion, 1880–1891.

Congressional Globe

Congressional Record

Record of Engagements With Hostile Indians Within the Military Division of the Missouri From 1868 to 1882. Chicago: Hqs. Mil. Div. of the Missouri, August 1882.

Report of the Secretary of War, 1868. Washington, D.C.: GPO, 1880–1901.

U.S. Statutes at Large 7.

HOUSE OF REPRESENTATIVES

Ex. Doc. 1, 30th Cong., 1st sess. "Executive Reports."

Ex. Doc. 45, 31st Cong., 1st sess. "Route From Fort Smith to Santa Fe; Report of Capt. R. B. Marcy."

Ex. Doc. 27, 35th Cong., 2d sess. "Protection of the Frontier of Texas."

Misc. Doc. 41, 39th Cong., 1st sess. "Issue of Arms to Kiowas and Other Indians."

Ex. Doc. 23, 39th Cong., 2d sess. "Protection Across the Continent; Reports of Gen. W. T. Sherman and D. B. Sackett."

Ex. Doc. 13, 40th Cong., 1st sess. "Special Report of Secretary of War."

Ex. Doc. 60, 40th Cong., 2d sess. "Information in Relation to Recent Raids and Outrages Upon Citizens of Texas."

Ex. Doc. 97, 40th Cong., 2d sess. "Report of Indian Peace Commission."

Ex. Doc. 1, 41st Cong., 2d sess. "Report of Hon. Vincent Colyer."

Ex. Doc. 240, 41st Cong., 2d sess. "Difficulties With Indian Tribes."

Ex. Doc. 123, 41st Cong., 3d sess. "Apache and Kiowa Indians."

Ex. Doc. 62, 42d Cong., 3d sess. "Depredations by Kiowa and Arapaho Indians."

Ex. Doc. 34, 46th Cong., 1st sess. "Duplicate Copies of Two Letters Received by the Indian Office From Agents Miles and Hunt, etc."

Report 1135, 48th Cong., 1st sess. "William Beddo and Others."

Report 2885, 49th Cong., 1st sess. "George Maxwell, F. C. Bulkley, and H. L. Newman."

SENATE

Ex. Doc. 1, 23rd Cong., 2d sess. Lt. T. B. Wheelock. "Col. Henry Dodge's Report of Leavenworth Expedition in the Summer of 1834."

Ex. Doc. 78, 33rd Cong., 2d sess. "Reports of Explorations and Survey to Ascertain the Most Practicable and Economical Route for a Railroad From the Mississippi River to the Pacific Ocean, 1853-54."

Ex. Doc. 23, 39th Cong., 2d sess. "U.S. War Department Protection Across the Continent."

Ex. Doc. 13, 40th Cong., 1st sess. "Indian Hostilities on the Frontier."

Ex. Doc. 60, 40th Cong., 2d sess. "Recent Raids and Outrages Upon Citizens of Texas by Bands of Kiowa and Comanche Indians."

Ex. Doc. 18, pt. 3, 40th Cong., 3d sess. "Indian Battle on the Washita."

Ex. Doc. 40, 40th Cong., 3d sess. "Copies of Reports Upon Indian Affairs in the Military Division of the Missouri."

MISCELLANEOUS

Message of the President [CSA] and Report of Albert Pike. Richmond: Enquirer and Job Press, 1861. Reprint Washington, D.C.: Ancient and Accepted Scottish Rite, 1968.

Report of Messrs. Butler and Lewis, Commissioners to Treat With the Camanches and Other Prairie Indians. Washington, D.C.: N.p., 1846.

Reports of the Commissioner of Indian Affairs, 1847-1875.

GOVERNMENT DOCUMENTS–UNPUBLISHED

Ltrs. Recd., Adjutant General's Office (RG-94)

Ltrs. Recd., AGO (Main Series), 1861-1870 (M619)

Correspondence relating to the implementation of the Medicine Lodge treaties, etc. (Roll 629)

Copies of reports by Gens. Sheridan and Custer and by other officers, etc. (Roll 812)

Papers relating to Cheyenne Indians (Roll 642)

Reports of Custer and Hancock, 1867 (Roll 563)

Ltrs. Recd. (Main Series), 1871-1880 (M666)

Correspondence relating to the arrest of Kiowa Chiefs Satanta, Satank, Big Tree, etc. (Roll 10)

Correspondence relating to raids by Comanche and Kiowa Indians in Texas, 1872-1873, etc. (Roll 60)

Papers relating to the attack by troops under Col. Ranald S. Mackenzie, etc. (Roll 86)

Papers relating to the 1874-1875 campaign against Arapahoe, Cheyenne, Comanche, and Kiowa bands, etc. (Rolls 159-184)

Correspondence of the Office of Indian Affairs (Central Office) and Related Records, Ltrs. Recd., 1824-1861 (M234)

Creek Agency (Rolls 224-231)

Kiowa Agency (Rolls 375-381)

Seminole Agency (Rolls 800–803)
Texas Agency (Rolls 858–861)
Upper Arkansas Agency (Rolls 878–882)
Wichita Agency (Rolls 928–929)

Records of the Bureau of Indian Affairs (RG-75)
"Atkinson's 1825 Expedition up the Missouri and His Treaty With the Indians, Including the Cheyenne." American State Papers, vol. 2, 19th Cong., 1st sess.
Wheelock, T. B. Proceedings of a Council Held at Fort Gibson, September 1834, by T. B. Wheelock Record Group 75, NA.

Records of the Superintendencies and Agencies of the Office of Indian Affairs
Central Superintendency (M856)
Southern Superintendency (M640)
Western Superintendency (M640)

Records of United States Army Continental Commands (RG-393)
Fort Arbuckle, Indian Territory, Post Returns
Fort Dodge, Kansas (M989)
Fort Hays, Kansas (T713)
Fort Sill, Indian Territory, Records (Bound)
Fort Supply, Indian Territory
Ltrs. Recd., Military Div. of the Missouri
"Special File," Division of the Missouri, Indian Territory

Records Relating to Indian Treaties
Documents Relating to Negotiations of Ratified and Unratified Indian Treaties, 1801–1869 (T494, Rolls 3, 4)
Ratified Indian Treaties, 1835–1837 (M668, Rolls 4, 5, 6, 8, 10)

NEWSPAPERS AND PERIODICALS

Arkansas Advocate (Little Rock)
Arkansas Gazette (Little Rock)
Arkansas Intelligencer
Army-Navy Journal
Cavalry Journal
Cherokee Advocate (Tahlequah)
Cheyenne Transporter
Chicago Times (Illinois)
Chicago Tribune (Illinois)
Cincinnati Commercial (Ohio)
Cincinnati Gazette (Ohio)
Daily Missouri Republican (St. Louis)
Daily National Intelligencer (Washington, D.C.)
Daily Oklahoman (Oklahoma City)
Daily Union (St. Louis)
Edmond Sun (Oklahoma)
Emporia News (Kansas)
The Friend (Philadelphia)

Friends' Review (Philadelphia)
Kansas Daily Tribune (Lawrence)
Kansas Weekly Tribune (Lawrence)
Leavenworth Conservative (Kansas)
Leavenworth Daily Conservative (Kansas)
Leavenworth Evening Bulletin (Kansas)
Leslie's Illustrated Newspaper
Missionary Herald (Philadelphia)
Missouri Republican (St. Louis)
National Republican (Washington, D.C.)
National Tribune (Washington, D.C.)
New York Times
New York Tribune
Niles' Register
Oklahoma Star (Caddo, Choctaw Nation)
St. Louis Post Dispatch (Missouri)
The Vindicator (Atoka, Choctaw Nation)
Washington Evening Star
Wichita Eagle (Kansas)
Winners of the West

THESES AND DISSERTATIONS

Buntin, Martha Leota. "History of the Kiowa, Comanche, and Wichita Indian Agency." Thesis, University of Oklahoma, 1931.

Mayhall, Mildred Pickle. "The Indians of Texas: The Atakapa, the Karankawa, the Tonkawa." Dissertation, University of Texas, 1939.

Northcutt, John Douglas. "Leadership Among the Kiowa 1833-1973." Thesis, University of Oklahoma, 1973.

Smalling, Linda D. "From Satank to Joshua Given, the Assimilation of the Kiowas." Thesis, University of Central Oklahoma, 1944.

Index